P9-CCX-369

Apostolicity Then and Now

An Ecumenical Church in a Postmodern World

John J. Burkhard, O.F.M. Conv.

A Michael Glazier Book

LITURGICAL PRESS

Collegeville, Minnesota

www.litpress.org

A Michael Glazier Book published by Liturgical Press.

Cover design by David Manahan, O.S.B. Illustration provided by PHOTODISC: World Religions.

Scriptures selections are taken from the **New American Bible** Copyright © 1991, 1986, 1970 by the Confraternity of Christian Doctrine, 3211 Fourth Street, NE, Washington, DC 20017-1194 and are used by license of copyright owner. All rights reserved. No part of the **New American Bible** may be reproduced in any form or by any means without permission in writing from the copyright owner.

© 2004 by the Order of Saint Benedict, Collegeville, Minnesota. All rights reserved. No part of this book may be reproduced in any form, by print, microfilm, microfiche, mechanical recording, photocopying, translation, or by any other means, known or yet unknown, for any purpose except brief quotations in reviews, without the previous written permission of the Liturgical Press, Saint John's Abbey, P.O. Box 7500, Collegeville, Minnesota 56321-7500. Printed in the United States of America.

1   2   3   4   5   6   7   8

Library of Congress Cataloging-in-Publication Data

Burkhard, John J., 1940–
    Apostolicity then and now : an ecumenical church in a postmodern world / John J. Burkhard.
        p. cm.
    "A Michael Glazier book."
    Includes bibliographical references.
    ISBN 0-8146-5121-6 (pbk : alk. paper)
    1. Church–Apostolicity. I. Title.

BV601.2.B87 2004
262'.72--dc22

                                                            2004007564

I dedicate this book in gratitude to my former professors,
and to my students, all of whom have helped me grow as a teacher,
scholar, and theologian.

Contents

Foreword

Christians have professed the apostolicity of the church—along with its unity, holiness, and catholicity—for nearly two millennia. Despite this long-standing affirmation of faith, the followers of Christ still do not agree on the exact meaning of apostolicity. It remains a church-dividing issue with far-reaching theological and pastoral implications. This creative study of apostolicity by John J. Burkhard is a welcome contribution to the debate.

John J. Burkhard, a Conventual Franciscan and former President of Saint Anthony-on-Hudson Seminary, is an associate professor of systematic theology at the Washington Theological Union in Washington, DC. He is well equipped to handle this complex question with his solid theological training at the Canisianum in Innsbruck (S.T.L.) and the University of Strasbourg (Dr.Sc.Rel.) and his many years of teaching. His theological vision is strengthened by his familiarity with contemporary European theology. Although this is his first book, systematicians know his major articles on the history and theology of the *sensus fidei* in Vatican II and the postconciliar period (*Louvain Studies* 1992 and *Heythrop Journal* 1993) and the meaning and application of subsidiarity in ecclesiology (*The Jurist* 1998).

The postmodern worldview provides the underpinning for Burkhard's understanding of apostolicity. He recognizes that postmodernism is a controversial topic with a wide variety of interpretations. Some reject it because of its destructive relativism, excessive subjectivity, and denial of foundational principles. Burkhard admits that these limitations exist in some versions of postmodernism, but argues that it is also possible to have a more positive understanding of postmodernism, one that emphasizes historicity, relationality, personhood, and pluralism. These qualities, he contends, can help situate apostolicity in a framework that does not compromise the uniqueness of Christianity and ensure a balanced view of Scripture, with its historical and ecumenical dimensions.

Burkhard skillfully relates the church as sacrament and communion in explaining the meaning of apostolicity. He agrees with Rahner that the church is the fundamental sacrament (not to be confused with Christ as the primordial sacrament). Every celebration of the seven sacraments—symbols of human encounter with the divine—is an ecclesial celebration. The divine gift of communion is expressed in the church as sacrament. The church is a communion of individual believers who share in the life of the Triune God through the sacraments and a virtuous life, with an openness to the Spirit. Ecclesial communion is rooted in the universal salvific will of God and the mystery of grace.

Apostolicity, Burkhard insists, does not refer just to ecclesiastical office or apostolic succession. Rather, it is an attribute of the entire church and includes the full life of the Christian community: its baptized members, sacred writings, and leadership structures. Likewise, the episcopate is not simply a collection of individuals who are successors of the apostles. In the words of St. Cyprian, "the episcopate is one and undivided" (*On the Unity of the Church*, 4). The bishops form a communion of pastoral leaders in apostolic ministry who serve the church. The episcopacy is essentially a collegial body, and the church is a communion of apostolic churches.

Apostolic succession, according to Burkhard, is not to be viewed as a linear unbroken line of individual bishops originating with the apostles. It is more accurate and theologically rich to see succession in the context of the apostolicity of the church. There is a succession of apostolic teaching, which Burkhard calls the "substance of apostolicity" or "apostolicity of life." His reference to Yves Congar is valuable: "Attention has been placed too exclusively on the validity of formal ordinations as such. . . . The episcopacy as function is not an object that one has control of outside the service it renders in the very bosom of the Church" (*Ministères et communion ecclesiale* [Paris: Cerf, 1971], 88).

In *Apostolicity Then and Now* we are taken on a tour d'horizon. Burkhard examines apostolicity from several vantage points. In addition to scriptural and historical evidence, he also presents in some detail how contemporary theologians treat apostolicity. Of special value is his discussion in chapter 7 of apostolicity in contemporary ecumenical dialogue. He also addresses several controversial issues: apostolic succession, recognition of ministry, meaning of validity, and the distinction between church and ecclesial community. He carefully presents his views in a balanced manner.

The book is designed for the educated reader: students, ecumenists, pastoral ministers, and those interested in the full import of apostolicity. A special feature of the book is the abundance of footnotes with copious references to theological literature. The footnotes give scholars, who wish to pursue in greater depth certain ideas, a rich source of information. It is hoped that this book on apostolicity will promote the cause of Christian unity. May it contribute to the vision of Vatican II, which noted that "almost everyone, though in different ways, longs that there may be one visible Church of God. . . (*Decree on Ecumenism,* 1).

Patrick Granfield, O.S.B.
The Shakespeare Caldwell-Duval Professor of Theology
The School of Theology and Religious Studies
The Catholic University of America

Preface

The genesis of this book was a semester in the fall of 1998 at the Institute for Ecumenical and Cultural Research, Collegeville, Minnesota, spent researching the relationship between the apostolicity of the church and postmodernity. I had been thinking about the impact of postmodernity on various formulations of the faith for several years, but had not had the opportunity to think the issue through regarding apostolicity. I planned to write an article on the topic, comparing pre-modern, modern, and postmodern worldviews. The project proved too complicated for a single article. I put it on hold until I realized that I would have to situate the question in the larger context of the very meaning of apostolicity in the Scriptures, in early church writings, as well as in recent writings of Roman Catholic, Anglican, Protestant, and Orthodox theologians. It also seemed natural to discuss the issue in the context of recent ecumenical dialogues. In the meanwhile, I was invited to write an entry on apostolicity for the second edition of the *New Catholic Encyclopedia,* and that project led to further rethinking of the topic. The present work emerged from these activities.

In the course of my research, I began to notice that in the early church, and then again in recent ecumenical documents, the whole church was the primary locus of apostolicity. It became clear to me that the apostolicity of the whole church did not threaten the doctrine of the apostolic succession of the bishops but that it put it in its proper ecclesial context. I saw that this insight, too, was reinforced by the growing acceptance by the churches of an ecclesiology of communion—an ecclesiology that acknowledged the Trinitarian nature of the church. I felt that growth in a common ecclesiology could lead to agreement on the divisive issue of official ministry in the churches.

Much of my research was readily available in scholarly books and journals, and in the many bilateral and multilateral ecumenical agreements that had appeared over the years since the conclusion of the Second Vatican Council, and yet the lack of progress on these issues was palpable. I decided to undertake a presentation that would examine the basic scriptural, historical, theological, and ecumenical issues. At the same time, it appeared increasingly important to me to place this valuable material in the wider cultural context of what was happening in the meltdown of modern philosophy which goes by the name of postmodernism. The thought forms of an emerging new worldview demanded investigation and testing. Could it be that postmodernity, as an underlying attitude and in its various forms in science, art, philosophy, literary criticism, popular entertainment, popular spiritualities, etc., was a possible resource in understanding and proposing the faith to our contemporaries? Could postmodernism help the churches better understand the divisive issue of apostolic succession? This book is an attempt to pursue these inviting clues.

I am grateful to my fellow teachers of theology at various seminaries and universities over the years for their supportive colleagueship: St. Anthony-on-Hudson Seminary, Rensselaer, New York; Washington Theological Union, Washington, D.C.; St. John's University, Collegeville, Minnesota; Catholic University of America, Washington, D.C.; and St. Peter's Regional Seminary, Cape Coast, Ghana. I am also grateful to Dr. Patrick Henry of the Institute for Ecumenical and Cultural Research, Collegeville, Minnesota, and to Dr. Theodor Dieter of the Institute for Ecumenical Research, Strasbourg, France, for their help and encouragement at different stages. Special thanks are due to the friars of my Province of the Immaculate Conception in the United States of America and to the Franciscan community of Strasbourg, France, for their fraternal support over the years. Finally, I am also indebted to the Liturgical Press for encouraging me to pursue this subject and its willingness to publish the results.

CHAPTER ONE

Who Were the Apostles?

The answer to the title of this chapter seems simple enough, but that impression is deceptive. One is inclined to point unthinkingly to the twelve Apostles, of course, and to Paul of Tarsus. The opinion of scholars, however, is that the answer to the question is more complicated than meets the eye.[1] Why? What is the evidence?

Our first written evidence in the New Testament is derived from a pre-Pauline creedal formula that Paul has incorporated in his first letter to the Corinthians. In chapter fifteen, we read:

> For I handed on to you as of first importance what I also received: that Christ died for our sins in accordance with the scriptures; that he was buried; that he was raised on the third day in accordance with the scriptures; that he appeared to Kephas, then to the Twelve. After that, he appeared to more than five hundred brothers at once, most of whom are still living, though some have fallen asleep. Then he appeared to James, then to all the apostles (15:3-7).[2]

After the creedal formula, Paul continues by speaking of his own experience of the risen Lord and of his calling to apostleship (vv. 8-11). An attentive reading of the text, then, reveals two groups (and possibly three, if one includes the five hundred brethren) of witnesses to the risen Lord. Though the relationship of the groups to each other is not clarified, the existence of two distinct groups is certain. There was a group of "twelve"

---

1. The best general introduction on the notion of the apostles is still Jürgen Roloff, "Apostel/ Apostolat/ Apostolizität, I. Neues Testament," in *Theologische Realenzyklopädie* [hereafter *TRE*], eds. Gerhard Krause and Gerhard Müller (New York/Berlin: Walter de Gruyter Verlag, 1978) 3:430–45.

2. The translation used throughout the book is from *The Catholic Study Bible/New American Bible,* General Editor Donald Senior (New York: Oxford University Press, 1990).

and a group of "apostles."[3] We must look elsewhere to discover the nature and composition of each group.

The Twelve

All the gospels mention a group of "twelve" men called by Jesus without further indication of their task or duties. Each member seems to have functioned in view of his participation in the group. The earliest written gospel, the Gospel of Mark, for instance, records ten such usages (3:14; 4:10; 6:7; 9:35; 10:32; 11:11; 14:10, 17, 20, 43). In general, these passages point to the calling of the Twelve to be with Jesus, to be his companions. Mark 3:13-15 makes the intention clearer. The context points to something momentous: "He went up the mountain and summoned those whom he wanted and they came to him. He appointed twelve (epoiēsen dōdeka) that they might be with him and he might send them forth to preach and to have authority to drive out demons." The mountain is probably an allusion to Mount Sinai/Horeb and God's entering into a covenant with the Hebrews there. In the context of something significant unfolding in the covenant life of Israel, Jesus chooses twelve men and "makes" or "fashions" them into the "true Israel" of the covenant. Henceforth, these twelve represent, by their very number but also by their actions in behalf of the proclamation of the kingdom of God now breaking in with Jesus' ministry, Israel healed and gathered as God intended the covenant people to be. Just like Israel's prophets, Jesus, too, performs a prophetic action[4] that is also a "word of God." To the Hebrews, God's word or dabhar[5] can be either a spoken word (an oracle) or

3. John P. Meier has discussed 1 Cor 15:3-7 at some length in his "The Circle of the Twelve: Did It Exist during Jesus' Public Ministry?" *Journal of Biblical Literature* 116 (1997) 635-72, at 659-63. He stresses the historicity of the group of twelve during the ministry of Jesus and concentrates on the eschatological symbolism of their number.

4. See Bruce Vawter, "Introduction to Prophetic Literature," in *The New Jerome Biblical Commentary* [hereafter *NJBC*], ed. Raymond E. Brown, Joseph A. Fitzmyer, and Roland E. Murphy (Englewood Cliffs, N.J.: Prentice Hall, 1990) 199 [=11:23 end].

5. On the Hebrew understanding of God's *dabhar,* see Edmond Jacob, *Theology of the Old Testament,* tr. A. W. Heathcote and P. J. Allcock (New York: Harper & Row, 1958) 127-38; Thorleif Boman, *Hebrew Thought Compared with Greek,* tr. Jules L. Moreau (Philadelphia: Westminster Press, 1960) 58-69; and John L. McKenzie, in "The Word of God in the Old Testament," *Myths and Realities: Studies in Biblical Theology* (Milwaukee: Bruce Publishing Co., 1963) 37-58. In the footnotes, I list the sources chronologically by date of publication rather than by alphabetical listing according to author. I begin with the earliest sources and proceed to the latest to have appeared.

a concrete action of God (a prophetic deed). In either case, it is God who speaks or acts in their behalf. The prophet is the instrument by which God effects the history of the covenant. God acts in history through the agency of the prophets. History becomes the revelation of God as Israel's covenant partner.[6] Something similar is unfolding in the ministry of Jesus. In him God is actively bringing the covenant to its appointed fulfillment. God's gracious mercy *(hesed)* will not be defeated by human actions but will be swept up and enfolded in God's own loving forgiveness. The sign of this divine mercy is the regathering of God's people of old (see Is 11:12; 59:15-20; 60:1-22; Ez 20:27-44; 36:22-24; 39:23-29; 47:13-14).[7] The twelve scattered tribes are being reunited among themselves and with their God.[8] Jesus' ministry is the sign of God's never-ending concern for the people. The kingdom of God Jesus proclaims is his expression of this divine intention.

In initiating God's kingdom and in Jesus' calling of twelve to represent the patriarchs of old (Gen 35 and 49), we are really in the sphere of the symbolic. It is not discursive reason that is operative in this context but a deeper, more immediate, experiential, comprehensive, and humanly satisfying knowledge. The Twelve, then, *are* the symbol of the covenant now entering into its final, eschatological realization by God's gracious will. The number itself is important.[9] Thus, after the defection of Judas Iscariot from the Twelve, Peter calls for the election of another to complete

6. On the importance of history as an expression of divine revelation, see the now classic thesis of Wolfhart Pannenberg, "Introduction" and "Dogmatic Theses on the Doctrine of Revelation," in *Revelation as History,* ed. W. Pannenberg, tr. David Granskou (New York: The Macmillan Company, 1968) 1–21 and 123–58.

7. Meier writes: "Even in OT and pseudepigraphic literature that is not itself apocalyptic (e.g., Tobit 13; Sir 36:1-17), the hope for the regathering or reconstituting of the tribes of Israel in the end-time is expressed. Such a hope fit perfectly into Jesus' proclamation of the coming of God's kingly rule, for Jesus addressed his proclamation not to the world indiscriminately but to Israel in its promised land. Reflecting his mission to all Israel in the end-time, Jesus created the group called the Twelve, whose very number symbolized, promised, and (granted the dynamic power thought to be present in the symbolic actions of prophets) began the regathering of the twelve tribes." See "The Circle of the Twelve," 657. Note footnote 56 on the same page for a treatment of the theme of Israel's hope for eschatological "regathering."

8. Meier treats this important biblical theme in extenso in *A Marginal Jew: Rethinking the Historical Jesus,* 3 vols. (New York: Doubleday, 2001) 3:148–54 ["The Twelve as Prophetic Symbols of the Regathering of the Twelve Tribes of Israel"].

9. Joseph A. Fitzmyer writes: "A nucleus of twelve—a number inspired by the twelve tribes of Israel—symbolizes the fact that the group is the New Israel." See "Jewish Christianity in Acts in Light of the Qumran Scrolls," in *Studies in Luke-Acts,* eds. Leander E. Keck and J. Louis Martyn (Nashville: Abingdon Press, 1966) 233–57, at 235.

the full number of the group, and thus the full complement of the "true Israel" (Acts 1:15-26).

Jesus' act of choosing the Twelve and Peter's reconstitution of the group after the Lord's passion and death point to similar symbolic decisions by their Jewish contemporaries. The Qumran community employed similar symbolism, though in a somewhat different way.[10] Reicke tells us that Qumran was organized in a strictly hierarchical way and that the Supreme Council of the community consisted of twelve men.[11] The symbolism of the twelve ancient tribes of Israel seems to have served both Qumran and the Jesus movement.[12] And yet, there was a difference. Whereas Qumran also saw itself as the "true Israel," its thought world and symbolic world were motivated by segregation from Jewish society as a whole in pursuit of the ritual and cultic purity characteristic of God's "holy" people. The members of Qumran saw themselves as preparatory to God's eventual coming to Israel.[13] This is not the case with Jesus and his movement.[14] In Jesus' proclamation of the kingdom, that kingdom is al-

---

10. See Bo Reicke, "The Constitution of the Primitive Church in the Light of Jewish Documents," in *The Scrolls and the New Testament,* ed. Krister Stendahl (reprint of 1957 edition; Westport, Conn.: Greenwood Press, 1975) 143–56; Joseph A. Fitzmyer, "Jewish Christianity in Acts in Light of the Qumran Scrolls," 233–57; and Raymond E. Brown, "Aspects of New Testament Thought," in *NJBC,* 1380 ["The Twelve and the Apostolate"] [=81:148].

11. The text is unclear, however, since the Supreme Council can be understood to be composed in fact of fifteen men. It reads, "In the Council of the Community (there shall be) twelve men and priests three, perfect in all that which is revealed from all the Law to do truth and righteousness and judgment and love of mercy and modesty. . ." (1QS 8:1-2). Apropos, Reicke writes: "There is to be 'council' in the community, consisting of twelve men and three priests (viii, 1). This looks like an analogue to the college of the twelve apostles of Jesus. It is, however, not clear from the text whether the three priests are inside or outside the circle of twelve. Perhaps the inclusion of the three priests is to be preferred, because it enables one to see in the expression 'priest' an especial mark of honor and to avoid the rather improbable result that the other twelve men were laymen." "Constitution of the Primitive Church," 151. Fitzmyer disagrees with Reicke: "Any normal reading of the line would suggest that the text mentions 15 persons." "Jewish Christianity in Acts in Light of the Qumran Scrolls," 246–47.

12. Fitzmyer writes: "In both Essene and Christian circles the number twelve is more plausibly explained as a derivative of the twelve tribes of Israel. The element that is common to the use of this number in both circles is its appearance in an eschatological context." "Jewish Christianity in Acts in Light of the Qumran Scrolls," 247.

13. Fitzmyer says, "Like the early Christians, the Essenes of Qumran considered themselves to be the Israel of the end of days." Ibid., 244.

14. Fitzmyer discusses the points of difference in ibid, 239–40. He turns his attention to parallels on pp. 240–51.

ready dawning in his ministry. Jesus' ministry is not some preliminary stage on the way to the real coming of the kingdom. With Jesus—and the twelve associated with him—the kingdom is present. Perhaps it is not present in its fullness, since the kingdom-proclamation sayings of Jesus point to both presence and future fulfillment, but it is not simply on its way as a still expected promise of God for an indefinite future. No, the kingdom is really encountered here and now in Jesus—in his words and actions.

The underlying eschatological framework of both Qumran and the Jesus movement also comes to expression in a saying of Jesus regarding the Twelve. In Luke, Jesus says of the Twelve: "And I confer a kingdom on you, just as my Father has conferred one on me, that you may eat and drink at my table in my kingdom; and you will sit on thrones judging the twelve tribes of Israel" (22:29-30).[15] Jesus sees the function of judging (or ruling) as a future activity.[16] The Twelve are not at this point in Jesus' ministry entrusted with real power of judging, but it is promised to them. They still remain in the perspective of symbolic activity. Another scriptural passage that points to the eschatological character of the Twelve is found toward the end of the process of the emergence of the New Testament, namely, Revelation 21:14: "The wall of the city had twelve courses of stones as its foundation, on which were inscribed the twelve names of the twelve apostles of the Lamb." The passage is found in a longer description of the New Jerusalem and is part of the author's description of "a new heaven and a new earth" (21:1). The context is clearly eschatological. Here, too, the Twelve—but now also identified as "apostles" and as "foundations"—are associated with the consummation of God's plan. Again, the group of the Twelve is presented to us as a symbolic figure. The Twelve do not appear to occupy an office in the early church, in the technical sense of an "office."[17] They are symbols of the

15. See Jacob Jervell, "The Twelve on Israel's Thrones: Luke's Understanding of the Apostolate," in *Luke and the People of God: A New Look at Luke-Acts* (Minneapolis: Augsburg Press, 1972) 75–112. Jervell writes: "In this discourse the future role of the Twelve is decisive since they will exercise ruling authority just as Jesus has. Above all, the Twelve are specially related to Israel (v. 30). They are not presented as ecclesiastical regents, but as Israel's eschatological rulers and judges." Ibid., 79.

16. Gerhard Lohfink, *Does God Need the Church? Toward a Theology of the People of God*, tr. Linda M. Maloney (Collegeville, Minn.: Liturgical Press, 1999) 184, opts for a present function by the Twelve. But see Matt 19:28, the parallel to Luke 22:29-30, where the future role of the Twelve is even more clearly expressed. Meier has discussed this text of Q (Matt 19:28/Luke 22:30) in "The Circle of the Twelve," 653–59.

17. Again, Jervell is insistent on this point, writing: "Luke's unique ecclesiology, the understanding of the church as the restored Israel, illumines another peculiarity in Acts. It

eschatological character of the kingdom Jesus proclaims. But what do we mean by a symbol?

Symbols and Symbolic Activity

The last century witnessed a genuine retrieval of the significance of symbols.[18] We had never really abandoned them, but in the modern period symbols tended to be little appreciated and rarely reflected on explicitly. Theoreticians of symbol point out how symbols differ from mere signs. The language used by scholars varies, but the general insight emerges that a sign remains at the surface level of our consciousness and is usually determined by human convention. Thus, the color red often represents "danger" or the need to stop (as at a traffic light), but logically we could have chosen another color for these purposes. However, the physical phenomenon we call "fire" operates differently. Its meaning is both immediate—exercise caution around it—and transcends our ability to fix its meaning—it has a depth of positive and negative meanings we cannot exhaust. Symbols are connected with who we humans are. To be human is to be bound to symbolic activity.[19] We are bound to many other dimensions anthropologically speaking, of course, but symbols must be

---

is usually claimed that the Twelve are the origin of ecclesiastical offices. It is not clear how this can be understood more precisely. If it is to be understood, for example, that the Twelve institute the offices, transfer authority and install office-holders, then it is mistaken. Luke has little interest in ecclesiastical institutions. For him the church is the continuation of Israel's history." "The Twelve on Israel's Thrones," 95. Meier also points out how short-lived the activity of the Twelve was in the post-resurrectional period. He writes: "[T]he group called the Twelve is never mentioned after Acts 6:2, while even references to 'the apostles' diminish notably after chap. 8, disappearing entirely after 16:4. . . .[T]he Twelve are prominent in the story of Jesus because that is where they actually played a significant role. On the basis of their close relationship with Jesus, which they claimed had been restored and confirmed by a resurrection appearance, the role of the Twelve continued into the earliest days of the church; but it declined and disappeared with surprising rapidity." "The Circle of the Twelve," 670–71.

18. On symbols, see the following general presentations: F. W. Dillistone, *Traditional Symbols and the Contemporary World*, The Bampton Lectures 1968 (London: Epworth Press, 1973); idem, *The Power of Symbols in Religion and Culture* (New York: The Crossroad Publishing Company, 1986); Gerald A. Arbuckle, "The World of Meaning: Culture," in *Earthing the Gospel: An Inculturation Handbook for the Pastoral Worker* (Maryknoll, N.Y.: Orbis Books, 1990) 26–43.

19. For an anthropologically sensitive presentation, see Bernard J. Cooke, "Anthropological Study of Symbol," in *The Distancing of God: The Ambiguity of Symbol in History and Theology* (Minneapolis: Fortress Press, 1990) 271–91.

listed prominently among our anthropological constants, that is, those dimensions that define what it is to be human, for example, freedom, reason, and language.

One very broad division of symbols might include the two general types I will call archetypal and conscious. Carl Jung theorizes that basically symbols are universal and transcultural.[20] They function in the human unconscious as archetypes that help explain human phenomena and meanings shared by all peoples. Dreams are attempts by our consciousness to enter into these archetypes and to direct their power. What we experience consciously as symbols, for example, blood, and how we react to it, is determined by our cultural assumptions, but ultimately it can only be "understood" at the more fundamental level of our unconscious life. Our "understanding" of symbols is really an ignorance of the full depth and power of the symbol. Archetypal symbols have the potential to be unitive (sym-bolical) or divisive (dia-bolical).

Conscious symbols are more directly under our human control. We have access to them at the level of our conscious processes—which include our understanding, willing, and feeling or emotions. We are somewhat directive in their regard, though never as much as we assume. Here the symbol operates in the important realm of our culture. What I call conscious symbols can be understood in two ways. To some, the symbol "participates" in another reality and communicates something of that other reality in sharing itself.[21] The general philosophical thrust comes from Plato; it is genuinely metaphysical. It is more "exemplaristic"[22] and so employs vocabulary such as substance, essence, and unity. Much of Catholic "sacramental" thought operates on this assumption of what a symbol is. Sacramental action is ultimately a form of symbolic activity

20. Cooke, ibid., 307–9. See Sandra M. Schneiders, *Finding the Treasure: Locating Catholic Religious Life in a New Ecclesial and Cultural Context* (New York: Paulist Press, 2000) 18–32 ["The Psychological Archetype: The Virgin"] for an application of the theory of Jungian archetypes.

21. This is the approach taken by Paul Tillich, "The Nature of Religious Language," *Theology of Culture,* ed. R. C. Kimball (Oxford: Oxford University Press, 1959) 107–16.

22. Exemplaristic causality is generally associated with St. Augustine (354–430) and the Franciscan school represented by St. Bonaventure (1221–1274). Exemplarity is not some purely extrinsic imitation but the expression outside of God of the mystery of God in the created order. The Son operates as exemplaristic cause of truth and salvation in the order of the incarnation, just as the Word is the *exemplum* of the Father in the Trinity. See Zachary Hayes, *The Hidden Center: Spirituality and Speculative Christology in St. Bonaventure* (New York: Paulist Press, 1981) 13–15 and 59–61.

that relates both to the transcendent ground of our existence and equally to the interpersonal and social sharing in that transcendent reality.[23] To others, a symbol operates "dialectically." Two realities are related and mutually define each other, not by sharing in the other's being but by standing in relation to it and in this way constituting it.[24] In this case, the causality, if I may use the term, is mutual, autonomous, and simultaneous. In the philosophical tradition, I would point to Aristotle and Hegel as representatives of this line of thought. It is more "oppositional" and so employs vocabulary such as dynamism, process, encounter, and finality to explain its insight. I am not convinced that one must choose between the two options. It might be that they operate much like the "quantum mechanical theory" of electricity as exhibiting the qualities of both waves and particles, i.e., ultimately we need both theories deriving from two different yet mutually interrelated "models."[25]

Roger Haight has proposed a division of symbols into first order symbols (which he also calls "concrete" symbols) and second order symbols (which he also calls "conscious" symbols).[26] A first order symbol refers to things taken from our empirical world: "things, events, or persons that make God present to the world and serve as media to communicate God to human consciousness."[27] They include a whole panoply of realizations: the human person in his or her very constitution as nature and freedom, or as spirit and matter; human interaction, for example, prayer, liturgy, fasting; things found in creation, for example, a mountain, a storm, a lamb for sacrifice; historical persons, for example, Moses,

23. See my "Ministry, Sacramentality and Symbolism," in *Franciscan Leadership in Ministry: Foundations in History, Theology, and Spirituality,* Spirit and Life: A Journal of Contemporary Franciscanism 7, eds. Anthony Carrozzo, Vincent Cushing, and Kenneth Himes (St. Bonaventure, N.Y.: Franciscan Institute, 1997) 79–95.

24. Here I would mention Haight's development of Jesus as symbol of God in his *Jesus Symbol of God* (Maryknoll, N.Y.: Orbis Books, 1999). See his earlier presentation in *Dynamics of Theology* (New York: Paulist Press, 1990) 136–38. Karl Rahner's symbolic theory of the *Realsymbol* would seem to belong in this category, though with a meaning peculiar to his systematic theology. See "The Theology of the Symbol," in *Theological Investigations,* 23 vols., tr. Kevin Smyth (Baltimore: Helicon Press, 1966) 4:221–52. We will return to Rahner's ideas regarding the *Realsymbol* and his theory of the church as *Ursymbol* in chapter 8.

25. On quantum theory and the use of "models" by scientists, see Ian G. Barbour, *Religion and Science: Historical and Contemporary Issues* (San Francisco: HarperSanFrancisco, 1997) 166–77.

26. Haight, *Dynamics of Theology,* 135–42. In order to avoid confusion of terms, I will use Haight's typology of first and second order symbols.

27. Ibid., 135.

Mary of Nazareth, Simon Peter, or an experience taken from personal encounters, for example, the presence of the Spirit, the resurrection appearances of the Lord; historical events, for example, the Exodus, Jesus' death on the cross; human artifacts, for example, the temple, bread and wine. The area of first order symbols is vast indeed. Second order symbols represent the inevitable human processing of the concrete realities referred to above. They include concepts, definitions, doctrinal propositions, creeds, scriptures, myths, narratives, theologies both speculative and practical, spiritualities, art and drama, and so forth.

I said above that Jesus communicated through symbols. Perhaps our symbol theory can now help us better understand why I said that Jesus employed the symbol of the kingdom of God in exercising his ministry. It really cannot be reduced to an idea or a definition, though attempts to understand and fix the symbol are not mistaken but will not be able ultimately to fully state the content of the kingdom as a first order symbol.[28] There is no need to apologize for using symbols or to speak of them as "mere" symbols. We would do better to speak of "mere ideas" than of "mere symbols." Our ideas and definitions draw their sustenance from the symbolic world. The Bible understands this, but we insist on forcing the symbolic thought of the Bible into our conscious cognitive categories. What is true of Jesus' proclamation of the kingdom is also true of his gesture in choosing twelve men and fashioning ("creating") them into a first order symbol for the gathering-in of the people of God at the end of times. This is no demotion or denigration of the Twelve. On the contrary, from this point of view they can truly emerge for us as a prophetic deed posited by Jesus to precipitate the arrival of God's kingdom—in part here and now in time and fully at the point that sums up all of time. Understanding the Twelve as symbol of the "true Israel" gathered around Jesus also helps us understand how their role is unique. There can be no succession to the Twelve and their indispensable role in salvation history. Thus, after the death of James of Zebedee (martyred by Herod Agrippa I around 43 C.E.; see Acts 12:2) we hear of no attempt to reconstitute the group of twelve. To have done so would have disrupted the symbolic communication intended by Jesus.

28. Compare the different approaches to the kingdom of God in Rudolf Schnackenburg's classic treatment *God's Rule and Kingdom,* tr. John Murray (New York: Herder and Herder, 1963), and in Norman Perrin's *Jesus and the Language of the Kingdom: Symbol and Metaphor in New Testament Interpretation* (Philadelphia: Fortress Press, 1976). John P. Meier, "The Kingdom of God: God Coming in Power to Rule," in *A Marginal Jew: Rethinking the Historical Jesus,* 3 vols. (New York: Doubleday, 1994) 2:237–506, should also be consulted.

Pauline and Lukan Understandings of the Apostle

It is now time to return to the question posed by the title of the present chapter. In Romans 16:7 we read: "Greet Andronicus and Junia, my relatives and my fellow prisoners; they are prominent among the apostles and they were in Christ before me." Paul seems to know a wider circle of apostles, and he even refers to this married couple as "outstanding apostles."[29] Rudolf Schnackenburg wrote of a pre-Pauline understanding of apostles, one that included a larger number of individuals than is usually assumed.[30] For some of these earliest apostles, we can point to the fact of their receiving a resurrection appearance of the Lord, for example, James, the brother of the Lord (1 Cor 15:7, cf. Gal 19). But many others are referred to as apostles without any indication as to whether they met certain criteria presumed by the earliest community.[31] In this group, Silvanus and Timothy (1 Thess 2:7—note the plural form, "apostles," which refers to the letter's opening greeting by Paul, Silvanus and Timothy), Titus and two unnamed brothers, called "the renowned brother" and "the earnest brother" respectively (2 Cor 8:18 and 22),[32] Epaphroditus (Phil 2:25), and possibly

29. On the woman Junia as an apostle, see the following articles: Elisabeth Schüssler Fiorenza, "The Apostleship of Women in Early Christianity," in *Women Priests: A Catholic Commentary on the Vatican Declaration*, eds. Leonard and Arlene Swidler (New York: Paulist Press, 1977) 135–40; Bernadette Brooten, "'Junia. . .Outstanding among the Apostles' (Romans 16:7)," in ibid., pp. 141–44; Ida Raming, "The Twelve Apostles Were Men. . .," *Theology Digest* 40 (1993) 21–25 [Source: "'Die zwölf Apostel waren Männer. . .': Stereotyp Einwände gegen die Frauenordination und ihre tieferen Ursachen," *Orientierung* 56:12 (June 30, 1992) 143–46. Joseph A. Fitzmyer, *Romans: A New Translation with Introduction and Commentary*, Anchor Bible 33 (New York: Doubleday, 1993) 737–40 also opts for the translation "who are outstanding among the apostles" rather than the possible "who are held in esteem by the apostles."

30. Rudolf Schnackenburg, "Apostles Before and During Paul's Time," in *Apostolic History and the Gospel: Biblical and Historical Essays Presented to F. F. Bruce on His 60th Birthday*, eds. W. Ward Gasque and Ralph P. Martin (Grand Rapids: Wm. B. Eerdmans Publishing Co., 1970) 287–303; idem, "Apostolicity—The Present Position of Studies," *One in Christ* 6 (1970) 243–73. The unnuanced presentation of Thomas M. Kocik, "Apostleship in the New Testament," *Apostolic Succession in an Ecumenical Context* (Staten Island, N.Y.: Alba House, 1996) 1–16, is regrettable. The author seems to be unaware of the historical and exegetical problems involved.

31. Apropos, Fitzmyer has written: "At least sixteen persons are called 'apostles' in the NT: the Twelve plus Barnabas and Paul (Acts 14:4, 14), unnamed persons (1 Cor 9:5; 12:28; 2 Cor 8:23; 11:13; Eph 4:11), as well as possibly Andronicus and Junia here." *Romans*, 739. I will argue that far more than sixteen such persons were called "apostles," but it is encouraging to read of Fitzmyer's support of the position that more than the Twelve and Paul counted as apostles in the early church.

32. I am following the exegesis of Victor P. Furnish, *II Corinthians: Translated with Introduction, Notes, and Commentary*, Anchor Bible 32A, 2nd ed. (Garden City, N.Y.: Doubleday & Co., 1984) 435–37.

Sosthenes (1 Cor 1:1) might be listed among those who are named. But 1 Cor 12:28, a famous passage that treats of various groups of persons in the local communities, speaks of apostles whom "God has appointed in the church." This, then, is the first—and possibly the largest—group of apostles in early Christianity. But what is the origin of the notion or the title "apostle"?

Unfortunately, we are no longer in a position to determine this.[33] What does appear certain is that apostleship is a post-resurrection phenomenon that developed during the earliest stages of nascent Christianity. Attempts to derive it from the Jewish institution of the *shaliach/sheluhim* have not met with widespread acceptance by scholars.[34] Recently, however, Francis H. Agnew has examined the modifications by scholars of the classical theory of Karl H. Rengstorf.[35] Agnew distinguishes two different notions in the *shaliach*. One is based on the practice called a "sending-convention" that is amply attested in the Hebrew Scriptures. The other derives from the later, juridical emissary—*shaliach*—of post-Second Temple rabbinic Judaism. Thus, the apostles were not so much understood as emissaries with juridical authority as figures who were modeled on the ancient prophets.[36] They spoke with the authority of God's word,

33. On this matter, too, Roloff, "Apostel/Apostolat/Apostolizität," in *TRE* 3:432-33 ["Zur Vorgeschichte des Begriffs 'Apostel'"] is worth consulting.

34. Karl H. Rengstorf developed the idea of the derivation of the Christian concept of an apostle from the first-century rabbinic institution of the authorized emissary of the rabbinate. See his classic article on apostleship in *Theological Dictionary of the New Testament,* 10 vols., eds. Gerhard Kittel and Gerhard Friedrich, tr. Geoffrey W. Bromiley (Grand Rapids: Wm. B. Eerdmans Publishing Co., 1964) 1:407–47, especially 414–20. For a handy summary, see *Theological Dictionary of the New Testament,* abridged in one volume by Geoffrey W. Bromiley (Grand Rapids: Wm. B. Eerdmans Publishing Co., 1985) 67–75. Francis H. Agnew, "The Origin of the NT Apostle-Concept: A Review of Research," *Journal of Biblical Literature* 105 (1986) 75–96 at 80, note 18, includes an extended discussion of the many authors who have employed Rengstorf's thesis. See the discussion of the wide variety of options regarding the origin of the term "apostle" by Andrew J. Kirk, "Apostleship since Rengstorf: Towards a Synthesis," *New Testament Studies* 21 (1974–75) 249–64. Kirk argues for a broad and fluid use of the title "apostle" that in the New Testament is not dogmatically determined but reflects the changing historical conditions of the emerging Christian church. He has no difficulty assigning the title to the Twelve also, maintaining that the use represents an early tradition, as witnessed to in Mark 6:30.

35. Agnew, "The Origin of the NT Apostle-Concept," 75–96. Among the major scholars Agnew studies are Birger Gerhardsson, "Die Boten Gottes und die Apostel Christi," *Svensk exegetisk årsbok* 27 (1962) 89–131, and Ferdinand Hahn, "Der Apostel im Urchristentum. Seine Eigenart und seine Voraussetzungen," *Kerygma und Dogma* 20 (1974) 54–77.

36. Agnew writes: "The use of the general sending-convention in the OT provides a variety of important analogues to apostleship as a religious phenomenon. . . .The

but now that word included the message of Jesus crucified and raised from the dead. They were indeed emissaries and messengers from God, and their lifestyle was fashioned on that of the wandering Jesus himself.

A second stage in the development of the notion of the apostle is met in the person of Paul of Tarsus. In the Christian imagination, Paul has emerged as *the* apostle par excellence. Where did Paul derive this unshakable conviction of his apostolic calling? The matter is not simple.[37] He first appears to have been initiated into "apostolic" work by Barnabas at Antioch (Acts 13:2-3 speaks of them as being "sent off"—*apelusan* from *apostellein*). Later, Paul again speaks of Barnabas and of a revelation he has received regarding the "gospel" (Gal 2:1-2). In Paul's own words, it seems, this revelation is the basis of his apostleship. But that apostleship was not without being contested, and it is from Paul's own defense of his apostolic calling that we learn from him how he understood the term.

For Paul there are genuine and spurious apostles. Not everyone claiming the title is ipso facto deserving of its authority and dignity (2 Cor 11:13). And so, Paul begins to delimit its use by determining appropriate criteria. Among these Paul mentions four. First, the apostle is a witness to the Lord's resurrection (1 Cor 9:1: "Am I not an apostle? Have I not seen Jesus our Lord?"). Paul is also a servant who has been "set apart for the gospel about his Son" (Rom 1:1-6). Next, the apostle strives to live and work in communion with the other genuine apostles (Gal 2:9-10). And finally, he strives to realize in his own life the very mystery of the Lord's dying (2 Cor 4:7-18; 11:23-29; 12:1-10; Gal 6:17). Unlike the actions of those whom Paul calls "super-apostles" (2 Cor 11:5 and 12:11), Paul's physical weakness, insignificant stature and bearing, his lack of eloquence, and the absence of amazing deeds of healing, and so forth, are the signs of true apostleship he points to. Paul also employs several images

---

importance of prophetic vocation is paramount. Hahn calls special attention to the fact that NT use of *apostellein/pempein* frequently echoes OT usage of *šlh* with reference to prophetic sending. In what is among the most innovative sections of his essay, he calls attention to the particular importance of Isa 61:1 in this regard. This usage is first christological, but the NT connection of all sending with the sending of Jesus makes it important for consideration of apostleship as well. This is especially so in view of the well-known fact that Paul describes himself in his vocation as apostle in terms derived from OT description of prophetic vocation." "The Origin of the NT Apostle-Concept," 95.

37. See Roloff, "Apostel/Apostolat/Apostolizität," in *TRE* 3:436–40 ["Paulus und sein Apostolat"], and James D. G. Dunn, *The Theology of Paul the Apostle* (Grand Rapids: Wm. B. Eerdmans Publishing Co., 1998) 571–80 ["Paul's Apostolic Authority"].

to communicate the meaning of apostleship. Noteworthy among them are "ambassador" (2 Cor 5:20), "servant/slave" (Rom 1:1; 2 Cor 4:5), "steward" (1 Cor 4:1), "master-builder" (1 Cor 3:10-15), "one who plants" (1 Cor 3:6-8), a "father" (1 Cor 4:15), and a "mother" (Gal 4:19).[38] These images do not define logically what an apostle is but attempt to communicate allusively a richer, more satisfying understanding by way of imagination, employing Old Testament literary allusions and political associations.

In his Gospel and Acts, Luke moves in another direction. It is approximately twenty-five years after the deaths of the originary apostles, who certainly included Paul, Peter, James, and others.[39] Luke is writing for another generation of Christians, during a period scholars today refer to as "subapostolic."[40] In Luke's theological vision, the Twelve no longer function principally as a symbol of Israel's fulfillment but as the witnesses to the life, death, and resurrection of Jesus. The symbolic number twelve recedes into the background, as the individual members of the group are singled out as reliable witnesses to the traditions relating to Jesus. Luke's literary invention is to stylize the events associated with Jesus' life and ministry and the emergence and growth of Christinanity. In this effort, the Twelve become apostles for Luke. The Lukan apostle is primarily a witness to the second generation of Christians of who Jesus was and what he did. The Twelve, even though there was no evidence of

---

38. See Jürgen Becker, *Paul: Apostle to the Gentiles,* tr. O. C. Dean, Jr. (Louisville: Westminster/John Knox Press, 1993) 76–81 ["Paul's Self-Designations and Self-Understanding"].

39. I have chosen to use the somewhat unusual expression "originary apostles" to emphasize the open and fluid character of apostleship in the first generation of Christians. In addition to the major apostolic figures like Peter, Paul, James, Barnabas, et al., the expression includes many other figures the first generation of Christians also regarded as "apostles," e.g., Apollos. The expression "originary apostles" aims at naming apostleship before Luke defined the term to include preeminently the original Twelve, augmented by Matthias after the defection of Judas Iscariot. As I have tried to demonstrate, Luke is responsible for developing what has come to be the traditional idea of the identity of the apostles, a definition that classically came to mean the Twelve and Paul. According to the classical definition, every other person who is named an "apostle" in the New Testament is such in a secondary or inappropriate sense. As I am trying to show, the so-called classical understanding of an apostle begs the question of what Christians in the first century understood by the term "apostle." I submit that the term was quite broad, even though it was not without boundaries. My expression "originary apostles" attempts to point to this phenomenon, especially as regards the first generation of Christians.

40. I am using the terms "subapostolic" and "post-apostolic" in the sense defined by Raymond E. Brown. See *The Churches the Apostles Left Behind* (New York: Paulist Press, 1984) 14–16 and *NJBC,* 1343–44 [=80:21–26].

the fact, have become for Luke the apostles tout court. They are now designated regularly as "the apostles" (Luke 6:13; 9:10; 11:49; 17:5; 22:14; 24:10). There is, of course, no attempt to dissimulate or mislead the second generation of disciples—or us. Instead, Luke employs a different symbolism in association with the apostles—the symbol of "foundations." The emerging and growing communities of Christians rest securely on their preaching. It is their kerygma—the apostolic kerygma in Luke's sense—that is all-important. The symbolism of being a foundation favored by Luke can be discerned in the opening chapter of Acts where the *conditio sine qua non* for the election a new member of the Twelve is developed. In the opening verses the sense of eschatology is palpably present: "Lord, are you at this time going to restore the kingdom to Israel?" (v. 6). A few verses later, however, the sense of time changes. We read: "Therefore, it is necessary that one of the men who accompanied us the whole time the Lord Jesus came and went among us, beginning from the baptism of John until the day he was taken up from us, become with us a witness *(martyra)* to his resurrection" (vv. 21-22). Luke develops a theology of the church that can be at home in time, however indefinite its expanse might be, without denying the Lord's parousia.

This irrefragable witness, based as it is on the twelve apostles' personal knowledge of the events, functions, too, as the basis of their authority. In Acts no important actions are undertaken without either the decision or the concurrence of the twelve apostles, or simply "the apostles" (Acts 6, 8:14ff., 11, and 15). They are now leaders of the community as well as witnesses. This leadership is retrojected by Luke back into the period of the ministry of Jesus. The public ministry of Jesus and the ministry of the Twelve who co-direct the Jerusalem community (together with the "elders" and James) are bridged perfectly. Luke's theological insight works marvelously for his community and his generation but for us can cause a myopic vision of the first-century church. One cannot generalize on Luke's insight, which was valid for his contemporaries but not necessarily in an exclusive sense for us today. We need to read Luke's understanding of an apostle in conjunction with the other evidence of the New Testament, especially Paul's.

The Wider Spectrum of Meanings of the Term "Apostle"

The development of the notion of an apostle does not end with Paul and Luke. There is a trajectory of images of the apostle well into the second century. As with the Petrine and Pauline trajectories, here, too, it is best to begin with the end-point and follow it backward to the source of the trajectory.[41] Interpretation based on a trajectory theory asks the question, "What situation were Christians facing at any given time or in particular circumstances, and how did the figure of an apostle help them to resolve their difficulties?" For Luke the situation was one of assuring his community and future generations of the authoritative witness value of the apostles. It made eminent sense to see the Twelve in a new light, as apostles. By the second generation, the originary apostles certainly represented what we today would understand as an "office" in the church. Their authority and influence would continue to be needed in the struggling and precarious Christian communities. Their teachings and example would provide material for solidifying new offices for the period following the writing of the gospels, the so-called post-apostolic period or third generation of Christians. Instead of the term "apostle" or its cognates disappearing from Christian vocabulary, it can be found in abundance well into the second century. What are some of these uses?

In the pseudonymously Pauline Pastoral epistles,[42] "Timothy" and "Titus" are no longer spoken of as themselves apostles but as close collaborators with Paul whose authority is dependent on him. By a procedure of laying hands on them, "Paul" communicates some of his apostolic authority to them. In 1 Tim 6:11, Timothy is now addressed as a "man of God" (*anthropos theou*, that is, a human being made by God). The authority of Timothy and Titus extends primarily to safeguarding the teachings of the Christian church, under attack from various quarters: mistaken interpretations of the faith, continued misunderstandings with Jews in various cities (Titus 1:14-15 and 3:9), and the inevitable

41. On trajectories in the New Testament, see James M. Robinson and Helmut Koester, *Trajectories through Early Christianity* (Philadelphia: Fortress Press, 1971), who developed and popularized the approach in the mid to late 1960s. It was frequently adopted by New Testament exegetes after that. The theory is presented in the first chapter of the book. The trajectories approach to the Scriptures has shown itself highly successful in developing both new insights and common ground that can be shared by former adversaries. The ecumenical study *Peter in the New Testament*, eds. Raymond E. Brown, Karl P. Donfried, and John Reumann (New York: Paulist Press and Minneapolis: Augsburg Publishing House, 1973) in using just such an approach has effected broad interdenominational consensus on the figure of Peter in the gospels and in the early church. See "Presuppositions of the Study," ibid., 7–22.

42. On the notion of literary pseudonymity in antiquity, see Raymond E. Brown, "Canonicity" in *NJBC*, 1051–52 [=66:8–89], and Robert A. Wild, "The Pastoral Epistles" in ibid., 892 [=56:6–8].

syncretism of a church moving ever more deeply into the empire and its thought world (1 Tim 1:3-7; 4:1-16; 6:3-5; 2 Tim 2:2, 14-18, 23-26; 4:1-5; Titus 1:10–2:1). Timothy and Titus are described as having authority to co-opt into the ranks of the "presbyters" (but referred to in the alternate Greek form *episkopoi* ("overseers") in 1 Tim 3:1-7 and Titus 1:5-9) only candidates who evince certain qualities deemed appropriate to the offices. The same holds true for co-opting deacons into the ministry.

According to many New Testament scholars, Ephesians is another subapostolic text. In three places it refers to "apostles." We need to examine each of these passages. In 2:20 the apostles are mentioned together with the prophets. The context speaks of the image of their being the once-for-all foundations of the church.[43] "The apostles" are the originary apostles whose preaching of the gospel accounts for the faith community's very existence. The same interpretation is probable for 3:5, where the apostles mentioned appear to be the originary apostles (again together with the prophets). However, in 4:11-12 the situation is somewhat different: "And he gave some as apostles, others as prophets, others as evangelists, others as pastors and teachers, to equip the holy ones for the work of ministry, for building up the body of Christ." The list of office-holders is much longer than in 1 Cor 12:28, which mentions only apostles, prophets and teachers. Evidently, the community has witnessed the development of a more extensive corps of leaders to help meet its needs. As always, the apostle holds first place among church offices. But if we are some twenty-five years after the fact of the death of the great originary apostles, who are the apostles mentioned as active in the community of the mid to late 80s? Many commentators interpret this mention of apostles and prophets, too, as referring to the apostles and prophets whose faith and proclamation of Christ are at the origin of the church's faith.[44] But

43. For the image of "being a foundation," see 2 Tim 2:19 also.

44. Among the helpful commentaries on Ephesians, see Markus Barth, *Ephesians: Introduction, Translation, and Commentary,* The Anchor Bible 34 and 34A (Garden City, N.Y.: Doubleday & Co., 1974) 43–40 and 477–84; Joachim Gnilka, *Der Epheserbrief,* Herders theologischer Kommentar zum Neuen Testament (2nd ed.; Freiburg: Verlag Herder, 1977) 210–14; Rudolf Schnackenburg, *Ephesians: A Commentary,* tr. Helen Heron (Edinburgh: T & T Clark, 1991 [German ed., 1984]) 180–84; Pheme Perkins, *Ephesians,* Abingdon New Testament Commentaries (Nashville: Abingdon Press, 1997) 99–102; and John Muddiman, *The Epistle to the Ephesians,* Black's New Testament Commentaries (New York: Continuum, 2001) 198–201. My interpretation departs from the common one by understanding the "apostles" in 4:11 as referring to persons who were contemporary with the composition of the document and not to the originary apostles. Ferdinand Hahn also speaks about the

the context is clearly one of present offices "to equip the holy ones for the work of ministry, for building up the body of Christ." The apostles of Eph 4:11 appear to be active here and now in proclaiming the gospel of the reconciliation of Jew and Gentile in the community of Ephesus. The effect and the continuing process of working for reconciliation is, in fact, one of the main themes of the epistle. Is it reasonable to infer, then, that apostles were still active—in some sense or other—even at this relatively late first-century date? There is evidence that this is the case.

For instance, we read in the *Didache* that apostles were still active in the church.[45] These apostles are wandering charismatic figures[46] and they are not expected to remain too long in a community, but are to be soon on their way.

> Now concerning the apostles and prophets, deal with them as follows in accordance with the rule of the gospel. Let every apostle who comes to you be welcomed as if he were the Lord. But he is not to stay for more

"apostles" mentioned in Eph 4:11 as contemporary with the community and calls them "wandering charismatic apostles." See "Der Apostolat im Urchristentum," 60–61. However, Hahn's point is to exclude these "wandering charismatic apostles," together with apostles entrusted with tasks by a Christian community ("Gemeindeapostel," e.g., 2 Cor 8:23), from the full notion of what an apostle is—one who has been called by the Risen Lord for this ministry for life, e.g., Paul. I consider this restriction by Hahn to be exaggerated but welcome his threefold distinction of an apostle.

45. The *Didache* is notoriously difficult to date, in part because of its composite nature. Since the discovery of the *Didache* in 1873 and its publication ten years later, various theories about its date of composition have been presented. There are three general positions: an early date, from 50–70 (proposed by Jean-Paul Audet in 1958—an earlier formulation of an early date was proposed by Paul Sabatier in 1885), a middle date, from 90–150 (proposed by Rudolf Knopf) or around 100 (proposed by J. B. Lightfoot in 1893 and recently by Kurt Niederwimmer in 1989), and the late date from 135–165 (proposed by Adolf von Harnack in 1902—earlier Archbishop Philotheos Bryennios, the discoverer of the manuscript, had proposed a late date of 120-160). See Jonathan A. Draper, "The *Didache* in Modern Research: An Overview," in *The Didache in Modern Research*, ed. J. A. Draper (Leiden: E. J. Brill, 1996) 1–42. Also worth consulting on the *Didache* are Clayton N. Jefford, ed., *The Didache in Context: Essays on Its Text, History and Transmission* (Leiden: E. J. Brill, 1995), and Kurt Niederwimmer, *The Didache: A Commentary*, Hermeneia—A Critical and Historical Commentary on the Bible, tr. Linda M. Maloney (Minneapolis: Fortress Press, 1998 [1st German ed., 1989; 2nd ed., 1993].

46. The idea of wandering charismatics of the early church has been appropriated and developed extensively by Gerd Theissen in numerous publications. See his early essay "Legitimation and Subsistence: An Essay on the Sociology of Early Christian Missionaries," in *The Social Setting of Pauline Christianity: Essays on Corinth*, ed. and tr. by John H. Schütz (Philadelphia: Fortress Press, 1982) 27–67. Ferdinand Hahn had already referred to these figures as "wandering charismatic apostles." See "Der Apostolat im Urchristentum," 60–61.

than one day, unless there is need, in which case he may stay another. But
if he stays three days, he is a false prophet. And when the apostle leaves, he
is to take nothing except bread until he finds his next night's lodging (11:3-6).

What would their task have been? Clearly, it is different from what we
have heard in Paul's letters and in the deutero-Pauline literature, but it
probably still had to do with giving witness to the gospel. Also, their status is still quite high: they are compared with the Lord. Nevertheless, we
are left with many questions. How are they related to the prophets? Has
the term "apostle" become interchangeable with the "prophet"? The text
goes back and forth between them.

Another late first-century, or early second-century, source also makes
reference to "apostles." In the Book of Revelation we read: "I know your
works, your labor, and your endurance, and that you cannot tolerate the
wicked; you have tested those who call themselves apostles but are not,
and discovered that they are impostors" (2:2; cf. 18:20). Are these apostles
the same as those mentioned in the *Didache,* charismatic wanderers whose
authenticity needs to be tested?[47] Perhaps the last canonical book in the
New Testament, the Second Letter of Peter,[48] also mentions "apostles" as
late figures in the post-apostolic period. At 3:1-2 we read: "I am trying to
stir up your sincere disposition, to recall the words previously spoken by
the holy prophets and the commandment of the Lord and savior through
your apostles." Is it unambiguously clear that the apostles mentioned
here refer to the originary apostles of the first generation? And who are
the apostles mentioned in Jude 17-18: "Remember the words spoken be-
forehand by the apostles of our Lord Jesus Christ, for they told you, 'In
the last time there will be scoffers who will live according to their own
godless desires.'" Is this a recollection of the teaching of the originary
apostles or of the teaching of later apostles who had to confront the con-

47. Adela Yarbro Collins writes: "Traveling charismatic leaders who were visiting
Ephesus considered themselves commissioned by the risen Lord or by particular congregations to this work. Such itinerant leadership was common in the early Church; Paul
and John himself fit into that pattern. . . .John calls these apostles false because he rejects
their teaching or because they rival his leadership or both." "The Apocalypse (Revelation)," *NJBC,* 1001 [=63:22].
48. Jerome H. Neyrey opts for the turn of the century (see "The Second Epistle of
Peter," *NJBC,* 1017 [=65:2]), as did Thomas W. Leahy in the 1st edition of the *Jerome Biblical Commentary* (Englewood Cliffs, N.J.: Prentice-Hall, 1968) 495 [=65:4], whereas earlier
critical scholarship suggested about 120 (Wikenhauser-Schmid) or the second quarter of
the second century (Werner Kümmel).

fusion among Christians regarding the delay of the Lord's parousia? If the Letter of Jude is also pseudonymous,[49] then the apostles mentioned might simply be an anachronism designed to reinforce its pseudonymous character. But there is another possibility, namely, that this document from the post-apostolic period is also speaking about real apostles late in the first century. It appears as though the evidence for apostles in early Christianity extends well beyond the classical and originary figures of Paul, Peter, James, and others, even if it is now impossible to know exactly what their status and responsibilities were.[50]

Conclusions

The first result of our investigation must be the distinction between "the Twelve" and the apostles. They represent two different groups of individuals in early Christianity with two very different functions. The Twelve were the symbolic expression of Jesus' conviction that in his proclamation of the kingdom of God the end times had begun. God was reuniting and healing the people of the covenant, and Jesus himself was inseparably a part of the process of renewal of the "true Israel." The apostles, on the other hand, represented the emergence of a community more or less distinct from Judaism, its parent. Their function was to be the once-for-all foundations of the confession of early Christians regarding the life, death, and resurrection of Jesus and his inseparable connection with God's kingdom in its ultimate or eschatological phase. Confusion results when we try to force these two categories of individuals—the Twelve and the apostles—into one cohesive group.[51]

49. Jerome H. Neyrey, "The Epistle of Jude," *NJBC*, 917 [59:2–3], considers Jude to be pseudonymous and dates it "late 1st century." However, Neyrey regards the apostles mentioned in verse 17 as "figures of the distant past," thus the originary apostles and not late first-century wandering apostles found in the *Didache* and possibly, too, in the Book of Revelation and 2 Peter.

50. *1 Clement* also alludes to a second group of apostolic men that might also be referenced in regards to naming a later category of apostles, but I propose to examine the appropriate text in some detail in chapter 3 when I discuss apostolicity in the early church.

51. Gerald O'Collins falls prey to such confusion in his article "Did Apostolic Continuity Ever Start? Origins of Apostolic Continuity in the New Testament," *Louvain Studies* 21 (1996) 138–52, at 142–44. He writes: "Attentive reading of the Gospels shows, then, multiple witness for the fact that at some point in his ministry Jesus chose twelve leaders from among the wider ranks of his followers and gave them some kind of authoritative office" (143). In his desire to overcome an anti-hierarchical tendency among certain authors, a desire understandable on its own, O'Collins falls into the trap of using the "twelve" as an office both in the ministry of Jesus and in the post-Easter church.

Secondly, we have had to confront the wide diversity of apostles in first-century Christianity. Scholars have long known of the distinction between "apostles of the Lord" and "apostles of the churches," but have failed to note still further distinctions among the ranks of those called apostles in the New Testament and early extra-canonical literature. In general, the impression created was that only the "apostles of the Lord" were apostles in the strict sense. "Apostles of the churches" were representatives or delegates of communities of Christians. The result has been that the other apostles mentioned throughout the New Testament have been forced into this twofold mold.[52] In the process, the richness of the notion of apostle has gone unnoticed. The trajectories approach to ancient texts, beginning with later texts and working backward to a point of origin, has proven helpful in this context. As a result, we can distinguish between originary apostles and a later first-century category of apostles. We can also distinguish better between pre-Pauline, Pauline, and Lukan understandings of the originary apostles, and between sub-apostolic and post-apostolic meanings of the later apostles. Perhaps future scholars will be able to better interpret other thorny issues, namely, the possibility of women apostles in the period of originary apostles and the issue of succession to the apostles.

Finally, we are now in a better position to understand the issue of office in early Christianity. The Twelve do not represent an office yet,[53] the apostles certainly do. It is an incipient understanding of office—use of titles, ascription of real authority, a certain permanency, the connotation

52. John Muddiman is a good example of this tendency. "In Paul, the term [apostolos] is used in two ways: of representatives or delegates sent from one congregation to another ('apostles of churches', 2 Cor. 8.23); and of representatives of the risen Christ, sent by him to preach the gospel (1 Cor. 15.8-10; 1 Cor. 1.20). 'Apostle' in this exalted sense seems to incorporate elements of a role equivalent in the new dispensation to that of the Old Testament prophets (cf. Gal. 1:15f.)." *The Epistle to the Ephesians,* 57–58.

53. John P. Meier writes with admirable clarity about the symbolic function of the Twelve: "[T]he Twelve as a group faded quickly from the scene after Easter. But what we can discern of their activity—basically from the Acts of the Apostles—argues for their more or less permanent residence and activity in the holy city of Jerusalem, the spiritual capital of Israel and the locus of Jesus' crucifixion and claimed resurrection. It is in Jerusalem that the Twelve apparently gave corporate witness to Jesus before the temple authorities, the citizens of Jerusalem, and the throngs of Jews from all over the world who crowded into Jerusalem during the great pilgrimage feasts. Neither Acts nor any other NT source gives the slightest indication that, during the early days of the church, the Twelve as a group were active in Galilee or traveled around Israel on any sort of corporate, organized mission." *A Marginal Jew,* 3:158f.

of certain "rights"–but an office nonetheless. An office can be succeeded to, at least in certain respects. But the character of apostolic office in the early church also emerges more clearly. I really do not see the strictly collegial character of the group of apostles in the first century. The group of "twelve apostles," with Peter as the head, are not a primordial form of the episcopal college with the pope as its head.[54] But this does not mean that collegiality is altogether absent either. There was a real concern for communion among the apostles.[55] This is unambiguously clear in the incident at Antioch involving Peter and Paul (see Gal 2:11-14), but even earlier in Paul's concern to be at one in proclaiming the gospel with "the pillars" [of the church] (Gal 2:1-10). Communion is more flexible and allows for greater diversity, and yet is still open to being realized in "collegial" terms. One notes communion among the apostles and subsequently among the presbyter-bishops and eventually among the threefold hierarchy of bishop, presbyters, and deacons–but this is another matter which we have yet to consider. Still, it is important to note that collegiality is adumbrated in the experience of the first century of Christianity.

54. See Vatican II, the Dogmatic Constitution on the Church (LG): "These apostles he [the Lord Jesus] established as a college or permanent group over which he placed Peter, chosen from among them" (art. 19). Throughout the book I quote from the translation in Norman P. Tanner, ed., *Decrees of the Ecumenical Councils,* 2 vols. (Washington, D.C.: Georgetown University Press, 1990) here at 2:863. See also LG, art. 18 and art. 22.

55. On the notion of communion in the New Testament, see Michael McDermott, "The Biblical Doctrine of *KOINONIA,*" *Biblische Zeitschrift* 19 (1975) 64–77; Schuyler Brown, "*Koinonia* as the Basis of New Testament Ecclesiology?" *One in Christ* 12 (1976) 157–67; and Josef Hainz, "*koinônia* community; fellowship; participation" in *Exegetical Dictionary of the New Testament,* 3 vols., eds. Horst Balz and Gerhard Schneider (Grand Rapids: Wm. B. Eerdmans Publishing Co., 1991) 2:303–5.

CHAPTER TWO

Why the Early Churches Understood Themselves as Apostolic

In 1999 an ecumenical event of singular importance took place—the signing of the mutual agreement on justification by the Lutheran World Federation and the Roman Catholic Church. The doctrine of justification was at the very center of the Reformation. Over the centuries, Catholic and Lutheran positions hardened and differences were seen as heresy and grave errors. Even in the ecumenical climate of the post-Vatican II era, arriving at agreement between Lutherans and Catholics proved elusive. But in the end, due to patient dialogue and the courage to move beyond the words of formulas that were too restrictive, the impossible happened. A formula was found that represented fairly and without caricature the belief of both Lutherans and Roman Catholics on God's justification of the sinner.[1]

Unlike justification, the topic of this book continues to elude a common solution, even though all sides yearn for it. The theologically intractable issue is apostolic succession. Issues of church offices, ministry, and ordination are theological hot potatoes. It is my contention that just as Roman Catholics and Lutherans had to find new language for new insights on justification, the same will have to be the case for apostolic succession. In the various bilateral and multilateral dialogues much has been accomplished, but the goal of full communion among the churches con-

---

1. See "Joint Declaration on the Doctrine of Justification," *Origins* 28/8 (7/16/98) 120–27 for the text itself. The official signing of the declaration took place in Augsburg, Germany, on October 31, 1999.

tinues to evade us because issues of ministry are so divisive. I do not think this should be the case. At the base of the Reformation were abuses of office, but the issue of ecclesiastical office itself was not a major one.[2] Much changed in this regard as the Reform bogged down. Eventually, the Reform splintered into innumerable movements. It is important for both Catholics and Protestants to remember that ecclesiology and ministry were secondary issues. We, too, should not give them central status. Apostolic succession need not be a church-dividing issue.

What Is Apostolicity?

The Christian churches confess the same Nicene-Constantinopolitan Creed, in which they say: "We believe in one, holy, catholic, and apostolic church."[3] Yet it is not entirely clear what claim we are making about

2. See Edgar M. Carlson, "The Doctrine of the Ministry in the Confessions," *The Lutheran Quarterly* 15 (1963) 118–31. Carlson writes: "The doctrine of the ministry, or the office of the ministry, was incidental and secondary to the real controversy which is at the heart of the [Lutheran] Confessions" (119). Many years ago, Walter Kasper confirmed this sentiment when he wrote: "Neither the Reformers nor the Council of Trent decisively made the question of ecclesiastical office a central issue." See his "Zur Frage der Anerkennung der Ämter in den lutherischen Kirchen," in *Evangelium–Welt–Kirche,* ed. Harding Meyer (Frankfurt: Verlag Otto Lembeck, 1975) 401–14, at 401. See also George A. Lindbeck, "The Lutheran Doctrine of the Ministry: Catholic and Reformed," *Theological Studies* 30 (1969) 588–612. Yves Congar, too, stresses this point, especially with regard to John Calvin's theology of ministry. See "Apostolicité de ministère et apostolicité de doctrine: Essai d'explication de la réaction protestante et de la tradition catholique," in *Ministères et communion ecclésiale* (Paris: Les Éditions du Cerf, 1971) 51–94, at 56–58.

3. H. Denzinger and A. Schönmetzer, *Enchiridion symbolorum, definitionum et declarationum de rebus fidei et morum* [hereafter, DS], 33rd ed. (Freiburg im Breisgau: Verlag Herder, 1965) #150. The Nicene-Constantinopolitan Creed continues to be the criterion that governs the ecumenical movement. The first consultation between Lutherans and Roman Catholics in the United States chose the Creed as its point of departure. See Paul C. Empie and William W. Baum, eds., *The Status of the Nicene Creed as Dogma of the Church* (Washington, D.C.: National Catholic Welfare Conference Publications Office, 1965). See also the World Council of Churches Commision on Faith and Order, "The Ecumenical Importance of the Nicene-Constantinopolitan Creed, Odessa Report, 1981," in *Apostolic Faith Today: A Handbook for Study,* Faith and Order Paper 124, ed. Hans-Georg Link (Geneva: WCC Publications, 1985) 245–56. The importance of the Creed remains undiminished even in our day. See the following studies: André de Halleux, "La réception du symbole oecuménique de Nicée à Chalcédoine," *Ephemerides theologicae Lovanienses* 61 (1985) 5–47; Frederick Norris, "The Nicene-Constantinopolitan Creed," in *The Apostolic Faith: Protestants and Roman Catholics* (Collegeville, Minn.: The Liturgical Press, 1992) 45–59; and Christopher R. Seitz, ed., *Nicene Christianity: The Future for a New Ecumenism* (Grand Rapids, Mich.: Brazos Press, 2001) for recent contributions on the Creed.

the church when we say it is apostolic. The descriptor "apostolic" was, in fact, the last of the so-called notes of the church to be included in a creed.[4] Unity and holiness were clearly scriptural claims for the church. Catholicity and apostolicity are not biblical terms but would be coined to make certain points about the church as it emerged from Judaism and defined itself over against the various religions in the Roman empire.

In general, theologians point to apostolicity as guaranteeing the identity of the church of a later period with the early Christian community.[5] The church as we know it today was determined by the apostles' witness to Christ and by decisions they made in the light of their understanding of the Christ event. Their witness and their decisions pertain to the areas of belief and doctrine, sacramental practice, the sense of mission, and day-to-day discipleship (which includes morality, spirituality, life in the secular polis, and customs practiced by Christians). The cause that precipitated the emergence of the importance of apostolicity was the conflict with Gnosticism in the mid to late second century. The various Gnostic teachers who espoused Christianity claimed that they had received privileged knowledge of Christ's intentions and significance from the apostles.[6]

4. It can be found in the creed of the church at Salamis from 374. See DS #42. Jared Wicks has examined the antecedents of the use of the phrase before Salamis and Constantinople I, especially in Alexander of Alexandria (324), Nicaea's anathemas of Arius (†336), and Athanasius (340–362), in "Ecclesial Apostolicity Confessed in the Creed," *Pro Ecclesia* 9 (2000) 150–64, and has given us the best study to date on the Nicene-Constantinoplitan confession of the church as "one, holy, catholic, and apostolic." He argues that Constantinople I did not draw upon the creed of Salamis as a conciliar draft text, but upon the antecedents just mentioned, as well as the use of the phrase by the *Apostolic Constitutions,* Basil of Caesarea (ca. 375), and Gregory of Nazianzen (ca. 379–380). What emerges is a more organic understanding of the third part of the creed, which treats of the Holy Spirit. As Wicks writes: "This formulation of a connection between the 'economy' of the Spirit's work and the ecclesial article helps overcome any impression that the final part of the creed contains simply juxtaposed affirmations, which have few or no organic links with each other. The elements or articles are linked by the operation of the Holy Spirit among the saints from the beginning, who forms them into a holy community, imparting the forgiveness of sins and a share in the kingdom of heaven, leading to resurrection and the life of the world to come" (163).

5. Werner Löser is typical, writing: "By the apostolicity of the church is meant the oneness of the present-day church with the original apostolic church. Due to its apostolicity the church remains identical through all places and times." See "Apostolicity of the Church," in *Handbook of Catholic Theology,* eds. Wolfgang Beinert and Francis Schüssler Fiorenza (New York: The Crossroad Publishing Company, 1995) 25–26, at 25.

6. See Pheme Perkins, *The Gnostic Dialogue: The Early Church and the Crisis of Gnosticism* (New York: Paulist Press, 1980), and idem, *Gnosticism and the New Testament* (Minneapolis: Fortress Press, 1993).

This secret knowledge, however, was to be entrusted only to certain initiates, so that a two-tiered structure of ordinary versus elite believers characterized the various Gnostic systems. If the deepest, purest, and most important salvific Christian truths were known only to the leaders and their initiates, the universality of Christian faith was imperiled. Christ came to save some, not all, men and women, as 1 Tim 2:3-4 claimed: "[Prayer for all people] is pleasing to God our savior, who wills everyone to be saved and to come to knowledge of the truth." Thus, Irenaeus of Lyons insisted on the public character of Christian beliefs and practices. The term "apostolic" came to be used to make just such a claim to the public accessibility of Christianity. The apostles—here understood as the Twelve and Paul—had either known the Jesus of the public ministry personally or, like, Paul had received revelation of salvific truth from the Risen One. Yet, even Paul made efforts to bring his gospel into conformity with what the other apostles preached.

Apostolicity of Origin

The notion of apostolicity may be examined from four of its expressions. The first is that a church is apostolic by reason of origin. It was founded by an apostle and thereby endowed by the apostle with the truth of faith and the appropriate expressions for living it. Among the understandings of an apostle examined in the previous chapter, missionary apostles were responsible for founding churches. By the third century, churches directly founded by an apostle began to refer to themselves as "apostolic." In the early centuries, Christians distinguished between communities clearly established by an apostle and those that were founded in turn by these same churches. The former were considered primary apostolic churches, for example, Rome, Antioch, Alexandria, Corinth, Ephesus, and so forth, while the latter were secondary apostolic churches. James F. McCue detailed this practice in an important contribution to the dialogue of Lutherans and Roman Catholics in the United States.[7] He examined the writings of Irenaeus of Lyons and Tertullian of Carthage, and determined that the churches of directly apostolic origin were considered "norm churches" by the other churches. On Irenaeus he wrote:

7. J. F. McCue, "Apostles and Apostolic Succession in the Patristic Era," in *Eucharist and Ministry,* Lutherans and Catholics in Dialogue 4, eds. Paul C. Empie and T. Austin Murphy (Washington, D.C.: United States Catholic Conference and New York: U.S.A. National Committee of the Lutheran World Federation, 1970) 138–77.

Irenaeus does not seem to require an apostolic pedigree for the existence of a church; at least he nowhere says that this is necessary. That is, a church not established by an apostle is validated according to the Irenaean scheme of things not (or at least not primarily) through a succession of ordinations going back to an apostle. It is validated by being in agreement and harmony with the norm churches, those of apostolic foundation and public episcopal succession.

In Irenaeus' conception the apostolic church or apostolic *cathedra* is more central than the idea of conferral of power from one bishop to another through episcopal consecration or ordination.

. . . If it is not putting too fine a point on the matter, we might say that one becomes a successor to the apostles through ordination for an apostolic church rather than simply through ordination by any bishop whatsoever.[8]

Regarding Tertullian's views, McCue limited himself to Tertullian's Catholic period (193–207). He wrote:

. . . Certain churches are apostolic because they were founded by apostles and are united under bishops in succession to these apostles. But churches which are not of apostolic foundation are said to be apostolic for a variety of reasons. Sometimes he considers a church which was founded as an offshoot from a church that is apostolic in its foundation as being *eo ipso* apostolic. At other times apostolicity is defined, in the Irenaean fashion, in terms of doctrinal agreement and peace with the principal churches.[9]

. . . It is the reception of the orthodox faith that makes a community a church. It may very well be that the practice with which Tertullian was familiar required that the bishop of a new church be consecrated *(inter alia)* by the laying on of hands by other bishops; but his understanding of apostolic succession does not bring this to the fore or even, strictly speaking, require it. Secondary apostolic churches would be derived from the preaching and missionary efforts coming from the original apostolic churches, the handing on of their *regula fidei* and of their scriptures.[10]

---

8. Ibid., 159–60.

9. McCue quotes Tertullian's *De praescriptione* 20 in this regard: "To this test, therefore, will they be submitted for proof by those churches who, although they derive not their founder from apostles or apostolic men (as being of much later date, for they are in fact being founded daily), yet since they agree in the same faith, they are accounted as not less apostolic because they are akin in doctrine."

10. Ibid., 161–63. The picture of apostolic churches painted by McCue is substantially the same as the one presented by J.N.D. Kelly in a paper read to members of the World Council of Churches and the Roman Catholic Joint Theological Commission in the course of their meetings from 1967 and 1968. The paper, "'Catholic and Apostolic' in the

Earlier, Joseph F. Mitros had written of Tertullian's understanding of the Christian faith: "In the public oral tradition of the apostolically founded churches and in their unanimity Tertullian saw the guarantee for the authenticity of the transmission of the original apostolic tradition."[11] Mitros' examination of Tertullian confirms what McCue would later propose, namely, that the quality of apostolicity was to be found primarily—though not exclusively—in the faith of the whole community considered to be apostolic. At the origin of this faith was the preaching and founding activity of the missionary apostles, and it was perpetuated to the extent that it was still believed and inasmuch as it was expressed in further missionary activity of the "apostolic churches." Apostolicity is based on two things. The first is communion among the churches, with primacy attributed to the norm or principal churches. The second is mutual reception of their understandings of the contents and practical implications of the faith. These two ideas are at least as important as episcopal consecration as an expression of apostolic succession in the patristic period.

Early Centuries," can be found in *One in Christ* 6 (1970) 274–87. Kelly writes: "The form that the argument took was to appeal to the succession of bishops in the famous sees (a characteristically second-century doctrine of 'apostolic succession', not to be confused with the types of that doctrine to be evolved in later times). People could be sure, it was contended, that the catholic Church offered them the authentic apostolic revelation because, while the alleged tradition purveyed by the Gnostics was confessedly secret, the catholic rule of faith had from the beginning been proclaimed publicly by an unbroken line of bishops in Churches which could trace their descent lineally from the apostles. So Tertullian arguing in a famous passage (*De praescr.* xix–xx) that the real question is who are the legitimate possessors of the faith and the Scriptures, reminds his readers that Christ himself commissioned the apostles, and they thereupon founded Churches in every city, and other Churches borrowed from them the tradition of faith and doctrine. Thus he distinguishes two kinds of 'apostolic Churches', those directly established by apostles and those which derive their title-deeds from such Churches. Later (*ibid.,* xxxii) he distinguishes a third kind, Churches which, although not founded by apostles or apostolic men, *tamen in eadem fide conspirantes non minus apostolicae deputantur pro consanguinitate doctrinae* ["nevertheless, churches that live by the breath of the same faith are considered no less apostolic by reason of the affinity of their doctrine"—my translation added]. The same line of thought is found repeatedly in Irenaeus, and it is this which explains the second century preoccupation with the compiling of episcopal succession lists. It is interesting to find Augustine, two hundred years later, denying apostolicity to the Donatists because they cannot trace their succession back to the apostles" (285–86).

11. Joseph F. Mitros, "The Norm of Faith in the Patristic Age," *Theological Studies* 29 (1968) 444–71, at 456.

Apostolicity of Doctrine

From the second century onwards, the issue of the content of Christian belief was of central importance. The church could only be church to the extent that it proclaimed and taught what the originary apostles themselves had taught. Fidelity to the apostolic kerygma became the hallmark of Christian belief. The importance of belief emerged concretely out of conflicts with Marcion (d. 160) and other Gnostic teachers whom Irenaeus of Lyons was compelled to refute. The influence of Gnosticism can also be seen in the large number of Gnostic apocryphal works in the second century.[12] The third century also witnessed the need on the part of the churches to interpret the Christian faith. As more and more adherents became affiliated with the church, issues of acculturation and inculturating the faith became urgent, particularly in the encounter with Stoicism[13] and the neo-Platonism[14] of the day. In the context of the sensitive questions that began to emerge, the witness of the churches to what they believed and how they understood the faith grew in importance.[15]

12. See Raymond E. Brown and Pheme Perkins, "Apocrypha; Dead Sea Scrolls; Other Jewish Literature," in *New Jerome Bible Commentary,* ed., Raymond E. Brown, Joseph A. Fitzmyer, and Roland E. Murphy (Englewood Cliffs, N. J.: Prentice Hall, 1990) 1055–82, at 1065–68 ["Christian Apocryphal Gospels"] [=67:53–77], for a brief discussion of second-century apocryphal literature, much of which was influenced by Gnosticism.

13. The philosophical school known as "Stoicism" thrived from the third century B.C.E. to the fourth century C.E. It stressed the cosmic role of *logos* or rationality which pervaded the universe and imparted meaning and order. The cosmic *logos* or "reason" possessed quasi-divine qualities. Stoic thinkers contributed to moral philosophy especially. See Richard Tarnas, *The Passion of the Western Mind: Understanding the Ideas That Have Shaped Our World View* (New York: Ballantine Books, 1993) 75–79 ["The Decline and Preservation of the Greek Mind"], and Carlo Tibiletti, "Stoicism and the Fathers," in *Encyclopedia of the Early Church,* 2 vols., ed. Angelo Di Berardino, tr. Adrian Walford (New York: Oxford University Press, 1992) 2:795–97.

14. Neo-Platonism was a revival and extension of Plato's philosophy that flourished from the third to the sixth century C.E. It stressed unity as the ultimate transcendent principle of all reality, which was understood to have emanated from the divine source. The goal of the world and of human affairs is to contemplate this oneness, to be in harmony with it, and so to return to it. Neo-Platonic thought was hostile to multiplicity and plurality and had no room for genuine history. It resulted in a primarily mystical view of the world. See Richard Tarnas, *The Passion of the Western Mind,* 84–87 ["Neoplatonism"], and Colin E. Gunton, *The One, the Three and the Many: God, Creation and the Culture of Modernity* (New York: Cambridge University Press, 1993) 136–41 ["The One as Transcendental"].

15. Tertullian offers a pertinent example, namely, the apostolic authority of the various Christian scriptures. If the faith of Christians is based on the teachings of the apostles, then it is imperative to determine which writings come from the apostles. Tertullian poses the question regarding the Epistle to the Hebrews and the *Shepherd of Hermas,* whose final written form

With the gradual emergence of mono-episcopacy[16] almost everywhere in the second and third centuries, the bishops, too, began to play an important role in explaining the faith.[17] They did not do so in isolation from others in their churches, for example, the presbyters and thinkers like Clement and Origen for Alexandria, or Tertullian for Carthage, but the center of gravity was definitely shifting to the bishops. Many were well-educated and came to their office with considerable administrative experience. Little by little, they came to speak for their churches and to convene at regional synods to discuss and resolve divisive issues. Gradually, the "apostolic churches" came to see themselves represented in the person of their bishops. This came to expression in the rite of episcopal ordination, the center of which was the expression of the Christian faith by the ordinand. In the course of the ordination, the episcopal candidate professed his faith, the people responded to the profession with shouts of recognition ("*Axios!* He is worthy!"), and the neighboring bishops received him into the communion of the churches. The representativity of the bishop vis-à-vis his church had nothing to do with modern democratic ideas or with juridical notions of delegation, but was rooted in the experience of being one body in Christ and in the unity which was the gift of the Holy Spirit. The bishop's ministry of representing his community was of a different order—one we now recognize as deeply symbolic and which we call "sacramental." However important the office of bishop came to be, we need to remember that at the very heart of the of-

---

is dated today about 150 C.E. Their teaching regarding the exclusive forgiveness of sins in baptism was regulative of Christian practice in this regard in the third century. Hebrews 6:4-6 seems to exclude the possibility of a second forgiveness of sins. If the work is clearly of apostolic origin, then its teaching cannot be put aside in favor of a more lenient policy, even one approved by Bishop Callistus of Rome (or Bishop Agrippinus of Carthage?). In "On Chastity," §20, Tertullian concludes to the apostolicity of the teaching of Hebrews since he judges that Barnabas (an apostle according to 1 Cor 9:6 and Acts 14:14) was its author. See G. G. Blum, "Der Begriff des Apostolischen im theologischen Denken Tertullians," *Kerygma und Dogma* 9 (1963) 102–21, at 110.

16. "Mono-episcopacy" refers to the practice of a local church being led by a single bishop together with its presbyterium and a group of deacons. The local church stands in the foreground of mono-episcopacy. It differs from the later practice of "monarchical episcopacy" which understood the bishop's office as the one source of ministry of a local church with the bishop being assisted by his presbyters, deacons, and other ministers.

17. The history of the emergence and development of episcopacy has been admirably presented recently by Francis A. Sullivan, *From Apostles to Bishops: The Development of the Episcopacy in the Early Church* (New York: Paulist Press, 2001).

fice and its responsibility was the faith of the whole community. The bishop, in fact, was supported by the faith of those he served.

Gradually, the centrality of the community's faith faded into the background as the church became more highly organized and specialization of ministries became the order of the day. The result was the clericalization of the ministry.[18] The proper balance between the official minister and the community of believers was lost. Over a period of centuries, many social factors and complex issues contributed to this sad outcome, with the result that the primacy of the content of apostolic faith (the material dimension), was lost, while the authority of the bishops as teachers of the faith (the formal dimension) came to predominate. One can understand the reform set in motion by Martin Luther and John Calvin as an attempt to re-establish the proper balance between both elements of apostolicity of doctrine, the material and the formal. The sad history of the subsequent development of the Protestant reform and of the Roman Catholic Tridentine reform was the increasing separation of these two elements that make sense only in relation to one another. Primacy must be accorded the content of the faith, along the lines of the early church, but it is not absolute and certainly not able to be isolated from the authoritative witness of official ministers in the church.

Apostolicity of Life

In the third place, we need to consider how Catholic theologians after Vatican II have paid greater attention to other elements of apostolicity that they had neglected heretofore. The result of the Protestant reform and the Roman Catholic Tridentine reform was a tendency toward the polarization of apostolic doctrine and apostolic succession in episcopal office.[19] The churches of the magisterial reformation stressed the former, while Roman Catholics accorded primacy to the latter. In their attempt to broaden the concept of apostolicity after Vatican II, Catholic theologians took into account the whole fabric of life of a Christian community. In short, they realized it was important to look at the concrete

18. See Michel Meslin, "Ecclesiastical Institutions and Clericalization from 100 to 500 A.D.," in *Sacralization and Secularization,* Concilium 47, ed. Roger Aubert (New York: Paulist Press, 1969) 39–54.

19. Alexandre Ganoczy, "'Splendors and Miseries' of the Tridentine Doctrine of Ministries," in *Office and Ministry in the Church,* Concilium 80, ed. Roland Murphy and Bas van Iersel (New York: Herder and Herder, 1972) 75–86.

life of a community to determine its genuineness.[20] What its doctrines are, its sacred writings, its sacramental practices, its style of leadership, its exercise of charity, its moral principles, its internal discipline, its leadership structure, and so forth—all of this must be considered. The community in its entirety and in all its richness must be examined. The focus moved from isolating ecclesiastical office or sacraments or ordinations as the source of a church's apostolicity, to the *doctrine, life,* and *praxis* of the community itself. A certain warrant was found in the documents of Vatican II. In the Decree on Ecumenism, the bishops at Vatican II had written:

> Moreover some, and even most, of the significant elements and endowments which together go to build up and give life to the church itself, can exist outside the visible boundaries of the catholic church: the written word of God; the life of grace; faith, hope and charity, with the other interior gifts of the holy Spirit, and visible elements too. All of these, coming from Christ and leading back to Christ, properly belong to the one church of Christ.
>
> Our separated brothers and sisters also celebrate many sacred actions of the christian religion. These most certainly can truly engender a life of grace in ways that vary according to the condition of each church or community, and must be held capable of giving access to that communion in which is salvation (UR 3).

This passage goes beyond finding a certain degree of apostolicity in the teachings of the apostles as maintained in the non-Catholic communities

---

20. The notion of "life" is a very rich one and is not so easily reduced to a simple idea. It might be helpful to pause for a moment to reflect on it. Drawing on Wilhelm Dilthey's ideas of "life" in his *Lebensphilosophie,* Bernard Lonergan has provided an excellent description of what postconciliar Catholic theologians were trying to express in terms of taking the whole life of a believing community or church into consideration. Lonergan writes: "Living expresses itself. In the expression there is present the expressed. So the data of human studies are not just given; by themselves, prior to any interpretation, they are expressions, manifestations, objectifications of human living. . . . The many expressions of individual living are linked together by an intelligible web. To reach that intelligible connectedness is not just a matter of assembling all the expressions of a lifetime. Rather, there is a developing whole that is present in the parts, articulating under each new set of circumstances the values it prizes and the goals it pursues, and thereby achieving its own individuality and distinctiveness. . . . As there is intelligibility in the life of the individual, so too is there intelligibility in the common meanings, common values, common purposes, common and complementary activities of groups. As these can be common or complementary, so too they can differ, be opposed, conflict. Therewith, in principle, the possibility of historical understanding is reached. For if we can understand singly our own lives and the lives of others, so too we can understand them in their interconnections and interdependence." Lonergan, *Method in Theology* (New York: Herder and Herder, 1972) 210–11.

of faith. Many other elements of ecclesial existence, and hence of the genuine apostolicity of the community, are pointed out. In his important commentary on article 3 of the Decree on Ecumenism, Johannes Feiner wrote:

> The second and third paragraphs of this article now emphasize the constitutive elements of the church which also exist in the communities separated from the Catholic Church. . . .The decree proceeds from the view that the form and body of the church is built up from a complex whole of invisible and visible endowments, which Christ has bestowed upon his church and effects within it. In the wholeness (not perfection) accorded by Christ to his church these endowments are found, according to Catholic belief, only in the Catholic Church. But they are to be found also in varying, reduced degrees in other Christian communities, and still possess their power to create and maintain communion. These endowments, values and realities, which are essential constituents of the church, are referred to in the second paragraph of this article as (ecclesial) elements. The term is also used in documents of the World Council of Churches. . . .The Decree on Ecumenism recognizes in non-Catholic communities more than Calvin does in the papal church, more than mere scanty "vestiges" or miserable "relics"; it sees in them essential structural elements of the church. And in such communities it even recognizes "very many of the most significant elements". The decree makes no attempt to give a full list of these elements; this makes it all the more important that it makes specific mention of the written word of God and then of the life of grace, of faith, hope and charity. The holy Scripture is the "institutional element" through which Christianity is constantly led to recognize its calling to the communion of the church, and by which its recognition of other constitutive elements of the church willed by Christ, such as the sacraments and the ministry, is maintained. And the life of grace, consisting of faith, hope and charity, which the decree mentions, forms the primary inner gift of grace, which links Christians with one another in the communion of the church, and which all outward elements of the church ultimately exist to serve.[21]

21. Johannes Feiner, "Commentary on the Decree," in *Commentary on the Documents of Vatican II*, 5 vols., ed. Herbert Vorgrimler, tr. R. A. Wilson (New York: Herder and Herder, 1968) 2:74. Feiner's comments on paragraph 3 are also appropriate. He writes: "Whereas the Orthodox Churches maintain all seven sacraments which are recognized by the Catholic Church, and the Catholic Church acknowledges the validity of all the sacraments of the Orthodox Churches, most of the Reformation Churches only recognize baptism and the Lord's Supper. This is the reason why the Catholic Church, for example, regards the Eucharist of the Orthodox Church in a different light from the Lord's Supper of the Protestant Churches, as is made clear in Chapter III of the decree. This does not mean that the Catholic Church denies the effectiveness for grace of the Protestant Lord's Supper—as

Apostolicity treated in this holistic and comprehensive manner is concerned about the very substance of apostolicity and might be called "substantive apostolicity."[22] It is the living *traditio apostolica,* and is more than purely doctrinal since it is also based on the right praxis of lived discipleship. The "Pullach Report" (1972) of the Anglican-Lutheran Conversation gives an admirable formulation of what I am trying to express by the phrase "substantive apostolicity." We read there:

> The succession of apostolicity through time is guarded and gives contemporary expression in and through a wide variety of means, activities and institutions: the canon of Scriptures, creeds, confessional writings, liturgies, the activities of preaching, teaching, celebrating the sacraments and ordaining and using a ministry of Word and Sacrament, the exercising of pastoral care and oversight, the common life of the church, and the engagement in mission to and for the world (74).[23]

---

indeed it also considers marriage between Protestant Christians as a sacrament effecting grace, even though the Reformation Churches do not share this conviction without qualifications. But the statement made in this paragraph ought not to be limited to sacramental actions in the strict sense. Preaching, blessings and other liturgical actions affect grace and create access to the communion of salvation, albeit in a different way from the sacraments." Ibid., 75.

22. The expression "substance of apostolicity" was used in an early postconciliar ecumenical document to express the stress in the early church on apostolic tradition. The document, usually referred to as the "Malta Report," says the following: "The basic intention of the doctrine of apostolic succession is to indicate that, throughout all historical changes in its proclamation and structures, the church is at all times referred back to its apostolic origin. The details of this doctrine seem to us today to be more complicated than before. In the New Testament and the early fathers, the emphasis was obviously placed more on the substance of apostolicity, i.e., on succession in apostolic teaching" (57). "Report of the Joint Lutheran-Roman Catholic Study Commission on 'The Gospel and the Church,'" (1972). See Harding Meyer and Lukas Vischer, ed., *Growth in Agreement: Reports and Statements of Ecumenical Conversations on a World Level* (New York: Paulist Press and Geneva: World Council of Churches, 1984) 181. The somewhat later document in the same dialogue between Lutherans and Roman Catholics entitled "The Ministry in the Church" (1981) says: "The starting point must be the apostolicity of the church in the substantive sense" (60). Ibid., 267. Francis A. Sullivan speaks of "a more comprehensive notion of apostolicity." See *The Church We Believe In: One, Holy, Catholic and Apostolic* (New York: Paulist Press, 1988) 189. It is just this sense of apostolicity in a more comprehensive or all-inclusive way that I am trying to express in the phrase "substantive apostolicity." I intend the phrase to mean more than the teachings of the apostles in the sense of the doctrines they bequeathed to the church. The *traditio apostolica* includes the whole "life" of the church.

23. See H. Meyer and L. Vischer, ed., *Growth in Agreement,* 24.

Substantive apostolicity is founded on the importance of apostolic witness to the Christian mystery as expressed in all the dimensions of the life of the early church.[24]

Another dimension that the notion of substantive apostolicity tries to retrieve is the accent in the early church on the authentic witness of the whole of the local church, and not simply the isolated authoritative witness of its leadership, however important or indispensable. The postconciliar ecumenical documents uniformly state the apostolicity of the whole church, that is, of all its members. The Reformed-Roman Catholic report "The Presence of Christ in Church and World" is typical of many: "The whole Church is apostolic" (94).[25] Substantive apostolicity attempts to retrieve some of the breadth and depth of the early Christian interpretation. It is open to understanding the church as a communion of apostolic churches.

Apostolic Succession

Finally, the church is apostolic by reason of ordained apostolic ministry. This is usually referred to as apostolic succession and means the succession of bishops in the course of the church's history. Yves Congar has pointed out that apostolic succession is not simply a matter of an historical chain of episcopal ordinations stretching back unbroken to the first bishops. It also possesses an element that transcends history and yet

24. The Greek Orthodox theologian John D. Zizioulas develops a similar idea when he speaks about valid apostolic ministry in terms of "the entire structure of the community." He writes: "The first and fundamental consequence of the method of looking at the community first and then at the criteria is that the recognition of ministries becomes in fact a *recognition of communities* in an existential sense. Thus one's primary question in facing another ministry would be a question concerning *the entire structure of the community* to which it belongs." *Being as Communion: Studies in Personhood and the Church* (Crestwood, N.Y.: St. Vladimir's Seminary Press, 1985) 244. Italics are the author's.

25. Ibid., 457. In his contribution to the Symposium on "Apostolic Continuity of the Church and Apostolic Succession," Centro Pro Unione, Rome, November 23–24, 1995, Gerald O'Collins, professor at Rome's Gregorian University, writes in similar vein: "I must join the Porvoo Statement and our other speakers in acknowledging the life and worship of the whole community to be the primary expression of 'the faith that comes to us from the apostles' (First Eucharistic Prayer) and of the continuity in/of that faith. In this sense of continuing to be apostolic in faith and life, apostolic succession is an attribute of the whole Church and is wider than mere episcopal succession." See O'Collins, "Did Apostolic Continuity Ever Start? Origins of Apostolic Continuity in the New Testament," *Louvain Studies* 21 (1996) 138–52, at 152.

does not negate it.[26] He pointed to the opinion of some emigré Russian
Orthodox theologians he had heard in conversations who expressed a
surprising lack of interest in apostolic succession as purely historical continuity. The history of the church shows that in emergency situations the
Holy Spirit might very well intervene to preserve apostolic office by another, an extra-institutional principle,[27] the principle of *oikonomia,* or "economy," as an expression of the Spirit's radical freedom-in-fidelity vis-à-vis
church order.[28] Congar also pointed out that apostolic succession is not
merely a matter of the sacramental validity of episcopal ordinations either. Instead, he speaks of the legitimacy of episcopal ordinations. Episcopacy as the expression of apostolic succession has to do with assuming
a pastoral charge that is founded in the missionary activity of the apostles.
Episcopal succession includes the notion of mission and not simply the
reception of a certain sacramental dignity. Congar faulted the Western
Church for adopting the practice of allowing absolute ordinations,[29] which

26. Congar speaks of an element that is "métahistorique," but which I have translated as "transcendence without negation." See "Composantes et idée de la Succession
Apostolique," *Oecumenica* 1 (1966) 61–78, at 64.

27. It is referred to as the principle of *oikonomia.* See K. Duchatelez, "La notion
d'économie et ses richesses théologiques," *Nouvelle revue théologique* 92 (1970) 267–92, and
Ladislas Orsy, "In Search of the Meaning of *Oikonomia:* Report on a Convention," *Theological Studies* 43 (1982) 312–19.

28. Gerald O'Collins and Edward G. Farrugia define "economy" or *oikonomia* as follows: "In Eastern theology, economy also denotes concessions to human weaknesses made
by the Church, which in particular cases dispenses from its own canonical prescriptions."
A Concise Dictionary of Theology (rev. and expanded ed.; New York: Paulist Press, 2000) 72.

29. The ordinary practice for ordinations in both East and West in the first thousand
years was what is called "relative ordination," i.e., ordination of a person with a view to a definite pastoral assignment. By contrast, "absolute ordination" became a more regular practice
in the second millennium. This practice had been proscribed by the Council of Chaldedon
(451) in its 6th canon, ostensibly to prevent vagabond bishops and presbyters, i.e., clergy not
attached to a particular church community. The validity of such ordinations led to reinforcing the idea that ordination had to do primarily with the individual ordinand and the imparting of certain powers to him independent of a specific pastoral charge. This led to the
theory that the priesthood resided in the powers of consecrating the Eucharist and other
sacramental powers. But it also led to the decline in a viable theology of the sacramental character of the office of bishop. The problem is very much with us today, as seen in the phenomenon of a multiplicity of auxiliary bishops of larger dioceses and the ordaining of bishops
for the Roman Curia and as Vatican diplomats. I think a case can be made for a true group
exercise of episcopal functions by a number of bishops for larger dioceses, but not according
to the current theology of an Ordinary bishop assisted by his auxiliaries. The Ordinary truly
has a pastoral charge, but the same can hardly be said of his auxiliaries who really assist him
but do not share the pastoral responsibilities on an equal footing. Often, their duty is to act as
executants of the Ordinary's decisions or to act as his sacramental representatives.

have resulted in the loss of the sense of pastoral charge and mission as intrinsic to apostolic office. None of this calls into question for Congar the fact that apostolic office is communicated by the imposition of hands in the sacrament of Orders, but is rather his attempt to spell out the inseparable relationship between apostolic office and its service of the teaching bequeathed by the apostles.

Equally indispensable for episcopal office is fidelity to the teachings of the apostles and the handing on of the *traditio apostolica*. In this respect, at least, the reformers of the sixteenth century were correct to challenge the sorry state of knowledge of the tradition by folk and leaders. Episcopal ordinations always call for the profession of the faith of the church by the candidate. Congar wrote: "The teaching of the bishops is indeed a norm for the faithful, but it, too, obeys a norm: the office includes authority, but it is not its own criterion of authority, for it is conditioned by its fidelity to the tradition of the apostles."[30] But, according to Congar, the Western understanding of episcopal office as apostolic succession has also suffered from symbolical and liturgical impoverishment. Instead of being attuned to the meanings in the ordination rite, Western theology tended to concentrate exclusively on the juridical aspects of ordination.[31] Finally, the Western Church also lost sight of the dimension of episcopal communion. The office of bishop in succession to the apostles only makes sense in the context of its being exercised with the other bishops for the building up of the whole church. The bishops do not succeed to any individual apostle, but apostolic succession as taught by Vatican II pertains to the college of bishops[32] succeeding to the mission of the apostles of the

30. "Composantes et idée de la Succession Apostolique," 67.

31. Ibid., 67–69. "The sense of liturgy was lost, i.e., the sense of a supernatural ontology and of the mutual interiority of things. Instead, it was replaced by a taste for allegory and for ceremony" (69).

32. The Dogmatic Constitution on the Church refers at several points to the bishops as a group, order, or college succeeding to the pastoral tasks of the apostles. In art. 22, we read: "However, the order of bishops, which succeeds the college of apostles in teaching authority and pastoral government, and indeed in which the apostolic body continues to exist without interruption, is also the subject of supreme and full power over the universal church, provided it remains united with its head, the Roman pontiff, and never without its head." Earlier, in art. 19, the bishops wrote: "These apostles (see Lk 6:13) he established as a college or a permanent group over which he placed Peter, chosen from among them." And in art. 20 they said: "Just as the office that was given individually by the Lord to Peter, the first of the apostles, is permanent and meant to be handed on to his successors, so also the office of the apostles of nourishing the church is a permanent one that is to be carried out without interruption by the sacred order of bishops. Therefore,

early church—in those matters and to the extent that they can do so. In this regard, Congar maintains that apostolicity here reconnects, as it must, with the church's catholicity.[33]

Apostolicity in the full sense includes all four dimensions discussed above. There is apostolicity of origin, which in the early church was understood in terms of the norm or principal churches and the communion of all the churches among themselves. The recovery of the notion of communion by the Second Vatican Council and in postconciliar thought points the church in the same direction, namely, the indispensable value of the communion of the churches as the expression today of its apostolic origins. Second, as a result of the *ressourcement,* or "return to the sources," movement in the theological disciplines in twentieth-century Catholicism, and most especially the renewal of scripture studies, the central importance of faith in the teachings of the apostles has reemerged. The Scriptures remain the primary expression and the point of reference of apostolic teaching. To say this is not to deny the need for interpretation of the Scriptures, even for authoritative interpretation by the magisterium, but it points to the character of such reflection and teaching as truly in service the Word of God. Third, apostolicity is to be found primarily by examining the full life of a church and not by isolating one element at the expense of all other dimensions. The faith preached by the apostles engendered communities of prayer, worship, service, and witness—communities that reflected on God's Word and the teachings of the Lord Jesus, charismatic as well as permanent ministries, the celebration of the Eucharist, the experience of God's Spirit and living in a way that was open to the Spirit, a lifestyle of discipleship that included acts of justice, forgiveness, penance, and love of neighbor, including one's enemies. One looks for the contours of the life communicated by the risen Lord in apostolic communities. Finally, there is apostolicity of the ordained ministry. Apostolic succession of the bishops is not an affair of a historically unbroken chain of episcopal leaders, but of proper, sacramental succession to the leadership of an apostolic community. This leadership is equipped with its own ministry of symbolizing, defending, and confirming that church's internal apostolic character. Apostolic suc-

---

the synod teaches that by divine institution the bishops have succeeded to the place of the apostles as shepherds of the church." I will return to Roman Catholic postconciliar theologies of episcopal succession in chapter 8.

33. "Composantes et idée de la Succession Apostolique," 69–70.

cession points to the very sacramentality of the church, that is, the church as the fundamental sacrament.

Conclusions

First, the inadequacy of the older, and what had become the classic, interpretation of apostolic succession as an unbroken chain of valid episcopal ordinations has been largely modified as the principal way of understanding apostolicity.[34] Moreover, the image of a chain of episcopal ordinations assuring the validity of ministry that this rather mechanical theory entailed has been largely abandoned. Catholic theologians who have expressed serious reservations as to the adequacy of this theory of apostolic succession include Yves Congar, Joseph Ratzinger,[35] and Francis A. Sullivan, among many others. The succession of the church's bishops

34. Even the Council does not speak of an "unbroken chain" of episcopal ordinations. In art. 20 we read: "Among the different ministries that have been carried on in the church right from the earliest times, as tradition witnesses, the chief place belongs to the task of those who, having been appointed to the episcopate through a succession that goes back to the beginning, possess the shoots that have grown from the apostolic seed." In his translation of this section, Austin Flannery has overzealously translated it as follows: ". . . through their appointment to the dignity and responsibility of bishop, and in virtue consequently of the unbroken succession, going back to the beginning. . . ." The Latin text contains no reference to an "unbroken" succession. See A. Flannery, *Vatican Council II: The Conciliar and Post Conciliar Documents* (Dublin: Dominican Publications, 1992) 371. The image it conjures up is no longer appropriate or necessary. The image of a chain is far too mechanical and creates too much misunderstanding.

35. Ratzinger has characterized the efforts of some individuals to assure the fact that their episcopal ordination is in strict historical apostolic succession by seeking out validly ordained bishops from another church to ordain them as "apocryphal." He writes of some who have "a longing for a link with the origins of Christianity; a feeling of dissatisfaction with communities that cannot, as such, be traced back to these origins; and a need to demonstrate, in a visible way, their membership in the Church of all ages. These sentiments are, in themselves, perfectly legitimate and helped break down many barriers even while being, at the same time, responsible for the fact that those who held ministries in these churches managed somehow to arrange an imposition of hands by bishops who could demonstrate a connection with the imposition of hands in the Catholic Church and were thus able to claim a formal legitimacy of apostolic succession. As a result, there are, today, a number of persons holding such ministries whose succession is, if I may so phrase it, apocryphal. Wherever such 'high-church' ordinations are conferred or received thus 'apocryphally', the fundamental nature of the imposition of hands has been totally misunderstood. . . . It is nothing without the Church—an imposition of hands that is not an entering into the existential and traditional context of the Church is not an ecclesial imposition of hands." *Principles of Catholic Theology: Building Stones for a Fundamental Theology,* tr. Mary Frances McCarthy (San Francisco: Ignatius Press, 1987) 245–46.

throughout the centuries is understood in terms of the episcopal college succeeding to the college of apostles, and not a succession of one bishop to his predecessor.[36]

Second, Catholic theologians are paying increased attention to the importance of apostolic doctrine. In the effort to reconnect apostolic doctrine with apostolic office, they are paying greater attention as well to the material aspects of apostolic doctrine, that is, the content of what Scripture and tradition witness to. The formal aspect of apostolicity, that is, the papal and episcopal magisterium, is not denied outright but is no longer seen in isolation from the material aspect.[37]

Third, apostolic succession is now considered in relation to the broader, more fundamental idea of the apostolicity of life. It is a fuller understanding of apostolicity and one that is more concrete, less abstract. This approach, too, opens new avenues of mutual understanding among the churches, that is, among Catholics, Christians of the Reform, and Oriental and Orthodox Christians, because the base for understanding has been broadened and is more realistic in terms of the actual life of the churches. It holds out better promise of relating the real beliefs and practices of the churches to the question of how they understand their apostolicity.

36. The recent encyclical on the Eucharist by John Paul II (April 17, 2003) addresses the relationship of the Eucharist to apostolicity and shows the tension that still inheres in the church's official theology of orders. After a section that summarizes the teaching on apostolicity of the *Catechism of the Catholic Church* (§857) and that is admirable in many ways, the pope's explanation becomes hard to understand when he speaks of episcopal succession in terms of the bishop's inclusion in the college of bishops and then proceeds to state: "Succession to the apostles in the pastoral mission necessarily entails the sacrament of holy orders, that is, the uninterrupted sequence from the very beginning of valid episcopal ordinations. This succession is essential for the church to exist in a proper and full sense" (28). The appropriate passage in the *Catechism* does not mention how the succession of bishops occurs. Instead, it merely speaks of the bishops' "successors in pastoral office: the college of bishops." The question of the manner of episcopal succession is not even raised in this paragraph of the *Catechism*. It is not entirely clear how these two "explanations" of episcopal orders, i.e., sacramental incorporation into the body of bishops and an "uninterrupted sequence [of ordinations] from the very beginning," are related to one another in the pope's encyclical. See *"Ecclesia de Eucharistia," Origins* 32/46 (May 1, 2003) 753–68, at 760.

37. The Dogmatic Constitution on Divine Revelation *(Dei Verbum)* of Vatican II needs to be recalled at this point. The Council did not develop its teaching on the nature of the church in isolation from other important teachings, e.g., the Word of God and the church in the world. The Council fairly forces us to examine the interrelationships among these central teachings.

Finally, theologians are seeing better the connections between the church's notes or marks. The attributes of the church as one, holy, catholic, and apostolic are not items on a list of characteristics considered as extrinsically related to each other. Instead, they mutually influence one another. A church's apostolicity needs to be examined in face of the holiness of the church and in light of the catholicity of its belief and doctrines. The attributes of apostolicity and catholicity in particular are seen as mutually conditioning one another. To consider apostolicity in isolation from catholicity is seen as representing a disembodied, almost dualistic, approach to the church.

CHAPTER THREE

Apostolicity in History

The Epistle of the Romans to the Corinthians[1] (1 Clement)

We honestly do not know when the anonymous letter called *1 Clement* was written. The more or less common opinion that its date of composition was around 95 C.E. is the date that most scholars have rallied around, but other possibilities have been suggested. Sometime in the 70s, between 118–125, and between 125–135 are the options usually cited.[2] The importance of deciding on a possible date of its writing is wrapped up with the question of the form of official ministry in the Roman church at that time. Was it the older collegial form of presbyter-bishops, or the form that emerged clearly later in the second century of a single bishop together with a group of presbyters, that is, mono-episcopacy? The answer is important because of its implications for the office of bishop and the growth of papal primacy. Was the author of *1 Clement* an anonymous presbyter writing on behalf of the governing body of Roman presbyters, or was he the presiding bishop of the church of Rome? The implications for the question of apostolic succession should be self-evident. Accepting the early date (70s) and the intermediate date (around 95) would align the leadership of the Roman church nicely within close proximity to the activity of the originary apostles Peter and Paul, both of whom were martyred in Rome. The two late dates (118–125 and 125–135) are already

---

1. James S. Jeffers explains how the anonymous letter was given this title according to some early sources. See *Conflict at Rome: Social Order and Hierarchy in Early Christianity* (Minneapolis: Fortress Press, 1991) 97, and the literature he cites. A word also needs to be said about designating *1 Clement* an "epistle." Harry O. Maier argues that it might be more accurately characterized as a "treatise." See *The Social Setting of the Ministry as Reflected in the Writings of Hermas, Clement and Ignatius,* Dissertations SR 1 (Waterloo, Ont.: Wilfrid Laurier University Press, 1991) 91.

2. See Jeffers, *Conflict at Rome,* 90–94.

too far removed from decisions regarding the form of offices that could be attributed to the originary apostles or their co-workers. The interpreter's assumptions about how all-important decisions were made in the early church—(1) by Christ who in turn gave his apostles specific directions; (2) by the originary apostles in terms of their fuller understanding of Jesus' intentions and thus without the need to attribute all their decisions to Christ directly; (3) by later post-apostolic disciples who were guided by the Lord's teachings and by the Spirit as they confronted their own historical circumstances—will be largely determinative of how one tells the story of ministry in the early church.

Most scholars have shown an interest in *1 Clement* because of the occasion of the letter.[3] The author announces this at several points, most succinctly and without grandiloquent polemics, in the following two passages:

> **44:6** For we see that you have removed certain people, their good conduct notwithstanding, from the ministry which has been held in honor by them blamelessly.

> **47:6** It is disgraceful, dear friends, yes, utterly disgraceful and unworthy of your conduct in Christ, that it should be reported that the well-established and ancient church of the Corinthians, because of one or two persons, is rebelling against its presbyters.[4]

The letter, however, is concerned with broader issues facing the church of Corinth, issues of peace, unity, right order, and concord.[5] But it is the topic of church ministry, the terms in which Clement frames the ministry, and the question of apostolic succession that have preoccupied

---

3. Numerous attempts have been made to determine what precisely had happened in Corinth to elicit the response of the church of Rome. Maier has offered a theory that is appealing. He writes: "It is possible that the dispute arose independently of any particular theological dispute and that, as Harnack suggested, the division was merely between 'personal cliques'. . . .We suggest that these groups collected around relatively wealthy householders who then began to hold their own celebrations. . . . It also explains why the division involved only a section of the presbyter-bishops (44:6), for not all the house churches were directly involved in the schism." *The Social Setting of the Ministry*, 93–94.

4. The translation is that of J. B. Lightfoot and J. R. Harmer, edited and revised by Michael W. Holmes, *The Apostolic Fathers* (2 ed.; Grand Rapids, Mich.: Baker Book House, 1989) 53 and 55.

5. Barbara Ellen Bowe has put it this way: "Communal cohesion and harmony is, thus, the real issue for Clement—not abstract principles of ecclesiastical office." *A Church in Crisis: Ecclesiology and Paraenesis in Clement of Rome*, Harvard Dissertation in Religion, No. 23 (Minneapolis: Fortress Press, 1988) 149.

commentators. In the past, two schools of thought have governed the interpretation. The Catholic interpretation saw *1 Clement* in terms of mono-episcopacy and as an early exercise of the papal magisterium. It confirmed a strong tendency toward ultramontanism before and after Vatican I. Most Protestants saw it is an example of an illegitimate early Catholicism that was usurping the earlier charismatic understanding of office in the post-apostolic church. This interpretation confirmed the traditional Protestant anti-Roman attitude that emerged in the years following the Reformation. Recent scholarship has taken its distance from both of these interpretations as oversimplifications.[6]

It is imperative at this point that we recall the focus of our study, namely, the apostolicity of the church and apostolic succession, not the study of the emergence of the episcopacy.[7] The two themes are very closely intertwined, of course, but it is precisely here that the danger of deciding matters too hastily needs to be confronted. If we choose to pursue the emergence of episcopacy in the early church, we will be predisposing ourselves to accepting a very specific understanding of apostolic succession, one that is not shared by all the participants in the dialogue. Instead, let us limit ourselves to investigating only those disputed passages of *1 Clement* that will help us determine the more fundamental question for us: Does *1 Clement* inculcate a principle of apostolic succession? In other words, is *1 Clement* the appropriate place to begin the history of an explicit principle of apostolic succession? What, then, do the pertinent passages from *1 Clement* state?

> **42.** (1) The apostles received the gospel for us from the Lord Jesus Christ; Jesus the Christ was sent forth from God. (2) So then Christ is from God, and the apostles are from Christ. Both, therefore, came of the will of God in good order. (3) Having therefore received their orders and being fully assured by the resurrection of our Lord Jesus Christ and full of faith in the

6. See the discussion of the various opinions by John Fuellenbach, *Ecclesiastical Office and the Primacy of Rome: An Evaluation of Recent Theological Discussion of First Clement,* The Catholic University of America Studies in Christian Antiquity, No. 20 (Washington, D.C.: The Catholic University of America Press, 1980) 4–7, with the excellent footnotes [nos. 24–59] explaining the wide variety of opinions. For an in-depth examination of each approach, see the appropriate chapter in ibid., 25–71 ["Church Structure in 1 Clement: Recent Protestant Studies"], and 73–117 ["Church Structure in 1 Clement: Recent Catholic Studies"].

7. See the excellent treatment of this issue by Francis A. Sullivan, "The *Didache* and *I Clement,*" in *From Apostles to Bishops: The Development of the Episcopacy in the Early Church* (New York: Paulist Press, 2001) 91–102 ["The Letter of the Romans to the Corinthians *(I Clement)*"].

Word of God, they went forth with the firm assurance that the Holy Spirit gives, preaching the good news that the kingdom of God was about to come. (4) So, preaching both in the country and in the towns, they appointed their first fruits, when they had tested them by the Spirit, to be presbyter-bishops *[episkopous]* and deacons *[diakonous]* for the future believers. (5) And this was no new thing they did, for indeed something had been written about presbyter-bishops and deacons many years ago; for somewhere thus says the Scripture: "I will appoint *episkopous* in righteousness and [their *diakonous*] in faith" (Is 60:17).[8]

44. (1) Our apostles likewise knew, through our Lord Jesus Christ, that there would be strife over the presbyter-bishop's office. (2) For this reason, therefore, having received complete foreknowledge, they appointed the officials mentioned earlier and afterwards they gave the offices a permanent character; that is, if they should die, other approved men should succeed to their ministry. (3) Those, therefore, who were appointed by them, or, later on, by other reputable men with the consent of the whole church, and who have ministered to the flock of Christ blamelessly, humbly, peaceably, and unselfishly, and for a long time have been well spoken of by all–these men we consider to be unjustly removed from their ministry. (4) For it will be no small sin for us, if we depose from the presbyter-bishop's office those who have offered the gifts blamelessly and in holiness. (5) Blessed are those presbyter-bishops *[presbyteroi]* who have gone on ahead, who took their departure at a mature and fruitful age, for they need no longer fear that someone might remove them from their established place. (6) For we see that you have removed certain people, their good conduct notwithstanding, from the ministry which had been held in honor by them blamelessly.[9]

These passages are concerned with a divinely willed orderliness in the church [42:2]. The key to understanding God's will in regard to officeholders is the will of Christ, but as understood in the Spirit of the Lord by the apostles [44:1-2]. Of the three options for the apostles making all-important decisions after the Lord's resurrection that I listed above, (3) seems to come closest to what the author of *1 Clement* is claiming. The apostles had a determinative or constitutive role to play in establishing the ministry in the church, but their contribution was guided by the Holy Spirit, that is, "having received complete foreknowledge" according to the text. But the passages do not teach that this is the case for all the churches. The letter is addressing a definite situation in a specific church,

8. See Lightfoot and Harmer, *The Apostolic Fathers,* 51.
9. See ibid., 52–53.

Corinth. It does not say that the apostles made the same determination for all the churches. That is often the meaning we read into the passage, because we cannot imagine that *1 Clement* would treat the apostles as anything other than universal legislators. However, we know that this was not the case in regards to Paul, who often rendered decisions that were quite particular. Somewhere in the back of our minds as we read the above passage, we picture all of the apostles—and probably the twelve apostles at that—making a common decision for all times.

Second, there is the matter of the appointment of presbyter-bishops by the apostles [42:4]. I have altered the translation somewhat, changing Lightfoot and Harmer's "bishops" to "presbyter-bishops." The reason is simple. There is no indication that the church of Corinth had as yet anything resembling the figure who would eventually be called a "bishop." At this stage, the two Greek words *presbyteros* and *episkopos* were probably still synonyms.[10] They could be used interchangeably. This form of local leadership by a group of presbyters is generally referred to today by the phrase "presbyter-bishops."[11] The translation of *episkopos* by the English "bishop" would probably be misleading to most readers. Moreover, at this stage of the development of the classical form of episcopacy, it is entirely possible that some presbyter-bishops were more fully engaged in the ministry of leadership than others. First Timothy 5:17-18 gives a hint of this with its formulation: "Presbyters who preside *(proestōtes presbyteroi)* well deserve double honor *(diplēs timēs)* [material support?], especially

---

10. The view of Harry O. Maier is rather common: "Given Clement's usage which treats *episkopoi* and *presbyteroi* as synonyms (e.g., *1 Clem* 44:4-5; 47:6), it is unlikely that these terms refer to two distinct orders within the church." *The Social Setting of the Ministry,* 63. One finds the same parallel use of these two terms in the earlier New Testament literature, e.g., Acts 20:17 and 28, where *presbyterous* (accusative plural) is used in verse 17 and *episkopous* (accusative plural) in verse 28 as referring to the same ministry. The passage is Luke's version of a sermon delivered by Paul at Miletus. Acts 14:23 gives us another example of Luke's understanding of how Paul appointed presbyters. There is no explicit reference in any of the authentic Pauline literature that his regular practice was to appoint local leaders. We simply do not know from Paul himself how he recognized the stable, local leadership of his churches. That there were such leaders, however, is beyond dispute. How they were recognized and/or installed, we do not know from Paul.

11. For the meaning of the term, see Eric G. Jay, "From Presbyter-Bishops to Bishops and Presbyters," *The Second Century* 1 (1981) 125–72; Raymond E. Brown, "*Episkopē* and *Episkopos:* The New Testament Evidence," *Theological Studies* 41 (1980) 322–38, at 330–37 ["The Presbyter-Bishops and the Succession to the Apostles"], and idem (co-authored with John P. Meier) *Antioch and Rome: New Testament Cradles of Catholic Christianity* (New York: Paulist, Press, 1983) 163.

those who toil in preaching and teaching. For the scripture says . . . 'A worker deserves his pay.'" However, we must not conclude hastily that this means a dual hierarchy of presbyter-bishops at this point. We are still probably at the level of the emerging solidifying of general institutions in the churches.

Third, there is the question of whether apostolic succession is explicitly addressed in these passages. On the surface, it certainly seems as though we have an equivalency between Christ appointing the apostles and the apostles appointing presbyter-bishops. Just as Christ knew he would have to die before the final coming of the kingdom he preached, so, too, the apostles knew that they would die before they had accomplished their missionary task. And so, just as Christ appointed the apostles to succeed him, so, too, the apostles appointed presbyter-bishops, or as the text says "other approved men" *[heteroi ellogimoi andres]*, to succeed them. How close is the correspondence of ideas of succession in the passages? Some scholars today maintain that the author's intention was to inculcate a general idea of orderly succession in the presbyteral office but not the technical understanding of apostolic succession[12] that emerged only later.[13] Others, however, deny any underlying idea of succession in

12. The technical term for "succession" that emerges in the second century is the Greek word *diadochē*. More about this term below.

13. Barbara E. Bowe writes: "The absence of any mention of individual apostles and their specific connection with individual churches argues against interpreting these chapters as a statement of 'apostolic succession.'" *A Church in Crisis,* 147–48. So, too, Georg G. Blum: "It is not a question of apostolic succession except in so far as the author strives to assure the legitimacy of the cultic ministry and therefore of church structures handed down by the apostles. There is no mention of their teaching or personal authority." "Apostel/Apostolat/Apostolizität. II: Alte Kirche," in *Theologische Realenzyklopädie* [henceforth *TRE*], eds. Gerhard Krause and Gerhard Müller (New York/Berlin: Walter de Gruyter Verlag, 1978) 3:445. Blum locates the emergence of the technical understanding of "succession" with Papias (ca. 60–130) and Hegesippus (second century). Blum characterizes this inchoate understanding of succession among Christians as "archaic" and as tributary to late Jewish rabbinic thought with its lists of students who eventually succeed to their teachers as "individuals who hand on the fund of knowledge" ("Tradenten"). Ibid., 446–47. Blum sees the final emergence of the principle of apostolic succession as the end product of a very complex process that involved the early church's efforts to come to terms with a whole series of issues. These issues included the role and value of direct pneumatic experience in some forms of Gnosticism, while other Gnostics insisted on a fixed fund of saving truth albeit esoterically communicated from an apostle to an authoritative teacher; the effort by Marcion to determine the extent of a biblical canon on the authoritative witness of only one apostle, Paul; and the subsequent efforts by the de facto historic church ("die Grosskirche") to work out an understanding of canonicity that included apostolicity in a sense wider than the witness of the individual apostles but that also included the proc-

office but point to the author's overriding concern of assuring the divine
order in the Corinthian church. Above all else, the divine order must not
be breached.[14] Raymond E. Brown has offered an intermediate position.
He has introduced distinctions among functional succession, succession
by apostolic appointment, and apostolic succession in its classic meaning
as sacramental or episcopal in the full sense. He writes:

> The idea of succession *(diadochē)* goes beyond insistence on rank or order
> *(tagma)* assigned by God—an order of Christ, apostles, bishops and deacons.
> Succession concerns the origin of the episcopate. A distinction should be
> made between functional succession (the presbyter-bishops take over the
> pastoral care of churches founded by apostles once the apostles die) and
> succession by apostolic appointment. Furthermore, an appointed sequence
> in legitimate authority is still not the same as a chain of succession to sacra-
> mental power—an idea that will later come into the Christian picture.[15]

Brown's suggestion has merit. It permits us to accept the emergence of
ideas of succession without being committed to the full understanding of
the term that he characterizes as "sacramental." Its advantage, however,
also imposes care in speaking about "apostolic succession" in *1 Clement*
and in other Christian documents of the same period. We cannot do so
without careful nuancing of the term.

Irenaeus of Lyons

The pivotal figure in determining the emergence of a fuller understanding of apostolicity and of apostolic succession is Irenaeus (ca. 115–ca.

---

ess of reception of apostolic witness by the church as a whole, i.e., in terms of the catholicity of the church ("die Gesamtkirche"). One of the peculiarities of Blum's theory of apostolic succession is the "Grosskirche." The traditional interpretation has been that Irenaeus
and others adopted the idea of "succession-lists" *(diadochai)* as a defensive tactic against the
Gnostic assault. As Blum reads the evidence, there was no single or unitary Gnosticism
but rather a pluralism of Gnosticisms. Ibid., 447–49.

14. See, recently, J. S. Jeffers, *Conflict at Rome,* 148–52 ["Traditional Authority in *1
Clement*"]. He writes in conclusion: "Thus, *1 Clement* offers a clear example of traditional
authority. Absent are the rational arguments of Paul. Absent also is Paul's appeal to divine
inspiration as the ultimate source of his authority. Rather than appeal to reason or to
charisma, Clement appealed to traditions that appeared to support his views, even though
they came from widely disparate sources: Jewish, Christian, and pagan." Ibid., 152. Harry O.
Maier also emphasizes the author's concern for general order rather than attempts on his
part to preserve a specific apostolic order. See *The Social Setting of the Ministry,* 91.

15. R. E. Brown, *Antioch and Rome,* 174, footnote 368.

195), bishop of Lyons in the later years of the second century.[16] Irenaeus did not approach apostolicity and its forms as a speculative question but as a concrete issue in the life of the church. The issues Irenaeus confronted were not of his choosing; he had to operate on two fronts dictated to him by his adversaries. Thus, on the one hand, Marcion (d. 160) and his followers posed the problem of what constituted Scripture for Christians. To this Irenaeus will point to the apostolic writings, for example, the four Gospels, Acts of the Apostles, the epistles of Paul, and so forth. The matter was complicated by the fact that there was no fixed canon of Scripture. On the other hand, there were the various Gnostics who pointed to the immediacy of the pneumatic experience of God or to the authority of some teacher who had received privileged but secret knowledge of revelation from an apostle. Regarding this threat to the faith, Irenaeus countered with the apostolicity of the tradition, that is, what Christians believed and preached as part of a living source of their faith and way of explicating the meaning of their Scriptures. "Tradition" is a slippery theological word that prejudices the understanding of the reader or interlocutor. To say the least, it is a controversial word in theology and in the understanding of the faith by Catholics and Protestants. It needs to be defined with care. At the time of Irenaeus the word did not have

16. The literature treating Irenaeus on apostolic tradition and apostolic succession is extensive. I can give only a few important references, arranged chronologically by date of publication. Einar Molland, 1950, "Irenaeus of Lugdunum and the Apostolic Succession," reprinted in *Opuscula Patristica* (Oslo: Universitetsforlaget, 1970) 161–79; idem, 1954, "Le développement de l'idée de succession apostolique," reprinted in *Opuscula Patristica*, 181–206; H. E. W. Turner, "Orthodoxy and Tradition," in *The Pattern of Christian Truth: A Study in the Relations between Orthodoxy and Heresy in the Early Church*, The Bampton Lectures 1954 (London: A. R. Mobray & Co., 1954) 307–78; André Benoît, "L'apostolicité au second siècle," *Verbum Caro* 58 (1961) 173–84; Antonio M. Javierre, "Le thème de la succession des apôtres dans la littérature chrétienne primitive," in *L'Épiscopat et l'Église universelle,* Unam Sanctam 39, ed. Y. Congar and B. D. Dupuy (Paris: Les Éditions du Cerf, 1962) 171–221; Georg G. Blum, *Tradition und Sukzession: Studien zum Normbegriff des Apostolischen von Paulus bis Irenäus,* Arbeiten zur Geschichte und Theologie des Luthertums 9 (Berlin: Lutherisches Verlagshaus, 1963); Jaroslav Pelikan, *The Emergence of the Catholic Tradition (100–600),* The Christian Tradition: A History of the Development of Doctrine 1 (Chicago: University of Chicago Press, 1971) 108–20 ["Criteria of Apostolic Continuity"]; J. N. D. Kelly, *Early Christian Doctrines* (Rev. ed.; San Francisco: HarperSanFrancisco, 1978) 35–41 ["Irenaeus and Tertullian"]; Georg G. Blum, "Apostel/Apostolat/Apostolizität," in *TRE,* 3:449–52 ["Die Entfaltung der Konzeption des Apostolischen durch Irenaeus"]; Maurice Jourjon, "La tradition apostolique chez saint Irénée," *L'Année Canonique* 23 (1979) 193–202; and Jacques Fantino, "La réflexion théologique et sa mise en oeuvre," in *La théologie d'Irénée. Lecture des Écritures en réponse à l'exégèse gnostique: une approche trinitaire,* Cogitatio Fidei 180 (Paris: Les Éditions du Cerf, 1994) 7–83, esp. 15–54.

the technical meanings that would later accrue to it, especially in the modern period.[17] Because using the word "tradition" almost inevitably leads to misunderstanding, for the period under discussion I think it best to employ the terms used by Irenaeus and his translator—*paradosis* and *traditio*.

According to Irenaeus, *traditio* encompasses the life of the church. In terms of the controversies he faced, *traditio* is related to a series of critical issues involving the Hebrew Scriptures, the newer Christian writings that emerged after the resurrection of the Lord, the statements of the faith, the so-called *regula fidei* and *regula veritatis,* the understanding of doctrine, and "succession" *(diadochē)*. All of these elements together constitute the one complex reality of *traditio*. Thus, on the front dictated by Marcion, the issue was what really constituted Scripture for Christians. Marcion refused to accept the Hebrew Scriptures, identifying its revelation with God the Creator who was other than God the Father revealed by Jesus Christ. He also refused to accept most of the newer writings that were also being read by Christians and commented on by them. Any new Christian Scripture would have to conform to Marcion's understanding of the God revealed by Jesus Christ in contrast to the God of the Old Testament. These writings included the letters of Paul, especially Galatians, and the Gospel of Luke. Irenaeus rejected the exclusivity of Marcion's choice of Scripture because it really was an attack on the apostolic character of Christian faith. The writings that were coming to be included in the Christian understanding of Scripture went back to the witness of the originary apostles or to writers closely associated with them and their proclamation *(kerygma)*. It is also clear from the apostolic *kerygma* that the apostles formulated it with the help of the Jewish Scriptures. Belief in

17. The modern meaning of "tradition" is associated with the two-source theory often proposed by Catholic theologians and its rejection by Protestant thinkers. The controversy has generated a vast bibliography. I will only mention James P. Mackey, *The Modern Theology of Tradition* (New York: Herder and Herder, 1963); Yves Congar, *Tradition and Traditions: An Historical Essay and a Theological Essay,* tr. Michael Naseby and Thomas Rainborough (New York: The Macmillan Company, 1966); and Josef Rupert Geiselmann, *The Meaning of Tradition,* Quaestiones Disputatae 15, tr. W. J. O'Hara (New York: Herder and Herder, 1966). There is also the issue of the difference between "Tradition" (capitalized) and "tradition" (lower case), "tradition" (sing.) and "traditions" (pl.), as well as the retrieval of the importance of tradition for human thought and culture by such thinkers as Hans-Georg Gadamer and Alasdair MacIntyre. Recent important works include John E. Thiel, *Sense of Tradition: Continuity and Development in Catholic Faith* (New York: Oxford University Press, 2000), and Terrence W. Tilley, *Inventing Catholic Tradition* (Maryknoll, N.Y.: Orbis Books, 2000).

Christ did not mean the rejection of the Jewish Scriptures but that they were now to be interpreted in light of the life and ministry of Christ. The notion of apostolicity came to be employed in a technical sense, namely, that which had the authority of the apostles of the early church behind it. "Apostolic" now included a certain claim to authority. The newer writings were considered to be "apostolic" and so enjoyed authority when considering what Christians believed. On the other hand, on the front dictated by the various Gnostics, the Scriptures represented the public proclamation of what the apostles had seen, experienced, and witnessed to. Unlike the claims of the Gnostics to special and secret knowledge, the apostolic *kerygma* was open for all to hear and consider. This *kerygma* was available in the church's Scripture, but it could also be encountered in the day-to-day life of Christian churches. To a certain extent, however, Gnostics and Christians, unlike the followers of Marcion, shared the same Scriptures. Thus, in the controversy with the Gnostics the issue was less what constituted the Scriptures and more how one was to understand their message. To this task, Christians and Gnostics shared in different thought worlds which governed their presuppositions for understanding Scripture. Jacques Fantino has pointed out how the role of doctrine gained importance in addressing the issue.[18] Simple recourse to Scripture was no longer adequate. Each group could quote the Scriptures as the depositary of the apostles' *traditio*. Something else was needed. That other element was doctrine, or in the words of Irenaeus and others at the time, the *regula fidei* and the *regula veritatis*. But what do these terms mean?

The church's *symbola* or creeds, which would be formulated in the context of the baptismal liturgy as professions of faith, did not yet exist. The Scriptures included various kerygmatic formulations, for example, the sermons of Peter in Acts of the Apostles, but they were lengthy and included a great deal of reflection of Israel's history and its fulfillment in Christ. There were also shorter kerygmatic formulas that could be found in the writings of Paul, for example, Romans 1:3-4, but these were often short in the extreme or focused on one issue, for example, the Lord's resurrection (see 1 Cor 15:3-7). Such kerygmatic formulations were not helpful in meeting the challenges of people like Marcion or the various Gnostic thinkers. For these situations "rules of belief or of truth," *regulae fidei* or *veritatis*, would have to be formulated. These *regulae* were con-

---

18. J. Fantino, *La théologie d'Irénée,* 12–14.

cerned with establishing doctrinal points of reference and so differed from the earlier kerygmatic formulas with their primarily proclamatory function. The *regulae,* which were communicated to the faithful in the context of baptism, also came to be used in a consciously apologetical way. But even in this new context of exploration of the faith, the believer must never forget the basic truths communicated to him or her at baptism. These truths are summed up in the "rule of truth." The *regulae* used terms and formulas that were quite specific and not necessarily found as such in the Scriptures.[19] Those who employed them, men like Justin, Irenaeus, and Tertullian, saw them as an integral element in understanding the Scriptures correctly. They were not meant to replace or supercede the Scriptures but to assist the believer in understanding the Scriptures, which always remained the point of reference.[20] In the more culturally diverse world of Christianity after 150 C.E., doctrine would become a necessary factor in proclaiming and explicating the Christian faith. Reflection on the faith could not be avoided, and so the "rule of faith" aided reflection by anchoring the Christian thinker in the essentials of the church's faith. The Fathers of this period never tried to substitute the "rule of truth" for the primary claims of the kerygma as found in the Scriptures.[21] The *regulae* helped assure the recognition of what constituted Scripture and how it should be understood. Doctrine (*hypothesis* in the Greek) was no substitute for faith or for the language of faith, but it could serve the faith by safeguarding it from false interpretation. Fantino expresses the mutuality of Scripture and the *regulae* in these words: "The rule of truth and the rule of faith are formulated with the help of the Scriptures and thanks to these rules the believer who remains true to them is given the ability to interpret the Scriptures correctly."[22] The *traditio apostolica* according to

---

19. An example can be found in AH ("Against Heresies") 3,11,1: ". . . to establish the rule of truth in the church, that there is one Almighty God, who made all things by His Word, both visible and invisible; showing at the same time, that by the Word, through whom God made the creation, He also bestowed salvation on the men included in the creation." The passage then continues with a long, composite quotation from the first chapter of John. See *Ante-Nicene Fathers: Translations of the Writings of the Fathers down to A.D. 325* [henceforth *ANF*], 10 vols., ed. Alexander Roberts and James Donaldson (reprint of 1885 edition; Peabody, Mass.: Hendrickson Publishers, 1994) 1:426.

20. J. Fantino writes: "The formula 'rule of truth' has a precise objective reference. In this way it acts as a principle and guide for interpreting Scripture and the faith. If it is not followed, the result is a purely subjective understanding of the faith." *La théologie d'Irénée,* 18.

21. Today we would speak of the "first order" and "second order" language of faith.

22. J. Fantino, *La théologie d'Irénée,* 24.

Irenaeus is an interlocking whole that includes the inseparable elements of the church's Scriptures (both the Hebrew Scriptures and the New Testament), the "rule of truth" communicated at baptism, and the role of doctrine as aiding in the effort to understand the faith. But it includes yet another element for Irenaeus, the idea of "succession."

Interpretation of a normative text, "rules" or reference points that contribute to the interpretation, and "doctrine" *(hypothesis)* as the context that determines the interpretation—all these elements point to the phenomenon of a school of thought. Fantino understands the Irenaean *traditio apostolica* as an expression of faith shared by the adherents of a community of belief that understood those beliefs in terms of certain doctrines, generally summarized in the "rule of truth." This helps us better understand the final element in Irenaeus' conception of "apostolic tradition," a succession of *doctores* or master teachers. In the thought world of Irenaeus' time, ideas would emerge, flourish, and be advanced within a "school of thought." But schools have masters or leaders.[23] By the time Irenaeus became bishop of Lyons, the collegial system of presbyter-bishops was quickly disappearing and the system of a single *episkopos* at the head of a body of presbyters (mono-episcopacy) was becoming the universal practice.[24] It is likely that Irenaeus was made a bishop by his presbyters, probably by a process of election that included the faithful and the presbyters and within the context of a liturgical celebration.[25] Christians of this era would instinctively have thought of their bishop as a *doctor* or *magister*. It would have been the dominant image governing the office. When Irenaeus and others, like Tertullian, speak about the *episkopos*, there would have been no incompatibility between the bishop's teaching responsibilities and his liturgical actions. They wouldn't spontaneously have associated the office of bishop with something sacerdotal or cultic. The bishop was the master teacher who taught his community about Jesus Christ, and that knowledge came to him within the *traditio*. Christians would have expected the bishop to expound the Scriptures to them when the community gathered to celebrate

23. On the general background regarding schools of thought in Hellenism, see ibid., 39–45, where the author shows how both Judaism and Christianity drew upon a common notion of a succession of teachers.

24. J. Fantino has also briefly traced the history of the development of mono-episcopacy in the second century. See ibid., 45–49.

25. We know that this was the procedure in Alexandria up to the time of the Council of Nicaea (325). See W. Telfer, "Episcopal Succession in Egypt," *Journal of Ecclesiastical History* 3 (1952) 1–13.

the Eucharist. The teaching activity would have extended to the process of baptismal catechesis and the celebration of baptism.

What did the custom of teacher following teacher look like in antiquity? It was called *diadochē,* and often lists of teachers reaching back to the first one following the Master who originated the movement or school of thought—but not including him—were composed. To the outsider, Christianity in the second and third centuries would have resembled a philosophical school in many respects. Of course, it is not simply the Christian form of a philosophical school—Christianity was much more than that— but it also wasn't entirely dissimilar from such a school. Moreover, post-Second Temple rabbinic Judaism, too, was organized around the synagogue and its teachers and interpreters of Torah. The home of Christianity was just such a form of Judaism, though of course it took years for rabbinic Judaism to assume its final form. It did not happen overnight, just as mono-episcopacy didn't happen overnight within Christianity. When Hegesippus, Irenaeus, and others referred to the bishop's "succession," the referents are those teacher-leaders (originally presbyter-bishops) who "succeeded" to the apostles. The succession did not include the apostles themselves, who always remained the masters who could not be superceded, just as they could not supercede the Lord who alone was always "the Teacher" (see Matt 23:8).

At this stage of the development of episcopacy, "succession" would not have been interpreted as sacramental ordination of someone who in turn succeeded to the sacramental role of the originary apostles. That development will eventually emerge; it just was not present at the end of the second century. The idea of an authoritative teacher of the *traditio apostolica* was the dominant insight. In this respect, the Irenaean interpretation of a tradition of faith and its understanding would not have differed in its essentials from that of the Gnostics or the Marcionites. The tradition would have been at its base, and the tradition needed its official teachers "in succession" with the apostles. The same was true for the Gnostics and Marcionites, however. It was not the practice of "succession" that distinguished the Great Church from the dissident groups. The practice was common to both.[26] The difference for Irenaeus lay in the understanding of the tradition and which "school of thought" therefore was truly in continuity with what the apostles themselves taught.

26. See J. Fantino, *La théologie d'Irénée,* 37.

The key to discovering this, as we have already noted, is the underlying doctrinal context. Is the governing doctrine, and the theology that conveys it, the church's? Who would be able to judge this matter?[27] In the period before the emergence of mono-episcopacy it was the presbyter-bishops. In the transitional period that Irenaeus represents, it is increasingly (but not yet exclusively) the bishops. The way of looking at matters proposed by Fantino helps to resolve a number of problems. For instance, when Irenaeus speaks of "succession," sometimes he refers to the "succession of bishops,"[28] while at other times he speaks of the "succession of presbyters."[29] Both successions seem to act as guarantors of correct faith. Which is it? Is it perhaps both?

We saw earlier that for many years the terms "presbyter" and "*episkopos*" were synonymous. They could be used interchangeably without confusing matters. Is this ancient usage by Christians still operative in Irenaeus' texts? Or is there really only one succession—that of the bishops? Some years ago, Harry J. McSorley argued that in Irenaeus a twofold succession was to be found.[30] He argued that the Reformers were aware of this Irenaean evidence and used it to justify the ordination of their ministers by those priests who had come over to the Reform, when the (Catholic) bishops refused to ordain these Lutheran and Reformed ministers. The ministers of the Reform were, therefore, in correct apostolic succession. The Reformers were certainly aware, too, of the influential opinion of Jerome that there was no essential difference between a priest and a bishop. To Jerome the Scriptures were clear on this point. I think McSorley was right to point to the twofold character of the succession texts in Irenaeus, because it is a matter of a period of transition in determining the form of the church's ministry. There was no single form yet for assuring that one was in succession. What McSorley was not then able to emphasize was that the reason for two forms of succession had to do with the *traditio* itself, not with sacramental powers per se. Presbyters, that is, the older presbyter-bishops, were also still intimately involved in the act of handing on the faith by

27. Fantino writes: "Is there a way of proving that one tradition is more authentic than another? It was just this debate that was the reason for advancing the argument of apostolic succession." Ibid., 33.

28. See Irenaeus, *Adversus haereses* 3, 3, 1; **4**, 33, 8; and **5**, 20, 1.

29. See ibid., **3**, 2, 2; **4**, 26, 2. 4. 5; and **5**, 20, 2.

30. Harry J. McSorley, "Recognition of a Presbyteral Succession?" in *The Plurality of Ministries,* Concilium 74, ed. Hans Küng and Walter Kasper (New York: Herder and Herder, 1972) 23–32.

teaching within the *traditio*. This would not change immediately either, since the presbyters continued to be involved in the baptismal catechesis.

Tertullian of Carthage

The North African layman Quintus Septimus Florens Tertullianus (ca. 160–ca. 220) is of interest to theologians for his many contributions to Western theology.[31] They include theological vocabulary, theological style and tone of arguing, his passion for the faith, unforgettable aphorisms,[32] and so forth. But he is also relevant because of the many details of church life he records and for the fascinating course of his life.[33] Tertullian's reflections on apostolicity, too, remain extremely important.[34]

Highly creative, Tertullian was not a systematic thinker. He preferred to develop ideas from different perspectives and often succeeded with brilliant theological insights. In the previous chapter, we saw how Tertullian stressed apostolicity primarily from the point of view of the principal or norm churches. These are the churches directly founded by the preaching and teaching of the originary apostles themselves.[35] Secondly,

31. See Hans von Campenhausen, "Tertullian," in *The Fathers of the Latin Church*, tr. Manfred Hoffmann (London: Adam & Charles Black, 1964) 4–35, and more recently Eric Osborn, *Tertullian, First Theologian of the West* (New York: Cambridge University Press, 1997). Timothy David Barnes, *Tertullian: A Historical and Literary Study* (Oxford: At the Clarendon Press, 1971 [reissued in 1985 with corrections]) 11, discusses the evidence pro and con on whether Tertullian was a presbyter. Barnes accepts Tertullian's own statements regarding his status as a layperson.

32. Tertullian's influence on the vocabulary of Christians continues into our day. We still speak of "the blood of the martyrs is the seed of the faith," "human flesh is the hinge on which salvation rests," "the human soul is by nature Christian," "What has Athens to do with Jerusalem?" and "Nothing is so worthy of God as the salvation of human beings," to name only a few.

33. Tertullian converted to Christianity in 193. Then, in 207, he left the Great Church to join the Montanist movement. His writings are often divided into his "Catholic" and his "Montanist" periods. On Montanus and Montanism, see Jaroslav Pelikan, *Emergence of the Catholic Tradition*, 98–108; and Eric Osborn, *Tertullian*, 209–13.

34. Georg G. Blum, "Der Begriff des Apostolischen im theologischen Denken Tertullians," *Kerygma und Dogma* 9 (1963) 102–21, is foundational for the study of apostolicity in Tertullian. See also the briefer studies by Blum, *Offenbarung und Überlieferung. Die dogmatische Konstitution* Dei Verbum *des II. Vaticanums im Lichte altkirchlicher und moderner Theologie*, Forschungen zur systematischen und ökumenischen Theologie 28 (Göttingen: Vandenhoeck & Ruprecht, 1971) 93–95, and "Apostel/Apostolat/Apostolizität," in *TRE* 3:452–53.

35. In *De praescriptione haereticorum* ["Prescriptions against Heretics"] 36, Tertullian refers to five such norm churches: Corinth, Philippi, Thessalonika, Ephesus, and Rome. Earlier, in *De praescriptione* 32, he spoke of Smyrna and Rome as norm churches.

he considered a church apostolic if it had been established by one of the norm churches.[36] Finally, apostolicity is to be found in the agreement of the churches with one another in maintaining the teaching and discipline of the apostles.[37] In cases where doubts arise, questions of the apostolicity of the beliefs, practices, and the Christian Scriptures are to be referred to the norm churches. They have been endowed with the fullness of apostolic truth and practice. Thus, to Tertullian there was no single criterion for judging the apostolicity of a church. Although Tertullian's teaching regarding apostolicity lacks rigorous consistency, the abundance of theological perspectives more than makes up for this lack. It might be well for Christians today to remember this in their ecumenical discussions.

In the light of Tertullian's polyvalent understanding of a church's apostolicity, what role does he attribute to the bishop of a church? Does the succession of bishops fulfill the same role as in the case of Irenaeus? In his study of Tertullian's understanding of apostolicity, Georg G. Blum maintains that Tertullian diverged considerably from the Irenaean understanding. Blum says that for Irenaeus the bishop is central to apostolic teaching and practice because his preaching of the *traditio apostolica* is a present activity. In the bishop's kerygmatic teaching and preaching, the living voice of the apostles still resounds. As we saw above, it is the Spirit who assures the living and saving effect of the bishop's teaching in this new moment in time. Episcopacy is understood as a pneumatic reality.

36. *De praescriptione* 20: "[The apostles] then in like manner founded churches in every city, from which all the other churches, one after another, derived the tradition of the faith, and the seeds of doctrine, and are every day deriving them, that they may become churches. Indeed, it is on this account only that they will be able to deem themselves apostolic, as being the offspring of apostolic churches. Every sort of thing must necessarily revert to its original for its classification. Therefore the churches, although they are so many and so great, comprise but the one primitive church, (founded) by the apostles, from which they all (spring). In this way all are primitive, and all are apostolic." *ANF*, 3:252.

37. *De praescriptione* 32: "For their [the heretics'] very doctrine after comparison with that of the apostles, will declare, by its own diversity and contrariety, that it had for its author neither an apostle nor an apostolic man; because, as the apostles would never have taught things which were self-contradictory, so the apostolic men would not have inculcated teaching different from the apostles, unless they who received their instruction from the apostles went and preached in a contrary manner. To this test, therefore will they be submitted for proof by those churches, who, although they derive not their founder from apostles or apostolic men (as being of much later date, for they are in fact being founded daily), yet, since they agree in the same faith, they are accounted as not less apostolic because they are akin in doctrine. Then let all the heresies, when challenged to these two tests by our apostolic church, offer their proof of how they deem themselves to be apostolic. But in truth they neither are so, nor are they able to prove themselves to be what they are not." *ANF*, 3:258.

This is not the way Tertullian speaks about the bishops.[38] First of all, Tertullian acknowledges the office of the bishops in the church and speaks of their succession.[39] However, according to Blum, their teaching is no longer the ever-new proclamation of the gospel or apostolic kerygma but the guarantee of the apostolic truth as communicated to one of the norm churches. The difference is that between an act in continuity with apostolic power in the here and now (Irenaeus) and episcopal actions as offering assurance and guaranteeing the truth of the community's inheriting salvific truth (Tertullian). Blum characterizes Tertullian's interpretation as preoccupied with historico-empirical verification, as a "functional" understanding of the office, which he contrasts to Irenaeus' "dogmatic" understanding, and as concerned with apostolic teaching and practice in terms of a "pragmatizing of tradition" ("Traditionspragmatismus"). Given Tertullian's clearly polemical purpose in the *Prescriptions against the Heretics,* his approach is not surprising. It is the approach of the apologist, not the systematician.

What does seem to emerge from Tertullian's more limited approach to episcopal succession is a narrowing of the concept. In his understanding of the apostolic norm churches and the other churches, the succession functions in the full sense only in the principal or norm churches. There, the bishop's function of guaranteeing the church's apostolic truth and practice makes sense. The office is not at the origin of the truth, only the apostles themselves are. Yet, the founding apostles have poured out this truth and life into the community, which remains the primary witness and source of the endowment by the apostles. This doesn't render the office of bishop useless. That office makes sense in reference to the apostolic faith, and the apostolic faith is in need of the authoritative witness of the bishop. The two dimensions are not of equal weight, of course,

---

38. R. F. Refoulé stressed the similarity of ideas, if not style, between Irenaeus and Tertullian. See "Introduction," in *Tertullien, Traité de la Prescription contre les Hérétiques,* Sources chrétiennes [henceforth, *SC*] 46, ed. R. F. Refoulé, tr. P. de Labriolle (Paris: Les Éditions du Cerf, 1957) 58–66 ["Tertullien et Irénée"].

39. See *De praescriptione* 32: "Let them [the heretics] produce the original records of their bishops, displaying the succession from the beginning in such manner as that [first] bishop can show for his originator and predecessor one of the apostles or apostolic men [*edant ergo origines ecclesiarum suarum, euoluant ordinem epispocorum suorum, ita per successionem ab initio decurrentem ut primus ille episcopus aliquem ex apostolis uel apostolocis uiris, qui tamen cum apostolis perseuerauerit, habuerit auctorem et antecessorem*]. . . . For this is the manner in which the apostolic churches transmit their registers." See ibid., 46:130 for the Latin text. I have emended somewhat the English translation found in *ANF,* 3:258.

but neither are they unrelated. Apropos of the relationship, as early as 1957, R. F. Refoulé had written:

> . . . Can we say that it is the material continuity of the episcopacy that ac-
> counts for the apostolicity of the Churches, or does a more theologically
> developed understanding of episcopacy rather claim that it is 'the effica-
> cious sign of apostolicity, that is, of the Church's faithfulness to the mis-
> sion of the apostles'? . . . The bishops play a necessary role in the
> governance of the Churches and in the maintenance of discipline. But he
> does not accord them any charism connected to the episcopal function. . . .
> Tertullian only recognizes the authority of the bishops inasmuch as they
> personally participate in the Spirit who animates the Church. In this way
> of looking at things, apostolicity of persons is entirely conditioned by apos-
> tolicity of doctrine and remaining in the Church. Tertullian would cer-
> tainly have refused to acknowledge as a successor of the apostles a bishop
> who, though ritually ["régulièrement"] ordained, had nonetheless subse-
> quently become a heretic, a schismatic, or had committed a sin that ex-
> cluded him from the community of believers. *A fortiori* this is true for the
> bishops who would have ordained him.
>
> Already in the *De praescriptione,* Tertullian's insistence on the apostolic-
> ity of the Churches leads us to consider that the apostolicity of persons is
> totally subordinated to the apostolicity of the objects it transmits. The
> bishops can only claim apostolic succession to the extent that they lead an
> apostolic Church. In other words, apostolic succession is the possession of
> the Church that has it, and not of the bishop alone who finds himself ex-
> ercising leadership over the Church. . . .
>
> . . . Tertullian's intention was to show how the Churches today are vi-
> tally connected to the apostles and to Christ. He wanted to show how this
> identity throughout the centuries, this dynamic and vital continuity, was to
> be understood. In his eyes, the continuity of the bishops was only the sign,
> the witness, and the guarantee of a deeper continuity.[40]

Is it appropriate to consider whether this means that episcopacy in the churches that are not norm churches differs somehow from that of the norm churches? It is imperative that the former remain in communion with the latter.[41] Communion is central to apostolicity—communion among the norm churches and between the norm churches and all others.

40. Refoulé, *SC,* 46:60–64.
41. Apropos of the heretical groups, Tertullian writes: "Nor are they admitted to peaceful relations and communion by such churches as are in any way connected with such apostles." *De praescriptione* 32.

According to this logic, the duty of those bishops who lead churches other than the norm churches is to test their faith and practice against that of the norm churches and to foster communion in their churches and among the churches. No easy task then and no easy task today!

The Collection Known as the "Traditio Apostolica"

The work that interests us in this section is usually referred to according to what has come to be its Latin title, the *Traditio apostolica*. Authorship of the work is usually assigned to a presbyter of Rome named Hippolytus, who died in exile in Sardinia under the emperor Maximinus (235–38 C.E.). Unfortunately, the matter of authorship is complicated by references in Eusebius and Jerome to another figure, sometimes called Josipos, who was a bishop of an unidentified church in the East, and not a presbyter in Rome. We are dealing with the double attribution of certain works, mostly fragments, from the third century.[42] Though scholars now tend to accept the probability that there were two different authors of these disputed works, one a presbyter in Rome and the other a bishop somewhere in the East, their relationship to the author of the *"Traditio apostolica"* is not the least bit clear. It seems that the author of this latter work will remain anonymous.[43]

42. See Pierre Nautin, "Hippolytus," in *Encyclopedia of the Early Church,* vol. 1, ed. Angelo Di Berardino, tr. Adrian Walford (New York: Oxford University Press, 1992) 383–85; idem, "Apostolic Tradition," in ibid., 63; and Emanuela Prinzivalli, "Hippolytus, Statue of," in ibid., 385. For a clear and concise summary of the essential elements of this confusing situation, see Christopher O'Donnell, "Apostolic Tradition," in *Ecclesia: A Theological Encyclopedia of the Church* (Collegeville, Minn.: The Liturgical Press, 1996) 26–28.

43. See Marcel Metzger, "Nouvelles perspectives pour la prétendue *Tradition apostolique,*" *Ecclesia orans* 5 (1988) 241–59. Metzger has drawn on the research of several scholars, and principally on the doctoral work of Jean Magne, *Tradition apostolique sur les charismes et Diataxeis des saints Apôtres. Identification des documents et Analyse du rituel des ordinations* (Origines chrétiennes I) (Paris, 1975). The traditional view regarding Hippolytus as the author of the *Traditio apostolica* is represented by Aimé Georges Martimort in "Nouvel examen de la 'Tradition apostolique' d'Hippolyte," *Bulletin de littérature ecclésiastique* 88 (1987) 5–25, and "Encore Hippolyte et la 'Tradition apostolique,'" *Bulletin de littérature ecclésiastique* 92 (1991) 113–37. These issues are enormously complex and cannot be decided fully, given the current state of our knowledge. But the questions are so weighty as to impose caution on us in terms of the kinds of claims we make. This is especially true since the *"Traditio apostolica"* is one of the most important works of the third century that figured prominently in several documents of the Second Vatican Council and in much postconciliar literature treating the liturgy and questions of church ministry. In much of the popular literature, it is simply assumed that Hippolytus of Rome was its author, and that it represents the liturgical

Georg G. Blum, whose writings on apostolicity we have already had occasion to study, has shown how the "*Traditio apostolica*"[44] both departs from the perspectives of Tertullian and seems to build upon and extend those of Irenaeus.[45] He argues that the author shows little interest in "apostolic tradition" as authoritative teachings and practices handed down by clearly accredited teacher-successors, as was the case with Irenaeus. Clearly, the ecclesial situation addressed by the "*Traditio apostolica*" has changed. Blum argues that the enemies envisioned are no longer a group of thinkers more or less clearly outside the Great Church and who are in competition for adherents to its form of religious belief—as was the case with the Gnosticisms Irenaeus opposed—so much as with thinkers within

traditions and ecclesial structures in Rome at the end of the second century or the beginning of the third, even though its traditional date of composition has been ca. 220. None of this, however, is certain. Even the work we have today is a reconstruction by the twentieth-century scholars Gregory Dix and Bernard Botte. The text can be found in Gregory Dix, *The Treatise on the Apostolic Tradition of St. Hippolytus of Rome,* Corrections, Preface and Bibliography by Henry Chadwick (Harrisburg, Pa.: Morehouse Publishers, 1992), and in Bernard Botte, *Hippolyte de Rome, La Tradition Apostolique d'après les anciennes versions,* SC 11bis (2nd ed.; Paris: Les Éditions du Cerf, 1984). In the theologies of ministry and liturgy, rarely have so many weighty claims been made on the basis of so few certitudes. If we keep these caveats in mind and remember, too, that our interest is in the teaching about apostolicity in a work whose authorship de facto is disputed, we can still study the interpretation of apostolicity in it. Its teaching is not substantially altered by its place of origin or by the identity of its author, though of course its implications are very much affected by our answers to these questions. In what follows, I will refer simply to "the author" of the *Traditio apostolica,* even though my sources often identify him with Hippolytus. Whoever the author was, it was surely not the presbyter Hippolytus of Rome. Metzger places the work in the genre of canonical literature intended to organize the pastoral, ministerial, and liturgical life of a community, a genre in which the regulations are anonymous, even though someone evidently must have compiled them.

After completing my text, an important article was published that treats in detail the complicated issues of authorship, dating, place of composition, and the text's meaning. Interested readers should consult John F. Baldovin, "Hippolytus and the *Apostolic Tradition:* Recent Research and Commentary, *Theological Studies* 64 (2003) 520-42.

44. Taking up a suggestion made by Magne, Metzger shows how the title "*Traditio apostolica*" is contrived. There was no separate document entitled the *Traditio apostolica* but only a collection of ecclesiastical regulations that were incorporated into other collections of canonical material. Metzger prefers to refer to the work—which he refers to throughout his article as "*document x*"—according to the Greek word for "regulations," *diataxeis,* but he realizes that the conventional designation is by now so deeply engrained as to be resistant to widespread acceptance of a new title—*The Diataxeis.* For this reason, I have taken the liberty to continue to refer to it as the "*Traditio apostolica*," but always in quotation marks.

45. Blum, "Apostolische Tradition und Sukzession bei Hippolyt," *Zeitschrift für die neutestamentliche Wissenschaft und die Kunde der älteren Kirche* 55 (1964) 95–110. See also idem, *Offenbarung und Überlieferung,* 96f.; and idem, "*Apostel/Apostolat/Apostolizität,*" in *TRE,* 3:453.

the very ranks of the church—or those we have come to call "heretics." Secondly, the perspective on apostolicity has changed. The author envisions apostolicity in more pneumatic terms than did Irenaeus. The instructions regarding the office of bishop and the prayer of ordination both point to the bishop as a pneumatic or spirit-endowed person. We read:

> *Prologue:* . . . The Holy Ghost bestows the fullness of grace on those who believe rightly that they may know how those who are at the head of the Church should teach the tradition and maintain it in all things.
> *Rite of the Ordination of a Bishop:* . . . With the agreement of all let the bishops lay hands on him and the presbytery stand by in silence. And all shall keep silence praying in their hearts for the descent of the Spirit. After this one of the bishops present at the request of all, laying his hand on him who is ordained bishop, shall pray thus, saying:
> *Prayer of the Ordination of a Bishop:* . . . And now pour forth that Power which is from Thee, of the princely Spirit which Thou didst deliver to Thy Beloved Child Jesus Christ, which He bestowed on Thy holy Apostles who established the Church which hallows Thee in every place to the endless glory of Thy Name . . . that by the high priestly Spirit he may have authority to forgive sins according to Thy command, to assign lots according to Thy bidding, to loose every bond according to the authority Thou gavest to the Apostles, and that he may please Thee in meekness and a pure heart, offering to Thee the sweet-smelling savour, through Thy Child Jesus Christ Our Lord. . . .[46]

According to Blum, the ordination of a bishop is really an act of creation, since the ordination is seen as part of a series of interconnected typological events that include the baptism of the Lord (with the coming of the Spirit to Jesus), the event of Pentecost (with the pouring out of the Spirit on the apostles), and episcopal ordination (with the bestowal of the Spirit on the bishop). Each is understood as a new creative act in the Spirit. In Blum's own words:

> . . . The bishop's charism of office is understood both christologically and apostolically in terms of its content, its origin, and its transmission. However, the prayer of ordination does not mention succession to the apostles.

46. Metzger has pointed to the composite character of the *"Traditio apostolica."* Repetitions and doublets in the text point to its regulations deriving from different times and changed circumstances. See Metzger, "Nouvelles perspectives pour la prétendue *Tradition apostolique,*" 247 and 255–57. Magne discusses the composite character of chapter 3 in his "En finir avec la 'Tradition' d'Hippolyte!," *Bulletin de littérature ecclésiastique* 89 (1988) 5–22, here at 19–22 ["Le rituel des ordinations"].

Where, then, is the connection between the apostles' receiving the Spirit and the ordination of a bishop? The answer lies in the fact that the church for whose service someone is ordained and is given the Spirit was itself founded by the apostles. . . . In the face of this idea of the presence of the Spirit and participation in the Spirit, the historico-linear aspect of succession recedes into the background. It is no longer a matter primarily of succession and reception of an office. Episcopal ordination is envisioned much more as a creative act of imparting the Spirit, analogous to the baptism of Jesus and the event of Pentecost, through which the ordinand is added to the college of the apostles as an *alter apostolos*—another apostle. . . . An entirely new perspective on apostolicity opens up before us. Whereas earlier it was the component of historical succession associated with apostolicity that predominated, now the accent is strongly on the pneumatic aspect. What was earlier with Irenaeus already present here unfolds fully by reason of the application of the idea of apostolicity to the liturgical action of ordination. The apostolic character of the bishop's office consists in participating in the Spirit of Christ here present. The realm of the Spirit is constituted by the imparting of the Spirit of the apostles and their founding of the church, in so far as with each bishop's ordination the Spirit is effectively real.[47]

This theology of the episcopacy is quite startling when examined from later, more juridically conceived, perspectives. The vision does not concentrate on historical givens or on juridical determinations—though neither is entirely excluded as entirely pointless; they simply are not seen as central. Instead, the church is understood as the creation of the Spirit, but with the Spirit understood in terms of salvation history and its culmination in Jesus Christ and its continuation by the Spirit.

Vita Apostolica et Evangelica *in the Middle Ages*

Finally, a source for our understanding the apostolicity of the church that is often neglected is the movement in the church during the Middle Ages to live "the apostolic life." Is it only a source for the history of spirituality and devotion in Catholicism, or does it also tell us something about how the church itself is apostolic, that is, in the life of all believers and not just of the hierarchy? But what does the phenomenon known as the *vita apostolica et evangelica* movement mean,[48] and what significance does it have for our discussion of apostolicity today?

47. Blum, "Apostolische Tradition und Sukzession bei Hippolyt," 106–7.
48. Material on the movements called *vita apostolica* and *vita evangelica* can be found distributed in vols. 3 and 4 of the *Handbook of Church History,* ed. Hubert Jedin and John

In the twelfth century, a number of factors coalesced to bring about important changes in the church of the feudal period.[49] After the fall of Rome (476) and the breakup of the empire in the West, life in the cities declined and the feudal society that emerged from the chaos was predominantly agrarian. However, between 1070 and 1220 feudalism began to lose its grip on Europe. The population increased dramatically, the cities began to be repopulated and new ones began to spring up, education was extended to more and more persons, the arts and architecture gained new vitality and new forms, and ordinary people yearned for religious renewal. The Crusades unlocked new knowledge and influences on Europe's population; more participatory forms of local government emerged in movements to establish city communes; and artisans and laborers found strength in guilds and voluntary associations. The leadership in the church, especially the papacy, began to address the scandals of ignorance, laziness, and moral laxity, the clergy.[50] It was felt that one of the causes of the scandals was the undue influence of lay princes and lesser nobles in determining who would be candidates for the priesthood and who would be appointed bishops. Popes Nicholas II (1059–61) and Gregory VII (1073–85) in particular addressed the papacy's struggle against "lay investiture." The twelfth century also witnessed the reform of monastic life with the birth of the Cistercians, the Camaldolese of Fontebuono, the Order of Grandmont, the Order of Vallombrosa, and so forth.[51] Some of the diocesan clergy also began to live

Dolan, trans. Anselm Biggs (New York: Herder and Herder, 1969 and 1970). The most important chapters and sections include: Friedrich Kempf, "The 'Vita Evangelica' Movement and the Appearance of New Orders," 3:453–65; and Hans Wolter, 4:86–88 ["Crusade Piety"]; idem, "Lay Movements in the Twelfth Century, Christian Knighthood, Pastoral Care, Popular Piety, and Mysticism," 4:104–112; idem, "The Mendicant Orders," 4:172–83; and idem, "Christian Fanaticism in the Thirteenth Century," 4:240–46.

49. See Prospero Rivi, "The Historical Context: A Century and One Half of Great Changes," in *Francis of Assisi and the Laity of His Time,* ed. Regis J. Armstrong and Ingrid Peterson, trans. Heather Tolfree, *Greyfriars Review* 15, Supplement (2001) 2–19.

50. On the state of the clergy in the Middle Ages, see Edward Schillebeeckx, "The Priest from the Eighth to the Thirteenth Century," in *The Church with a Human Face: A New and Expanded Theology of Ministry,* tr. John Bowden (New York: The Crossroad Publishing Company, 1985) 161–94.

51. On the various reforms of orders and the founding of new orders in the twelfth century, see Friedrich Kempf, "The 'Vita Evangelica' Movement and the Appearance of New Orders," in *Handbook of Church History,* 3:453–65.

a common life in support of their ideals and their ministry by constituting a canonical form of life, and came to be called "canons regular."[52]
The Premonstratensians, or the canons regular of Prémontré, still active
to our day, were one of the most successful experiments. But the yearn-
ing for rebirth and reform was far from limited to the clergy and religious in the church. The ordinary faithful sought new activities and new
ways of living out their Christian faith more enthusiastically.[53] The century abounded in charismatic individuals who roamed the countryside
or adopted ascetical lifestyles in the towns and cities.[54] In a word, the
Crusades and the breakdown of feudal ideals elicited revivals and new
experiments.

Scholars group these experiments under the rubric of the *vita apostolica et evangelica* movement because they were all inspired by the life of
the early church as depicted in the Scriptures, and in the Acts of the
Apostles in particular. There they read that:

> All who believed were together and had all things in common; and they
> sold their possessions and goods and distributed them to all, as any had
> need. And day by day, attending the temple together and breaking bread

52. On the canons regular, see Friedrich Kempf, *Handbook of Church History*, 3:460–64
["The Canons Regular"]; Grover A. Zinn, "The Regular Canons," in *Christian Spirituality:
Origins to the Twelfth Century,* World Spirituality: An Encyclopedic History of the Religious
Quest, vol. 16, ed. Bernard McGinn and John Meyendorff, in collaboration with Jean
Leclercq (New York: The Crossroad Publishing Company, 1985) 218–28; and Gerd Tellen-
bach, *The Church in Western Europe from the Tenth to the Early Twelfth Century,* tr. Timothy
Reuter (New York: Cambridge University Press, 1993) 120–21.

53. See André Vauchez, "The Religion of a New Era: From the Late Eleventh to
the Early Thirteenth Century," in *The Spirituality of the Medieval West: The Eighth to the Twelfth
Century,* Cistercian Studies 145, tr. Colette Friedlander (Kalamazoo, Mich.: Cistercian
Publications, 1993) 75–143; and Prospero Rivo, "The Laity in Search of Their Own Spirituality," in *Francis of Assisi and the Laity of His Time,* 20–36.

54. These include Robert of Arbrissel (d. 1117), Bernard of Thiron (d. 1117), Gerard of Salles (d. 1120), Vitalis of Savigny (d. 1122), Stephen of Muret (d. 1124), the Hu-
miliati in Lombardy, the *pauperes catholici* of Peter Waldo (d. between 1205–18), and the
followers of Bernard of Primus. On these figures, see Duane V. Lapsanski, "The 'Gospel
Life' as Source of New Ecclesiastical Communities" and "The 'Evangelical Life' as the Inspiration of Lay Apostolic Movements," in *Evangelical Perfection: An Historical Examination of
the Concept in the Early Franciscan Sources* (St. Bonaventure, N.Y.: The Franciscan Institute,
1977) 14–30 and 31–46, and George H. Tavard, "Apostolic Life and Church Reform," in
Christian Spirituality: High Middle Ages and Reformation, World Spirituality: An Encyclopedic
History of the Religious Quest, vol. 17, ed. Jill Raitt (New York: The Crossroad Publishing Company, 1987) 1–77, here at 6–10.

in their homes, they partook of food with glad and generous hearts, prais-
ing God and having favor with all the people (Acts 2:44-47).

Now the company of those who believed were of one heart and soul
and no one said that any of the things which he possessed was his own,
but they had everything in common. And with great power the apostles
gave testimony to the resurrection of the Lord Jesus, and great grace was
upon them all. There was not a needy person among them, for as many as
were possessors of lands or houses sold them, and brought the proceeds of
what was sold and laid it at the apostles' feet; and distribution was made to
each as any had need (Acts 4:32-37).

In other words, Christian life was seen as itself "apostolic" and "according to the gospel," that is, evangelical. This represented a real departure
from their proximate experience, since up to then the gospel was seen to
be enshrined in monasticism or in the ordained ministry. Monasticism,
or the *ordo monasticus,* in particular was dominant at the time. Marie-Dominique Chenu has shown how the evangelical movement represented a
breakthrough on three fronts: the discovery of the world as a value, a retrieval and a deepening of evangelical poverty, and the need to hear, pon-
der, and preach the word of God.[55]

The spirituality that had characterized the faith after the dissolution
of the empire in the West is often referred to as *fuga mundi*–a fleeing or
repudiation of the world.[56] The world was the domain of the devil,
whereas the monastery represented the ideal "city of God" where everything the monk did converged on the centrality of God. Such an ideal
was not available to the ordinary lay person. A new understanding of
the world began to develop, one that opened up the possibility of the
world's autonomy and a rediscovery of its inherent goodness. The Middle
Ages inherited a sacralized universe that was an undifferentiated mix of
the sacred and the secular, and was unthinkingly assumed to be immutable. Thus, the papacy's struggle for its independence from lay influence tended to separate the world and the church, the secular and the
sacred. This represented a blessing in disguise: the church was free to be
itself–it had its own goal and institutions, and it did not need to become

55. See M.-D. Chenu, "Monks, Canons, and Laymen in Search of the Apostolic
Life" and "The Evangelical Awakening," in *Nature, Man, and Society in the Twelfth Century: Es-
says on New Theological Perspectives in the Latin West,* ed. and trans. Jerome Taylor and Lester
K. Little (Chicago: University of Chicago Press, 1968) 202–38 and 239–69.

56. See the discussion by Prospero Rivi, "The Historical Context," 5–6.

embroiled in the power game of the world. The world also gained by separation from the church because it, too, discovered its God-given nature and purpose. The process of self-discovery by church and secular world was often conflictual and confrontational, but it was the price each had to pay to gain its own sense of autonomy. For the first time in Christian history, the "world" emerged on its own, and this meant that the laity, who lived and worked in the world, were not necessarily at a disadvantage vis-à-vis monastics and the clergy. There was a basis for the laity's own characteristic spirituality, not a world-defying but a world-building one.

There was also a deepening of poverty as an ideal. Chenu characterizes it as "social poverty."[57] The ideal in monasticism was the spiritual value of being poor and its relationship to life in common. In the twelfth century, with the widespread ecclesiastical scandal caused by spiritual tepidity, moral laxity, and woeful ignorance among the clergy, poverty emerged as a measure designed to counter the low standards in place. The freely espoused poverty of groups of itinerant lay preachers served to reinforce the credibility of their message. Unfortunately, the pursuit of poverty often included hostility toward the institutional church and heretical dissent from the validity of the church's sacraments. Needless to say, the bishops, and a papacy bent on intra-ecclesial reform, looked on these popular movements with alarm and often reacted with condemnation. However, as the pace of social change increased in the twelfth and thirteenth centuries, the dire consequences on European society gained in urgency. Not everyone benefited from the emancipation of the serfs and the emergence of a prosperous middle class. Many people were unable to cope with the changes in society and were reduced to destitution. The poverty movements of the thirteenth century understood apostolic poverty more in terms of living poorly by associating with the poor and helping to alleviate their material needs. As I have written elsewhere: "Poverty was not seen in overly personal and idealistic terms, that is, poverty as the way back to the ideal existence of the early church, but in social terms, that is, poverty as sharing in the fate of those who are inevitably left behind in a period of social transformation."[58] This more socially conscious

---

57. See Chenu, "The Evangelical Awakening," 243.
58. Burkhard, "Defining Gospel Life in Postmodern Culture," in *Franciscan Identity and Postmodern Culture,* Washington Theological Union Symposium Papers 2002, ed. Kathleen A. Warren (St. Bonaventure, N.Y.: The Franciscan Institute, 2003) 35–54, at 43. See also Chenu, "The Evangelical Awakening," 240–44.

form of poverty came to expression in the Order of Preachers—popularly known as the Dominicans—and the Order of Friars Minor (more literally, the Lesser Brothers)—the Franciscans. It is really a form of poverty in solidarity with the poor and the disadvantaged.

Finally, the *vita apostolica et evangelica* movement addressed the lack of preaching in the late Middle Ages.[59] With little formal training in theology and Scripture, priests resorted to edifying stories of saints and miracles often verging on the superstitious. For their part, many bishops were absent from their dioceses or absorbed in other affairs. Illiteracy precluded the ordinary folk from direct access to the Scriptures, yet there was a great thirst for the word of God. The founding of the medieval universities began to correct the issue of ignorance of the Scriptures, but the benefits were far from widespread. Again, the itinerant lay preachers addressed the issue by their popular preaching. Clearly, devotion to the word of God was a primary value of the early apostolic church. The popular movements of the twelfth century aspired to revive this devotion but ran afoul of the right of the bishops alone to preach.

In the early apostolic church, the ministry of the word was shared by apostles, teachers, evangelists, and prophets—not all of whom could be considered as holding an office. After the emergence of episcopacy in the second century, the bishops shared the ministry of the word with others, for example, the presbyters and teachers like Clement and Origen of Alexandria. The bishops held no monopoly on preaching. A reform-minded papacy saw in the itinerant lay preachers and certain canons regular the possibility of addressing the woeful state of preaching and allowed some to preach alongside the bishops. This ad hoc arrangement was permanently established in the thirteenth century with papal approbation of the Order of Preachers and the entrusting of preaching tasks to the Friars Minor. In spite of opposition by the bishops and clergy, this new stable form of ministry of the word was introduced into the church.[60]

59. See Chenu, "The Evangelical Awakening," 244–45, and Edward Schillebeeckx, "The Right of Every Christian to Speak in the Light of Evangelical Experience 'In the Midst of Brothers and Sisters,'" in *Preaching and the Non-Ordained: An Interdisciplinary Study,* ed. Nadine Foley (Collegeville, Minn.: The Liturgical Press, 1983) 11–39.

60. See John W. O'Malley, "Priesthood, Ministry, and Religious Life: Some Historical and Historiographical Considerations," *Theological Studies* 49 (1988) 223–57, at 231–37 ["The Dominicans and Franciscans"]; Karl Suso Frank, "The Mendicant Orders," in *With Greater Liberty: A Short History of Christian Monasticism and Religious Orders,* tr. Joseph T. Lienhard, Cistercian Studies 144 (Kalamazoo, Mich.: Cistercian Publications, 1993)

The fact that the Dominicans were a clerical community from the start and that the Franciscans yielded to the clericalization of a largely lay movement facilitated the institution of more available and often popular preaching by the friars.

The *vita apostolica et evangelica* movements of the twelfth and thirteenth centuries tapped into new energies as feudal Europe lost its grip on society. Not the least of the energies was a deep thirst for a spirituality the laity could share and for new ministries of charitable works, fighting for the freedom of the shrines in the Holy Land, living in communities that were sometimes associated with monasteries and at other times were independent, living a poor life after the example of Christ and the Apostles, serving the materially poor, and popular preaching in response to the desire for God among many. Much of this vitality and energy would culminate in the wake of the mendicant movements of the thirteenth century, but to pursue the subsequent history would take me too far afield. The point I want to make is that the *vita apostolica et evangelica* movement and its subsequent flowering has theological significance for the apostolicity of the church. What postconciliar theologians have emphasized in terms of the apostolicity of the life of a church is confirmed in the *vita apostolica et evangelica* movements of the late Middle Ages. Their importance is more than devotional, it is also doctrinally significant.

107–30; David N. Power, "Theologies of Religious Life and Priesthood," in *A Concert of Charisms: Ordained Ministry in Religious Life,* ed. Paul K. Hennessy (New York: Paulist Press, 1997) 61–103, at 71–76.

CHAPTER FOUR

Apostolicity and the Theologians

In the twentieth century, especially in the years immediately before Vatican II and in the postconciliar period, many outstanding theologians from the various ecclesial traditions have studied the apostolicity of the church and the question of apostolic succession. In the present chapter, I will attempt to survey the most important positions developed. I will look at representative theologians from the Roman Catholic Church, from the churches of the Reform, and from the Orthodox Church. I will leave to a future chapter the ecumenical dialogues and the degree of consensus that has been reached. At any rate, the consensus that has emerged in the years following the Council would not be possible without the efforts of the following theologians, and many other scholars who have been actively involved in official ecumenical consultations and informal discussions.

Yves Congar, O.P.

Among Catholic theologians, perhaps no one has contributed more to the theme of apostolicity than the French Dominican, Yves Congar (1904–1995). His theological career was fruitful and long, over sixty-five years of teaching and writing, and ecclesiology stood at the center of his work. He was undoubtedly the twentieth century's premier theologian of the history of ecclesiology, its movements, principal writers, and schools of thought.[1] Congar's contributions to Vatican II included the

---

1. See Yves Congar, *Vraie et fausse Réforme dans l'Église,* Unam Sanctam 20 (2nd ed., Paris: Les Éditions du Cerf, 1969); *L'ecclésiologie du Haut Moyen Age* (Paris: Les Éditions du

nature of episcopacy, especially collegiality, the church as a communion, the role of the laity, and ecumenism. He showed how the church in the second millennium had adopted a juridical model of understanding itself. He outlined its effects on the church's concrete life, including a mentality of triumphalism, a clericalism that beclouded the ministry's call to service, and what he called a "hierarchology," that is, a mentality that saw the hierarchy at the center of the church and the church in all its dimensions as derived from the hierarchy. Consequently, at Vatican II, he championed the biblical image of the church as the People of God. After the Council, he devoted increased attention to the Holy Spirit and tried to develop a pneumatology to help counterbalance the christomonistic ecclesiology he saw as characteristic of the Western Church.[2]

In the years immediately following the Council, Congar studied the questions of apostolicity and ministry in great detail. His knowledge of the long theological tradition helped him better appreciate the central importance of apostolic doctrine. In several essays he pointed out the following about apostolicity.[3] First, he indicated the primacy of the apostolicity of the whole church, and he maintained that apostolic succession is inseparable from apostolicity in this more fundamental sense, which he also called the "tradition" in the full and real meaning of that term.[4] Second, he claimed that we must not isolate apostolicity and apostolic succession from the church as a community. If the Catholic Church ran

---

Cerf, 1968); *L'Église: De saint Augustin à l'époque moderne* (Paris: Les Éditions du Cerf, 1970 [reprinted 1997]; *Études d'ecclésiologie médiévale* (London: Variorum Reprints, 1983).

    2. *I Believe in the Holy Spirit*, 3 vols., tr. David Smith (New York: The Seabury Press, 1983), and *The Word and the Spirit*, tr. David Smith (San Francisco: Harper & Row, 1986). On Congar's theology and theological output, see Aidan Nichols, *Yves Congar,* Outstanding Christian Thinkers Series, ed. Brian Davies (Wilton, Conn.: Morehouse-Barlow, 1989).

    3. Yves Congar, "Composantes et idée de la Succession Apostolique," *Oecumenica* 1 (1966) 61–78; *L'Église une, sainte, catholique et apostolique,* Mysterium Salutis, vol. 15 (Paris: Les Éditions du Cerf, 1970) 181–224; "Ministères et structuration de l'Église," in *Ministères et communion ecclésiale* (Paris: Les Éditions du Cerf, 1971) 31–49; "Apostolicité de ministère et apostolicité de doctrine. Essai d'explication de la Réaction protestante et de la Tradition catholique," in ibid., 51–94; "Quelques problèmes touchant les ministères," *Nouvelle revue théologique* 93 (1971) 785–800.

    4. Before and during Vatican II, Congar also wrote one of the most significant works on tradition, entitled *Tradition and Traditions: An Historical Essay and A Theological Essay,* tr. Michael Naseby and Thomas Rainborough (New York: The Macmillan Company, 1966). It appeared in French in two volumes, *An Historical Essay* appeared in French in 1960, and *A Theological Essay* in 1963. Both texts were influential in the formulations of the Dogmatic Constitution on Divine Revelation *(Dei Verbum)* at Vatican II.

the risk of isolating the authoritative magisterium from the believing community, the churches of the Reform ran the risk of stressing apostolicity of doctrine in a way which was open to exaggerating excessively the private interpretation of the content and meaning of apostolic doctrine by each individual believer. The solution is to be found in an understanding of the church as a communion in which one finds the certainty of true doctrine and the validity of formal succession in mutual relationship. Each supports and provides balance to the other. He wrote: "Attention has been placed too exclusively on the validity of formal ordinations as such. . . .The episcopacy as function is not an object that one has control of outside the service it renders in the very bosom of the Church."[5] On the side of the bishops, an understanding of episcopacy as collegiality, that is, communion as a body of pastoral leaders in the apostolic ministry and not as isolated individual successors to the apostles, is indispensable. On the side of the body of believers, this implies some form of participation by the whole church, including the notion of reception of doctrine by all. Finally, the way to an integrated and balanced understanding of the apostolicity of the church is inseparable from the recovery of a sacramental sense of the church. The church as sacrament excludes an overly mechanical or automatic understanding in as much as it sees itself as the sacramental expression of God's covenant with humankind. The sense of covenant assures God's freedom and sees the covenant as an expression of grace and God's fidelity to the divine word of covenant. In view of such a sacramental understanding, the church's structures are not comparable to laws of nature but are concrete forms of the graces of God who calls the church to accept them as gift but also to realize them as task. A good summary statement of Congar's views on apostolicity is the following:

> In short, in this matter as in others, a healthy understanding of apostolicity consists in inserting ecclesial ministries into the whole reality of the Church whose mystery is found in each particular authentic Church. Apostolicity is the apostolicity of these churches, just as collegiality is the collegiality or the communion of the churches. But these churches are structured by the Lord's will and the Lord's institution has been mediated by a history that has been directed by divine providence. God wills a people that is one, holy, catholic, and apostolic in accord with the structures of the covenant

5. Congar, "Apostolicité de ministère et apostolicité de doctrine," 88.

of grace. The community cannot be separated from its pastors, and the pastors cannot be divided from their communities. . . . By the grace of the Holy Spirit, the pastors receive the task of serving the community according to the structures that derive from the apostles. This ministry is a responsibility, mission, and a function with all the "powers" that are connected with it.[6]

Congar contributed admirably and constructively toward a new understanding of apostolicity, and yet forty years after Vatican II the official Roman Catholic position has remained substantially the same as the preconciliar one. How are we to understand this immobility on the theology of apostolicity? Could Congar have done something better? I don't think it is the elements that Congar singled out. Two things, however, were not properly attended to. The first was the notion of collegiality itself. The bishops at the Council and in the postconciliar period were not able to agree on a convincing understanding of collegiality. This lack leaves a gaping hole at the very center of the discussion, and it is sensed by the leaders of the other churches as well. Second, Congar did not develop adequately his pneumatological insights in the service of apostolicity. His reflections on the Spirit at this stage are still too tentative and fleeting. Only later did he develop his pneumatology in its own right, but without really integrating it into his theory of apostolicity.

Hans Küng

Perhaps no Catholic theologian is as well known internationally as the Swiss theologian Hans Küng (1928–). He was a young peritus at Vatican II and has been a tireless advocate of the Council's call for aggiornamento and ecumenism. He has always cut something of a figure of a theological enfant terrible, and this has tended to limit his effectiveness in leading the movement for renewal. However, he is enormously popular among his Catholic and non-Catholic, and, indeed, his non-Christian readers. Most of his writings on apostolicity are from the sixties and early seventies of the twentieth century, the period that saw the appearance of his influential writings on the church, *Structures of the Church* (1964) and *The Church* (1967).

Küng has made a number of points on the nature of apostolicity. First, he showed how the four attributes or marks of the church listed in

6. "Apostolicité de ministère et apostolicité de doctrine," 93.

the Creed are not arbitrary or unrelated to one another. Unity, holiness, catholicity, and apostolicity help realize each other and in this way constitute the church itself. They interpenetrate and mutually realize one another. In *Structures of the Church* he makes this point forcefully: "The attributes of the church are not static labels. Rather, as different dimensions of one and the same church they dynamically penetrate each other at every point (in a *circumincessio* and *circuminsessio* of a unique kind)."[7] Küng repeated this idea more rhetorically later in *The Church:*

> [These four attributes] are dimensions which at a very deep level are interdependent; indeed, as we have often noted, they overlap and must necessarily overlap. What is ecclesiastical unity without the breadth of catholicity, the power of holiness and the original impulse of apostolicity? What is ecclesiastical catholicity without the links of unity, the distinction of holiness and the vitality of apostolicity? What is ecclesiastical holiness without the binding power of unity, the generosity of catholicity and the long roots of apostolicity? What finally is ecclesiastical apostolicity without the brotherhood of unity, the diversity of catholicity and the spirit of holiness?[8]

Second, Küng pointed out that apostleship existed in the church within and with a view toward the whole community. The apostle did not act in a manner entirely independent of others and other ministries. "He gives his [apostolic] witness not on his own, but surrounded by the witness of all those who have received the Spirit."[9] Third, there is a certain unrepeatability to the apostolic office in so far as the church is derived from the apostles' own authoritative witness to the Risen Christ. "The Church is founded on this apostolic witness and ministry, which is older than the

7. *Structures of the Church*, tr. Salvator Attanasio (New York: Thomas Nelson & Sons, 1964) 69–70. Latin authors employed two different translations of the Greek *perichoresis*, i.e., "the reciprocal presence, interpenetration, or interrelationship of the three persons of the Trinity." See Gerald O'Collins and Edward G. Farrugia, *A Concise Dictionary of Theology* (rev. and expanded ed.; New York: Paulist Press, 200) 199. *Circumincessio* is a more literal rendering and means the mutual being-in-and-with each other of the trinitarian persons. *Circuminsessio* is a metaphor and attempts to present the trinitarian persons pictorially as "sitting around each other in a circle."

8. *The Church*, tr. Ray and Rosaleen Ockenden (New York: Sheed and Ward, 1967) 359. George H. Tavard also points to the mutual relations among the church's attributes. See *The Church, Community of Salvation: An Ecumenical Ecclesiology* (Collegeville, Minn.: Liturgical Press, 1992). On pp. 113f. he writes: "They stand together in mutual implication. The Church is not one apart from or in addition to being holy, catholic, and apostolic . . . . Each mark includes all the others."

9. Kung, *The Church,* 353.

church itself. The apostles are the beginners, the continuing foundation-stones of the Church, the cornerstone and keystone of which is Christ himself."[10] They are, therefore, the constant reference points for all future generations of Christians. Fourth, though the apostles' witness to the Risen Christ is once and for all, their mission perdures throughout the centuries. "The mission of the apostles was more than the persons of the apostles themselves. The apostolic mission is now no longer instituted directly by the Lord, but indirectly by men. Since this apostolic mission remains, so too does the apostolic ministry."[11] There must be succession to the apostolic ministry. Fifth, the whole church is the successor to the continuing apostolic mission. The primary referent to the apostles' mission is the church as such and only secondarily a more limited apostolic ministry of leadership. Küng writes: "The authorized mission of the apostles has been handed on to the Church which the apostles summoned together; the authorized ministry of the apostles has been handed on to the Church which the apostles ministered to. The Church is the successor of the apostles in obedience, and from this obedience it derives its authority."[12] Sixth, the church's obedience must be more than an external listening to the apostles, it must also include following the apostolic witness by the appropriate responses of respecting, believing, confessing, and following. In other words, the apostolicity of the church as a whole is constant, dynamic, and found primarily in fidelity to the apostles' witness as communicated in the Scriptures. "Apostolic succession therefore entails a continuing and living confrontation of the Church with the original, fundamental testimony of Scripture; apostolic succession is achieved only if this biblical witness is faithfully followed in preaching, faith and action. . . . [God's word] is to be heard and believed here and now as a message of joy, of liberation, of good news."[13] Seventh, ecclesial apostolicity points beyond itself and envisions the church's mission as inclusive of service to the world and to all human beings. "To be a Church and to have a mission are not two separate things. To be itself, the Church must follow the apostles in continually recognizing and demonstrating that it has been sent out to the world."[14] Finally, apostolicity participates

10. Ibid.
11. Ibid.
12. Ibid., 356.
13. Ibid., 357.
14. Ibid., 358.

·in human history. "It is an historical dimension, a dimension which has constantly to be fulfilled in history. Apostolicity . . . must continually be achieved afresh, must be a recurring event in a living history."[15]

In an article written about the same time as *The Church*, Küng rehearses many of the points just mentioned.[16] However, in the article he dedicates more space to ecclesiastical office as an expression of apostolic succession. In particular, Küng shows how the threefold order of ministry of bishop, presbyter, and deacon is a legitimate expression of apostolic leadership in the church. Other legitimate, possibly more charismatic or "Pauline," ways cannot be excluded entirely, and this is not a limitation but a benefit for the church.

What in particular has Küng contributed to the discussion and why has it, too, not been effective in reshaping the Catholic theology of apostolic succession? I find Küng's suggestion regarding the mutuality of the four attributes of the church a very fruitful avenue in the process of rethinking this doctrine, but Küng does not really pursue it. If the attributes of their nature realize each other through mutual relations, the idea that some churches which have undervalued apostolic succession by episcopal ordination but which are truly outstanding in holiness or openness to full catholicity, is rich in the possibility for arguing another mode of the realization of apostolicity itself.[17] Then, too, no one better than Küng has stressed the idea of apostolicity as an attribute of the whole church and of each individual in the church. This idea, too, seems to retrieve the sense of the early church that first of all the churches themselves were apostolic, so that apostolicity could then be discerned in the various

15. Ibid.

16. Hans Küng, "What is the Essence of Apostolic Succession?" in *Apostolic Succession: Rethinking a Barrier to Unity*, Concilium 34, ed. Hans Küng (New York: Paulist Press, 1968) 28–35.

17. Miroslav Volf, an outstanding Baptist theologian, gives us an example worth pondering. He writes: "I am thinking . . . of the observation that the dynamic life and the orthodox faith of the many, quickly proliferating Free Churches make it difficult to deny them full ecclesiality. Let me illustrate this difficulty by referring to a situation that, although doubtless atypical, must nonetheless be the touchstone of any ecclesiology precisely because it is a borderline case. Should, for example, a Catholic or Orthodox diocese whose members are inclined more to superstition than to faith and who identify with the church more for nationalistic reasons– should such a diocese be viewed as a church, while a Baptist congregation that has preserved its faith through the crucible of persecution *not* be considered such?" *After Our Likeness: The Church as the Image of the Trinity* (Grand Rapids, Mich.: Wm. B. Eerdmans Publishing Company, 1998) 133–34.

dimensions of the church's life, doctrine, ministry, and so forth, as signs of its apostolicity.

Theologians of the Reform

The topic of apostolicity has been an important one for the Reformation churches also. Both Martin Luther (1483–1546) and John Calvin (1509–1564) addressed issues of apostolic ministry in the church of their time. It is not the scope of this book to pursue their teachings in depth. Instead, I am interested in the contemporary discussion among post-Vatican II Lutherans and Reformed theologians.

The discussion of apostolicity in the church among Protestants must surely begin with the 1957 talk by Edmund Schlink to the Ecumenical Commission of the United Lutheran Church of Germany. His important presentation appeared later in a collection of his talks and articles as "Apostolic Succession."[18] It has been referred to often in the theological literature, and Warren A. Quanbeck has provided an excellent summary of its contents.[19] Instead of concentrating on this essay, I will examine a contribution made several years later, a study of ecclesiastical office, ordination, and apostolic succession in the exegesis and systematic theology of Evangelical Lutherans, Reformed Theologians, and Roman Catholics by Heinz Schütte.[20]

In his study, Schütte attempted to demonstrate the following two points. First, the widespread perception that Luther and Calvin rejected the necessity of a ministry of leadership and denied the sacramentality of ordination is really a misconception. Second, within a broad variety of interpretations of the positions of Luther and the Lutheran confessional statements, a majority opinion has emerged in the post-Vatican II period. It is more problematic to establish these two points as regards Calvin and the Reformed theological tradition but by no means is it excluded entirely.

---

18. *The Coming Christ and the Coming Church* (Philadelphia: Fortress Press, 1968) 186–233.

19. Warren A. Quanbeck, "A Contemporary View of Apostolic Succession," in *Eucharist and Ministry,* Lutherans and Catholics in Dialogue 4, eds. Paul C. Empie and T. Austin Murphy (Washington, D.C.: USCC Publications Office, 1970) 178–88, at 182–85.

20. Heinz Schütte, *Amt, Ordination und Sukzession im Verständnis evangelischer und katholischer Exegeten und Dogmatiker der Gegenwart sowie in Dokumenten ökumenischer Gespräche* (Düsseldorf: Patmos Verlag, 1974).

Regarding the Lutheran confessions, Schütte has shown that office is constitutive of the church and as such is of divine institution. Though it is oriented toward a function of service of word and sacrament, it also involves the whole person and is in this sense "personal" as well as "functional." The confessions do not hesitate to refer to it as an *ordo*. Service and ministry do not exclude real authority in so far as the minister represents Christ by teaching and acting in accord with the gospel. On the issue of the assumption of office, the confessions view it as a sacramental ordination, even though the term *sacramentum* is reserved for baptism, the Eucharist and the forgiveness of sins. Lutherans tended to avoid mention of ordination as a sacrament because they were intent on excluding any misunderstanding of the office as a priesthood that offered sacrifice as though somehow the sacrifice of Christ was inadequate. They also had difficulties with the late scholastic understanding of a *character indelebilis*. Moreover, ordination was to be administered only by those who themselves occupied the ministry. Ordinarily, this meant the bishops, but in exceptional conditions, such as the circumstances of the Reform itself, it could include the pastors. The priesthood of all believers, then, is not the basis for the ministry of preaching and administering the sacraments, even though its importance for a full understanding of the Christian's dignity and status is unquestioned.[21]

The issues are less clear for the Reformed churches stemming from John Calvin's thought.[22] Schütte refers to two general positions as representative of Reformed theology of the ministry. The first position, or the minority opinion, is represented by Jean-Jacques von Allmen especially, and corresponds closely with the Lutheran and the Catholic positions. The majority position, represented by the German Otto Weber (1902–1966), departs from this understanding at certain points.[23] Recently, David Fergusson, too, cautioned against forcing Reformed theology, characterized by

21. See also Arthur Carl Piepkorn, "The Sacred Ministry and Holy Ordination in the Symbolical Books of the Lutheran Church," in *Eucharist and Ministry,* eds. Paul C. Empie and T. Austin Murphy, 101–19, and George A. Lindbeck, "The Lutheran Doctrine of the Ministry: Catholic and Reformed," *Theological Studies* 30 (1969) 588–612.

22. Other Reformation figures who contributed to the formation of Reformed theology include Martin Bucer (1491–1551), Huldrych Zwingli (1484–1531), Johann Heinrich Bullinger (1504–1575), and Theodore Beza (1519–1605). See R. W. A. Letham, "Reformed Theology," in *New Dictionary of Theology,* ed. Sinclair B. Ferguson, David F. Wright, and J. I. Packer (Downers Grove, Ill.: InterVarsity Press, 1988) 569–72.

23. Other Reformed theologians of this tendency mentioned by Schütte include Karl Barth, W. Kreck, and A. J. Bronkhorst.

a broad spectrum of views, into a homogeneity that it does not possess.[24] It is necessary to proceed with greater caution when generalizing on the Reformed theology of ministry. The majority view according to Schütte includes an authoritative ministry, especially of the word. This ministry is a gift from God and is not generated from within the church or from below. In Reformed theology, ministry is seen as shared in a collegial manner ("kollegiale Gemeinsamkeit"), namely, pastors, elders, teachers, and deacons, and entrance to the pastoral ministry takes place through ordination by other ordained pastors. Apostolicity of succession in ministry by episcopal ordination is not eo ipso excluded so long as it is understood as a sign of fidelity to the apostolic teaching. The pastor is not a cultic priest and his office is not an ecclesiastical state. On sacramental ministry, Fergusson adds the following important observations:

> . . . [I]t is hard to deny that priority was generally attached to the preaching of the Word over against the sacraments which tend to confirm the former in more visible and tangible forms. The view thus emerged that the weekly gathering of God's people must always involve the speaking and hearing of the Word, but not always the dispensing of the sacraments. Although the latter as divine gifts are not to be neglected, they are largely annexed to the proclamation of the gospel. Ecumenical theology, however, tends to move in the direction of juxtaposing Word and sacraments to the extent that the celebration of the Lord's Supper becomes an integral part of the weekly diet of worship. Yet this is still largely foreign to the worship of most Reformed communities in the world today, and, if ecumenical progress is to be achieved, a commitment to the more frequent celebration of the Lord's Supper is probably required alongside a reassessment of its theological significance.[25]

24. David Fergusson, "The Reformed Churches," in *The Christian Church: An Introduction to the Major Traditions,* ed. Paul Avis (London: SPCK, 2002) 18–48. Fergusson writes: "It has been pointed out that even in formal bilateral dialogues several different and conflicting Reformed theologies of ministry operate. These range from positions which emphasize congregationalist themes through those which articulate classical Reformed approaches to others which adopt something approaching a traditional Catholic model of ministry" (41). Earlier, he had spoken of "the pluralism and fragmentation of Reformed Christianity in today's world. This diversity within the modern Reformed tradition accounts for much of the frustration expressed by our dialogue partners when they fail to receive clear delineation of the Reformed position on any given doctrine" (40).

25. Ibid., 41. See Fergusson's discussion of the ecumenical document "God's Reign and Our Unity: The Report of the Anglican-Reformed International Commission 1981–1984" on pp. 37–40. The document can be found in Jeffrey Gros, Harding Meyer, and William G. Rusch, eds., *Growth in Agreement II: Reports and Agreed Statements of Ecumenical*

According to the minority opinion represented by von Allmen, ministry is seen more clearly as constitutive of the church ("wesenhaft"), but in total dependence on Christ. This opinion, too, accords greater place to the notion of apostolic succession, not merely in the sense of an historical claim to an unbroken succession of the ordinations of its pastors, but as a divinely given sign of the church's apostolicity of doctrine and life. Both dimensions are interrelated. The Reformed tradition has always paid special attention to the calling of its pastors and to the fact that it takes place in a way that is ritually proper, that is, as conforming to the church's traditional ritual of ordination. Moreover, the opinion represented by von Allmen is clearer about ordination by the imposition of hands and the calling down of the Holy Spirit (epiclesis). At the remove of thirty years from his presentation of the Reformed theology of ministry, Schütte's insights regarding the minority opinion seem to be confirmed, when he wrote: "[The position of von Allmen] offers genuine possibilities of arriving at convergence with the Lutheran confessional statements and Catholic teaching, as appears to be the case in the light of recent ecumenical discussions."[26] Despite all its diversity and the richness of its theologies of ministry, under the pressure of ecumenical conversations with a variety of other churches, the Reformed tradition seems to be moving in the direction outlined by von Allmen and others.

Wolfhart Pannenberg

Over the years, theologians have come to expect much from the thought of the German Lutheran theologian, and now professor emeritus of the University of Munich, Wolfhart Pannenberg (1928–). His theological insights are characterized by daring speculation together with creative originality and a deep reading of the Christian tradition in equal measure. He is uncommonly well-versed in modern and contemporary philosophy as well as in the scientific outlook on the world and reality. Perhaps G.W.F. Hegel has been the principal philosophical influence on his thought, in particular Hegel's view of history and its dynamic character. In theology proper, undoubtedly the principal influence has been the eschatological character of Jesus' ministry and teaching, as well as

---

Conversations on a World Level, 1982–1998 (Grand Rapids, Mich.: Wm. B. Eerdmans Publishing Company, 2000) 114–54.

26. Heinz Schütte, *Amt, Ordination und Sukzession,* 197.

that of the early church. In his understanding of apostolicity, we find the same insistence by Pannenberg on the eschatological nature of apostolicity.

In an essay prepared for the dialogue of the Joint Working Group of the World Council of Churches and the Roman Catholic Church on catholicity and apostolicity, Pannenberg points out immediately that the church's apostolicity has to do with the mission of the church and not primarily with pure fidelity to the early church's teaching or ministry.[27] He is not arguing against fidelity to apostolic teaching but rather against its self-sufficiency and its lack of complete corresponding to the eschatological mission that the emergence of the church represents. This is the case because of the church's foundation in the fact of the Lord's resurrection—a thoroughly eschatological event that truly anticipates the final fulfillment of God's plan for humankind's salvation yet without sacrificing the genuinely historical element of its realization in time by the church.[28] Christ's resurrection necessarily implies eschatological mission. Only this fact can be an adequate foundation of the church's permanence, fidelity, and continuity in history. In fact, the calling of the apostles in the early church by the risen Lord is itself a dimension of the Lord's resurrection. "That the risen Christ called apostles and sent them forth is thus not something that was incidental to his resurrection appearances. . . . [which] do not constitute only the confirmation of Jesus' own mission but also the reaffirmation of that mission for his disciples."[29] The apostolate of the apostles is ordered toward eschatological mission, and there can be a succession to this mission by the post-apostolic church.

> The work of the apostle . . . points toward the goal of accomplishing the content of the eschatological promise itself, preparing the way for the coming of the Kingdom. . . . Jesus' message was that the power of God's lordship was determinative for the present age through Jesus' own life and

27. Wolfhart Pannenberg, "The Significance of Eschatology for the Understanding of the Apostolicity and Catholicity of the Church," *One in Christ* 6 (1970) 410–29. A different translation was reprinted in the collection of Pannenberg's essays *The Church,* tr. Keith Crim (Philadelphia: The Westminster Press, 1983) 44–68. Subsequent references are to this reprint.

28. Pannenberg's theology of the resurrection as a "prolepsis" or real anticipation of the end is bound up with his general philosophical principle of the "ontological priority" of the future. See idem, *Theology and the Kingdom of God,* ed. Richard John Neuhaus (Philadelphia: The Westminster Press, 1969), and "The God of Hope," in *Basic Questions in Theology,* 2 vols., tr. George H. Kehm (Philadelphia: Fortress Press, 1971) 2:237–49.

29. "The Significance of Eschatology for the Understanding of the Apostolicity and Catholicity of the Church," 50–51.

work. It could be continued by his apostles only as the proclamation that ultimate reality had broken through in Jesus himself. The ultimate reality that was manifest in Jesus, however, was made effective for the present age by the world mission of the church.[30]

Pannenberg realizes that his rethinking of the apostolicity of the church can lead to a misunderstanding of the relationship of the present church vis-à-vis the church of the apostles. He obviates the misunderstanding by pointing to the nature of faith as directed toward what is ultimate—God—and hence as literally still outstanding and not possessed by us. The only way we can grasp the truth of faith—which, too, is ultimate—is to rethink our faith in the light of contemporary human experience, understand it anew at a deeper level in the light of our experience, and formulate it in language that is valid for us.[31] "We cannot bring against the church the comprehensive charge that in the development of doctrine the eschatological orientation of the apostolic mission was lost. In reality, this apostolic motif has always remained active in the history of the church and in its teachings."[32]

On the question of apostolic succession in office, Pannenberg does not see anything that definitively precludes Lutherans today from accepting episcopacy in the Roman Catholic sense, *so long as* episcopacy, as an expression of the apostolicity of the whole church, follows the criterion that the bishops exercise their office and authority in accord with the "eschatological nature of the apostolic mission." Pannenberg spells this out in further detail:

> [This eschatological character] determines the necessity and also the direction in which this mission is continued beyond the age of the apostles. This provides, then, the basis for the institutional form which such a mission should take in order to accomplish its purpose in each historical situation of the whole church, that is the specific organization of the one mission in a multiplicity of offices. The number of such offices, the division of labor among them, and the lines of authority do not always need to remain the same.[33]

30. Ibid., 51–52.

31. Pannenberg shows how this was the case with respect to Christology, the Trinity, and the theology of grace.

32. Ibid., 54.

33. Ibid., 59. Within such an understanding of episcopacy and ecclesiastical leadership, Pannenberg makes it clear that both Roman Catholicism and Lutheranism need to courageously examine their official structures for any authoritarian exercise of them.

Given his focus on the primacy of apostolic mission as the hallmark of the church's apostolicity, it is hardly surprising that Pannenberg eventually turns his attention to the church's catholicity as well. But catholicity, too, for Pannenberg is intrinsically eschatological. Geographical extension and increase in the numbers of Christians are only signs of catholicity that point to its true nature, the eschatological fulfillment of the church. Catholicity sweeps up and encompasses all generations of Christians, from the apostolic church to the church of the present. The richness of catholicity is seen in the necessary diversity of its forms. "In the relationships of the various Christian groups to one another, catholic unity can only be expressed if they acknowledge and respect in one another the presence of the fullness of catholic truth in their specific modes of life, traditions, ordinances, and creeds."[34] Pannenberg goes even further in demanding of each church that, in accepting the necessary diversity of catholicity, each one accepts "responsibility, not just for its own tradition, but for the whole of Christian history and its heritage."[35] Though he never says so, Pannenberg appears to treat the attributes of unity, catholicity, and apostolicity as so mutually interrelated that they can only be realized in conjunction with one another. Pannenberg's principal contribution to the discussion on apostolicity—and catholicity, too, for that matter—is his clear vision of eschatology as the very wellspring of Jesus' ministry and the ultimate explanation of his resurrection. The same is true for the origins of the church. The eschatological focus is so rich because it can provide solid ground for continuity within real change and for the mutuality and non-competitiveness of the various Christian churches. I will return again to the importance of history for understanding apostolicity in Chapter Six.

Miroslav Volf

We are not accustomed to think that the question of apostolic succession is a central issue for the so-called Free Churches of the Reform. But they, too, profess the Nicene-Constantinopolitan Creed and so are also committed to the apostolicity of the church, even though they might

---

Genuine authority is demanded by apostolicity but not an authoritarian exercise of it. Both communities have been guilty of such authoritarianism in the past.

34. Ibid., 64.
35. Ibid., 65.

not bother themselves overly much with the question of succession in its more narrowly understood meaning, namely, episcopal succession in office. Recently, however, in his important ecclesiological study, the Croatian Baptist Miroslav Volf, professor at Yale University Divinity School, has broached the topic.[36] His book is a valiant attempt to show both his fellow Baptists and other Christians that the Free Church tradition is not inimical toward or bereft of its own valid ecclesiology.[37] In the course of making his argument, Volf engages ecumenically in lively and highly informed discussion with other Protestant, Orthodox, and Roman Catholic theologians. His book will undoubtedly become the standard work on the ecclesiology of the Free Churches.

In general, Volf does not speak explicitly of apostolic succession but prefers to explain his understanding of official ministry in the Baptist tradition. When he does address apostolic succession directly, it is to engage in a critical discussion of the ideas of Cardinal Joseph Ratzinger[38] and Metropolitan John Zizioulas.[39] It is easy to read these pages as a dismissal of the Roman Catholic and the Orthodox positions, but that would be to read too much into the presentation. Volf's point is to open the discussion of office in a way that goes beyond the traditional understanding in an exclusively hierarchical sense. He shows how the theology of the Baptist thinker John Smyth (c. 1570–1612)[40] is another possible reading of the church's apostolicity of office understood in the broadest or most inclusive sense. As we have seen, this meaning is not to be neglected in the general discussion of the apostolicity of the church. Volf

36. Miroslav Volf, *After Our Likeness: The Church as the Image of the Trinity* (Grand Rapids, Mich.: Wm. B. Eerdmans Publishing Company, 1998).

37. See Timothy George, "Toward an Evangelical Ecclesiology," in *Catholics and Evangelicals: Do They Share a Common Future?* ed. Thomas P. Rausch (Downers Grove, Ill.: InterVarsity Press, 2000) 122–48. See also the recent comparison of ecclesiologies by Veli-Matti Kärkkäinen, *An Introduction to Ecclesiology: Ecumenical, Historical and Global Perspectives* (Downers Grove, Ill.: InterVarsity Press, 2002), with special attention to Pentecostal ecclesiology. On apostolicity in Pentecostal theology in particular, see his "The Apostolicity of Free Churches," *Pro Ecclesia* 10 (2001) 475–86.

38. Volf, *After Our Likeness,* 53–61 ["Office and Communion"].

39. Ibid., 117–23 ["Apostolicity and Conciliarity"].

40. Neither John Bowden, *Who's Who in Theology: From the First Century to the Present* (New York: The Crossroad Publishing Company, 1992), nor Wilfried Härle and Harald Wagner, *Theologenlexikon. Von den Kirchenvätern bis zur Gegenwart* (Munich: Verlag C. H. Beck, 1987), has any mention of John Smyth. Volf cites W. T. Whitley as the editor of *The Works of John Smyth* (Cambridge: Cambridge University Press, 1915).

shows that there are points of contact between the Baptist and the Catholic and Orthodox understandings. Ecumenical dialogue on apostolicity and on ecclesiastical office is not out of the question. But what precisely does Volf present for our consideration?

First, Volf shows that the Catholic and Orthodox positions regarding apostolic succession follow from their understandings of the mystery of the Trinity. Ratzinger, as one representative of the Catholic position, tends to understand the Trinity in terms of the total relationality, or pure activity, of the divine persons. Dialogue constitutes the Trinity, or perhaps better, the Trinity is the expression of the "dialoguing" of the divine persons. The oneness of the Trinity must be understood from the mystery of their being relations one to another. As Volf interprets Ratzinger, this means that the traditional Western emphasis on the unity of the divine substance over the plurality of the divine persons once again dominates Ratzinger's Trinitarian theology. And yet Volf senses an unresolved tension in Ratzinger's thought in as much as he prefers to explain the divine unity in terms of the "perpetual, dynamic intertwining and mutual interpenetration of spirit to spirit, love to love, than in the image of the one divine monarchy."[41] Naturally, this starting point has implications for Ratzinger's understanding of the unity of the church. The same unresolved tension is found in Ratzinger's ecclesiology as well. Thus, on the one hand, Ratzinger forcefully defends the primacy of the universal church over the local church, while, on the other, his theology of the pure relationality of persons—divine and human—really pulls his thought in the direction of greater openness of the hierarchy to the charisms, insights, and contributions of the laity and to fuller participation by all in the church. In the end, however, the weight of the long Western tradition on stressing the unity of the divine substance prior to any consideration of the diversity of persons in the Trinity wins the day. It comes to expression ecclesiologically in the indispensability and priority of the hierarchy, and even within the hierarchy of the pope over the college of bishops.[42]

41. Volf, *After Our Likeness,* 71, quoting Ratzinger in part.

42. It is not my intention in presenting Volf's thought to judge whether his interpretation of Ratzinger is correct or mistaken. Such an examination would take us far afield. My only point is to show how Volf is searching in his own Free Church tradition for a possible explanation of office in the church other than one that has resort immediately to a divinely willed hierarchical structure grounded in the mystery of the Trinity itself.

Volf engages in a similar analysis of the trinitarian thought of John Zizioulas, whom we will study at greater length below. For the present, however, Volf is interested in Zizioulas' thought as yet another trinitarian theology of relations, but different from the pure relationality of Joseph Ratzinger. How is it different? Not in its stress on the Trinity as relational or the radical *perichoresis* [mutual indwelling] of persons. In fact, Zizioulas defines "being" *(esse)* by way of "relations." Personal reality has priority over "being." It doesn't negate "being," but it emphasizes that being-as-necessity is transcended in being-as-freedom, that is, as person. How? Volf interprets Zizioulas in terms of the perennial philosophical question of the one and the many.[43] Which has priority, the one over against the many, or the many as constituting the one? To Volf, Zizioulas' thought, too, is characterized by an unresolved tension between unity and plurality. Zizioulas clearly wants to stress the notion of communion as the deepest explanation of reality, while at the same time remaining true to his Greek patristic sources—the Cappadocian fathers, who stressed the person of the Father as the absolute point of departure for an understanding of the Trinity.[44] The Father is *monarchos*—the monarchical principle which grounds unity and calls forth superabundant divine fruitfulness in the Son/Word and Spirit. They in turn constitute the trinitarian mystery by reason of their subsistent relations as Son/Word and Spirit vis-à-vis the Father or, perhaps better, the "Unoriginate Origin." Volf's difficulty with Zizioulas' interpretation is that the Trinity is not really symmetrical by reason of the three divine persons—since the Father alone has ontological priority—contrary to Zizioulas' own intentions.[45] Again, this trinitarian theology has ecclesiological ramifications for an understanding of apostolic office.[46] In the church, the bishop acts in a way analogous to the Father in the Trinity. The bishop, understood in terms of a eucharistic ecclesiology, however, is the principle of the unity of the local church,

43. M. Volf, "Zizioulas: Communion, One and Many," *After Our Likeness,* 73–123. See also Paul McPartlan, "The One and the Many," in *The Eucharist Makes the Church: Henri de Lubac and John Zizioulas in Dialogue* (Edinburgh: T&T Clark, 1993) 166–86.

44. McPartlan is particularly good on retracing the process followed by Zizioulas to retrieve the genuine thought of the Cappadocians and the breakthrough this represented in his thought. See "Greek Philosophy," *The Eucharist Makes the Church,* 144–65.

45. See Volf, *After Our Likeness,* 78–80.

46. Volf speaks about the polycentric structure of the congregation vis-à-vis the asymmetrical structure advocated in their different ways by Ratzinger and Zizioulas. See ibid., 240, 247.

whose diversity and variety is expressed in terms of a communion of persons. Bishop and community are coordinated to one another: there is no church without a bishop, and episcopacy makes no sense apart from the assignment of a real community of believers.[47]

As with Ratzinger, it is not the validity of Zizioulas' interpretation that interests me, but rather whether the Free Church interpretation of Volf is really excluded by the Orthodox understanding. In other words, does the asymmetrical point of departure for an understanding of the immanent Trinity really exclude a certain polycentrism? If the Son/Word and the Spirit really constitute the Trinity in equal measure with the action of the Father as Divine Principle of the Trinity, does this not imply a certain polycentrism of the Trinity? In terms of an ecclesiological correspondence, does this not mean that the role of believers in choosing and installing the leaders of their communities is just as constitutive of the church as the actions of the leaders themselves? In other words, Volf's Baptist interpretation cannot be so easily dismissed as heterodox.

Volf's second argument can be presented more briefly. Just because he argues for a polycentric understanding of the Trinity, it does not follow that, when examining its ecclesiological implications, believers act only in their own name and under their own initiative in determining officeholders in the church. The Free Church tradition has always maintained a high regard for the immediate agency of the Holy Spirit. The Spirit's freedom must never be restricted. Of course, when Christians determine their leaders in the apostolic faith and the apostolic tradition, it is by way of responding to the inspiration of the Holy Spirit.[48] It is the Spirit who ultimately chooses the leaders of the church. Is this really that different from what Catholics and Orthodox are trying to say by way of the official theologies in their communions? Are the positions really diametrically opposed? Isn't there room for different theological interpretations that do not cancel each other out? Might this approach be a way of coming to agreement on apostolic succession?

47. In technical theological terms, "absolute ordination" makes no theological sense.

48. Volf explains the roles of the supervening Spirit and the responding believers of a congregation in terms of an "interactional model" of divine-human activity. The interactional model is explained in *After Our Likeness,* 233, see also 242. To this he adds a more basic understanding of the process of reception, using it as a theological foundation for the decentralized participatory practices of Baptists. See ibid, 252–57 ["Ordination and Election"].

John D. Zizioulas

John D. Zizioulas (1931–) is a prominent Greek Orthodox theologian and one of the most frequently cited theologians of our day, quoted with admiration by Orthodox, Protestants, Anglicans, and Roman Catholics alike. After he finished his doctorate at the University of Athens, he was a staff person on the Faith and Order Commission of the World Council of Churches. He has taught successively at the Universities of Edinburgh and Glasgow. He was made Metropolitan of Pergamon in 1986 and a member of the Ecumenical Patriarchate based in Istanbul, Turkey.[49] Zizioulas' influence depends on his facility with ancient and modern philosophy as well as theology. His creative theological contributions rest on his attempts to return to the sources of Greek Orthodox theology, especially Maximus the Confessor and the Cappadocian Fathers, in an effort to overcome the hold that a rationalistic late Scholasticism had on orthodoxy in recent centuries. What, then, does Zizioulas teach about apostolicity?

In the first place, Zizioulas distinguishes two fundamental senses of what he calls "apostolic continuity": historical and eschatological. The historical meaning points toward the apostles and the post-apostolic church as missionaries who bring humankind to faith in Christ in the course of history. Here, the apostles are conceived as individuals. More important for Zizioulas is the eschatological meaning which points in the direction of the anticipated end of history in the person of Christ. Here, the apostles must be seen as a college, and their role is iconic, a role that is fulfilled primarily in the eucharistic liturgy. The Western Church has favored the historical meaning, the Eastern Church the eschatological. One is not wrong while the other is right, however. But each does result in a different way a church understands itself when one exclusive way is seen to characterize the church's apostolicity. Here is where the tension lies between the two great Christian traditions of East and West. As long as the church was united, these ways complemented each other. After the break

---

49. For the basic biographical facts of the life and education of John Zizioulas, I have relied on the presentation by Patricia A. Fox, *God as Communion: John Zizioulas, Elizabeth Johnson, and the Retrieval of the Symbol of the Triune God* (Collegeville, Minn.: The Liturgical Press, 2001) 3–10. The book as a whole is a very reliable guide to the thought of the two theologians named. Paul McPartlan, too, is a reliable expositor of Zizioulas' theology of church. See *The Eucharist Makes the Church*, 123–235 ["Part Two. John Zizioulas"]. See my reviews of McPartlan in *Worship* 72 (1996) 560–63 and of Fox in *Worship* 76 (2002) 468–71.

between East and West, the tendency of exclusivity inherent in each took on unhealthy forms of separate existence.

In fashioning his argument, Zizioulas interprets Ignatius of Antioch (2nd century) in the Eastern sense. To Ignatius, a bishop makes sense only in terms of his presbyterate and the whole local church. Episcopacy is to be understood primarily in terms of the Eucharist, for the church is found where the Eucharist is celebrated. Apropos of Ignatius, Zizioulas writes:

> . . . The apostles are a united college and they surround Christ in His Kingdom. For this reason it is in the *college of presbyters* surrounding the bishop, who sits 'in the place of God' or is the image of Christ, that Ignatius sees the image of the apostles. Continuity here is guaranteed and expressed not by way of succession from generation to generation and from individual to individual, but in and through the convocation of the Church in one place, i.e. through its *eucharistic structure*. It is a *continuity of communities* and *Churches* that constitutes and expresses apostolic succession in this approach.[50]

And when Zizioulas compares these two approaches, important conclusions emerge. First, on the notion of apostolic continuity itself, the historical approach tends to emphasize in an exclusive way the normativity of the apostles' teachings and prescriptive decisions. Apostolicity is seen from the point of view of the past. But when apostolic continuity is understood as eschatological, it is seen from the point of view of the future as consummation. The differences are profound. Profound, too, is the relationship between Christology and pneumatology. From the historical point of view, the Spirit is understood as the divine person who executes in a kind of linear salvation history the decisions transmitted already by Christ. As Zizioulas puts it: "In such an approach Pneumatology indicates an *agency;* the Spirit is the *agent of Christ* and is dependent on Him."[51] While in the eschatological perspective, the Spirit as "Lord" (according to the Nicene-Constantinopolitan Creed) is creative and the one who engages the church's *anamnesis,* that is, the memory of the future which beckons to fullness and consummation. Only in the second sense, really, can a genuine pneumatology emerge and be transformative of the church: "Unless the church lets Pneumatology so condition Christology that the

50. John Zizioulas, "Apostolic Continuity and Succession," in *Being as Communion: Studies in Personhood and the Church* (Crestwood, N.Y.: St. Vladimir's Seminary Press, 1985) 171–208, at 177.

51. Ibid., 179.

sequence of 'yesterday-today-tomorrow' is transcended, she will not do full justice to Pneumatology."[52]

How is a synthesis of the historical and the eschatological understanding of apostolicity to be effected? At this point we must step back and survey some of Zizioulas' fundamental philosophical and theological insights. The West, and other cultures influenced by the West, has succumbed to a temptation already inherent in the philosophical ethos of antiquity, namely, the priority of the individual understood in terms of "substance" and "being." The Cappadocian Fathers came to the unanticipated insight that what Jesus realized for humankind at the deepest level was not the saving of men and women as individuals but their recreation as "persons." Their wrestling with the mystery of the triune God led them to an understanding of God as a "communion" of Father, Son/Word, and Spirit. At the center of the mystery of God is found the relations of the persons of the Trinity. For Zizioulas, this insight meant that the Cappadocians realized that the categories of substance and being had to be transcended by an ontology of persons—an ontology which necessarily was founded on the notion of communion. God is communion. The church, then, is a communion of persons. Human isolation, radical individuality, or total autonomy are not our calling; communion with others or our mutual relations with one another is. Zizioulas uses the concept of communion to rethink the basic issues involved in the question of the apostolicity of the church also. Let us examine how he does so.

First, the mystery of Christ is itself a mystery of communion. Christ, too, is not an isolated individual but the "first born of creation," the "New Man," the "final Adam," that is, a corporate personality in biblical terms, a representative of humankind in philosophical terms, the Exemplar in theological terms. But Christ fulfills even this role in solidarity with us. We too—together with Christ—constitute the mystery of Christ as a mystery of communion. He writes:

> . . . In a pneumatologically constituted Christology, an event can never be defined by itself, but only as a relational reality. It is this that allows the Biblical notion of 'corporate personality' to be applied to Christ: *Christ without his body is not Christ but an individual of the worst kind.* Our continuity, therefore, with the Christ event is not determined by sequence of response based on distance; it is rather a continuity in terms of *inclusiveness*: we are *in*

52. Ibid., 180.

Christ, and this is what makes Him be *before* us. . . . He is the eschatological Man—yet, let me repeat, not as an individual but as Church, i.e., because of our being included in Him.[53]

Applying these same key ideas to the question of the church, Zizioulas
sees that a synthesis of the historical and the eschatological understandings of apostolicity is best approached from the Eucharist in orthodox
theology. The memorial celebrated in the Eucharist truly recalls the events
of Jesus' self-giving but also is a participation already in communion
with the blessings of the eschaton or the kingdom of God that has arrived in its fullness. The Eucharist is both "tradition" and "memorial."
Already in time and history the eschaton is not only seen as a distant
blessing but shared in here and now in an anticipatory way. But that anticipatory participation in the consummation of all things must include
God's ultimate purpose for humankind—its being called into the oneness
of communion with God and with each other. The Eucharist is the expression of God's eschatological "gathering in" of men and women from
all times and cultures.[54] This is true of every Eucharist. In terms of the
apostolicity of the church, "the eucharist [is] the moment in which the
church realizes that her roots are to be found *simultaneously* in the past and
in the future, in history and in the eschata."[55] This is possible, once
again, only in the Spirit. The Eucharist as a sacramental action is the
calling on the Holy Spirit in prayer (epiclesis) to bring about what God
has promised us. "The *epiclesis* means ecclesiologically that the church
*asks to receive from God what she has already received historically in Christ as if she
had not received it at all,* i.e., as if history did not count in itself. This includes her continuity with the apostles in all its forms."[56]

In the conclusions of this important study, Zizioulas concentrates
on how the synthesis of the two perspectives—the historical and the
eschatological—might be achieved. He remains firmly committed to his
principle of the simultaneity of both principles. The problem up to the
present has been that all the churches seem to have forgotten the existence of the eschatological interpretation. The answer, therefore, is not as-
serting it at the expense of the historical, but bringing the historical into

53. Ibid., 182–83.
54. This is the meaning of the church's self-designation as *ekklesia*-assembly, or, as
Zizioulas puts it, "convocation."
55. Ibid., 188.
56. Ibid., 185.

better alignment with the eschatological. But how does the church do this precisely? First of all, by returning to the insights of such early thinkers as Ignatius, Hippolytus, and Eusebius of Caesarea, all of whom saw the episcopate in corporate terms, that is, as succeeding to the corps of apostles and not to individual apostles. Second, by recovering the second century's understanding of the bishop as a member of his presbyterium with the unique role of symbolizing their unity and thereby the unity of the local church. Third, by situating episcopacy firmly in the context of the Eucharist. Primarily this last point summarizes for Zizioulas the unity and simultaneity he so desires. Synoptically, he writes:

> It is not, therefore, an accident that the eucharist provided the early Church from the beginning with (a) the basic concept and framework of her structure, and (b) the context for the perpetuation of this structure in history. This leads to a real synthesis between the historical and the eschatological dimensions of the Church's existence without the danger of "institutionalization." For the eucharist is perhaps the only reality in the Church which is *at once an institution and an event;* it is the uniquely privileged moment of the Church's existence in which the Kingdom comes epicletically, i.e., *without emerging as an expression of the historical process, although it is manifested through historical forms.* In this context the Church relates to the apostles simultaneously by looking backward and forward, to the past and to the future—always, however, by letting the eschaton determine history and its structures.[57]

What can be said about Zizioulas' understanding of apostolicity in this essay rich in ideas? The essay is demanding for all parties concerned. It shows how all have minimized the important dimension of eschatology in their understanding of the church. Here is where Zizioulas challenges all of us to come to terms with how we understand eschatology and how we might reintegrate an eschatological outlook into our thought and praxis. This rethinking cannot happen at a superficial level, but must reach down deep into how we have appropriated our Christian faith. It will involve the rethinking of the Eucharist, the nature of sacraments, the apostolicity of the whole church, the unity of office in the church, the nature of tradition, the priority of the Word of God, and so many other questions. And finally, Zizioulas also challenges us to examine our long-held philosophical assumptions in the West by rethinking being in terms of communion and relationality. These are no small tasks, and they will

57. Ibid., 206–7.

require many years of pondering them. But it will also involve going through the painful process together—all of us—and not as isolated churches. Not only is the individual determined by the ontology of communion, but all of social reality is so characterized.[58]

---

58. For another positive, albeit brief, appraisal of Zizioulas' ecclesiology by a giant among Catholic ecclesiologists, see Yves Congar, "Two Theologies of Apostolicity: W. Pannenberg and J. D. Zizioulas," in *I Believe in the Holy Spirit*, 2:50–51.

CHAPTER FIVE

Apostolicity and the Classical and Modern Worldviews

Apostolicity has been variously understood in the church's history. There are three basic models for expressing the meaning of the church's apostolicity: the model of identity, of continuity, and of coherence. Each of the models operates within a different worldview. The first two models are characteristic of the ancient and medieval world, as well as modern times. The model of coherence is just emerging and is associated with a postmodern view of the world. I propose to examine only the first two models in the present chapter. I will treat the model of coherence in Chapter Six.

Worldviews, Paradigms, and Models

What I have called models of apostolicity must be understood against a broader background—that of worldviews and of the paradigms that express them. Such worldviews and paradigms help to organize the vast amount of information available from long periods of human history. However, the definition of these basic terms is not uniform. There is less difficulty with organizing the data according to periods, which in the case of the church would include the earliest Jewish Christian period, then the Hellenistic culture of antiquity, followed by the feudal and medieval period. Finally, there is the modern period characterized by the breakup of a once united Western church, the emergence of modern science, and the Enlightenment with its "turn to the subject." Though thinkers sometimes disagree as to when these periods officially begin, the periodization is fairly standard. The same cannot be said for the terms "worldview" and "paradigm." The meanings of these terms need to be carefully defined.

How might we characterize the periods we are considering in a way that respects the complexity and rich diversity of each one and yet sees it as fitting into a broader framework of shared meaning? Is it possible to take such a long period like antiquity and medieval culture and consider it as somehow unified or organic? Scholars customarily refer to epochs, eras or ages to unite complex realities into wholes. The intent is not to deny particularities and specific differences but to gain a sense of a period as a totality. In other words, there are underlying points of interconnectedness and unity that are as undeniable as the real differences. To grasp both unity and difference helps us better understand the time frame. What language can we use to grasp the underlying unity? I propose the terms "worldview" and "paradigm."

The term "worldview"[1] is of rather recent coinage. It is a loan translation from the German *Weltanschauung,* a term that became enormously important in the nineteenth century.[2] Some thinkers felt the need to coin a new term that would encompass reality in as comprehensive a way as philosophy but without philosophy's heavy overtones of "speculation," "theory," and "systematizing." Philosophy was seen to pertain to the realm of the universal, the necessary, that which can be established by critical and scientific reason. Besides, philosophy seemed to be a matter of objective reason divorced from subjective feelings, reasons, or reactions. Individuals like Søren Kierkegaard (1813–55), Wilhelm Dilthey (1833–1911), Heinrich Rickert (1863–1936), and Karl Jaspers (1883–1969) helped to develop the meaning of worldview.[3] Little by little the word came to find its place, especially in the human and social sciences, for example, sociology, philosophy of religion, cultural anthropology, and so forth. In English, *Weltanschauung*

1. Various spellings of the term can be found, viz., "world view," "world-view," and "worldview." The last spelling now seems to be fairly standard in current English usage.
2. See Albert M. Wolters, "On the Idea of Worldview and Its Relation to Philosophy," in *Stained Glass: Worldviews and Social Science* (Lanham, Md.: University Press of America, 1989) 14–25, at 15 ["History of the Concept of Worldview"]. In general, on the notion of a worldview see Marcel Reding, "World, Views of the," in *Sacramentum Mundi: An Encyclopedia of Theology,* 6 vols., ed. Karl Rahner (New York: Herder and Herder, 1970) 6:388–90.
3. On these figures and for a typology of the understandings of "worldview," see Wolters, "On the Idea of Worldview and Its Relation to Philosophy," 16–17. Jacob Klapwijk has expressed some reservations about the typology. See Klapwijk, "On Worldviews and Philosophy," in, *Stained Glass,* 41–55, at 48–50.

was simply translated as "worldview." It attempts to express a comprehensive understanding of reality that includes particularity, is open to more personal perceptions, and adverts to historical conditions. A worldview is also something that is shared with others and that influences society and social relationships. It is concerned with the "human" (the *humanum*) over rationalism's "reason" *(ratio)* and with the "person" over the Enlightenment's "subject." A worldview is also more immediate to individuals, attempts to unify reality, and relies more on "experience" in its perceptions.[4] With these qualifiers in mind, the popular phrase that speaks of a person's "philosophy of life" comes very close to expressing the content of what a worldview is, but without the stress on what is culturally or socially shared and that does come to expression in "*world*view." Another term often used to stress the individual's worldview, as contrasted with his or her sharing in a socially defined worldview, is "mindset." It comes very close to a person's "philosophy of life" without sounding pretentious. However, one also detects nowadays the use of worldview in this more individualized, subject-oriented sense, akin to one's "philosophy of life." In the latter case, society is rather amorphous, consisting of a loose aggregation of persons each having his or her own worldview.

In this chapter I want to employ worldview in its meaning of what is socially shared and affects the cultural forms of a society.[5] Thinkers frequently refer to the role of religious beliefs and practices as constituting

4. This statement intends to claim only that late modern philosophy, e.g., Immanuel Kant's transcendental analysis and Hegel's system of the Absolute Spirit, had become divorced from the ordinary person's concerns. It makes no claim that these limitations are inherent to philosophy or that philosophy has always been pursued in its late modern forms.

5. Marcus J. Borg draws on the work of Huston Smith, who refers to a "root image" of a people. Smith identified two basic root images, the "primordial tradition" and "the modern world-view." Borg writes, "A root image is a fundamental image of how reality is, our most basic 'picture' of reality. Perhaps most often called a 'world-view,' it consists of our most taken-for-granted assumptions about what is possible. It is an idea (a mental construct) with immense power." Borg, "Root Images and the Way We See: The Primordial Tradition and the Biblical Tradition," in *Jesus in Contemporary Scholarship* (Valley Forge, Pa.: Trinity Press International, 1994) 127–39, at 127. Borg is here drawing on Smith's *Forgotten Truth: The Primordial Tradition* (New York: Harper & Row Publishers, 1976). For further discussion on worldview, see Thomas Luckmann, *The Invisible Religion: The Problem of Religion in Modern Society* (New York: The Macmillan Company, 1967). Jack B. Rogers, "Worldview: A Source of Conflict," in *Claiming the Center: Churches and Conflicting Worldviews* (Louisville: Westminster/John Knox Press, 1995) 1–21, discusses the relationship and the difference between a believer's worldview and his or her religion.

an indispensable element of a worldview. The religious dimension might be either explicit in naming or calling upon the deity or implicit in referring only to the Transcendent or the Ultimate. N. T. Wright, in his ambitious study of Christ and the early Christians, uses a theory of worldview to organize the vast amount of material to be studied.[6] What does one do with all the New Testament sources in their luxuriant diversity? How does one sift through the innumerable interpretations and opinions voiced by exegetes, historians, and systematic theologians? Which interpretations are to be followed and built upon? To help him decide such questions, Wright employs a theory of worldviews that distinguishes story, symbols, questions, and praxis as the four basic elements of a society's worldview. If the reader has some grasp of the worldview that predominated in Palestine in Jesus' lifetime, he or she is in a better position to make choices about valid interpretations of the actions and the sayings of Jesus. The worldview does not tyrannically dictate the reader's interpretation but positively interacts with the data and traditions being considered. It is just some such theory that might help us better understand today how earlier generations of Christians understood apostolicity and apostolic succession. Their understanding must have fitted into the broader context of what they thought about the world, society, authority, God, faith, time, and possibly, too, a life beyond death.

A theory of worldview demands further theories. Thus, paradigms break down the all-encompassing, interrelated, and unified worldview into constitutive "parts" or dimensions that are manageable for humans. This procedure helps the person come to a better understanding of the worldview by his or her ability to isolate certain elements in order to later reintegrate them into the unified worldview. The theory of paradigms developed by Thomas Kuhn stresses the social and communal aspect of human understanding. In his study of how science proceeds, Kuhn shows how changes in scientific outlook are determined by how the scientific community explains reality. Science consists of more than empirical observation and hypotheses that lead willy-nilly to fixed positions or laws. Changes in science have come about by what Kuhn calls

6. N. T. Wright, "Theology, Authority and the New Testament," in *Christian Origins and the Question of God,* vol. 1, *The New Testament and the People of God* (Minneapolis: Fortress Press, 1992) 121–44; and "Worldviews and Mindsets," in *Christian Origins and the Question of God,* vol. 2, *Jesus and the Victory of God* (Minneapolis: Fortress Press, 1996) 137–44.

"scientific revolutions" or paradigm shifts. At a certain point, some scientists realize that the regnant theory can no longer either accommodate anomalies and discordant data or yield more fruitful explanations. A new conceptual framework is needed. The insight results in substituting a new generalized theory for the old–a "revolution" or the emergence of a new paradigm.[7] A paradigm, then, is a global theory that is shared by a community of scientists and that demonstrates inherent heuristic value. Kuhn defined a paradigm as "an entire constellation of beliefs, values, techniques, and so on shared by the members of a given community."[8] It is not an absolute or timeless law, since it, too, will eventually be replaced by yet another paradigm. A theory of paradigms can help us in treating religious questions also.[9] Paradigms help us see how our most general truth and faith claims make sense regarding very particular issues. Thus, paradigms refract the worldview we share, in order to live more meaningfully from its claims, convictions, and assumptions. The worldview is the most general horizon of our living and understanding, whereas paradigms draw on that global intelligibility and mediate it to us in historically concrete forms.

Finally, just as a worldview needs to be broken down into paradigms, they in turn are in need of further division into models. Models, paradigms, and a person's worldview are all interrelated and mutually elucidate one another. Models are among the most basic explanatory and exploratory elements of human understanding and for successfully finding truth and meaning. Like paradigms, the language of "models" was first employed by scientists, and subsequently adopted by social scientists,

7. It is also important to remember that for Kuhn the "revolution" does not mean starting absolutely from scratch. Some of the data and observations from the earlier viewpoint will be able to be integrated into the new paradigm. The past is not rejected as purely and simply erroneous.

8. See Thomas Kuhn, *The Structure of Scientific Revolutions* (2nd ed.; Chicago: University of Chicago Press, 1970) 175. Commenting on Kuhn, Ian G. Barbour writes: "A paradigm . . . is a cluster of conceptual and methodological presuppositions embodied in an exemplary body of scientific work, such as Newtonian mechanics in the eighteenth century or relativity and quantum physics in the twentieth century. A paradigm implicitly defines for a given scientific community the kinds of questions that may fruitfully be asked and the types of explanations to be sought." *Religion and Science: Historical and Contemporary Issues* (San Francisco: HarperSan Francisco, 1997) 108. For further material on paradigms, see Nancey Murphy, "Paradigm," in *A New Handbook of Christian Theology*, eds. Donald W. Musser and Joseph L. Price (Nashville: Abingdon Press, 1992) 344–46.

9. See Hans Küng and David Tracy, eds., *Paradigm Change in Theology: A Symposium for the Future*, tr. Margaret Kohl (New York: The Crossroad Publishing Company, 1989).

anthropologists, economists, and theologians. The word has become one of the most frequently employed terms in all of theology. But what does it mean precisely?

In the realm of the physical sciences, it became increasingly clear to its practitioners that scientific knowledge was not only about empirically observable reality.[10] Science also had to do with speculative theory and not only with inductive theory. Induction works from laws governing reality to the experience of that reality in the here and now. Science is enormously helpful in this regard, but is not limited to it. Science also wants to understand the deeper structures of reality and not merely predict how reality "works" in the practical order. In their quest for knowledge of reality, scientists began to employ models or constructs to help them better understand partial aspects of complex realities. Ian G. Barbour has defined them as "abstract symbol systems, which inadequately and selectively represent particular aspects of the world for specific purposes. . . . [Models] are neither literal pictures nor useful fictions but limited and inadequate ways of imagining what is not observable."[11] In the realm of understanding divine revelation, as theologians came to the conviction that faith involves a person's total relationship to God, the approach that stressed propositional formulas and doctrines as primary began to give ground to more personalist approaches. The models approach seemed to offer promise of understanding reality as ultimately inaccessible to the knower. Models have come to exercise great appeal as a way for theology to be of service to revelation understood as the divine-human dialogue and faith as commitment. Many realities of faith are so multifaceted and complex that they demand a variety of approaches at understanding: logical definition, discursive reason, imagination leading to metaphor and symbol, and models that both explain and explore the faith. Such approaches mutually enrich one another, so that the limitations of one method are offset by another method's greater promise of understanding.

In summary, we share, broadly speaking, a worldview with all those who participate in our culture. The worldview gives us a global orientation toward reality and includes presuppositions that are rarely adverted

10. The history of religion and science from the Middle Ages into the twentieth century has been admirably told by Barbour, *Religion and Science*, 3–74. This section is a reworking of his *Issues in Science and Religion* (Englewood Cliffs, N.J.: Prentice-Hall, Inc., 1966) 15–114.

11. Barbour, *Religion and Science*, 117. See also Barbour, *Myths, Models, and Paradigms: A Comparative Study in Science and Religion* (San Francisco: Harper & Row, 1974), chapters 3 ("Models in Science"), 4 ("Models in Religion"), and 5 ("Complementary Models").

to but that exercise a profound impact on our thinking and acting. In turn, paradigms help us to surface these presuppositions and to test them against reality. The paradigms can change while the worldview remains basically intact. In general, though, multiple changes of paradigms, especially rapidly successive paradigms, lead to a revision of the worldview. Finally, together with our efforts to define reality in logical terms and predictive laws, models help us better understand aspects of the world mediated to us through our broader and more inclusive paradigms.

The Premodern Worldview

It is time to apply the theory of worldview, paradigms, and models in order to better understand the apostolicity of the church. At the beginning of the chapter, I called the first way of speaking about apostolicity the model of identity because it defines apostolicity in terms of sameness. The church is the same today as it has always been. Christ had a mental blueprint for the constitution of the church which he delivered to his apostles. Subsequent generations of Christians are expected to maintain the ecclesiastical constitution exactly as given by Christ. This understanding is often intended when someone says that something in the church is "according to the mind," or "according to the will," of Christ. Certain aspects of church life and teaching are considered immutable, unable to be changed, irreversible. But why should this be the case? It is not evident to many contemporary Christians why some things in the church cannot be changed. We are inclined to see change as something desirable, as long as it can be justified in faith and is not arbitrary. But how do we decide between what is justifiable in faith and what is not?

In the case of the two worldviews to be studied in this chapter, I intend to look at each from four points of view. First, I will consider the general cultural assumptions of the worldview. Then, I will examine what some of the operative theological criteria were that governed the worldview. Next, in the light of the assumptions of the worldview, I will discuss how someone who shared these assumptions would have understood Scripture and practiced exegesis of the text. Finally, I will single out a representative thinker who best exemplified the worldview. Before proceeding further, I need to remark that whole books could be written on how these many aspects of worldviews impact the church's teaching on apostolicity. My treatment must be brief and it will give the impression of simplifying long and complex periods in the church's life. My intention is not to force the understanding of the data at the expense of its richness, but to acknowledge that my interest lies elsewhere. The review of the material is intended to show that the teaching on apostolicity is not able to be understood in isolation from its interconnection with other doctrines and with the dominant assumptions of the world and our ability to understand that world and the meaning of our existence in light of it.

I begin with the worldview that is a long-lived and rich one—the premodern or classical.[12] It has brought many opportunities and blessings to the church. This worldview emerged out of the classical culture of antiquity at the same time that the nascent Christian community was distancing itself from its Jewish roots and adopting its own distinctive symbols, practices, doctrines, and structures. It did so with the help of the rich, multifaceted, and flexible synthesis known as Hellenism.[13] The church's reworking of its founding experiences can be viewed in the emergence of the New Testament Scriptures and the eventual formulation of a canon, as well as in the genesis of a "system" of orthodox teachings.[14]

12. I am leaving out of discussion a worldview that predates the classical one, viz., the archaic or mythic worldview. I do not discuss it because it had been transformed in the classical premodern worldview that emerged largely out of the experience of what Karl Jaspers called "the axial period." See Jaspers, "The Axial Period," in *The Origin and Goal of History*, tr. Michael Bullock (New Haven: Yale University Press, 1953) 1–21. I need to clarify the fact that one worldview is never entirely superseded by its successor worldviews. Vestiges or elements of the former worldview are always creatively maintained and interwoven in successive worldviews.

13. On Hellenism, see the observations of Jaroslav Pelikan, "De-Judaization and Hellenization: The Ambiguities of Christian Identity," in *The Dynamic in Christian Thought,* The Villanova University Series 1, ed. Joseph Papin (Villanova, Pa.: Villanova University Press, 1970) 81–124; and Bernard J. Lonergan, "The Transition from a Classicist World-View to Historical-Mindedness" and "The Dehellenization of Dogma," in *A Second Collection* (Philadelphia: The Westminster Press, 1974) 1–9 and 11–32. For a general overview of the Hellenistic period and its thought-world, see Richard Tarnas, "The Transformation of the Classical Era," in *The Passion of the Western Mind: Understanding the Ideas that Have Shaped Our World View* (New York: Balantine Books, 1991) 73–90. Also worth consulting is Jean Daniélou, *Gospel Message and Hellenistic Culture*, vol. 2: *A History of Early Christian Doctrine before the Council of Nicaea*, tr. John Austin Baker (Philadelphia: The Westminster Press, 1973).

14. On the gradual emergence of what is called "orthodoxy" in the first centuries of the church, see Walter Bauer, *Orthodoxy and Heresy in Earliest Christianity* (Philadelphia: Fortress Press, 1971); David J. Hawkin, "A Reflective Look at the Recent Debate on Orthodoxy and Heresy in Earliest Christianity," *Église et théologie* 7 (1976) 367–78; Rowan Williams, "Does It Make Sense to Speak of Pre-Nicene Orthodoxy?" in *The Making of Orthodoxy: Essays in Honour of Henry Chadwick*, ed. R. Williams (New York: Cambridge University Press, 1989) 1–23; and Arland J. Hultgren, *The Rise of Normative Christianity* (Minneapolis: Fortress Press, 1994).

Orthodoxy established the boundaries between its distinctive system of practices and beliefs and other formulations which represented views incompatible with the truth of the emerging synthesis. It did so with the help of social forces and currents of thought mediated by the general culture of Hellenism. None of this was simple or monolithic. There was tremendous room for variations and options, as the gradual development of Eastern and Western Christianity shows.[15]

As the process advanced, however, the system adopted certain markers that were considered beyond question. This inevitable process necessarily meant the adoption of certain points of view that were increasingly assumed as constitutive of the system rather than as historically and culturally determined factors in handing on the Christian faith. The sense of the inner logic, adequacy, and totality of the system is what constitutes the premodern or classical worldview. What is astounding to us today is how this worldview survived as long as it did. By contrast, we moderns are accustomed to rapid changes and to crossing boundaries by engaging in dialogue. I propose to look first at some of the cultural assumptions of the classical worldview in late antiquity.

Cultural Assumptions

Up to Constantine (275–337 C.E.) and his successors, Christians constituted a tiny minority in the Roman empire.[16] Gradually, Christianity as the official religion became coextensive with the empire. The lines of demarcation between state and church were blurred as the church assumed more and more responsibility for certain civil functions. Since most citizens were baptized Christians, there were few boundaries between church and state. Christianity was Christendom. This sense of belonging to a Christian people communicated a powerful sense of a shared identity and a common destiny. At the same time, the price of maintaining

15. See Yves Congar, "Ecclesiological Awareness in the East and in the West from the Sixth to the Eleventh Century," in *The Unity of the Churches of God,* ed. Polycarp Sherwood (Baltimore: Helicon Press, 1963) 127–84.

16. See Rodney Stark, *The Rise of Christianity: A Sociologist Reconsiders History* (Princeton: Princeton University Press, 1996); and Keith Hopkins, "Christian Number and Its Implication," *Journal of Early Christian Studies* 6 (1998) 185–226. According to Hopkins' estimate, by the early fourth century Christians constituted only 10% of the empire's citizens, or approximately six million persons, but this was up dramatically from a mere 0.36%, or approximately two hundred thousand persons, at the beginning of the third century. See p. 193 for Hopkins' chart.

this identity was uniformity of practice and belief. The formulas used to express the Christian faith were more and more fixed, and the practices and customs which expressed the faith in specific personal and communal actions were increasingly uniform and regulated by law. Uniformity acted to bind Christians together cohesively and to limit the weakening of their bonds by outside influences. These two goals of unity and uniformity were in turn served by two further assumptions, hierarchy and authority.

Hierarchy explained why some people in Christendom possessed the power to render decisions concerning others.[17] A hierarchical view of power, both secular and sacred, maintained that it was divinely entrusted to leaders and was exercised in degrees that are descending and interlocking. A higher person always possessed de jure what someone at a lower grade exercised de facto, and therefore the higher person could limit the exercise of the power as he saw fit. Ideally, hierarchical power was exercised by a harmonious interplay of jurisdictions. Hierarchy constituted the order needed for social cohesiveness. Authority, on the other hand, represented the claim to the intellectual allegiance of believers. In a world where very few were formally educated, knowledge was identified with the great thinkers and writers who were determinative of the culture. These giants represented the real "authorities" *(auctores* and *auctoritates)* in classical culture,[18] and subsequent thinkers exercised their authority derivatively to the extent that they had access to the thought of the giants and were able to communicate their truth faithfully to others. This view of authority explains the tremendous influence of the likes of Plato and Aristotle, the sacred writers of Scripture, the bishops of Ni-

17. See Ghislain Lafont, "The Gregorian Form of the Church," in *Imagining the Catholic Church: Structured Communion in the Spirit,* tr. John J. Burkhard (Collegeville, Minn.: The Liturgical Press, 2000) 37–64. See also ibid., 14–21 [on Hellenism and hierarchy]; and Garrett J. Roche, "Hierarchy: From Dionysius to Trent to Vatican II," *Studia Canonica* 16 (1982) 367–89.

18. On the terms *"auctor"* and *"auctoritas,"* see the entries in Lewis and Short, *A Latin Dictionary,* revised, enlarged and in great part rewritten by Charlton T. Lewis and Charles Short (Oxford: At the Clarendon Press, 1962) 198–200. See also Marie-Dominique Chenu, *Toward Understanding St. Thomas,* tr. Albert M. Landry and Dominic Hughes (Chicago: Henry Regnery Company, 1964) 126–39 ["The Procedure of Authority in the Middle Ages"], and 139–49 ["The Technical Handling of Authorities"]; Yves Congar, *A History of Theology,* tr. Hunter Guthrie (Garden City, N.Y.: Doubleday & Company, 1968) 55–56; and Jacques-Guy Bougerol, "The Church Fathers and *auctoritates* in Scholastic Theology to Bonaventure," in *The Reception of the Church Fathers in the West: From the Carolingians to the Maurists,* 2 vols., ed. Irena Backus (Leiden: E. J. Brill, 1997) 1:289–335; and Leo J. Elders, "Thomas Aquinas and the Fathers of the Church," in ibid., 337–66.

caea, Augustine, Gregory the Great, and Pseudo-Dionysius to subsequent generations. Later Christians saw their task rather as composing "commentaries" on the writings of the genuine authorities.[19] We might call this interpretive procedure a "hermeneutic of authority." It was not one of discovery. In an age of the limited diffusion of knowledge in society at large, a "hermeneutic of authority" is not necessarily inappropriate. One could extend the knowledge of the giants but never substantially alter it. Deeper insight by ever more assiduous study of the "authorities" was always possible, but the possibility of transcending their knowledge was out of the question.

In such a culture of Christianity as Christendom, a culture of unity-in-uniformity, hierarchy, and authority, how would apostolicity have been interpreted? Apostolicity would have been a timeless truth, somehow independent of historical change and possessing a fixed and immutable doctrinal content. The historical argument of a succession of bishops going all the way back to the apostles would have served as a model for reinforcing the worldview of stability, timelessness, and purity of truth. The strengths of the classical understanding of apostolicity arise out of the strengths of the culture. Those very strengths, however, also reveal the worldview's limitations.

The power of the classical worldview for Catholicism is shown by its incredible survival until very recently. As late as the second half of the nineteenth century with the emergence of neo-Scholasticism, and together with the more historically minded retrievals of such Thomists as Jacques Maritain (1882-1973) and Étienne Gilson (1884-1978) in the first sixty years of the twentieth century, the classical worldview provided the natural

---

19. On the role and importance of commentaries written in late antiquity and during the Middle Ages, Yves Congar has written: " . . . the Middle Ages considered itself as having received a heritage and so was obliged to safeguard and assimilate it. As to the Middle Ages, historians have observed a certain passivity in the use of sources, the scarcity of new translations from ancient works, a kind of closed world. . . . The Middle Ages gives us a datum which must be taken as it is and which calls for nothing more than a commentary. This was their view of themselves. Intellectual work was simply assimilation of a text, the commentary on an accepted author. Teaching, in the schools, was essentially the explanation of a text. The essential act and the normal procedure of medieval pedagogy was reading, *lectio;* the teacher, the doctor, was called *lector." A History of Theology,* 54–55. Beryl Smalley, *The Study of the Bible in the Middle Ages* (Notre Dame, Ind.: University of Notre Dame Press, 1964), and Gillian R. Evans, *The Language and Logic of the Bible: The Earlier Middle Ages* (New York: Cambridge University Press, 1984), have studied many of these commentaries in the period prior to the period of high Scholasticism.

ambience for Catholic thought and life. Its influence can be discerned in theology, preaching and catechesis, the academic curricula of Catholic colleges and seminaries, the focus of interest of academic journals and professional societies, and so forth. To this day, it continues to exercise a powerful attraction to many.

Theological Criteria

Which general theological criteria operate as founding principles of the classical Christian worldview and help explain how the church in the premodern period would have understood apostolicity? First of all, there is the emergence of a propositional understanding of revelation.[20] Under the pressure of the doctrinal controversies that raged in the first five centuries of Christianity, the perspective of salvation history, so vibrant at the start of the church, disappeared. The Christian faith increasingly was restricted to statements about the faith. For example, the baptismal creeds of the early centuries were transformed into confessional formulae, to which anathemas were appended.[21] Propositions became the most appropriate vehicle for expressing God's revelation. Furthermore, a growing anti-Jewish and, after the rise of Islam, an anti-Islamic polemic led to the need for Christians to reinforce their identity. In practical terms, this meant the devaluation of the literal or historical sense of Scripture. Paradoxically, this led to a simplistic view of the church's origins by attributing its foundational acts to an omniscient Christ, for example, the calling of a group of twelve apostles, the primacy of Peter and his successors, the sacramental system accepted by Catholics, including the ordination of bishops and priests, and so forth. What resulted was a Christian faith narrowly focused on doctrine and fixed liturgical acts, practices, and ecclesial structures that could be explained in christological terms.

Because the richness of salvation history was lost, a static view of history emerged, one which conformed neatly to the substantialist view of nature and the world in its Aristotelian form, or as shadowy and in-

---

20. See Avery Dulles, "Model One: Revelation as Doctrine," in *Models of Revelation* (Garden City, N.Y.: Doubleday & Company, 1983) 36–52; and idem, *The Assurance of Things Hoped For: A Theology of Christian Faith* (New York: Oxford University Press, 1994) 170–72 ["Propositional Model"].

21. See H. J. Carpenter, "Creeds and Baptismal Rites in the First Four Centuries," *Journal of Theological Studies* 44 (1943) 1–11; Joseph Crehan, *Early Christian Baptism and the Creed: A Study in Ante-Nicene Theology* (London: Burns Oates & Washbourne Ltd., 1950); and J.N.D. Kelly, *Early Christian Creeds* (3rd ed.; London: Longman Group Ltd., 1972).

substantial, pointing to the true reality of the eternal ideas, in its Platonic form. Since nothing could really change in the flux of history, the values of sameness and immutability became the basic expressions of reality. Thus, Christ had formulated once and for all a charter for the church and handed it over to the apostles and their successors, the bishops. The offices of bishop and pope were meant to preserve the purity of doctrine and the identity of the church and its structures. The early literature of Christianity was subsequently read out of this optic, for example, papal primacy was seen as already enshrined in *1 Clement,* as we saw above in Chapter Three. There has been no real development since Christ and the apostles, the executors of his will.

The will of Christ and his apostles was interpreted against the unquestioned assumption that society was organized hierarchically and pyramidally. Only in this way could the immutable fixed order of the cosmos and social reality be maintained. That very order was itself sacred *(hieros)* and consequently its manifestation in sacred persons and institutions was unquestioned too. Fixity and immutability were not limitations according to this worldview but divine guarantees of the physical and social order. Finally, the Catholic appropriation of the premodern worldview saw the church as a society, even as a "perfect society" in the supernatural order, alongside the other "perfect society," the state, in the natural order.[22] A theology that tended to neatly dichotomize reality into the distinct orders of nature and supernature separated the church from the world as well.

With these premodern assumptions of sameness, immutability, fixity, stability, order, and the lack of real historical change as a backdrop—assumptions which are expressed in the classical ideas of unity-in-uniformity, hierarchy, and authority—the implications of the meaning of apostolicity to Christians in an earlier era should be clear. Even today, some persons seem to regard apostolicity in the way just described. For many who have been formed by neo-scholastic principles and have never questioned them, it is impossible for the church to adopt new ways of thinking and new ecclesial forms. Changes would betray the identical character of the apostles' teachings and the offices they bequeathed to the church.

22. See Patrick Granfield, "The Church as *Societas Perfecta* in the Schema of Vatican I," *Church History* 48 (1979) 431–46; and Knut Walf, "Die katholische Kirche—eine 'societas perfecta'?" *Theologische Quartalschrift* 157 (1977) 107–18.

Scripture and Exegesis

The understanding and use of Scripture are also elements in the premodern worldview characteristic of Catholicism up to the Second Vatican Council. These uses emerged over many centuries and responded to changing circumstances in the church's life. In general, today we characterize the use of Scripture during these centuries as "precritical," not to dismiss it entirely as useless to the contemporary Christian, but to distinguish it from forms which emerged later and were concerned with explicitly "critical issues."[23] Of course, Christians during the long period of time marking the premodern or classical period were concerned with issues of criticism.[24] They, too, were concerned with establishing a reliable text, with textual inconsistencies and contradictions, with the straightforward meaning of the text in its original language, but in general these critical concerns were focused less on the text itself than on other important issues.[25] Modern critical study of the Bible focuses almost exclusively on the text itself, often to the neglect of wider issues. What, then, were some of the other dominant issues characteristic of the premodern period?

At first, scriptural interpretation was concerned with establishing the messianic meaning of the Hebrew Scriptures vis-à-vis the emerging Christian Scriptures.[26] This process was already going on in the New Testament itself, and the Gospel of Matthew is a particularly apt example

23. On the use of the terms "precritical" and "critical," see Avery Dulles, *The Craft of Theology: From Symbol to System* (2nd ed.; New York: The Crossroad Publishing Company, 1995) 3–5.

24. Robert M. Grant, "Historical Criticism in the Ancient Church," *The Journal of Religion* 25 (1945) 183–96. See also Robert M. Grant with David Tracy, *A Short History of the Interpretation of the Bible* (rev. ed.; Philadelphia: Fortress Press, 1984).

25. See Manlio Simonetti, *Biblical Interpretation in the Church: An Historical Introduction to Patristic Exegesis,* eds. Anders Bergquist and Markus Bockmuehl, tr. John A. Hughes (Edinburgh: T&T Clark Ltd., 1994); G. R. Evans, "Medieval Interpretation," in *A Dictionary of Biblical Interpretation,* eds. R. J. Coggins and J. L. Houlden (Philadelphia: Trinity Press International, 1990) 438–40; and John F. A. Sawyer, "Interpretation, History of," in ibid., 316–20; Karlfried Froehlich, "The Significance of Medieval Biblical Interpretation," *Lutheran Quarterly* 9 (1995) 139–50; and Karlfried Froehlich, Jerry H. Bentley, and James Barr, "Interpretation, History of," in *The Oxford Guide to Ideas and Issues of the Bible,* ed. Bruce Metzger and Michael D. Coogan (New York: Oxford University Press, 2001) 226–34 ["Early Christian Interpretation"], 234–37 ["Christian Interpretation from the Middle Ages to the Reformation"], and 237–46 ["Modern Biblical Criticism"].

26. See Frances Young, "Jewish Texts and Christian Meanings," in *Virtuoso Theology: The Bible and Interpretation* (Cleveland: The Pilgrim Press, 1993) 66–87.

of the promise/fulfillment relationship.[27] Once Christians had secured their messianic interpretation, the great controversies of the third through sixth centuries regarding the doctrines of the Trinity and Christ demanded the lion's share of the church's attention. Scripture was marshaled to unravel these mysteries of the faith, to oppose errors, and to work toward the formulation of an orthodox synthesis of faith-statements. But the church was also engaged in the process of structuring its liturgical life in sacramental rites and practices. In both respects, typology proved extremely helpful. Moreover, the concrete conditions under which Christians lived demanded expressions that could help them face persecution, moral and social issues, and the need for spiritual growth. Given the urgency of the questions and the extent of the needs, it is no wonder that teachers, theologians, bishops, and spiritual writers employed forms of interpretation that sought to get at another, deeper meaning beneath or within the literal one. In this way, the widespread use of allegory and the moral or tropological senses of the text prevailed.[28] There can be no doubt that such interpretive procedures helped the church survive and thrive.[29]

The more-than-literal meaning of the text of Scripture continued to be developed in the early and late medieval period. In general, it was a time of relative calm regarding the formulation of the faith. It was concerned with pastoral issues of preaching the faith and transforming society, as well as the sanctification of the believer. To these ends, allegory and the moral meaning continued to be used. Increasingly, too, a fourth sense was developed, the anagogical, concerned with what the text told the believer about life beyond death.[30] These senses were fed by the growth of education and the use of the liberal arts in the schools. Literary and rhetorical concerns began to emerge, however modestly. In the

---

27. See Jean Daniélou, *From Shadows to Reality: Studies in the Biblical Typology of the Fathers,* tr. Wulstan Hibberd (London: Burns and Oates Ltd., 1960); and Brian McNeil, "Typology," in *A Dictionary of Biblical Interpretation,* 713–14.

28. See Anders Jørgen Bjørndalen, "Allegory," in ibid., 14–16; Andrew Louth, "Allegorical Interpretation," in ibid., 12–14; and Gillian R. Evans, "Medieval Interpretation," in ibid., 438–40.

29. See David C. Steinmetz, "The Superiority of Pre-Critical Exegesis," *Theology Today* 37 (1980–81) 27–38; and Ignace de la Potterie, "Reading Holy Scripture 'in the Spirit': Is the Patristic Way of Reading the Bible Still Possible Today?" *International Catholic Review: Communio* 13 (1986) 308–25.

30. See Susan K. Wood, "The Spiritual Interpretation of Scripture," in *Spiritual Exegesis and the Church in the Theology of Henri de Lubac* (Grand Rapids: Wm. B. Eerdmans Publishing Co., 1998) 25–51.

Middle Ages, these four basic senses of Scripture were expressed in the following couplet:

Littera gesta docet, quid credas allegoria,
Moralis quid agas, quo tendas anagogia

"The meaning of the letter treats deeds, while allegory deals with what is believed.
And while the moral sense explains what should be done, anagogy points to the goal."

Saints Thomas Aquinas and Bonaventure represent the coexistence of two approaches to interpretation, the one more Aristotelian, the other more Platonic. Thomas placed greater stress on the literal or historical sense of the passage, given his intellectualist-theological project, while Bonaventure's more voluntarist-contemplative venture concentrated on the symbolical or figurative meanings.[31] The Middle Ages had room for both theologians during their lifetimes, but as the period wore on and urgent issues, such as church reform, were not attended to, the gulf between the approaches grew wider. Spiritual interpretations could help Christians cope with sin in the church itself, but were increasingly incapable of bringing about real reform. By the sixteenth century, a decadent allegorization and an impotent moralization of the text were no longer viable options. The thinkers of the magisterial Reformation[32] began to look for other, less subjective resources. But this meant returning to the

---

31. See Barnabas Lindars, *The History of Christian Theology,* vol. 2: *The Study and Use of the Bible,* ed. Paul Avis (Grand Rapids: Wm. B. Eerdmans Publishing Co., 1988) 286–88. On Thomas Aquinas, see Jacques Verger, "L'exégèse de l'Université," in *Le Moyen Age et la Bible,* Bible de tous les temps 4, ed. Pierre Riché and Guy Lobrichon (Paris: Éditions Beauchesne, 1984) 199–232, at 204–21. On Bonaventure, see Dominic V. Monti, "Symbolic Exegesis," in "Bonaventure's Interpretation of Scripture in His Exegetical Works" (Ph.D. dissertation, University of Chicago, 1979) 222–89; and Thomas Reist, "Saint Bonaventura and Sacred Scripture," in *Saint Bonaventure as a Biblical Commentator: A Translation and Analysis of His Commentary on Luke, xviii, 34–xix, 42* (Lanham, Md.: University Press of America, 1985) 29–65.

32. Today, scholars distinguish between the reforms undertaken by "mainstream thinkers" like Martin Luther, John Calvin, Martin Bucer and others from more radical thinkers associated with Anabaptism as the "magisterial Reformation" in contrast with the "radical Reformation." For an explanation of the terms, see Alister E. McGrath, *Historical Theology: An Introduction to the History of Christian Thought* (Oxford: Blackwell Publishers Ltd., 1998) 158–63 ["A Clarification of Terms"]; and idem, "Introduction," in *Reformation Thought: An Introduction* (2nd ed.; Oxford: Blackwell Publishers Ltd., 1993) 1–26.

primacy of the text, and that very project helped to bring about an entirely new paradigm.

A Case Study: Joaquín Salaverri, S.J.

An introductory word is in order regarding my choice of a representative of the neo-scholastic school of theology. I have chosen neo-Scholasticism, and Joaquín Salaverri, S.J., in particular, for two reasons. First, neo-Scholasticism represents the continuation of the scholastic synthesis of the Middle Ages and is thus allied to the premodern worldview. However, it also departed from Scholasticism in several important ways that proved deleterious to Catholic theology.[33] Second, many in the church today—including bishops, priests, and some theologians—still espouse a neo-scholastic theology or are at least influenced by its goals of certitude, authoritative teaching, and pronounced systematization. Neo-Scholasticism is clearly an influence in the Roman Catholic Church today.

In his volume of dogmatics, Salaverri treats apostolicity at five points.[34] The order of presentation is of interest. First, apostles are mentioned under the question of the office of bishop in the church. Second, Salaverri states that apostolicity is a necessary "property" of the church. Third, he gives certain responses to scholarly objections to apostolicity. Fourth, he argues that apostolicity is found in the Roman Catholic

---

33. Among many examples that could be cited, perhaps the most important is the neo-scholastic teaching on grace and on the relationship between nature and the supernatural. For a brief treatment, see Richard P. McBrien, *Catholicism* (rev. ed.; San Francisco: HarperSanFrancisco, 1994) 175–84. A more extensive treatment can be found in Stephen J. Duffy, *The Dynamics of Grace: Perspectives in Theological Anthropology* (Collegeville, Minn.: The Liturgical Press, 1993). Another major difference is represented by the methods each employed. Scholasticism used the method of posing questions that led to greater understanding, while neo-Scholasticism used the thesis method. This was based on gathering together the certain teachings of the church derived from conciliar statements and the papal magisterium. Its goal was less that of understanding than achieving certitude in an intellectual climate that was both rationalistic and polemical. Francis Schüssler Fiorenza presents a fair and balanced explanation of neo-Scholasticism in "Systematic Theology: Task and Methods," in *Systematic Theology: Roman Catholic Perspectives*, 2 vols., eds. Francis Schüssler Fiorenza and John P. Galvin (Minneapolis: Fortress Press, 1991) 1:3–87, at 27–35 ["Neo-scholasticism: Its Distinctive Characteristics"]. Bernard Lonergan shares brief but trenchant insights into the strengths and weaknesses of Scholasticism that show both appreciation for the achievements of Scholasticism while addressing its deficiencies. See his *Doctrinal Pluralism,* The 1971 Père Marquette Theology Lecture (Milwaukee: Marquette University Press, 1971) 28–33.

34. *Tractatus de ecclesia,* vol. 3 (2nd ed.; Madrid: Biblioteca de autores cristianos, 1952) §§330–82; §§1176–81; §§1201–3; §§1226–27; and §§1247–53.

church alone. And finally, he claims that other Christian churches lack authentic apostolicity *(vera apostolicitas)*.

With regard to the first section, the question in systematic theology of just who the apostles were is not examined in itself but in service of a thesis that the bishops are indeed successors of the apostles. This is by far the longest treatment given to apostolicity in the treatise.[35] Salaverri maintains two fundamental positions vis-à-vis episcopacy: the bishops succeed the apostles *iure divino*[36] and the office in their local churches is properly monarchical, not collegial. The content of this succession of the bishops is the *complexus potestatum* ("full complement of powers") of the apostles that they exercised in their teaching, sanctifying, and governing functions *(munera)*. Salaverri is aware of the scholarly non-Catholic literature and opinions on the important issues of apostleship, the emergence of episcopacy, the authorship of the Pastorals, and so forth. He cites the works of J. B. Lightfoot, O. Linton, E. Hatch, A. von Harnack, R. Sohm, K. L. Schmidt, M. Goguel, C. H. Turner, and others.[37] He informs us of their arguments faithfully, albeit with the utmost brevity. But in the end, he arrives at the certainty of his position on the basis of the "hermeneutic of authority," namely, the teaching of the Councils of Trent and Vatican I that the bishops are the successors of the apostles *iure divino*. As a result, he is never really able to address the historical arguments of the above-named scholars on their own merits. But to Salaverri's credit it must be remarked that he never places undue weight on the fact of an unbroken chain of episcopal ordinations going all the way back to the twelve apostles. Instead, he argues that the historical evidence from the New Testament up to Eusebius of Caesarea and Jerome, is sufficient to support the church's conciliar teaching regarding the succession of the bishops directly to the apostles. I think I am not unfair to Salaverri in

35. It consists of 17 out of a total of 23 pages on apostolicity.

36. On the concept of *ius divinum*, i.e., divine law, and its problematic status in theology, see Karl Rahner, "Reflections on the Concept of *Ius divinum* in Catholic Thought," in *Theological Investigations*, 23 vols., tr. Karl-H. and Boniface Krüger (Baltimore: Helicon Press, 1966) 5:219–43; Carl J. Peter, "Dimensions of *Jus divinum* in Roman Catholic Theology," *Theological Studies* 34 (1973) 227–50; Harald Wagner, "Zur Problematik des 'ius divinum,'" *Trierer theologische Zeitschrift* 88 (1979) 132–44; Avery Dulles, "*Ius Divinum* as an Ecumenical Problem," in *A Church to Believe In: Discipleship and the Dynamics of Freedom* (New York: The Crossroad Publishing Company, 1982) 80–102; and Yves Congar, "Jus Divinum,'" in *Église et Papauté. Regards historiques* (Paris: Les Éditions du Cerf, 1994) 65–80.

37. See also Salaverri, "La sucesión apostólica en la 'Historia eclesiástica' de Eusebio Cesariense," *Gregorianum* 14 (1933) 219–47.

concluding that he understands apostolicity primarily as the succession of the bishops in apostolic office.

Salaverri defines apostolicity as follows: "Apostolicity is the permanent identity of the church's mission as entrusted to the apostles when Christ instituted the church."[38] He specifies apostolicity in terms of "identity"— of origin, of teaching, and of legitimate succession in office. Nevertheless, he goes on to clarify the fact that such "identity" does not exclude all change, development, or modification. Moreover, he understands apostolicity globally and speaks of the church's "mission." Salaverri is more nuanced than, for example, Timotheus Zapelena, S.J., whose *De ecclesia Christi* insists on what he calls "numerical identity" (and not merely "specific identity") on "all essential elements which Christ instituted" for his church. Zapelena writes that "it is necessary that doctrine be identical, the sacraments be identical, the same sacrifice, the same sacred or hierarchical powers, and finally the same structure and social makeup."[39] The difference of emphasis between these two late preconciliar neo-Scholastics shows that neo-Scholasticism as the end-product of the premodern worldview did not lack all vitality of thought.[40] But the neo-scholastic paradigm of theology—with its hostility toward modernity, its suspicion of history and critical methods of research, and its over-reliance on arguments from authority—was too sterile in practice. It was rooted too firmly in the premodern worldview. Quite simply, a new worldview was needed. To that we now turn our attention.

The Modern Worldview

At the start of the chapter, I referred to the second model of apostolicity as the model of continuity. It is a model that is broadly shared by contemporary Catholic theologians, and is based on the assumption that

---

38. *Tractatus de ecclesia*, 3§1176.

39. "*Oportet ergo ut eadem sit doctrina, eadem sacramenta, idem sacrificium, eaedem postestates sacrae seu hierarchicae, eadem demum structura seu constitutio socialis.*" Zapelena, *De ecclesia Christi* (4th ed.; Rome: Apud Aedes Universitatis Gregorianae, 1946) 413.

40. On the subsequent history of neo-Scholasticism and its vitality, see Gerald A. McCool, *From Unity to Pluralism: The Internal Evolution of Thomism* (New York: Fordham University Press, 1989); idem, "The Tradition of St. Thomas since Vatican II," *Theology Digest* 40 (1993) 324–35; idem, *The Neo-Thomists* (Milwaukee: Marquette University Press, 1994); John F. X. Knasas, *Being and Some Twentieth-Century Thomists* (New York: Fordham University Press, 2003); and Serge-Thomas Bonino and others, *Thomistes ou de l'actualité de saint Thomas d'Aquin* (Éditions Parole et Silence, 2003).

organic development characterizes the personal and social actions of human beings. There might be moments of regression in the human search for knowledge and appropriate social activity, but in general the development is progressive and linear. Men and women who share the modern worldview simply expect continuity and progress. Thus, when believers try to explain the church's apostolicity, they will no longer do so in terms of the expectation of sameness or exact identity, but in terms of the continued growth of something that is given.[41] Thus, for the modern Christian change is the unfolding in history of what is already contained in the seed of Christianity planted centuries ago. The modern worldview does not run away from the challenge of change but understands it as fundamentally continuous with its past. Change is not something to be feared. Let us examine the modern worldview in greater detail, following the same procedure we did as regards the classical worldview.

Cultural Assumptions

By the fifteenth century, the adequacy of the late classical and medieval paradigms showed clear signs of being exhausted. In the church there were the strains of the Great Western Schism which pitted one pope against another and caused widespread confusion. A weakened papacy elicited conciliarist movements among the bishops and further provoked a crisis of leadership in Christendom itself. Urgently needed reform in the church was stymied. The Black Death decimated the population and sapped creative social and intellectual energies. Signs of new directions were awakened in the Renaissance and in the magisterial Reformation. There was new life, new possibilities. In the end, however, there was only bitter disillusionment. The French Catholic René Descartes (1596–1650) felt the growth of skepticism with particular pain. The internecine madness known to us as the Thirty Years War forced him to develop a new method of adjudicating truth claims. There had to be some solid basis for deciding between options. If skepticism was to be avoided and fanaticism contained, new foundations for determining truth were needed.[42] Descartes sought to accomplish this in his *Discourse on Method* (1637).

41. In neo-scholastic language, there is "specific" versus "numerical" continuity: the classical worldview anticipates "numerical" sameness; the modern worldview looks for continuity in the same species or "specific" identity.

42. See the discussion of the issues by Stephen Toulmin, *Cosmopolis: The Hidden Agenda of Modernity* (Chicago: University of Chicago Press, 1990) 69–80 ["1640–1660: The Politics of Certainty"].

Descartes was impressed with the use of mathematics in the newer models of physical science, exemplified in the writings of Johannes Kepler (1571–1630) and Galileo Galilei (1564–1642). Observation of external phenomena led inductively to certain conclusions or laws governing the physical universe. Once formulated, these laws could be used deductively to anticipate or predict the regularity of phenomena. Descartes felt that, in the face of so much uncertainty and even skepticism, a philosophical method modeled on mathematics could also reach certainty regarding intramental phenomena. He found this point of departure in the overpowering experience of his selfhood. If there was one thing he simply could not deny, it was the fact that he existed. His thinking led to the unassailable conclusion that he existed. *Cogito, ergo sum!* The activity of thinking gave him absolute certainty regarding his existence in an objective or physical universe. That knowledge became the very foundation of all his other knowledge. This certainty would support him if he further invoked a procedure of methodical doubt. With the certainty this foundational insight provided, Descartes could proceed to test other statements regarding reality. He could avoid falling into the inescapable skepticism he so dreaded.[43]

Supported by the twin pillars of scientific method and the philosophy of the subject, the hallmarks of the modern worldview, or as it is often called, "modernity," emerged. It is important to keep in mind that modernity draws equally from *both* scientific/observational *and* philosophical/introspective sources. Historians of the period generally admit that these hallmarks include the primacy of the subject, the sovereignty of reason, the foundation for a process of universalizing experience, and the inevitability of progress. Some scholars go on to further specify the innate dualism of Descartes' view of the subject, resulting in an extreme formulation of the subject/object dichotomy. These hallmarks explain why the period is marked by what is called "the anthropocentric turn." The worldview of classical antiquity and the Middle Ages was marked by "cosmocentrism." The human, until then lost in the cosmos, has emerged with modernity as the center of concern and the arbiter of reality

43. See Klaus Scholder, *The Birth of Modern Critical Theology: Origins and Problems of Biblical Criticism in the Seventeenth Century,* tr. John Bowden (Philadelphia: Trinity Press International, 1990) for a readable presentation of how the issues raised by modern science and scientific method intersected with and challenged theological method, exegesis, and the authority of the Bible and the church's magisterium.

and truth. Just as in astronomy there was a change from a geocentric to a heliocentric paradigm, so, too, modernity represents a revolution from a cosmocentric to an anthropocentric paradigm.

Moreover, the "turn to the subject" or "anthropocentric turn" had a number of definite implications for Western societies. With the emergence of the subject or the individual came the continuing challenge to authority, already unleashed with the magisterial Reformation. Now, the individual was at the heart of society. Society existed for him or her, and not the other way around. But to assume one's rightful place or autonomy meant that society also had to be reconceived. The American and French revolutions pointed away from authoritarian, monarchical forms of government to participative democracy. The individual truly realizes his or her potential as a "citizen." But democracy, and the responsibilities that citizens bear for its health, is achievable only if education is extended to as many individuals as possible. At no time in recorded history have so many benefited from extended formal education. At first, these benefits were restricted to men, but with time increasing numbers of women, too, benefited from education—primary, secondary, and graduate. Finally, the indispensability of the scientific method and a "hermeneutic of observation and testing" emerged as powerful cultural assumptions of the modern worldview. The emerging democracies of Europe and North America became powerhouses of industrialization, drawing on the technologies spawned by science. University education ceded more and more space to the physical and the new human and social sciences. The good citizen now had to assure not only the freedoms of democracy but the benefits of a thriving economy. The individual citizen was transformed into a consumer as well.[44]

Officially, the Catholic Church was never comfortable with modern paradigms. It resisted modernity throughout the period, giving special expression to its rejection with the "Syllabus of Errors" of Pius IX (1864).[45] Sporadic efforts of individual thinkers were countered by the official establishment of neo-Scholasticism in the nineteenth cen-

44. On the development briefly outlined in this paragraph, see Robert N. Bellah, et al., "The Political Economy: Market and Work" and "Education: Technical and Moral," in *The Good Society* (New York: Alfred A. Knopf, 1991) 82–110 and 145–78 respectively.

45. See Denziger-Schönmetzer, *Enchiridion symbolorum, definitionum et declarationum de rebus fidei et morum* (33rd ed.; Freiburg im Breisgau: Verlag Herder, 1965) §§2901–80 [*The Sources of Catholic Dogma*, tr. Roy J. Deferrari (St. Louis: B. Herder Book Co., 1957) 435–42 (§§1701–80)].

tury[46] under Popes Pius IX and Leo XIII and by the painful experience of the condemnation of Catholic modernism by Pius X at the beginning of the twentieth century.[47] After the Second World War, however, the situation was to change dramatically. Despite appearances that things were returning to the way they were before the trauma of European fascism and the war, thinkers and prelates of the church knew that a process of reconceptualizing the role of the church in modern nation-states was inevitable. Already under Pius XI, consideration was being given to the role of the laity in the "apostolate." The movement was officially called "Catholic Action," and shows that the regnant understanding of "apostolicity" was being rethought, however timidly at this point, to include the laity.[48]

Theological Criteria

A number of theological criteria are operative in the modern worldview. First, the understanding of revelation has been influenced by the transcendental thought of Immanuel Kant (1724–1804). When God is revealed, it is to the individual subject and to his or her consciousness. The certainty of revealed truth takes place internally and only secondarily in formulae and ecclesial confessions. Revelation is primarily "transcendental experience" that is inexhaustible and ultimately only partially understood in the historical process of development. Before we speak about the experience in human language, we have grasped it internally in a fuller and richer way. We can see how revelation is being rethought in terms of modernity's "turn to the subject." Thus, revelation is directed toward the individual subject, takes place in the sphere of a person's interiority, and is universal in extent, since every human being is a subject

46. The story is told admirably by Gerald A. McCool, *Catholic Theology in the Nineteenth Century: The Quest for a Unitary Method* (New York: The Seabury Press, 1977).

47. See Émile Poulat, *Histoire, dogme et critique dans la crise moderniste* (2nd ed.; Paris: Casterman, 1979); Gabriel Daly, *Transcendence and Immanence: A Study in Catholic Modernism and Integralism* (Oxford: At the Clarendon Press, 1980); Daniel L. Donovan, "Church and Theology in the Modernist Crisis," *Catholic Theological Society of America Proceedings* 40 (1985) 145–59; Marvin R. O'Connell, *Critics on Trial: An Introduction to the Catholic Modernist Crisis* (Washington, D.C.: The Catholic University of America Press, 1994); and Darrell Jodock, ed., *Catholicism Contending with Modernity: Roman Catholic Modernism and Anti-Modernism in Historical Context* (New York: Cambridge University Press, 2000).

48. On Catholic Action, see D. J. Geaney, "Catholic Action," in *New Catholic Encyclopedia,* 15 vols., ed. William J. McDonald (New York: McGraw Hill Book Company, 1967) 3:262–63; and Christopher O'Donnell, "Apostolate," in *Ecclesia: A Theological Encyclopedia of the Church* (Collegeville: The Liturgical Press, 1996) 18–19.

open to the claims of truth. There is no need for an apologetics of the faith in the traditional sense of criteria that point to external signs of the credibility of belief. Interior religious experience is the foundation of the truth-claims of belief and of the authenticity of the act of believing.

Second, history, which plays such an important role in Christian revelation, was also devalued as a dimension of revelation. The human mind is directed to what is universal and necessary and not to the contingencies of history. The mind searches for the fundamental principles and laws governing reality. According to Kant's critical transcendentalism, only a priori categories permit knowledge that is certain. History, which works from a posteriori facts, can never offer certitude. This was the point of Gotthold Lessing's reference to history as an "ugly ditch."[49] Religious truths must be beyond the limitations of history. As an historical religion, Christianity and its beliefs could never add anything to what the human mind already knows in its own spontaneous and interior experience. The facts of revelation and the claims of salvation history are at most a reduplication of what the mind already knows in a purer and more convincing way.

Not everyone influenced by the rational thought of the Enlightenment capitulated to the exclusion of history from genuine knowledge. Some felt that though the reliance of traditional apologetics on external criteria was overstated, the claims of historical knowledge needed to be integrated into the process of knowing and believing. History was more than a mere indicator of the truth of Christian faith, it also participated in that truth. But how? Weren't the claims of pure rationality and historically contingent truth mutually exclusive?

In theology, Karl Rahner accepted the challenge of trying to reconcile the contradiction or the tension. With Rahner, the primacy of internal evidence occurs only in a dialectic with history, which is not something secondary but of equal importance for knowing. In the Rahnerian sense, transcendental revelation is never purely internal, subjective, or individ-

---

49. Gordon E. Michalson writes: "The inherited problems, as well as the newer, more modern difficulties, were both graphically conveyed by G. E. Lessing's famous image of the 'ugly ditch' between the 'accidental truths of history' and the 'necessary truths of reason', which has become a shorthand symbol of the faith-history problem." See his "Faith and History," in *The Blackwell Encyclopedia of Modern Christian Thought*, ed. Alister E. McGrath (Oxford: Blackwell Publishers, 1993) 210–14, at 211. See idem, *Lessing's 'Ugly Ditch': A Study of Theology and History* (University Park: Pennsylvania State University Press, 1985), for an in-depth presentation.

ual. Thus, the kind of argument employed by exponents of a propositional view of revelation is so modified by Rahner that the so-called historical facts "out there" do not exist independent of a mental framework
or horizon against which alone they make sense. For Rahner, human consciousness is always consciousness of history. Our historical experience
actually mediates transcendence to us. Rahner understands transcendental method as a mutual ordering of the absolute and the contingent in such
a way that each truly helps the other to be realized. Transcendence and
history are mutually related. The Incarnation of the Word, then, is of
central importance for faith. It is not simply one among many truths but
expresses the full human reality of Christ. Like any human being, Christ
developed over his lifetime and that human life has permanent, even
unique, significance in human history. As incarnate, Christ challenges
humankind to fulfill its task in history as its own way to realizing its transcendence. For many today, transcendental thought along the lines of
Karl Rahner's rethinking of transcendentalism is the most appropriate
theological paradigm for understanding Christian faith within the modern worldview.[50]

In the light of these theological criteria, apostolicity points to the
historical character of the church itself. The church cannot extricate itself
from the historical process of development or from human entanglements.
Scholars have tended to concentrate on the whole sweep of the apostolic
period.[51] They have pointed out the uniqueness of the apostolic period
and its importance as a final point of reference. Issues of the apostolicity
of the tradition, of the praxis of early Christian communities, and of the
ministry as a whole have emerged as salient, rather than the succession
of individual bishops to apostolic responsibilities and authority in isolation from these other factors. A more global sense of apostolicity precedes

50. For Rahner's own statement regarding the transcendence of the modern subject
and the need for a transcendental method, see "Transcendental Theology," in *Encyclopedia
of Theology: The Concise "Sacramentum Mundi,"* ed. Karl Rahner (New York: The Seabury
Press, 1975) 1748–51; idem, "The Hearer of the Message," in *Foundations of Christian Faith,*
tr. William V. Dych (New York: The Seabury Press, 1976) 24–43; and idem, "What Is
Man?" in *Christian at the Crossroads,* tr. V. Green (New York: The Seabury Press, 1975)
11–20. Also helpful are Karl Lehmann, "Transcendence," in *Encyclopedia of Theology,*
1734–42; and Karl H. Neufeld, "Theologies, II. Transcendental Theology," in *Dictionary of
Fundamental Theology,* eds. René Latourelle and Rino Fisichella (New York: The Crossroad
Publishing Company, 1995) 1082–84.

51. In this regard, see Raymond E. Brown and John P. Meier, *Antioch and Rome: New
Testament Cradles of Catholic Christianity* (New York: Paulist Press, 1983).

and regulates specific realizations, such as the episcopal and presbyteral ministry. In this historical approach, the church itself went through a long period of gestation and emergence. What is characteristic of the development, according to the modern worldview, is continuity with its past. Development has been understood along the lines of the model of organic development. Change is the unfolding in history of what is already contained in the seed of Christianity planted centuries ago. The modern worldview does not flee from the challenge of change but understands it as always continuous with its past. Thereby, change is less frightening.

Scripture and Exegesis

How was Scripture used and interpreted during the modern period? And how did exegetes understand apostolicity during the same period? How were the hallmarks of modernity expressed in modern critical exegesis?

At the end of the premodern period, we saw the impasse reached by the free use of the fourfold sense of Scripture. Once fruitful, this method of interpretation succumbed to sclerosis. Gradually, the principles of a critical approach to Scripture emerged in the eighteenth century.[52] The center of attention became the literal or historical meaning of a passage.[53] Instead of treating this meaning quickly and moving on to the really interesting allegorical, moral, or anagogical senses, modern scholars mined the literal sense in ways that were unheard of in the early and medieval church. They employed the emerging academic disciplines of literary criticism, history, archaeology, and the history of religions ("Religionsgeschichte") as allies.

Up to the Enlightenment, dogmatic issues of orthodoxy determined biblical interpretation to a large extent. Catholicism was intent on shoring up its dogmatic definitions and the teaching authority of the pope and bishops, whereas the thinkers of the magisterial Reform employed scriptural interpretation to support their theological starting points. Both would soon be under attack by a religion of reason championed by Enlightenment thinkers who largely dismissed the need for a divine revelation in

52. See John W. Rogerson, "Biblical Criticism," in *A Dictionary of Biblical Interpretation,* 83–86; and Friedemann W. Golka, "German Old Testament Scholarship," in ibid., 258–64.

53. See Frances Young, "Literal Meaning," in ibid., 401–402.

addition to what the person could grasp as religious truth from the autonomous use of reason alone. The spirit of rationalism would take over the reins of interpretation and bequeath a legacy of biblical criticism based on objective and scientific methods. The inspired character of the Bible and the unity of the Hebrew and Christian Scriptures were excluded as presuppositions of these procedures. Scripture was to be approached as any other ancient document.

Thus, a whole series of issues emerged which the precritical method had largely ignored. These included authorship of a work, written or oral sources that the author used, the unity or composite character of a work, the meaning of a biblical book as an independent literary entity, and the historical conditions in Israel or in early Christianity that obtained at the time of the composition (the so-called "Sitz im Leben" of a text). All these questions were open to purely rational analysis and excluded divine influences as factors of interpretation. Other, less scientific and more ideological factors arising out of rationalism, for example, the impossibility of miracles, were also operative. By the end of the nineteenth century, Protestant scholars by and large worked with the biblical evidence on the basis of the theory of sources and the literary forms or genres ("form criticism").[54] The process of composing the work ("redaction criticism")[55] emerged in the second half of the twentieth century and has enjoyed wide acceptance.[56]

The historical-critical method continues to evolve, but by and large no longer operates on the assumption that its practice is value-free, purely objective, and rigidly scientific. It also struggles to assure its predominance in the growing field of methods of interpretation. It is not convinced that newer methods of interpretation bear a weight equal to its own or can operate independent of the historical meaning of the text. Are the

54. See Edgar V. McKnight, *What Is Form Criticism?* (Philadelphia: Fortress Press, 1969); and John Muddiman, "Form Criticism," in *A Dictionary of Biblical Interpretation,* 240–43.

55. See Norman Perrin, *What Is Redaction Criticism?* (Philadelphia: Fortress Press, 1969); and Christopher M. Tuckett, "Redaction Criticism," in *A Dictionary of Biblical Interpretation,* 580–82.

56. Roman Catholic scholars would adopt the methods of higher criticism only in the 1950s and 1960s. See Alexa Suelzer and John S. Kselman, "Modern Old Testament Criticism," in *NJBC,* 1126–27 [69:55–61]; and John S. Kselman and Ronald D. Witherup, "Modern New Testament Criticism," in *New Jerome Bible Commentary* [hereafter *NJBC*], ed. Raymond E. Brown, Joseph A. Fitzmyer, and Roland E. Murphy (Englewood Cliffs, N.J.: Prentice Hall, 1990) 1142–44 [70:71–77].

proponents of newer methods too eager to move beyond the literal sense, just as medieval exegetes preferred allegory, tropology, and anagogy?

How did the practitioners of higher criticism understand apostolicity? There were many questions about the historicity of the twelve apostles. Did they go back to the ministry of Jesus, or were they an invention of the emerging sect of Jewish Christians? Did Jesus ever call them "apostles"? Where did the term come from? It is not found in the Judaism of Jesus' day. Did it originate in the Jewish institution of the *sheluhim*[57] or was it an invention of the Gentile mission? Why are there various understandings of an apostle in the New Testament and how are they related to one another? Were the concerns for orderly succession, evident in Luke's Acts of the Apostles and in the Pastoral Epistles, theological devices designed to answer the question of the delay of Christ's parousia and the continued existence of the church in a longer expanse of history? These, and many other questions, could not be answered by exegetes with doctrinal or confessional presuppositions but would have to be argued for, denied, or clarified on the basis of the strength of the arguments brought forth by their exponents. This has led to a proliferation of points of view, without any one view in general able to convince all readers. In the end, higher criticism, like rationality itself, seems to pose more questions than offer answers. Once again, have we arrived at a point where a new paradigm is needed, given the impossibility of arriving at the vaunted purely rational solution?

A Case Study: Karl Rahner, S.J.

Rahner had been trained in the neo-Scholasticism of his day, but he had also attended the University of Freiburg for postgraduate studies, where he attended the lectures of Martin Heidegger (1889–1976). His doctoral thesis was an attempt to retrieve Thomas Aquinas' epistemology with the help of Kantian transcendentalism.[58] Upon returning to the

---

57. Karl H. Rengstorf thought the Jewish rabbinic practice of sending out plenipotentiary emissaries from Jerusalem was the source of the Christian adaptation of apostleship. *Sheluhim* ("apostles") is the Hebrew plural form of these official emissaries. See my discussion of Rengstorf's theory and Francis H. Agnew's reworking of it in ch. 1, pp. 11–12.

58. It was published in German as *Geist in Welt* and translated into English by William Dych, S.J., as *Spirit in the World* (New York: Herder and Herder, 1968 [reprinted by The Continuum Publishing Company, 1994]). On the stages in the emergence of Rahner's fundamental theology throughout his career, see Werner Winfried, *Fundamentaltheologie bei Karl Rahner. Denkwege und Paradigmen* (Tübingen: A. Francke Verlag, 2003).

University of Innsbruck, Rahner devoted years to the study of the Fathers of the church, especially the Greeks, and edited the 28th edition (1952) of the famous handbook of official church teachings, Denziger's *Enchiridon symbolorum*. Rahner knew the tradition well, but he had also breathed in deeply the spirit of modern philosophy. He was committed to bringing the two into dialogue with each other. Though he was not the first to do so, Rahner undoubtedly was the most influential theologian in the movement which came to be called Transcendental Thomism.[59] It stressed the dynamism of Thomas' thought and excluded the extrinsicism[60] connected with the division introduced after Thomas between nature and grace, the natural and the supernatural.[61] But unlike Thomas, it also introduced Kant's transcendental analysis of reality as known, or noumenal reality. Rahner thought that he could be true to the basic insights of Aquinas while engaging philosophy on its own terms. Rahner's orthodoxy was derived from his unquestioning support of the official teaching of the church, under the guidance of the *Doctor Angelicus*, and in dialogue with modernity's great thinkers, especially Kant and Hegel, and the contemporary representative of a return to an ontological starting point, Heidegger. How did Rahner employ his tools to address the issue of apostolicity?

Rahner took up the question of apostolicity in an essay that appeared in German in 1954. It was subsequently (1958) expanded into a short book, and became the first of what was to be a distinguished series edited by Rahner and Heinrich Schlier, *Quaestiones Disputatae*. In English Rahner's

59. See Otto Muck, *The Transcendental Method*, tr. William D. Seidensticker (New York: Herder and Herder, 1968); and Gerald A. McCool, "Rousselot's Intellectualism: The Internal Evolution of Thomism" and "Maréchal's Dialogue with Kant," in *From Unity to Pluralism*, 39–86 and 87–113 respectively.

60. See Stephen J. Duffy, *The Graced Horizon: Nature and Grace in Modern Catholic Thought* (Collegeville, Minn.: The Liturgical Press, 1992) 55–59, 86–89, and 170–72. "Extrinsicism" is the term often used to describe a theology of grace as not only unmerited by the graced person but also as superadded to a human nature that is assumed to be meaningful and complete in its own right. According to extrinsicism, the supernatural, or grace, adds nothing directly to nature but provides the human being with an additional goal or finality. Human nature is related to grace only negatively, i.e., human nature does not preclude the gift of grace by God, but human nature is not oriented toward grace in any positive sense either.

61. See Stephen J. Duffy, "Karl Rahner: Transcendental Anthropology," in *The Dynamics of Grace*, 261–341; and John P. Galvin, "The Invitation of Grace," in *A World of Grace: An Introduction to the Themes and Foundation's of Karl Rahner's Theology*, ed. Leo J. O'Donovan (New York: The Crossroad Publishing Company, 1981) 64–75.

book was entitled *Inspiration in the Bible*.[62] Instead of treating the inspiration of Scripture as an isolated divine act guaranteeing the inerrancy of the truth taught therein, Rahner envisioned inspiration in dynamic, historical, social, and christological terms. The divine acted in and through the real agency of the human, just as in the christological mystery, the hypostatic union. The two natures of Christ did not stand statically alongside one another, the human nature deferring to the divine in one circumstance, the divine nature deferring to the human in another. No, they acted in harmony because they were really ordered to each other. But the human, according to the thought of modernity, is thoroughly historical and therefore is involved in some form of growth or self-perfection. A process of inspiration, and subsequently a process of the development of the dogmatic understanding of the Scriptures, is inevitable. This process, in fact, *is* Scripture. There is a real history of revelation, just as there is a real history of salvation—not only a story or narrative about salvation but a continuing unfolding of that salvation in time. The history of revelation takes place paradigmatically in the church, as a tangible proclamation of what God is doing universally for humankind. Thus, the church comes to be historically in the process of the inspiration of Scripture.

In addition to historical, processive, and christological dimensions, inspiration is also a social process involving the community of believers. Scripture does not come to the church in some pure, antiseptic form—from heaven as it were—but only as mediated through human experiences expressed in human words. God's truth comes to us *in and through* our historical wrestling with this truth. As such, Scripture is no mere record of the church's early experience of Christ and of its institution by this same Christ, but is an act that is the very "constitution" of the church. It has normative character,[63] but, as the church's "constitution," is in constant dynamic unfolding, even as salvation is still unfolding in human history. Scripture is not on the sidelines, as it were, rooting for salvation, but, as grace, is dynamically effecting this very salvation. Apostolicity, then, is inseparable from the coming-to-be and the continuing existence of the church. To speak of apostolicity is first of all to speak of the whole church, even though the officeholders in the church will have their own unique and indispensable expression of this same apostolicity.

62. Tr. Charles H. Henkey (New York: Herder and Herder, 1961).
63. Theologians use the pleonasm that Scripture is *norma normans*, i.e., there is no higher norm of its teaching and its truth. Some even speak of a *norma normans non normata*!

The hallmarks of the modern worldview are evident. Though some of these characteristics have been modified, especially Rahner's stress on the social character of inspiration, his insistence on the inherent value of the human (the *humanum*) and of human agency, progress and development, and historicity should be noted. A little reflection also shows his harmony with the universalizing tendency of modernity. Scripture is the "constitution" of the church, while it is also the expression of what God is doing for the salvation of all humankind. Rahner's famous writings on non-Christians as "anonymous Christians" represent his attempt to include all of humankind in God's salvific will.[64] If God's will to save all is effective, then in some way or other all must be aggregated to Christ, and so, albeit anonymously and subconsciously, are "Christian." In this way Rahner is trying to be faithful to the teachings of Scripture itself. But his aim of total inclusiveness also shares in the spirit of modernity's worldview. Questions have been raised regarding the underlying purpose of such religious inclusiveness. Is its goal to colonize the other? Does it really pay attention to the differences of other religions? Does it understand the role of language and culture as differentiating human societies? Rahner appears to labor under these same limitations, and so might be counted a representative of a Catholic ecclesiology that operates under the assumptions of the modern worldview. Rahner's new paradigm of the inspiration of Scripture is a sign of his drawing on the worldview of modernity to mediate the Christian faith and to articulate his theology.

Conclusion

In the short period that Roman Catholic ecclesiology has accepted the challenge of modernity's worldview, what image of the church has emerged? Vatican II called for collegiality among the bishops, including

---

64. See Rahner, "Anonymous Christians," in *Theological Investigations,* tr. Krüger, 6:390–98; "Anonymous Christianity and the Missionary Task of the Church," in *Theological Investigations,* tr. David Bourke (New York: The Seabury Press, 1974) 12:161–78; "Observations on the Problem of the 'Anonymous Christian,'" in *Theological Investigations,* tr. David Bourke (New York: The Seabury Press, 1976) 14:280–94; "Anonymous and Explicit Faith," in *Theological Investigations,* tr. David Morland (New York: The Crossroad Publishing Company, 1983) 16:52–59. See also Karl-Heinz Weger, "Anonymous Christianity and God's Universal Revelation," in *Karl Rahner: An Introduction to His Theology,* tr. David Smith (New York: The Seabury Press, 1980) 112–41; and Gerald O'Collins, "Anonymous Christians," in *Dictionary of Fundamental Theology,* 10.

the Bishop of Rome as head of the college. The Council also called for a sense of the presbyters of the local church constituting a presbyterium, or body of presbyters, in lieu of a corps of ministers who act primarily as individual professionals. It also called for the laity to assume responsibility for both the world and the church. The coresponsibility of the laity in the church was expressed in the Council's teaching on the *sensus fidelium*— or the sense of the faithful.[65] The model which emerged approximated more closely that of a community of believers (a *congregatio fidelium*) than had ever been the case before in Catholic theology. In the postconciliar period, calls for more democratic forms of decision making, for the election of bishops, for respecting the "rights" of the faithful, for greater use of the principle of subsidiarity in the church itself,[66] for the establishment of parochial and diocesan pastoral councils, and for more public discussion of problems in the church came to be seen by some as threats to the unity of the church and to the legitimate authority of officeholders. The Council opened up a spirit of taking responsibility in the church that called for more participatory structures. But to many, the very idea smacks of a Congregationalist understanding of the church that is foreign to Catholicism, and the ecclesiology of Vatican II seems to breathe more modernity's spirit of democracy than the spirit of the gospel. Furthermore, the Council preferred to speak of God's salvific plans for all humankind and referred to the church as the universal "sacrament of salvation" rather than as the exclusive community of the redeemed. Some have wondered whether modernity's spirit of egalitarianism has not supplanted the understanding of the church bequeathed by Christ. And yet, despite the church's belated acceptance of the challenge of modernity and the conflicts the Council provoked within the church, the world seems to have moved on to yet another worldview—that of postmodernity. It is time to look at the emergence and meaning of this highly problematic worldview.

65. See John J. Burkhard, "*Sensus fidei:* Meaning, Role and Future of a Teaching of Vatican II," *Louvain Studies* 17 (1992) 18–34; idem, "*Sensus fidei:* Theological Reflection since Vatican II," *The Heythrop Journal* 34 (1993) 41–59 and 123–34 [with copious bibliography]; and idem "*Sensus fidelium,*" in *New Catholic Encyclopedia,* 15 vols., ed. Berard Marthaler (2nd ed.; Detroit: Gale Group and Washington, D.C.: The Catholic University of America, 2003) 12:916–18, and Ormond Rush, "*Sensus fidei:* Faith 'Making Sense' of Revelation," *Theological Studies* 62 (2001) 231–61.

66. See John J. Burkhard, "The Interpretation and Application of Subsidiarity in Ecclesiology: An Overview of the Theological and Canonical Literature," *The Jurist* 58 (1998) 279–342 [with copious bibliography]; and idem, "Subsidiarity in the Church," in *New Catholic Encyclopedia* (2nd ed.) 13:569–70.

CHAPTER SIX

Apostolicity in a Postmodern World

Few words today are employed more frequently in speech and writing than the term "postmodern." But what is postmodernism? Its bewildering uses seem to defy definition. One commentator has remarked: "Most of us would agree . . . that the 'postmodern phenomenon' eludes all clear conceptual definition. In a sense postmodernism is more of a cultural attitude and a point of view, and never a doctrinal platform that might lend itself to some kind of systematic survey. In this sense postmodernity then escapes any and all linear characterizations."[1] Another author has commented appropriately: "The postmodern era may be far from midday, but it is well past dawn."[2] Though it might be hard to define at this moment, it is becoming increasingly impossible to dispute that something quite new is emerging. It is my contention that postmodernity represents a new worldview, certainly for the cultures of the Western world, and perhaps globally. It is important then to spell out postmodernity carefully.

An Attempt to Delineate Postmodernism

In the 1970s, the terms "postmodern," "postmodernity," and "postmodernism" began to appear frequently in print. Gavin Hyman has indicated that "postmodernism" first appeared in relation to literary

1. J. Wentzel van Huyssteen, "Rationality and the Postmodern Challenge in Science," in *The Shape of Rationality: Toward Interdisciplinarity in Theology and Science* (Grand Rapids: Wm. B. Eerdmans Publishing Company, 1999) 17–60, at 29.
2. James B. Miller, "The Emerging Postmodern World," in *Postmodern Theology: Christian Faith in a Pluralist World*, ed. Frederic B. Burnham (San Francisco: HarperSanFrancisco, 1989) 1–19, at 8.

criticism—more precisely to Hispanic literary criticism which coined the term "postmodernismo." Next, the terms were applied to architecture, and finally they were employed in the context of philosophy, social and cultural analysis, and theology.[3] Though the acceptance of these terms is quite recent, the roots of the phenomenon go back to the nineteenth century and the thought of Friedrich Nietzsche (1844–1900) and in the early twentieth century to Martin Heidegger (1889–1976). The thrust of hermeneutics in Heidegger's philosophy led to the emergence of French deconstruction theory,[4] often associated with the French thinker Jacques Derrida (1930–).[5] Michel Foucault (1926–1984) also added to the radical positions of postmodern thought by his historico-sociological studies of madness, the modern penal system, power, and sexuality.[6] The terms gained increased frequency and popularity after the appearance in 1979 of Jean-François Lyotard's *The Postmodern Condition: A Report on Knowledge*.[7] Today, these terms are among the most prominent in the literary, cultural, sociological, philosophical, and theological lexicons. But the question remains: Is postmodernism something genuinely novel, or is it another manifestation of the modern worldview?

Several prominent cultural analysts and philosophers maintain that postmodernism is only a manifestation of late modernity and does not constitute in itself a separate movement. It is an extension of the modern spirit.[8] Others hold that postmodernism is truly a departure from, and

3. Gavin Hyman, *The Predicament of Postmodern Theology: Radical Orthodoxy or Nihilist Textualism?* (Louisville: Westminster John Knox, 2002) 11–19 ["Postmodernism: A Cultural and Philosophical (Hi)Story"]. Hyman draws heavily on Perry Anderson, *The Origins of Postmodernity* (London: Verso Press, 1998).

4. See Christopher Norris, *Deconstruction: Theory and Practice* (New York: Routledge, 1982); Samuel C. Wheeler, "Deconstruction," in *The Cambridge Dictionary of Philosophy*, ed. Robert Audi (2nd ed.; New York: Cambridge University Press, 1999) 211–12; and Roger Scruton, *Modern Philosophy: An Introduction and Survey* (New York: Penguin Books, 1994) 477–79 ["Deconstruction"].

5. See Martin C. Dillon, "Derrida, Jacques," in *The Cambridge Dictionary of Philosophy*, 223.

6. See Gary Gutting, "Foucault, Michel," in ibid., 320–21.

7. Tr. Geoff Bennington and Brian Massumi (Minneapolis: University of Minnesota Press, 1984).

8. Individuals who are often cited as representing the view that late modernity reveals characteristics that are called postmodern but do not constitute a newly emerging worldview or even a new paradigm, include, among others, Jürgen Habermas, *The Philosophical Discourse of Modernity: Twelve Lectures*, tr. Frederick G. Lawrence (Cambridge, Mass.: The MIT Press, 1987); Albrecht Wellmer, *The Persistence of Modernity: Essays on Aesthetics, Ethics, and Postmodernism*, tr. David Midgley (Cambridge, Mass.: The MIT Press, 1991); Charles Taylor, *The Sources of the Self: The Making of the Modern Identity* (Cambridge, Mass.:

even the rejection of, the spirit of modernity. The latter position appears to be in the ascendant, and if it is correct, we would have to consider the possibility that a new worldview is emerging. In the light of the question posed by this book, we need to ask what difference a new worldview might have on the topic of apostolicity. Before considering these ramifications, let us examine postmodernism in greater detail.[9]

Postmodernism manifests both positive and negative responses to modernity.[10] To many, its face is overwhelmingly hostile to much that modernity represents. Yet, it is not a wholesale rejection of modernity or a naïve desire to return to an earlier, premodern vision of the world. For instance, it does not desire to compromise human rights and democracy, or the benefits of universal education and modern medicine and technological advances. It does not argue for a return to patriarchal societies at the expense of the liberation women have already won. What, then, does it advocate?

Postmodern authors and commentators on postmodernism usually point to a whole series of ideas that characterize postmodernity. I cannot examine all of them in this chapter, since that would take me too far afield. However, I propose to study five postmodern characteristics, eventually with a view to examining how they impact on the book's topic, namely,

---

Harvard University Press, 1989); idem, *The Ethics of Authenticity* (Cambridge, Mass.: Harvard University Press, 1991); idem, *A Catholic Modernity? Charles Taylor's Marianist Award Lecture,* ed. James L. Heft (New York: Oxford University Press, 1999) 13–37; and John Thornhill, *Modernity: Christianity's Estranged Child Reconstructed* (Grand Rapids: Wm. B. Eerdmans Publishing Company, 2000).

9. A good thumbnail sketch of postmodernism can be found in Sandra M. Schneiders, "Religious Life in a Postmodern Context: Faith and Fidelity against the Grain," in *Finding the Treasure: Locating Catholic Religious Life in a New Ecclesial and Cultural Context,* Religious Life in a New Millenium, vol. 1 (New York: Paulist Press, 2000) 99–119. See my "Defining Gospel Life in a Postmodern Culture," in *Franciscan Identity and Postmodern Culture,* ed. Kathleen A. Warren (St. Bonaventure, N.Y.: The Franciscan Institute, 2003) 35–54, at 45–54 ["Postmodernism and Gospel Life"], together with the other essays in the collection of the Washington Theological Union Symposium Papers, May 24–26, 2002.

10. Helpful books on modernity include the following: Roy Porter, *The Creation of the Modern World: The Untold Story of the British Enlightenment* (New York: W. W. Norton & Company, 2000); Louis Dupré, *Passage to Modernity: An Essay in the Hermeneutics of Nature and Culture* (New Haven: Yale University Press, 1993); Robert B. Pippin, *Modernism as a Philosophical Problem: On the Dissatisfactions of European High Culture* (Oxford: Blackwell Publishers Ltd., 1991); Hans Blumenberg, *The Legitimacy of the Modern Age,* tr. Robert M. Wallace (Cambridge, Mass.: The MIT Press, 1985); and Peter Gay, *The Enlightenment, An Interpretation,* 2 vols. (London: Weidenfeld and Nicolson, 1967 and 1970).

apostolicity. The five topics are (1) the rejection of a dualistic view of the world, (2) the rejection of any form of "foundationalism," (3) the rejection of "totalization" and the role of metanarratives, (4) a threatening anti-human nihilism, and (5) the return of the "other."

Five Postmodern Characteristics

Rejection of a Dualistic View of the World

Modernity is associated with the emergence of modern science. In the premodern era, of course, there was such a thing as science, but its methods of observation, proof, prediction, and explanation were bound up with the assumptions of what constituted the world as dictated by the traditions of society. Modern science distinguished itself from earlier forms by its methodology of objective observation of the phenomena of the world. This meant that it paid no regard to the preexisting traditions of what constituted reality. Modern science liberated observation from the trammels of traditional theory and limited the influence of subjective factors in determining the structure and laws of reality. Modern science developed the distinction between object and subject in an unprecedented way. This is how on the one hand Isaac Newton could develop a "mechanical" view of the world and how René Descartes on the other hand viewed the human being dualistically as two separate things—"extended non-thinking substance" [*res extensa*] and "non-extended thinking substance" [*res cogitans*], that is, "body" and "mind."[11] There is no underlying unity in the cosmos or in the human being, only two antithetically related "things." This extreme opposition came to be associated with objective, physical, empirical reality, that is, science, and subjective, immaterial, spiritual reality, that is, the human person. Each has its own realm of activity and value, but the two realms are ultimately unable to be united or related to each other. Knowledge came to be associated exclusively with what is objectively, that is, scientifically, knowable. The subject ruled in the area of feelings, imagination, values, and faith, that is, in the areas of politics, art, religion, and ethics. Knowledge in the strict sense was not attributable to the latter.

Postmodern thinking has difficulty with the total separation of reality into objective and subjective spheres. Concretely, this separation is

11. The translations of *res extensa* and *res cogitans* are from Calvin O. Schrag. See "Pluralism," in *The Cambridge Dictionary of Philosophy*, 714.

experienced as harmful and threatening to the human species and to the environment. In science, this dualism leads to a view of nature as just so many "objects" to be dominated by humans. The threat of nuclear anni-hilation and the environmental crisis we are experiencing seem to be the direct result of a rigid separation of the world into objects and subjects. Human beings have felt free to manipulate the world of objects to their own advantage, with the result that the manipulation seems to spell dis-aster for the human race, for other species, and for the planet. Modern science is held responsible for a doomsday scenario that many of our contemporaries share. Postmodern science is in search of a newer and more adequate approach to the world that goes beyond the dualism in-herited from modernity.

Philosophy and the human sciences in general have also lost confi-dence in the unquestioned blessing of dividing the world neatly into ob-jects and subjects. The human being suffered by the various reductionistic attempts to explain subjecthood. Persons were understood simply in terms of objective and materialist forces. Men and women seemed to be in-creasingly determined by emerging technology. The specifically human appeared to be lost. Philosophy, particularly twentieth-century European existentialism, was flattened out and restricted to the realm of human in-teriority. It lost much of its customarily broad reach into the areas of cosmology, politics, esthetics, social ethics, and so forth. Also, the rich va-riety of methods in philosophy and the human sciences was sacrificed to the unidimensionality of scientific method.

Rejection of Foundationalism

In light of the search for "objective" knowledge of the universe and of the "world of truth," both science and philosophy had recourse to various forms of foundationalism.[12] As the term is used today, founda-tionalism refers to absolutely irreducible principles of knowledge and

---

12. See Paul K. Moser, "Foundationalism," in *The Cambridge Dictionary of Philosophy,* 321–23; and Nancey Murphy and James Wm. McClendon, "Distinguishing Modern and Postmodern Theologies," *Modern Theology* 5 (1988–89) 191–214, at 192–93. See also the reflections of John E. Thiel, *Nonfoundationalism* (Minneapolis: Fortress Press, 1994) 17–19, 82–84, 87–88, and 94–97; Thomas G. Guardino, "Foundationalism and Contemporary Theology," *Philosophy & Theology* 3 (1989) 241–52; idem, "Revelation and Foundational-ism: Toward Hermeneutical and Ontological Appropriateness," *Modern Theology* 6 (1990) 221–35; and idem, "Philosophy within Theology in Light of the Foundationalism De-bate," *Philosophy & Theology* 9 (1995–96) 57–69.

action whose truth imposes itself with irrefutable evidentiary power. They are "first" principles, since nothing can precede them, and as such they are unquestioned. The indispensable role played by tradition in the premodern worldview was assumed by "absolute" or "unquestionable" foundational principles. All of our human knowledge or striving "rests" on these foundations. Doubt the foundations and you call everything into question.

In light of the skepticism following on the conflicting claims of Protestant and Catholic Christians in the post-Reformation period, Descartes felt the need for just such unshakeable foundations. He found certainty in the fact that he could not deny his own existence as a thinking subject. That overwhelming fact, at the very least, could not be gainsaid. Its undeniable truth became the firm basis for practicing real methodical doubt regarding other issues. Out of this method came further truth, because it was based on solid foundations.[13] Likewise, the early scientists of the modern era experienced the increasing disparity between their observations, made with the help of the newly developed telescope and microscope, and the inherited theory buttressed by long tradition. They found the situation quite intolerable. Scientists, too, desired irrefutable foundations for understanding the physical world.

Both of these powerful intellectual movements happened around the same time and mutually reinforced each other's desire for certain truth. The search for foundations resulted in the acceptance of the existence of absolute and timeless truths. In modern science this meant the establishment of *universal laws* governing the universe, while in philosophy it meant the *exaltation of reason* over all other human dimensions. Science and philosophy eventually parted company and went their separate ways, but neither doubted its unassailable foundations. However, to philosophers science seemed to have success in its task of obtaining objective knowledge, while the philosophical pursuit of truth encountered one conflicting explanation after another. Scientific knowledge grew incrementally, while philosophy seemed to be hopelessly splintered and incapable of arriving at any truth all could agree upon. Increasingly, philosophy modeled itself on science's strict methods of observation and verification.

Postmodernism has shown itself unalterably opposed to all foundational principles. This is true not only for philosophy and the human

13. For Descartes the ideal of knowledge was still provided by mathematics. He wanted to replicate mathematical certitude for philosophy and understanding human affairs.

sciences but for modern physical science as well. For the latter, the discovery of quantum physics by Niels Bohr broke the hegemony of Newton's mechanical universe founded on general principles. Some aspects of the universe simply resisted explanation in terms of Newtonian physics. Werner Heisenberg's principle of indeterminacy and Albert Einstein's theory of relativity have shaken a scientific universe based on foundational principles. Moreover, the pure objectivity of modern science was called into question by the admission that science does not explain reality in an unobserved state but as always under study by a human investigator. We know reality only as studied or under investigation, never as simply given.

Philosophy, too, has rejected foundationalism, but for other reasons. In the second half of the nineteenth century and in the twentieth, philosophers gave greater attention to human freedom. It resists full explanation in terms of obeying the laws of nature or conscience. Human freedom is greater than simple obedience and always contains an element of creativity. Moreover, newer human sciences had emerged—history in the modern sense, sociology, cultural anthropology, and psychology. Absolute laws were simply not applicable in these fields, despite efforts to discover them.

Rejection of "Totalization" and the Role of Metanarratives

The modern ideal of rationally comprehending all of reality resulted in efforts to totally capture reality in universal formulas and propositions. Postmodern writers often speak of efforts at "totalization." Modernity tries to fix reality in one normative and superior form. All other understandings are deemed inferior and inadequate. Philosophically, the phenomenon can be seen in the various "systems" or complete explanations developed by modernist thinkers, for example, Karl Marx, Georg W. F. Hegel, and others. Politically, totalization assumed the forms of militarism, colonialism, and imperialism, by which modern nation states assumed the right to occupy other countries and confiscate their natural resources for their own national ends. Another example of such totalizing thinking was the various national totalitarianisms, for example, Nazi Germany or Communist Soviet Russia, which dominated the political scene in the twentieth century. Anything that did not serve the totalizing scheme was deemed unworthy and expendable.

Modern totalizing systems were always accompanied by narratives that recounted the ideals and absolute rights championed by the system.

Modernity's truth is communicated not only in propositions, universal principles, and general laws, but equally in powerful narratives. Post-modern thinkers have become especially sensitive to the inherent ideologies expressed in these master narratives. Their interpretations of national or religious grand narratives started from the assumption of the presence of a hidden ideology. Postmodern thinkers developed a hermeneutics of suspicion, a hermeneutics that aimed to unmask the covert prejudices and manipulations of the grand narrative.

Many postmodern thinkers paid greater attention to the structure and uses of language. Narratives were studied to discern the negative purposes of story telling, that is, to keep certain persons or groups in their place or to deprive them of their rights. These grand narratives are often referred to as "metanarratives." Gavin Hyman writes: "A metanarrative, precisely be-cause it is a metanarrative, must seek to 'explain' and 'position' *everything*, that is, every other narrative and every other interpretation of the world. This is because, for a metanarrative, there can be no *remainder* or *reserve*."[14] Hyman shows how the modern understanding of a metanarrative excludes the coexistence of competing or complementary narratives.

In modernity, grand narratives operate in all the fields of human understanding. Each area tells its own grand narrative. One of the most important is modernity's own grand narrative of endless human progress. The abstractions and generalizations of modern science, sociology, phi-losophy, and so forth are made available in the story that human beings are perfectible, can enjoy happiness, rid the world of conflict, and pro-vide unending material wealth for all the world's citizens. But when post-modern thinkers have searched for the signs of the fulfillment of such promises, they find the secular grand narrative illusory and deceptive. They find wars and genocides, a growing gap between rich and poor, spreading hunger among human beings, the depredation of the natural environment, increased militarism, widespread migration of uprooted peoples, the harshness of economic globalization and greed, unchecked violence in our cities, patriarchy and androcentrism, and so forth. Post-moderns have lost confidence in modernity's master narrative of human perfectibility and progress.

The world's major religions have their grand narratives, and post-modern thinkers have submitted them also to harsh criticism. Instead of promoting the harmony with self, with others, and with the cosmos that

14. Hyman, *The Predicament of Postmodern Theology*, 78. Italics are the author's.

the religious grand narratives promise, one often finds intolerance, persecution, witch hunting, and subservience to the national, political, or social agenda. Postmoderns do not presume the truth or the purity of motives of religious grand narratives. The hermeneutics of suspicion practiced on religious grand narratives helps account for the demise of public affiliation with religion, especially in the West. However, it also helps to understand the suspicion toward other religions. It is assumed that religion per se is self-serving, intolerant, and leads to deception. Religion is not liberative.

The response of postmodern thinkers has been to renounce the grand narrative and privilege what Lyotard calls "petits récits"–"modest narratives." Each one's story counts: the stories of individuals, small groups, tribes, nations small and great, the major religions and their religious denominations, women, the oppressed, and so forth. Which narrative holds the greater claim to attention, the narrative of Christian black American slaves longing for freedom or the Christian narrative as told by their white Christian masters? The narrative of black Christian South Africans or the Christian narrative as told by the white Christian supporters of apartheid? The narrative of early Christian origins that challenges us to consider the equality of men and women in the community or the narrative that stresses male superiority and a rigid hierarchy of roles? Narratives and their memories can be dangerous and subversive.[15]

Threat of Anti-Human Nihilism

Perhaps there is no more threatening aspect of postmodernity in the minds of many contemporaries than the claim of nihilism. Yet, many people today are not clear about what nihilism is. Is it absolutely opposed to value and meaning? Does it mean just one thing? Is it corrosive of all meaning? Is it intrinsically irrational? Does it commit us to nothingness? A glance into the origins and development of nihilism might be helpful.

The beginnings of nihilistic thought can be located in the second half of the nineteenth century.[16] In the wake of the political, social, and

15. See Johann-Baptist Metz, "The Dangerous Memory of the Freedom of Jesus Christ: The Presence of the Church in Society" and "Narrative," in *Faith in History and Society: Toward a Practical Fundamental Theology*, tr. David Smith (New York: The Seabury Press, 1980) 88–99 and 205–18 respectively.

16. Gavin Hyman presents an alternate explanation in *The Predicament of Postmodern Theology*, 96–98. This explanation places the origins of nihilism in the late thirteenth century and the fourteenth, in the thought of John Duns Scotus and William of Ockham. See

intellectual ferment of the time, the idea that there is one meaning to reality or one basic value in human acts was called into question. To some extent, the dominance of a bourgeois mindset and of bourgeois morality exacerbated the search for the underlying meaning of life. In the face of the threats posed by the questions of the day, society resorted all too easily to conformism—social, moral, and religious. A nihilistic attitude appealed to many intellectuals and artists as a way of counteracting a stultifying and reactionary conformism. Nihilism consisted in assuming a dismissive or a radical position. Dismissive nihilism refused to take social, moral, and religious conformism seriously, preferring to mock it or render it harmless by the doubt raised by a thousand questions. Radical nihilism, however, called the very foundations of humanism and society into question. It waged a frontal assault on the assumption that there is any inherent or fixed meaning/value in life. To the radicals, life is intrinsically empty of meaning. Radical nihilism came to expression in Russian authors in the nineteenth century, for example, Ivan Sergeevich Turgenev (1818–1883), who coined the word "nihilism" itself. But there have always been questions about the internal consistency of the concept. Is a position of radical nihilism intellectually tenable? Here, the example of Nietzsche is instructive.

Friedrich Nietzsche was no friend of Christianity, conventional morality, or the blessings of industrialization. He saw all these as trammels on human creativity and ingenuity. Nihilism was helpful to Nietzsche in undermining the prevalent humanism as false humanism. He declared God dead not in a purely rhetorical sense, but not in an absolute sense either. When he declared "God is dead," he intended the God of Christianity, a God whom he understood as limiting human greatness and a Christianity that focused on the beyond. The God of Christianity had to be declared dead for human beings to realize their true nature. Richard Schacht has pointed to the division among philosophers as to how to interpret Nietzsche. He discerns two groups. In Schacht's view, one group

take[s] seriously his concern to find a way of *overcoming* the nihilism he believed to result from traditional ways of thinking. . . . Notwithstanding

---

the differing interpretation of Adrian Pabst, "De la chrétienté à la modernité? Lecture critique des thèses de *Radical Orthodoxy* sur la rupture scotiste et ockhamienne et sur le renouveau de la théologie de saint Thomas d'Aquin," *Revue des sciences philosophiques et théologiques* 86 (2002) 561–99.

his frequent characterization as a nihilist, therefore, Nietzsche in fact sought to counter and overcome the nihilism he expected to prevail in the aftermath of the collapse and abandonment of traditional religious and metaphysical modes of interpretation and evaluation. While he was highly critical of the latter, it was not his intention merely to oppose them; for he further attempted to make out the possibility of forms of truth and knowledge to which philosophical interpreters of life and the world might aspire.[17]

In the literature on postmodernism, no one figures more prominently as a nihilist than Nietzsche, and yet it is not at all certain how extreme the form of nihilism was that he espoused. He just might have subverted nihilism from within.

In a fascinating chapter on nihilism, Gavin Hyman points to the need to make certain distinctions.[18] He distinguishes between "metaphysical" (or substantive) nihilism and "fictional" (or narrational) nihilism. Hyman reviews the various interpretations of Nietzsche's thought in Martin Heidegger, Jacques Derrida, and Gianni Vattimo, and concludes that a unitary understanding of Nietzsche regarding nihilism ultimately escapes us. Heidegger in particular cannot get beyond the metaphysical framework for understanding Nietzsche. Derrida comes closer in that he discerns the importance of "styles" of interpretations of being in Nietzsche rather than a fixed teaching regarding nihilism. Finally, Vattimo points out the inherent "polar tensions" in Nietzsche that can be given justice only by a hermeneutical reading of Nietzsche. There is no single or identifiable teaching regarding nihilism by Nietzsche, only perspectives and points of view. Hyman concludes:

> It would appear, then, that although interpretations of Nietzsche have been diverse and complex, it is nonetheless possible to identify two dominant readings: one that interprets Nietzsche as the last metaphysician, expounding a nihilistic metaphysical doctrine of "the way the world is," and another that interprets Nietzsche as the first philosopher to overcome metaphysics, clearing the way for a hermeneutic understanding of philosophy, where nihilism is just one story among others.[19]

17. Richard Schacht, "Nietzsche, Friedrich Wilhelm," in *The Cambridge Dictionary of Philosophy*, 614, 616.
18. Hyman, "(A/)Theology and Nihilism," *The Predicament of Postmodern Theology*, 95–118.
19. Ibid., 103.

Hyman maintains that behind attempts to express "metaphysical or substantive nihilism" lies a more fundamental and ultimately unattainable "pure nihilism." Pure nihilism appears to act like a "limit concept" in as much as it expresses something that cannot be represented but must be thought in order to make sense of "substantive nihilism." Hyman writes of it:

> But if metaphysical nihilism is indeed engaged in the act of representation, what exactly does it seek to represent? It is at this point and in answer to this question that I invoke a third form of nihilism, what I shall call a "pure" nihilism. It is, however, distinct from the other two forms of nihilism in that it cannot be expressed. Indeed, the more one speaks about it, the more one distances oneself from it. It is that which metaphysical nihilism yearns to represent, and in its attempt to do so, it ceaselessly moves further on. But this movement never reaches its goal; its journey never comes to an end. Metaphysical nihilism never reaches its goal of "pure" nihilism because the latter *cannot be represented.* Metaphysical nihilism thus has an impossible object, and as such, it is destined to die of its own impossible goal. Thus, in its (impossible) quest to achieve this pure nihilism, metaphysical nihilism undergoes a process of purification in which it purges itself of its metaphysical baggage.[20]

Postmodern nihilism is of a different sort. It accepts the fact of the impossibility of determining a nihilistic worldview in any substantive sense. Instead, it opts for the story or the fiction of nihilism. It "speaks" of the world as nihilistic, but cannot "define" it as such. Again, in the words of Hyman:

> In taking leave of this metaphysics, of this frustrated attempt at representation, nihilism is accomplished. It is also an overcoming of nihilism, however, because nihilism is now fictionalized along with everything else. Here, insofar as the nihilist story is still told, it is told precisely *as* a story. The absoluteness of nihilism is thus overcome, its privilege dissolved; for now nihilism is a story just like any other. Thus, the nihilism that once relativized everything else has now relativized itself.[21]

The stories of emptiness, of the void, of the absence of meaning, of moral relativism, and so forth are powerful and seem to be supported by the facts of how humans live and interact. But it also cannot exclude the telling of other stories, stories of meaning, value, life, and purpose. It

20. Ibid., 104. Italics are the author's.
21. Ibid., 105. Italics are the author's.

cannot, for instance, exclude the stories Christianity tells of life-giving death and transforming resurrection, of liberation and reconciliation. If it tried to exclude these other "absurd" stories, it would be hopelessly involved in self-contradiction. In making space for its stories of emptiness, it also makes space for stories of purpose and meaning. It is not at all clear, then, how disadvantaged Christianity is in the face of postmodern fictional nihilism. Unlike modernity, which sought to subordinate Christian faith to its exclusively rational vision, postmodernity cannot absolutely exclude faith. It is even possible that both narratives—that of nihilism and that of Christian faith—are free to communicate with each other.

Return of the "Other" and Relationality

One of the undisputed hallmarks of modernity is the focus on the human subject. This is commonly referred to as the "anthropocentric turn" or the "turn to the subject."[22] In the premodern worldview, the human being was understood primarily in terms of the cosmos and in terms of some theory of being. With modernity, the "subject" replaced the cosmos as the center of reflection and epistemology, that is, cognitional theory, displaced metaphysics at the center of philosophical reflection. Several consequences followed from this basic move toward the "subject." Modernity considered the person in terms of individuality—to be a person is to be autonomous and self-contained. Also, the primary act of being a person-as-individual is ethical conduct and not, as in the former worldview, reflection on ultimate realities, for example, being, goodness, truth, God, and so forth. Ethics, too, came to be understood in terms of (1) pragmatic acts, that is, acts not as reflecting some stable order or a tradition of good versus bad acts, (2) and autonomy, that is, ethics no longer flow out of a person's actions as constituting community or society but as constituting a "commonwealth of persons' rights." Postmodern thought opposes modernity on each of these points. Instead of the priority of the individual, postmodernity privileges interrelationships and community. Instead of absolute autonomy, postmodernity promotes various theories that draw upon traditions of human actions or practices.[23] And instead of theories of knowledge that advance discrete facts

22. See Nancey Murphy, *Theology in the Age of Scientific Reasoning* (Ithaca, N.Y.: Cornell University Press, 1990) 200–1.
23. The ethics of Alasdair MacIntyre have been described as "postmodern ethics." See MacIntyre, *After Virtue: A Study in Moral Theory* (2nd ed.; Notre Dame, Ind.: University

as constitutive of reality, postmodern epistemology and methodology stress holism and knowledge gained by scholars working in communities.[24] Two approaches in particular have come to characterize the post-modern subject—reflection on "the Other" and recourse to "relationality." Both notions have important repercussions on understanding faith today, and in terms of our topic, apostolicity, on how Christians can come to agreement on the church's apostolicity. Let us consider each.

Various theories of the "Other" are associated with the postmodern thinkers Emmanuel Levinas (1906–1995) and Paul Ricoeur (1913–). Their philosophical reflections challenge the extreme forms of autonomy of modernity by understanding the human subject in terms of some "Other."[25] In the course of his philosophical journey, Levinas has understood the "Other" in terms of some transcendent reality that stands over against the human being as the condition of the possibility of my human realization, and yet the "Other" does not surrender itself in its transcendence to me as subject.[26] Eventually, Levinas came to see the "Other" more in terms of other human beings who are the condition of the possibility of my human realization. Other human beings have claims on me—claims of justice and compassion especially.[27] "I" literally cannot exist as "human" without the human "Other." "I" am not diminished by

---

of Notre Dame Press, 1984); idem, *Whose Justice? Which Rationality?* (Notre Dame, Ind.: University of Notre Dame Press, 1988); and idem, *Three Rival Versions of Moral Enquiry: Encyclopedia, Genealogy, and Tradition,* The Gifford Lectures 1988 (Notre Dame, Ind.: University of Notre Dame Press, 1990).

24. On holism, see Murphy and McClendon, "Distinguishing Modern and Post-modern Theologies," 199–201 ["Postmodern Epistemology"]. The opposite of "holism" is "atomism," a view typical of modernity that sees reality as so many separated and non-unifiable entities.

25. Postmodern literature on the "Other" often speaks of "alterity," a philosophical term derived from the Latin adjectival forms meaning "other"—*alter, altera, alterum.*

26. Levinas concentrates on the "Other" in this first sense in his *Totality and Infinity: An Essay on Exteriority,* tr. Alphonso Lingis (Pittsburgh: Duquesne University Press, 1969 [original French edition, 1961]).

27. Levinas emphasizes this second understanding of the "Other" in his *Otherwise than Being, or Beyond Essence,* tr. Alphonso Lingis (The Hague: Martinus Nijhoff Publishers, 1981 [original French edition, 1974 and revised in 1978]. A word is in order on my practice of capitalizing "Other" in both instances of usage by Levinas. Sometimes Levinas capitalizes the French words *L'Autre* and *Autrui,* but often he does not. Levinas does not appear to follow any particular rule in capitalizing the words or not capitalizing them, according to his translator, Alphonso Lingis. I have preferred to simplify the matter by always capitalizing the words. Moreover, it should be noted that in the first instance of use by Levinas, the words are not capitalized because they refer to God in some cases.

the "Other," for the "Other" is an intrinsic dimension of "my" humanity.[28] Modernity's isolation of the person as "individual" is broken at its very base. I don't think it is necessary to make an unbridgeable distinction in Levinas's thought between the two understandings of the "Other"—in *my* terms, as the "Divine Other" and as the "Human Other." They are not mutually exclusive, and I don't think it is helpful to try to establish a priority of one over the other. The end result is a powerful postmodern humanism that shows its strength in the very teeth of such twentieth-century horrors as two world wars, innumerable regional wars, the Shoah, and ethnic cleansings. It is even possible that according to Levinas, both interpretations of the "Other" must be maintained. In either case, there is a transcendent quality to the "Other." As a result, Levinas has not rejected the centrality of ethics in modernity, but he has definitely redefined it.

Paul Ricoeur's approach is distinctive precisely in reference to Levinas' insistence on the centrality of ethics. In fact, Ricoeur's thought is framed in the light of Levinas' position, or at least he clearly reacts to it.[29] Ricoeur also stresses the Other but only after he has wrestled with dimensions of our human ontological structure. To Ricoeur the ethical is important, but only in conjunction with ontology.[30] Ricoeur is still strongly attracted to the dimension of the universal in the human as emphasized by modern philosophy, and yet he is open to the ideas of human interaction, social institutions, speech as communication, and identity-forming narratives as constitutive dimensions of human being. Whereas Levinas stresses the unconditional claim of the "Other" on me, Ricoeur stresses the need for solicitude and compassion. Dan Stiver writes of Ricoeur's thought as follows:

28. For an explanation of Levinas, see Richard Kearney, *The God Who May Be: A Hermeneutics of Religion* (Bloomington: Indiana University Press, 2001) 62–69 ["Phenomenological Readings—From Hegel to Levinas"]. See also Colin Davis, *Levinas: An Introduction* (Notre Dame, Ind.: University of Notre Dame Press, 1996), and Adriaan Theodoor Peperzak, *The Philosophy of Emmanuel Levinas* (Evanston, Ill.: Northwestern University Press, 1997).

29. See Paul Ricoeur, *Oneself as Another,* tr. Kathleen Blamey (Chicago: University of Chicago Press, 1992) 188–89 and 338–40.

30. Both Levinas and Ricoeur are exceptional phenomenologists, yet there are real differences in their approaches. Levinas continues in the tradition of Edmund Husserl (1859–1938) and in outright opposition to Martin Heidegger's ontologizing tendencies, while Ricoeur continues the trajectory traced by Emmanuel Kant and Georg W. F. Hegel, but augmented by the study of language as performative and by literary theory, so that for Ricoeur metaphors are rich in meaning. Given the fertility of his sources, Ricoeur's thought is hard to synthesize in simple terms.

The Other calls me to respect; the Other also calls me at times to compassion. Our capacity to respond is part of our humanity. Such feelings of sympathy are not peripheral or contingent but essential. Unlike Kant and much modern philosophy, we do not act apart from feeling but with it, raising again the embodied nature of our being. . . . Far from reason being able to rise above life's tragedies, knowledge is rooted in a tragic wisdom of the suffering self who inescapably suffers with others.[31]

While Levinas challenges us like a Hebrew prophet, Ricoeur's voice speaks as a gentler Old Testament sage or wisdom figure.[32]

The second strand of thought I referred to that challenges modern assumptions of the person-as-subject is twentieth-century relational thought. Ideas of relationship as constitutive of the human being were proposed by personalist thinkers such as Martin Buber (1878–1965).[33] Another, less known figure is the British thinker John Macmurray (1891–1960). In his *The Self as Agent*, Macmurray challenged modern ideas of human nature that stressed the subject as an isolated rational thinker and developed instead the human subject as agent.[34] Thinking can easily be understood as a purely interior act, while acting is open to exteriorization and to interaction. Macmurray saw the subject or self as personal, that is, as existing in interaction with other persons. At the center of his understanding of the person stands the notion of our "acts" as "relations." Macmurray later developed the idea of human agency in terms of human community. To be human is to be in relation with other persons.[35]

31. Dan R. Stiver, *Theology after Ricoeur: New Directions in Hermeneutical Theology* (Louisville: Westminster John Knox Press, 2001) 181.

32. For another voice challenging us to come to terms with the "Other," see Miroslav Volf, *Exclusion and Embrace: A Theological Exploration of Identity, Otherness, and Reconciliation* (Nashville: Abingdon Press, 1996), winner in 2002 of the prestigious Grawemeyer Award in Religion.

33. See Martin Buber, *I and Thou*, tr. Ronald Gregor Smith (2nd ed.; New York: Charles Scribner's Sons, 1958). On the importance of Buber, see Kenneth Seeskin, "Buber, Martin," in *The Cambridge Dictionary of Philosophy*, 104. Seeskin writes: "Buber rejects the idea that people are isolated, autonomous agents operating according to abstract rules. Instead, reality arises *between* agents as they encounter and transform each other. In a word, reality is dialogical." Italics are the author's.

34. See Macmurray, *The Self as Agent* (London: Faber and Faber Limited, 1957 [reprint 1966]).

35. See Macmurray, *Persons in Relation* (London: Faber and Faber Limited, 1961 [reprint 1967]).

Macmurray's ideas have been espoused by many contemporary theologians. This is the case especially for the areas of theological anthropology and the Trinity. Catherine Mowry LaCugna's writings on the Trinity have drawn on Macmurray's insights. In evident agreement, she writes: "Macmurray's argument removes the static and privatized connotations of person-as-selfhood, or being-in-itself or being-by-itself, and defines the person as being-in-relation-to-another. . . . *A person is a heterocentric, inclusive, free, relational agent.*"[36] In an earlier article that examines Thomas Aquinas' understanding of the divine, inner-trinitarian relations, LaCugna points to Aquinas' "ontology of relations."[37] The being of the Trinitarian God is "to-be-with" or "relational to-be." After examining Aquinas' teaching about relations in his philosophical and theological writings, especially in the *Summa theologiae*, LaCugna summarizes Aquinas in the following way: "On the one hand, God's nature might be to-be, but we cannot know by reason alone what such a to-be is like. On the other hand, we can know through revelation what God's to-be is like, namely, it is a relational to-be. To be God is to be related."[38] The lesson LaCugna wants to make is that relationality is at the very heart of divine being, and of course of the creature made in God's "image and likeness." LaCugna undercuts the false starting point of modernity itself, namely, the human being as isolated, self-sufficient subject.

Stanley J. Grenz, too, has pointed to the importance of Macmurray in helping him formulate his theological understanding of the human being and of the triune God. In a section in which he treats Martin Buber, Michael Polanyi, and John Macmurray, Grenz writes approvingly of the last:

> . . . In Macmurray's estimation, the starting point for philosophical reflection is not the theoretical attitude, the standpoint of the thinker or the observer, not the Cartesian cogito, the "I think." Rather, he sees as the primary certainty the "I do" and therefore launches his reflections by taking the standpoint of the agent or participant. This approach does not lead to "the isolated self, excluded from existence," but to "persons in dynamic

36. Catherine Mowry LaCugna, *God for Us: The Trinity and Christian Life* (San Francisco: HarperSanFrancisco, 1991) 259. Italics are the author's.

37. See LaCugna, "The Relational God: Aquinas and Beyond," *Theological Studies* 46 (1985) 647–63. In a footnote, LaCugna defines ontology in the following way: "Ontology is a description of the nature of existence. A relational ontology assumes that to-exist means to-exist-in-relationship." *God for Us,* 306, note 1.

38. LaCugna, "The Relational God: Aquinas and Beyond," 659.

relation. . . ." This perspective leads ultimately to the community of persons in relation.[39]

Finally, John Zizioulas, whose ideas on apostolicity we considered in Chapter Four, has also pointed to John Macmurray's insights as an aid in retrieving the genuine Christian tradition of personhood. In an article which treated the theological view of human being, Zizioulas wrote:

> Man's [*sic*] personhood should not be understood in terms of 'personality', that is of a complex of natural, psychological or moral qualities which are in some sense 'possessed' by or 'contained' in the human *individuum*. On the contrary, being a person is basically different from being an individual or 'personality' in that the person can not be conceived in itself as a static entity, but only as it *relates to*. Thus personhood implies the 'openness of being', and even more than that, the *ek-stasis* of being, that is a movement towards communion which leads to a transcendence of the boundaries of the 'self' and thus to *freedom*.[40]

I think that by now I have made the point that far from being entirely hostile to a Christian anthropological view, postmodernity opens up new possibilities of thought for Christian thinkers in arguing for an understanding of the human being different from that of modernity. Postmodernism shows itself to be less than entirely bent on nihilistic and anti-rational tendencies. It need not be destructive. In fact, postmodernism can be used in constructive ways.

It is now time to examine in greater detail some of the ways in which postmodernism can help us engage some fundamental problems in ecclesiology. How can postmodern thought help us understand apostolicity in ways that are impeded by modernity and its ideal of strict and objective control of the data available from the church's tradition of understanding apostolic life, doctrine, and ministry? I propose to exam-

---

39. Stanley J. Grenz, *The Social God and the Relational Self: A Trinitarian Theology of the Imago Dei* (Louisville: Westminster John Knox Press, 2001) 12.

40. John Zizioulas, "Human Capacity and Human Incapacity: A Theological Exploration of Personhood," *Scottish Journal of Theology* 28 (1975) 401–47, at 407–8. Italics are the author's. In a footnote to this section, Zizioulas writes: "The understanding of the person as a *relational* category in our time has marked a sharp contrast with the Boethian individualistic tradition. Some representative examples of this trend are to be found in M. Buber's *I and Thou*, [and] J. Macmurray's *Persons in Relation* and *The Self as Agent*." Ibid., 408. On Zizioulas, see also LaCugna, *God for Us*, 260–66 ["Persons as Ecstatic and Hypostatic: The Contribution of Contemporary Orthodox Theology"].

ine three general issues before turning to a proposal for a third model of understanding the church's apostolicity. The three issues are history, historicity and human freedom, and pluralism. In each case I will attempt to show how postmodernism provides a better context than modernity for understanding these basic personal and social issues.

History

Civilizations have long recorded their histories in one form or another—steles, wall paintings, chronicles, archival collections, and so forth. But history in the distinctively modern sense appeared rather late in the West.[41] Modern historiography is a product of the Enlightenment and modernity. Academic history is intimately connected with the emergence of the modern university, particularly in Germany, and is imbued with the spirit of objectivity and scientific rigor associated with modernity. What actually happened in the past is discoverable in its objectivity, without embellishment by ethical values, social conventions, human traditions, and so forth. Leopold von Ranke (1795–1886) expressed the ideal of the modern historian as one who searches for "just what happened"– "wie es eigentlich gewesen ist"–no more, no less. But it wasn't always so.

In antiquity, history was intended to edify more than to inform people about the facts. Society and individuals were in need of examples of personal and civic virtues. Historians were interested in heroes and important figures for the lessons they taught. And when facts were emphasized, it was usually for apologetic or polemical purposes.[42] The ideal of modernity, however, held that self-determination and knowledge of the world was something interior, intrinsically sustained by one's subjectivity. Tradition and authority external to the individual were of no intrinsic value. Historical facts concerning how human beings acted and what they did, like the scientific laws of the universe, would compel assent and lead to greater social concord. According to the parameters of the modern

41. See Robert Eric Frykenberg, "History as History: A Double Definition" in *History and Belief: The Foundations of Historical Understanding* (Grand Rapids: Wm B. Eerdmans Publishing Company, 1996) 19–37, for some of the complexities of the term "history."

42. On the writing of history in the classical and premodern period, see R. G. Collingwood, *The Idea of History* (New York: Oxford University Press, 1956 [©1946]) 14–85; R. L. P. Milburn, *Early Christian Interpretations of History* (London: Adam and Charles Black Limited, 1954); Michael Grant, *The Ancient Historians* (New York: Charles Scribner's Sons, 1970); Herbert Butterfield, *The Origins of History,* ed. Adam Watson (New York: Basic Books, Inc., 1981).

worldview, history was approached as something to be mastered by human reason. Knowledge for its own sake was now the goal, not edification. The result was the development of methods of research that would assure objectivity. Modern historical method stressed collecting facts, broadening the pool of available data by improved techniques of archeology and paleography, searching through libraries and archives for new information, reading memoirs and diaries, formulating criteria to judge the authenticity of documents, applying literary criteria to documents, establishing scholarly societies to share information, forming hypotheses about causes and consequences of actions in history, and so forth.[43]

Various movements emerged out of modernity's quest for objectivity. One goes by the name "historicism," but it is not always easy to separate out the various meanings of the term. Kai Nielsen has pointed out two meanings, which I shall call (1) scientific historicism and (2) hermeneutical historicism. Scientific historicism shows strong similarities to the Enlightenment's enthusiasm for establishing objective facts of history. This naïve theory is often called positivism and it can be found in the heyday of the Enlightenment's enthronement of reason alone.[44] Its appeal is perduring. In the twentieth century, positivist tendencies emerged in theories of laws of history. A theorist such as Carl G. Hempel (1905–1997) stressed the symmetry between scientific method and historical knowledge. More than many other thinkers, Hempel was inclined toward the possibility of predicting an individual's and society's acts based on the reading of history, and thus of discovering the general meaning and direction of history. Karl R. Popper (1902–1994) in particular criticized such scientific approaches to human actions as naïve, but did not escape ambiguity himself. The issue continues to be a vexing one among historians.[45]

43. On the different approaches of the modern view of historiography, see Collingwood, *The Idea of History*, 134–204 ["Part IV: Scientific History"] and 249–82 ["Historical Evidence"]; and Butterfield, "The Development of Historical Criticism" and "The Great Secularisation," in *The Origins of History*, 185–97 and 198–220 respectively. Bernard Lonergan has described the emergence of the tasks and methods of the modern historian in "History," in *Method in Theology* (New York: Herder and Herder, 1972) 175–96, at 181–84 ["Historical Experience and Historical Knowledge"].

44. See Collingwood, *The Idea of History*, 126–33 ["§ 9. Positivism"]; and René Latourelle, "Positivism, Historical," in *Dictionary of Fundamental Theology*, eds. René Latourelle and Rino Fisichella (New York: The Crossroad Publishing Company, 1995) 785–88. Auguste Comte (1798–1857) is often cited as a paragon of the epistemology of positivism.

45. Lonergan, too, examines the meanings of "historicism" in his chapter entitled "History and Historians," in *Method in Theology*, 214–220 ["5. Perspectivism"]. Drawing on

The second meaning, hermeneutical historicism, owes its prominence to Wilhelm Dilthey (1833–1911), who refused to make history con-
formable to science. He developed an approach to history and the other
humanistic branches of learning that stressed the uniqueness of the knowledge gained in humanistic studies and of the methodology for gaining such
knowledge. Kai Nielsen summarizes this form of historicism as follows:

> In the mid-nineteenth century certain German thinkers (Dilthey most cen-
> trally), reacting against positivist ideals of science and knowledge, re-
> jected scientistic models of knowledge, replacing them with historical
> ones. They applied this not only to the discipline of history but to
> economics, law, political theory, and large areas of philosophy. Ini-
> tially concerned with methodological issues in particular disciplines,
> historicism, as it developed, sought to work out a common philo-
> sophical doctrine that would inform all these disciplines. What is es-
> sential to achieve knowledge in the human sciences is to employ the
> ways of understanding used in historical studies. There should in the
> human sciences be no search for natural laws; knowledge there will
> be interpretive and rooted in concrete historical occurrences. As
> such, it will be inescapably perspectival and contextual.[46]

As the twentieth century unfolded, historicism took on distinct connotations of relativism, but we need to exercise caution in identifying this
narrow meaning with the wider concerns of historicism.[47]

With the benefit of more than a century of development of what he
calls critical history, Bernard Lonergan distinguished between "history
written about" or existential history, and "written history" or scientific
history.[48] The former aims at assisting in the complex process of identity

---

Karl Heussi's presentation in *Die Krisis des Historismus* (Tübingen: Mohr, 1932), Lonergan lists
four meanings of historicism: "(1) a determinate but simple-minded stand on the nature of objectivity; (2) the interconnectedness of all historical objects; (3) a universal process of development; and (4) the confinement of historical concern to the world of experience." Ibid., 214.

46. Nielsen, "Historicism," in *The Cambridge Dictionary of Philosophy*, 386.

47. See Patrick L. Gardiner, "Historicism," in *The Oxford Companion to Philosophy*, ed. Ted
Honderich (New York: Oxford University Press, 1995) 357. Calvin O. Schrag compares the
historicism of modernity with what he calls the "new historicism" and the "quasi-historicism"
of postmodernity. See "The Challenge of Postmodernism," in *The Resources of Rationality: A Response to the Postmodern Challenge* (Bloomington: Indiana University Press, 1992) 13–49, here at
42–49 ["A New Historicism"]. The entire chapter deserves a careful reading.

48. See the discussion in *Method in Theology*, 181–96. At the very beginning of his chapter on the functional specialty history, Lonergan introduces the distinction in a programmatic

formation, by individuals and their societies. Important, it is still not academic history. The latter demands the application of all the resources of human knowing and is reached, according to Lonergan, by a process he calls "transcendental method." It is beyond the scope of this study to enter into a lengthy explanation of transcendental method according to Lonergan. Suffice it to say that knowing something to be true involves many human operations (for example, attention to reality, asking questions, forming initial insights, asking more questions, deepening one's insights, asking more questions, forming provisional judgments on the way to more certain judgments, and finally deciding what to do on the basis of these judgments) that fit into a recurrent and lifelong process of learning about the world and defining it. In the technical sense, history is what Lonergan calls "written history" because when the historian performs his or her craft, the transcendental method in some form or other is employed. But note how different this critical understanding of history is for Lonergan. It isn't scientific in the normally accepted meaning of the term, but it isn't naively realist or positivist either. To Lonergan, as we contemporaries understand it, history is a never-ending critical process of learning and testing our "existential history." My contention is that history in such terms—those of Dilthey, Lonergan, and other hermeneutical philosophers—is really a different phenomenon than history in the sense of modernity. "Written history" is much more than gathering sources, collecting facts, and surrendering oneself to the objectivity of these historical elements. The best historian is not the one who amasses more and more data, but the one who asks better questions about the data. The kind of history Lonergan writes about might better be termed postmodern. It views cognitional theory and indeed the world very differently from the typically modern way of doing so.

Historicity and Human Freedom

This brings us to the next major distinction that emerges from postmodernity's rejection of modernity's tendencies toward positivism, narrow objectivism, and foundationalism, namely, historical consciousness, historicity, and freedom. Thinkers like Hans-Georg Gadamer (1900–2002)

---

way. He writes: "The word, history, is employed in two senses. There is history (1) that is written about, and there is history (2) that is written. History (2) aims at expressing knowledge of history (1)." Ibid., 175.

view the historicity of the human being as inescapable, inherent, constitutive.[49] What do I mean? Drawing on Heidegger, but going well beyond him, Gadamer stresses the impossibility of being human in any way
other than by our immersion in history itself—not as something unfolding all around us, but as that which affects us through and through.
Human beings can define themselves as creatures of history. We *are* historical. The word history used in this sense is often called "historicity" or
"historicality." Thus, the human being unfolds by way of his or her
openness to history, being formed by it, and in turn forming it. Historicity for the human being is more than simply being in history. It points to
how the very open-ended character of history impinges on and impacts
human existence in all its dimensions. Human historicity is not something fixed or determined but creatively open and dynamically unfolding. It involves risk, fallibility, and failure, but also human freedom,
some grasp of truth, and successful actions—more or less in equal measure. Historicity is open, unpredictable, and unable to be programmed.
There is no pure essence or substance of what it means to be human. In
a word, what we understand by human being can be summed up in our
historicity.[50] But is this so dangerous?

When the human person is aware of his or her historicity and interprets the world in terms of that ineluctably historical character, we
have what is called "historical consciousness." In other words, the human
being is not a form of "pure consciousness" along the lines of nineteenth-
century idealist thought. Idealism understood human subjectivity in terms
of consciousness.[51] Historical consciousness directs the subject outward,
into the world and toward others. We are inescapably defined by being
directed toward others—both for good and for ill. Historical consciousness also includes the ideas of the overwhelming complexity of the
world, of the unimaginable expanse of space and time, and of a sense of
threat from our not being able to master or dominate reality. Because
our world and the universe are so complex, we feel threatened with the
lack of meaning, or at least our inability to determine meaning. Because

49. See Gadamer, *Truth and Method*, rev. transl. Joel Weinsheimer and Donald G.
Marshall (New York: Crossroad, 1989) 164–69, 231–42, 297–301, and 340–79. The work
is generally acknowledged to be a philosophical classic of the twentieth century.

50. See Jörg Splett, "Die theologische Dimension der Geschichte," *Zeitschrift für katholische Theologie* 100 (1978) 302–17.

51. Remember my earlier reference to modernity's "turn to the subject," pp. 115–16.

of the urgency of the question of meaning for us, truth is considered beyond our ability to know it. Whatever meaning we can fasten on is entirely relative. Historical consciousness contributes to the sense of the relativism of all views and choices. This brings us to our last question regarding postmodernism—pluralism.

Pluralism

Like nihilism, historical consciousness, and relativism, the word pluralism is also viewed with apprehension by many. Some Christians instinctively feel that pluralism is incompatible with their faith. A closer look at Christian doctrines and a deeper probing of the concept of pluralism reveal a meaning that is considerably less threatening. Let us examine both of these issues. First of all, what do we mean today by pluralism?

Here is how one commentator, Calvin O. Schrag, defines pluralism: "[A] philosophical perspective on the world that emphasizes diversity rather than homogeneity, multiplicity rather than unity, difference rather than sameness."[52] In his exposition, Schrag demonstrates that pluralism is opposed to both monistic and dualistic forms for understanding the world, that is, systems of thought that insist on the primacy of the One to the exclusion of the many (monism) or that divide the world into two antagonistic and incommensurable realms (dualism). Pluralism views reality as heterogeneous—neither monistic nor dualistic. He concludes: "[Pluralism] is less concerned with traditional metaphysical and epistemological issues, seeking answers to questions about the nature and kinds of substances and attributes; and it is more attuned to the diversity of social practices and the multiple roles of language, discourse, and narrative in the panoply of human affairs."[53]

Pluralism is one of the hallmarks of postmodernism to the extent that postmodernism rejects modernity's version of reality as entirely objective, hence empirical and open to scientific explanation only, or purely subjective, hence radically privatized and incommunicable. A pluralistic vision is chary of scientific reductions of reality and of apodictic claims to truth. It tends to discern ideological distortions of reality and hence to invoke a hermeneutics of suspicion—perhaps too hastily, but not without reason. It tends to revel in multiplicity and polyvalence and hence to es-

52. Schrag, "Pluralism," in *The Cambridge Dictionary of Philosophy*, 714–15, at 714.
53. Ibid., 715.

chew systematic reason and premature closure of issues. It tends toward irony and fancy as defenses against the often unchallenged demands of the recent past for conformity. It tends to indulgence in the face of excesses—pleasure, leisure, culture, and so forth—or to indifference in the face of societal assumptions—consumerism, militarism, individualism, and so forth. It tends to value tolerance almost as an absolute, without sufficiently adverting to the sometimes harmful results and consequences of actions. But it also tends to avoid judgmentalism toward individuals or a sense of superiority associated with the colonialism and imperialism of modern nations vis-à-vis what were considered less developed countries. Pluralism has its shadow side, but it also tends to be more sympathetic to reality's shades of gray. But is this so dangerous? I propose to examine the meanings of pluralism in order to see if any might be applicable to the issues of belief today, the formulation of belief in the second-order language of doctrines,[54] and the question of the church's apostolicity.[55] This last point in particular points us in the direction of examining the possibility that there might be several ways of understanding and speaking about apostolicity that respect the multiplicity of traditions relating to apostolicity. My approach will be to examine theological pluralism in the context of postmodernity and the worldview that is emerging from it. Since that is my focus, I will not be able to examine the interesting and instructive questions of a pluralism of theologies in the Bible, theological pluralism in history, and the de facto pluralism in the concrete life of the church.[56]

54. Religious language is sometimes distinguished in terms of first-order and second-order language. First-order language is the language of faith, i.e., the language used in the spontaneous expression of what a community believes. It is usually concrete, often mythic; it draws on the imagination, is symbolic, and uses narratives. Second-order language is the language about faith, i.e., the language used in a more reflective expression of what a community believes. It is more abstract and general; it relies on the mind's ability to make distinctions, is analogical, and prefers propositions and definitions.

55. My interest is in the possibility and meaning of a pluralism of religious beliefs, doctrines, and theologies, not in the issue of the pluralism of religions. Important as this topic is, it does not really pertain to this chapter's concerns.

56. The literature on these questions is plentiful but hardly vast. I can mention only several more helpful works. On biblical theologies, see Raymond E. Brown, "The Unity and Diversity in New Testament Ecclesiology," in *New Testament Essays* (Milwaukee: The Bruce Publishing Company, 1965) 36–47; James D. G. Dunn, *Unity and Diversity in the New Testament: An Inquiry into the Character of Earliest Christianity* (2nd ed.; Philadelphia: Trinity Press International, 1990); Pheme Perkins, "Theological Implications of New Testament Pluralism," *Catholic Biblical Quarterly* 50 (1988) 5–23; and John Reumann, *Variety and Unity in*

One of the first Catholics to take note of the fact of pluralism after Vatican II was the Munich theologian Heinrich Fries (1911–1998). In spite of the reference to "the problem of pluralism" in the title of the article,[57] Fries understood pluralism less as a "problem" and more as a "simple fact" of modern thought. He does not bemoan pluralism, but considers the possibilities it opens to the church. Fries begins by defining pluralism:

> . . . The word "pluralism" . . . does not merely designate multiplicity, as the word "plurality" does; it makes multiplicity the very predicate of the one. . . .
>   . . . "Pluralism" expresses the fact that in the various areas of human existence multiplicity, plurality, is the dominant factor. Pluralism is the side-by-side-ness of the many.[58]

He makes no reference to any threatening character of contemporary pluralism and no reference to postmodernity. But he does note the changed conditions for the church as it leaves behind the cultural and sociological assumptions of its premodern worldview. He offered one of the earliest descriptions of postmodernity by a Catholic theologian:

> . . . The world in which we live is no longer determined by unifying basic concepts and institutions, by a universal tradition and atmosphere, by a milieu occasioned and motivated by the Christian faith. What we find is rather a motley multiplicity, a pluralism of world views: Christian faith and the Church are no longer the one and all, but merely the one among others, the one among the many. And in this situation the one among the many, that one which is still Christianity and faith and Church, is by no

---

New Testament Thought (New York: Oxford University Press, 1991). On pluralism in the history of theology, see Bernard Schultze, "Latin Theology and Oriental Theology," in *The Unity of the Churches of God,* ed. P. Sherwood (Baltimore: Helicon Press, 1963) 185–215; Emmanuel Lanne, "Pluralism and Unity: The Possibility of a Variety of Typologies within the Same Ecclesial Allegiance," *One in Christ* 6 (1970) 430–51; Mary Ann Fatula, "The Council of Florence and Pluralism in Dogma," *One in Christ* 19 (1983) 14–27, and idem, "The Holy Spirit in East and West: Two Irreducible Traditions," *One in Christ* 19 (1983) 379–86; Yves Congar, *Diversity and Communion,* tr. John Bowden (Mystic, Conn.: Twenty-Third Publications, 1985) 9–43; René Marlé, "La question du pluralisme en théologie," *Gregorianum* 71 (1990) 465–86; and Robert L. Wilken, "Religious Pluralism and Early Christian Thought," in *Remembering the Christian Past* (Grand Rapids: Wm. B. Eerdmans Publishing Co., 1995) 25–46.

57. Fries, "Theological Reflections on the Problem of Pluralism," *Theological Studies* 28 (1967) 3–26.

58. Ibid., 3–4.

means the dominant and overshadowing factor. By dominant factors very different from itself it has been challenged to a many-sided competition, factors which deny to Christianity any status of privilege and exception, which indeed outrank Christianity, which in any event demand equality with it.[59]

Fries then shows the opportunity that pluralism opens to the church. Again, to quote him: "No movement or ideology, no matter how it may originally be defined and devised, can live, can persist, can so long survive by error alone. All of this is possible only because of the truth, the reality, the undeniable value that inheres in, with, and under the *errores*. If I see the matter correctly, we are today on the threshold of making contact with this core of truth, of discerning it and laying it bare."[60] He points to modernity's valid discovery of the human being and insists that the Christian faith does not reject a correct understanding of the human: "What was never sufficiently observed and asserted was that there need not be any opposition between theocentrism and anthropocentrism; that there can in fact be a theologically conditioned anthropocentrism."[61] Fries warns against the tendency of pluralism to surrender to complete relativism, but he also maintains that this need not be so: "It is possible to accept pluralism as a form of modern society without lapsing into a religious relativism, without overlooking or sacrificing what is distinctively Christian."[62] In fact, because the church now acknowledges the insights of pluralism in the many areas of human existence means that the church is urgently called to be of service to an anthropocentric world. Gone are the church's militancy, antagonism, and competitiveness with the world. In terms of the other Christian churches, too, pluralism points the Catholic Church in the direction of tolerance for others' views, receptivity of their genuine insights into the faith, and dialogue.

What tasks does the situation of pluralism, even in the church, impose? Fries points to three. First, the need for dialogue with the world, especially regarding issues surrounding the peril that humankind faces.[63]

59. Ibid., 11.
60. Ibid., 14.
61. Ibid., 15. Theocentrism means "centered on God"–*theos* in Greek. Here, God has priority. Anthropocentrism means "centered on the human"–*anthropos* in Greek. Here, the human being has priority.
62. Ibid., 17.
63. In this regard, we need to recall the world situation at the time Fries wrote the article. It was the height of the Cold War and the threat of nuclear annihilation of the species was very real.

Second, pluralism calls us to a more genuine faith, not to its demise. And third, the church itself is challenged to welcome legitimate ecclesial pluralism. On this last point, Fries writes: "Since the Church's main striving and willing has until now been directed toward the realization of unity, she now faces a genuine need to recover something in articulating the plural."[64]

Fries's article betrays the naïve optimism of the immediately post-conciliar church. After so many centuries of resistance to modern thought and strenuous intra-ecclesial efforts at uniformity of practice and governance, the optimism of the period was refreshing. However, it also arrived a bit late on the scene. The Catholic Church was now open to modernity, but modernity was itself already in crisis. Fries, and many other theologians at the time, did not seem to be aware of this fact. But that would change very quickly with the emergence of new theologies: more philosophically critical, more sociologically and politically cautious, more liberationist in their view of the human being, more suspicious of hidden ideology and power plays.

Bernard Lonergan was one of the first to take note of the complexity of the task. Over the course of many years, Lonergan had developed what he called "transcendental method." He applied the method in his 1971 lectures at Marquette University on "Doctrinal Pluralism."[65] Lonergan tried to clear up the meaning of pluralism by situating it in terms of a theory of cognition. The lectures are relatively short but dense, and I must be as concise and succinct as possible.

Central to understanding Lonergan on pluralism is his teaching about undifferentiated and differentiated consciousness.[66] The pluralism of understandings and interpretations of reality can be accounted for by the variety of consciousnesses that human beings bring to understanding. There are two fundamental ways of understanding reality—in an undifferentiated and in a differentiated way. A person who regards the world on the basis of undifferentiated consciousness lives in a world of immediacy, reacting to the world without asking questions about its makeup and meaning. Things simply are the way they are presented to him or her. In the realm of undifferentiated consciousness a common sense understanding of reality presides. Few questions are asked and those that are do not penetrate to deeper levels of meaning. But Loner-

64. Ibid., 26.

65. Lonergan, *Doctrinal Pluralism* (Milwaukee: Marquette University Press, 1971).

66. Ibid., 12–22 ["Undifferentiated and Variously Differentiated Consciousness"].

gan understands the human being as not only living in the world as immediately presented to him or her, but as inhabiting another world, a world of meaning mediated by questions. The kinds of questions posed determine the world as it is meant to be understood. The sense of realism of this human world of meaning Lonergan calls "critical realism," in contradistinction to the "naïve realism" of undifferentiated consciousness alone. What, then, are these all-important questions human beings pose in their quest for meaning and truth?

Lonergan distinguishes four sets of questions. Scientific questions seek to understand the structure of things not so much in terms of their meaning for us as in terms of their meaning in themselves and in relationship to other things. Religious questions search for how reality relates to God or to transcendence. This is the realm of the believer, devotee, or mystic. Next, scholarly differentiated consciousness asks questions of how reality is to be understood in terms of another place and time, and not simply in terms of the here and now. This is the realm of the historian and the literary and art critic. Finally, humans ask modern philosophical questions that have their origins in different aspects of subjectivity. This is the realm of the philosopher especially, but also the sociologist and the psychologist. It is rare that an individual operates at all these levels of differentiated consciousness. Most relate to the world and others on the common sense level of immediacy, but some combine a common sense approach with one or two other approaches. The sheer variety of approaches to consciousness explains why Lonergan holds for an unavoidable pluralism of thought. As humans, we cannot help but ask questions in search of greater meaning. The kinds of questions we ask—scientific, religious, scholarly, and philosophical—and the openness of these questions to yet better questions in the same realm or in combination with other question-realms, accounts for the insurmountable pluralism of positions and explanations we encounter on a day-to-day basis. In Lonergan's way of thinking, to be human is to be involved in the never-ending process of discovering our individual world of meaning and of sharing that world with other worlds of meaning. Our human worlds of meaning have both personal and corporate dimensions. But this insight into the radically pluralistic way of our knowing has only been identified with a postmodern view of things in the last twenty-five years. The roots are there in Lonergan's system, but he continued to see this pluralism in terms of the modernity he tried to understand and to champion.

Second, how did Lonergan apply this general theory of consciousness to how Christians understand their faith? Is there pluralism in this area, too, or is faith exempt from it?[67] First of all, Lonergan points out that in a Christian perspective religious knowledge has a unique relationship to the act of God's self-revelation. Religious knowledge is not less authentically human because of this relationship. Two effects emerge from the divine-human relationship in human knowing. The first effect maintains that all the human questions we ask in forming a more differentiated understanding of the truths of our faith are always directed toward a divine meaning that can never be adequately seized by our understanding or by our human terms or images. The need for developing such terms and images is not contradicted by the content of God's self-revelation, however. This does not arise primarily out of human weakness, fallibility, or sinfulness so much as out of the sheer recognition of the transcendence of the mystery of God. In the world of religious meaning this fundamental datum must always be preserved. And yet, a second effect emerges out of the limitless insights and questions we pose in terms of how God's self-revelation impacts our understanding of its many layers of religious meaning. The first realm of God's self-revelation is primary and excludes pluralism. Lonergan speaks of its "permanence." The second realm, however, is vast and pluralistic through and through. And yet the two realms are also intertwined for us. Our experience of searching for the meaning of faith is one that is open-ended, developing, and revisable in terms of the words we employ, the doctrines we define, the images we form, and the practices we follow. Most of the divisive questions among Christians are from this realm of the second effects of religious knowledge, including the apostolicity of the church.

In the course of his lecture on doctrinal pluralism, Lonergan employs various meanings for the term pluralism, and this fact can account for some confusion in the presentation. First, there is the pluralism derived from the unavoidable differences between differentiated and undifferentiated consciousness. Second, there is the pluralism derived from the unavoidable differences among differentiated consciousnesses. Third, there is the pluralism in the realm of religiously differentiated consciousness among Christians at the level of their second-order expressions. And finally, there is a pluralism that emerges when the process of conversion that Lonergan describes is inauthentic. Conversion is the proc-

67. Ibid., 22–33 ["Pluralism and Theological Doctrines"].

ess by which differentiated consciousness emerges and affects the person intellectually, morally, and religiously. It is inauthentic when it fails to enter into the spirit of transcendental method by posing ever-better questions, when it fails to summon enough courage to adopt the new consciousness, and when it fails to realize the process of conversion on all three levels—intellectual, moral, and religious.[68]

Before concluding this section on pluralism, I want to consider an important point made by another theologian, Thomas G. Guarino. In the first chapter of his book *Revelation and Truth*, Guarino distinguishes between incommensurable and commensurable pluralism and considers how they relate to postmodernity.[69] Guarino forces us to consider the nature of the pluralism some Christians are prepared to admit into their rethinking and restating of the faith. How extreme or moderate is it? After examining the pluralism admitted by John XXIII and Vatican II, and after examining several documents emanating from Vatican congregations and from the Extraordinary Synod of 1985, Guarino examines the understanding of pluralism by several influential Catholic theologians—Karl Rahner, Hans Urs von Balthasar, Bernard Lonergan, and Walter Kasper. He shows how among Catholic sources the pluralism that has been espoused is "commensurable," that is, a pluralism that admits genuine differences in interpretation, expression, and the basic elements of a systematic theology, but does not reject the fundamental truth claim of an article of faith. The kind of pluralism associated with postmodernism, however, is more radical in character. The commensurable pluralism which many Catholics espouse is still foundationalist in nature, that is, it still rests on some inescapable foundation that grounds other elements of the process of understanding—in this case, on the fundamental articles of faith found in the church's creeds and conciliar definitions. To most postmodern thinkers, such a foundational point of departure excludes the

68. Lonergan puts it this way: "Now, in any individual, conversion can be present or absent; in the former case it can be present in one dimension or in two or in all three; it can be enriched by development, or distorted by aberration and the development and aberration may be great or small. Such differences give rise to another variety of pluralism. Besides the pluralism implicit in the transition from classicist to modern culture, besides the pluralism implicit in the coexistence of undifferentiated and variously differentiated consciousness, there is the more radical pluralism that rises when all are not authentically human and authentically Christian." Ibid., 37.

69. Guarino, "Pluralism: Key Word for Contemporary Catholic Theology," in *Revelation and Truth: Unity and Plurality in Contemporary Theology* (Scranton, Pa.: University of Scranton Press, 1993) 19–56.

Catholic understanding from making a genuine claim to being postmodern. It still remains bound to an earlier worldview. To most of these thinkers, pluralism in the postmodern sense is "incommensurable," that is, no single understanding can lay claim to expressing truth and meaning. They are entirely relative in the strong sense of that term. All of the options made available to us must be examined and considered on their own merits and the final resolution—always tentative and open to further revision—must be justified for reasons other than invoking some foundation or higher authority, for example, Scripture or the Nicene-Constantinopolitan Creed. By the standards of incommensurability, the postmodernism adopted by many Christians simply does not correspond to what most postmodern thinkers recognize as authentically postmodern. How valid is the argument against a Christian form of postmodernism?

In the course of his book, Guarino shows how for Catholics the matter is not as simple as the foundationalist versus a postfoundationalist option implies. The fundamental articles of faith are not the same as foundations in the philosophical sense. The latter are open to exhaustive understanding—even if this is rarely achieved. To believers, however, the articles of faith function precisely as foundations that really provide no foundation for reason, that is, as initiating the person into another realm of human activity, that of faith. While Christians do not consider faith irrational, neither is it simply interchangeable with reason[70]—faith as some other, perhaps higher, form of reason.[71] The complexity of the relationship of faith and reason is precisely the heart of the matter to a Christian, not an either/or option. In fact, recent reflection on faith is even more committed to its complexity because it sees faith in terms that go beyond reason to include all the dimensions of being human: a person's willing, loving, self-committing, acting, feeling, imagining, and so forth. It is not at all clear to me that the option between "incommensurable" and "commensurable" pluralism is completely applicable here. On the second point

---

70. This insight often tended to be lost under the influence of rationalism on how Christians understood their faith. This helps to explain the current popularity of Karl Barth's neo-orthodox theology for many theologians. See Ronald F. Thiemann, *Revelation and Theology: The Gospel as Narrated Promise* (Notre Dame, Ind.: University of Notre Dame Press, 1985).

71. This insight often tended to be lost under the influence of rationalism on Christians' understanding of the faith. This was true for Protestant liberalism and for Catholic neo-Scholasticism, both of which conceded too much to the spirit and method of modern rationalism.

made by Guarino, however, there are better grounds for the option. He has shown how the various structures of thought really are not interchangeable, for example, Augustinianism versus Thomism, Rahnerian transcendentalism versus neo-Thomism, Lonergan's transcendental method versus hermeneutical theologies, feminist theologies versus neoorthodoxy, process theology versus transcendental Thomism, and so forth. The issue is not to compare them and say which one has got it right—whatever that could possibly mean in matters of faith—but to judge the relative weight of a system on its own terms, namely, how effective has it been in elaborating the truth and meaning of the articles of faith? Is it ultimately true to faith's presuppositions? If Guarino is correct—and I think that he is—then there is a genuine sense in which these theologies are incommensurable and so measure up to the standard of postmodernist thinkers. Incommensurability need not mean "the contradictory of all other options" or a totally relativistic world, but the ultimate irreducibility of options based on their own assumptions. If "postmodern Christian theology" means anything, then it certainly points to a real pluralism of thought among Christians. And yet they remain within the same family of faith.

Apostolicity in a Postmodern Perspective

How do these reflections on postmodernism affect what Christians mean by apostolicity? I maintain that the meaning of apostolicity does not happen in a historical and cultural vacuum. Apostolicity fits into various contexts and especially into the shared worldview. In the case of postmodernity, many assume that the context is dismissive of all claims to apostolic authority. However, we have seen that postmodernism is a complex phenomenon, and is not really able to be identified completely with one postmodern movement or thinker. In fact, it makes sense to speak of postmodernism in the plural.[72] The world that is emerging and succeeding to modernity's project is really a congeries of postmodernisms, some more positive and constructive in spirit than others.[73] For a couple of generations now, some theologians have begun to think outside the

72. I have discussed this in my article "Defining Gospel Life in Postmodern Culture," 47–50.

73. Among those who hold a more positive evaluation of postmodernism, I might mention Paul Lakeland, *Postmodernity: Christian Identity in a Fragmented Age,* Guides to Theological

box of modernity by adopting other language, categories, and perspectives.[74] These influences are often marked by a rediscovery of biblical perspectives or the thought of earlier theologians, for example, Augustine, the Cappadocian Fathers, Anselm, Thomas Aquinas, John Henry Newman, and others. These thinkers no longer concede the right to modernity to dictate the terms of theological discussion or the language of faith. The pluralism of postmodernity is far more congenial to professing the Christian faith than the hostility to Christianity and organized religion, anti-traditionalism, and anti-dogmatism of modernity. The newly found appreciation for biblical language, images, and narratives, as well as the teaching of the early church councils, has cleared a space for a more consciously positive encounter with postmodernism, especially in its less negative and relativistic forms. In conclusion, I propose to examine several of these positive contributions to the discussion of apostolicity.

First of all, certain forms of Christian postmodern thinking are open to postmodernity's suspicion toward master narratives that exclude other, smaller narratives. The Christian narrative of Jesus Christ's life, death, and resurrection deserves to be heard just as much as modernity's grand narrative of innate human goodness and of humankind's inevitable progress. The Christian narrative of human sinfulness, redemption by Christ, and destiny for life with God has the power to call men and women to commitment to God in faith and to each other in justice and love. But there are also the smaller narratives that Christians tell. Some of these stories tell the narratives of the apostles, their fellow-workers, and apos-

Inquiry (Minneapolis: Fortress Press, 1997), especially xii; T. Howland Sanks, "Postmodernism and the Church," *New Theology Review* 11, No. 3 (August 1998) 51–59; Michael J. Scanlon, "Theological Studies at the Threshold of the Third Millennium: An Overview," in *At the Threshold of the Third Millennium,* Proceedings of the Theology Institute of Villanova University 30, ed. Francis A. Eigo (Villanova, Pa.: Villanova University Press, 1998) 1–29; idem, "The Postmodern Debate," in *The Twentieth Century: A Theological Overview,* ed. Gregory Baum (Maryknoll, N.Y.: Orbis Books, 1999) 228–37; and idem, "A Deconstruction of Religion: On Derrida and Rahner," in *God, the Gift, and Postmodernism,* ed. John D. Caputo and M. J. Scanlon (Bloomington: Indiana University Press, 1999) 223–28; and Merold Westphal, "Appropriating Postmodernism," in *Postmodernism and Christian Thought,* ed. M. Westphal (Bloomington: Indiana University Press, 1999) 1–10; idem, "Overcoming Onto-theology," in *God, the Gift, and Postmodernism,* 146–69; and idem, *Overcoming Onto-theology: Toward a Postmodern Christian Faith* [a collection of Westphal's essays from 1993–2001] (New York: Fordham University Press, 2001).

74. The theologian invariably mentioned is the great twentieth-century Swiss theologian Karl Barth (1886–1968), and the Barthians who have followed in his footsteps.

tolic ministry. Other stories are clearer in their claims about the role presbyters and bishops played in the early church, while still other stories
build on the Bible's references to the "imposition of hands" by "apostles"
and/or presbyters and incorporate a rite of ordination into the narrative.
These narratives are not history in the modern sense of critical or scholarly history as described, for instance, by Bernard Lonergan, and so we
need to relate to them primarily as narratives by allowing their expres-
sive and identity-forming power to operate. The narratives of the churches
which tell the story of the bishops and their successors need not suppress
the story of those churches which tell another story with roots in the earliest centuries of the united church. The narrative of these "episcopal
churches" also need not suppress the narratives of episcopal synodality
and conciliarity of many of the Orthodox churches of the East. If Christians in the twenty-first century can live their faith and coexist with postmodernity—and my claim is that they can and in fact are doing this—then
it is not unthinkable that we can each tell our story and listen respectfully to the stories of others, all the while learning from these other stories. The other Christian narratives do not overwhelm our own narrative,
but help us to come to terms with the ambiguity of Christian history and
story-telling in the face of a far more threatening relativism. In listening
respectfully to other narratives our own identity as Roman Catholics,
Anglicans, Presbyterians, Methodists, Greek Orthodox, and so forth is
strengthened in the face of extreme relativism's onslaught.

Secondly, the discovery of our historicity opens us up to change, development, and conversion, not only as individuals but as members of our
corporate ecclesial bodies. In the postmodern understanding, historicity
means more than simply being the product of historical forces. By historicity I mean the conscious efforts in all the domains of being human of realizing oneself in the face of constant change. Historical existence is not the
same as simple identity or sameness. Lonergan maintained both an invariant dimension and historical change in his insistence on human being as determined by "nature" and by "historicity." The dimension which is stable or
invariant exists in tension with what is equally human, our historicity. Stability and historicity mutually define what it is to be human. But the same
can be said of the institutions humans construct to help in realizing their humanity. They, too, are historical through and through, so that humankind
might survive and even thrive. Comparing the classicism of the premodern
worldview with the pluralism of the (post)modern worldview, Lonergan

writes: "[Classicism] is not mistaken in its assumption that there is something substantial and common to human nature and human activity. Its oversight is its failure to grasp that something substantial and common also is something quite open."[75] The "something quite open" he refers to is our human historicity. Of the pluralism characteristic of our contemporary situation, he says: "The pluralist, then, differs from the classicist inasmuch as he [sic] acknowledges human historicity both in principle and in fact. Historicity means—very briefly—that human living is informed by meanings, that meanings are the product of intelligence, that human intelligence develops cumulatively over time, and that such cumulative development differs in different histories."[76] Human historicity places an enormous burden on our shoulders, namely, to have the courage to move from a world of undifferentiated consciousness, that accepts the world and questions of truth simply on the basis of what appears to be so to common sense, to a world of meanings arrived at by the multiform and demanding activities of thinking, asking questions in pursuit of the truth, and making decisions and commitments on the basis of a differentiated consciousness. Such activity demands personal risk and courage, as well as mutual human support in the form of interpersonal relationships and social institutions. This is the realm of human historicity and it is every bit as "essential" or "constitutive" of human being as rationality considered as a formal cause of human nature. The church as the *congregatio fidelium*, or assembly of the faithful, is as historical as the "faithful" themselves. The fact that the church is the Body of Christ does not absolve the church as People of God of its historicity. "Body" and "People" exist in the life-giving tension that characterizes all human existence. The church's apostolic character then is defined by the church's historicity. It pertains not only to the stable factor of the church's nature—its identity—but also to its changeable factor—its historicity.[77] When the church defines itself as apostolic, in our contemporary situation we are referring primarily to the church's inherent historicity.[78]

75. Lonergan, *Doctrinal Pluralism*, 8.

76. Ibid., 7–8.

77. On the role of history in forming our understanding of apostolicity, see Wolfgang Beinert, "Die Apostolizität der Kirche als Kategorie der Theologie," *Theologie und Philosophie* 52 (1977) 161–81; and idem, "Apostolizität der Kirche," in *Lexikon für Theologie und Kirche,* ed. Walter Kasper (3rd ed.; Freiburg: Herder Verlag, 1993) 1:881–82.

78. See my "Apostolicity," in *New Catholic Encyclopedia*, 15 vols., ed. Berard Marthaler (2nd ed.; Detroit: Gale Group and Washington, D.C.: The Catholic University of America, 2003) 1:595–98.

A postmodern reading of apostolicity embraces genuine pluralism, not as inevitable confusion or an indifferent relativism of perspectives, but as the way differentiated consciousness necessarily deals with the world as a world of meanings and not simply of "brute facts." The complexity, richness, and mystery of the universe is better rendered for us by a pluralism of perspectives and insights into it. Pluralism does not mean deafening cacophony or crushing chaos, but the wealth of shared insight and wisdom gained by men and women over the centuries. In light of this less threatening postmodern understanding of pluralism, perhaps Christians can understand apostolicity better by sharing their experiences of apostolic faith, apostolic life, and apostolic ministry with each other. We can each learn from one another what the church is by listening to each other's insights, by challenging each other to live more authentically, and by supporting each other in the necessary ambiguity of the postmodern search for truth and meaning, even of the Christian world of meaning and truth in its fullness.

Finally, I propose that we might call this model of apostolicity the model of coherence. It avoids the naïve reading of history found in the model of identity, while also avoiding the "strong unity" of the model of continuity. The latter model is still too confined by the demands of modernity for laws of predictability, the certitude of our knowledge, and the primacy of reason isolated from our other human faculties. The model of coherence tries to make space for the richness of reality and the pluralism of our human explanations and interpretations, while respecting our human historicity and relationality.[79] It aims at what might be called a "weak unity," but one that nonetheless challenges cultures, religions, human beings, and believers to strive for a genuine sense of the underlying coherence or meaningfulness of reality.[80] I suggest that this "weak unity" is not a limitation or a weakness, but offers us the very possibility of dialogue with others and opportunities to truly evangelize in a postmodern world.

79. Whereas the model of identity operates out of an understanding of apostolicity in terms of "substance," the model of continuity thinks more in terms of "laws." I suggest that the model of coherence I am proposing is based on the priority of "relations" in the postmodern worldview.

80. See Johannes A. van der Ven, *Ecclesiology in Context* (Grand Rapids: Wm. B. Eerdmans Publishing Co., 1996) 97–98 ["Coherence and Meaning"]; and Gerhard Sauter, *The Question of Meaning: A Theological and Philosophical Orientation*, ed. and tr. Geoffrey W. Bromiley (Grand Rapids: Wm. B. Eerdmans Publishing Co., 1995).

CHAPTER SEVEN

Apostolicity in Ecumenical Dialogue

After examining the broader meaning of the apostolicity of the church in Roman Catholic, Lutheran, Baptist, and Orthodox theologians (Chapter 4), how apostolicity has been understood against earlier worldviews (Chapter 5), and the challenge of contemporary postmodern thought to how Christians talk about apostolicity (Chapter 6), I propose to examine how the topic has been broached in the conciliar and postconciliar ecumenical documents. Apostolicity has figured prominently in the ecumenical discussions of the last forty years, but the literature is too vast to cover in a single chapter. I will single out for discussion the understanding of apostolicity between Roman Catholics and Anglicans, Roman Catholics and Lutherans, its meaning in the multilateral document *Baptism, Eucharist, Ministry* (1982) and in the *Porvoo Common Statement* (1992), and finally the meaning of apostolicity in the Orthodox-Roman Catholic Dialogue. Also, I propose to examine in the various documents the emergence of the insight that has been growing since Vatican II and that I have called "substantive apostolicity." I do not intend to ignore entirely the question of apostolic succession in ordained ministry, but it will be a secondary, though co-constitutive, element of ecclesial apostolicity. I intend to pay closer attention to the underlying ecclesiologies elaborated in the documents.

The Roman Catholic-Anglican Dialogue

The results of the Anglican-Roman Catholic dialogue are rich and complex. The international and national dialogues have reaped much theological and pastoral fruit.[1] And yet they are also troubled by older and more recent issues—the document *Apostolicae Curae* (1896) of Leo XIII which rejected the validity of Anglican orders and which has never been revoked by the Vatican[2] and, since the 1980s, the practice of the various provinces of the Anglican communion of ordaining women to the priesthood, a practice that Pope John Paul II has rejected. The main reason for the pope's rejection is that the ordination of women to the priesthood is contrary to what the Christian Scriptures permit and to Christian practice of the last twenty centuries.[3] I mention these issues only as back-

1. See Mary Tanner, "Anglican-Roman Catholic Relations from Malta to Toronto," *One in Christ* 36 (2000) 114–25; and Mary Cecily Boulding, "Anglican-Roman Catholic Relations since Vatican II," *The Downside Review* 121 (2003) 26–38.

2. The literature on this thorny and divisive issue is very extensive. I can refer only to several important studies. John Jay Hughes, *Absolutely Null and Utterly Void: The Papal Condemnation of Anglican Orders, 1896* (Washington/Cleveland: Corpus Books, 1968); idem, *Stewards of the Lord: A Reappraisal of Anglican Orders* (London: Sheed & Ward, 1970); Edward Yarnold, *Anglican Orders—A Way Forward* (London: Catholic Truth Society, 1977); George H. Tavard, *A Review of Anglican Orders: The Problem and the Solution* (Collegeville, Minn.: The Liturgical Press, 1990); idem, *"Apostolicae Curae,"* in *New Catholic Encyclopedia,* 15 vols., ed. Berard Marthaler (2nd ed.; Detroit: Gale Group and Washington, D.C.: The Catholic University of America, 2003) 1:592–94; R. William Franklin, ed., *Anglican Orders: Essays on the Centenary of 'Apostolicae Curae,' 1896–1996* (Harrisburg, Pa.: Morehouse Publishing, 1996); Cecily Boulding, Roger Greenacre, John Muddiman, and Edward Yarnold, *"Apostolicae Curae:* A Hundred Years On," *One in Christ* 32 (1996) 295–309; and Margaret O'Gara, *"Apostolicae Curae* after a Century: Anglican Orders in Light of Recent Ecumenical Dialogue," *Canon Law Society of American Proceedings* 60 (1998) 1–18.

3. The statement by John Paul II is firm on this point. It is not clear that the pope rejects the practice of ordaining women to the official ministries of priesthood and episcopacy as something that is positively or directly contrary to the faith as enunciated in the Scriptures or because it was taught in this form previously by the papal magisterium or in the teachings of the Councils. Instead, the pope says somewhat obliquely that he cannot see how it is possible to act in a way that goes beyond the church's traditional belief and practice: "Wherefore, in order that all doubt may be removed regarding a matter of great importance, a matter which pertains to the church's divine constitution itself, in virtue of my ministry of confirming the brethren (cf. Lk. 22:32) I declare that *the church has no authority whatsoever* to confer priestly ordination on women and that this judgment is to be definitively held by all the church's faithful." See John Paul II, "Apostolic Letter on Ordination and Women" [*Ordinatio sacerdotalis*], §4. English translation in *Origins* 24/4 (June 9, 1994) 49, 51–52, at 51 (my italics). "Ministry" from *Baptism, Eucharist, and Ministry* of the Faith and Order Commission of the World Council of Churches nods in this direction when in its commentary on §18 it says the following: "Those churches which do not practise the ordination of women consider that the force of nineteen centuries of tradition against the ordination of women must not be set aside. They believe that such a tradition cannot be dismissed as a lack of respect for the participation of women in the church. They believe that there are theological issues concerning the nature of humanity and con-

ground to the discussion of the dialogues between Anglicans and Roman Catholics. They are far too complicated to be discussed in detail in the context of this chapter, but to ignore their existence entirely would be misleading.

"The Final Report"

At the international level, Anglicans and Roman Catholics have been conducting bilateral discussions for over thirty years. There have been two conversations thus far at the international level. The first concluded in 1981 with the submission of the "Final Report" to the Vatican and the authorities of the Anglican Communion.[4] The "Final Report" collates the separate studies undertaken by the Commission on "Eucharistic Doctrine" (Windsor, 1971), "Ministry and Ordination" (Canterbury, 1973), and "Authority in the Church I" (Venice, 1976) and "Authority in the Church II" (Windsor, 1981), together with two sets of "Elucidations" (1979 and 1981). The whole collection is accompanied by a "Preface," an "Introduction," and a "Conclusion" that attempt to tie the otherwise separate elements together.

---

cerning Christology which lie at the heart of their convictions and understanding of the role of women in the Chruch." See *Growth in Agreement: Reports and Agreed Statements of Ecumenical Conversations on a World Level,* eds. Harding Meyer and Lukas Vischer (New York: Paulist Press, 1984) 500. Divine revelation in Scripture does not directly teach that only men can be ordained, but it does appear to be indirectly taught by the constant tradition of the church. It seems that the argument for John Paul II is predicated on how tradition is to be understood. On the nature of tradition as it relates to this sensitive intra-catholic and ecumenical issue, see Hervé Legrand, " *Traditio perpetuo servata?* The Non-ordination of Women: Tradition or Simply an Historical Fact?" *Worship* 65 (1991) 482–508. Ernst Dassmann also expresses himself cautiously as regards the final character of recent Vatican teaching on the exclusion of women from ordination in his examination of *Inter insigniores* (1976) and *Ordinatio sacerdotalis* (1994). See "Die frühchristlichen Tradition über den Ausschluss der Frauen vom Priesteramt," in *Ämter und Dienste in den frühchristlichen Gemeinden,* Hereditas. Studien zur alten Kirchengeschichte 8 (Bonn: Verlag Norbert M. Borengässer, 1994) 212–24. Much more needs to be done on the central notion of tradition, and although the differences among Christians on the ordination of women now complicate ecumenical relations, perhaps our understanding of tradition will be deepened by the challenge this issue poses. In fact, "Ministry" of *Baptism, Eucharist, and Ministry* points in this direction when it adds to the commentary quoted above: "The discussion of these practical and theological questions within the various churches and Christian traditions should be complemented by joint study within the ecumenical fellowship of the churches." *Growth in Agreement,* 501.

4. For a brief but highly informed statement of the Anglican Communion, see Paul Avis, "The Churches of the Anglican Communion," in *The Christian Church: An Introduction to the Major Traditions,* ed. Paul Avis (London: SPCK, 2002) 132–56.

Before the authorities of both churches could respond officially to the "Final Report," Canterbury and Rome agreed to a second round of official conversations in 1982. Known as ARCIC-II, it has thus far offered studies on "Salvation and the Church" (Llandaff, 1986), "Church as Communion" (Dublin, 1990), "Life in Christ: Morals, Communion and the Church" (Venice, 1993), and "The Gift of Authority" (Palazzola, 1998). I propose to examine the studies of ARCIC-I and ARCIC-II to the extent that they have bearing on the topic of the apostolicity of the church.[5] I will also refer occasionally to reactions to these studies from the Anglican-Roman Catholic Dialogue in the United States.

The statements of ARCIC I and II prefer to speak about apostolicity in very concrete and comprehensive terms. The "Final Report," "Church as Communion," and "The Gift of Authority" refer often to "apostolic tradition," the "apostolic community," "apostolic faith," "apostolic teaching," "apostolic doctrine," "apostolic witness," "apostolic preaching," "apostolic writings," "apostolic mission," "apostolic authority," "apostolic mandate,"

---

5. The significance of what ARCIC has achieved needs to be acknowledged. The Commission has claimed that on the issue of what Anglicans and Roman Catholics believe regarding the Eucharist and ministry there is "substantial agreement." It means that both communions are in agreement on all matters that pertain to the essentials of the apostolic faith regarding these doctrines. There is no fundamental divergence on the substance of what Roman Catholics and Anglicans believe about the Eucharist and ministry. Thus, "The aim of the Commission has been to see whether we can today discover substantial agreement in faith on the eucharist. Questions have been asked about the meaning of *substantial* agreement. It means that the document represents not only the judgement of its members–i.e. it is an agreement–but their unanimous agreement 'on essential matters where it considers that doctrine admits no divergence' (*Ministry and Ordination* para. 17)–i.e. it is a substantial agreement. Members of the Commission are united in their conviction 'that if there are any remaining points of disagreement they can be resolved on the principles here established' (*Eucharistic Doctrine* para. 12)" ("Elucidation" on *Eucharistic Doctrine,* 1979, §2). And, "Mutual recognition presupposes acceptance of the apostolicity of each other's ministry. The Commission believes that its Agreements have demonstrated a consensus in faith on eucharist and ministry which has brought closer the possibility of such acceptance" ("Elucidation" on *Ministry and Ordination,* 1979, §6). Subsequent questions and official statements of both communions have not called this claim to "substantial agreement" on essentials into question. Nor did the Commission try to hide the fact that other sensitive and important issues needed further reflection, especially on issues relating to ecclesial authority where it spoke of their "significant convergence" at most (see *Authority in the Church I,* §25). On the essentials of the Eucharist and ministry, Anglicans and Roman Catholics have every right to rejoice in their common faith, and this fact must never be blurred. On the degree of agreement reached by ARCIC-I and an attempt to explain the rather negative response of the Vatican to the "Final Report," see Francis A. Sullivan, "The Vatican Response to ARCIC I," *Gregorianum* 73 (1992) 489–98.

"apostolic body," "apostolic group," "apostolic inheritance," "apostolic ministry," "apostolic order," "apostolic leadership," and "apostolic succession" or "succession to the apostles." Less frequently, but importantly, they refer to "apostolic" in a general sense and to the "apostolicity of the Church."[6] It is evident that the church's profession that its life is "apostolic" as enunciated in Scripture and by Nicaea and Constantinople is central to ARCIC. The statements also refer to *episkopē*, the "ministry of oversight," and "episcopal succession." Let us examine more closely several issues connected with the interpretation of ARCIC's understanding of apostolicity.

The "Final Report" added an introduction that situates the various statements of ARCIC-I within the context of an ecclesiology of communion or *koinonia*. In the postconciliar period communion ecclesiology emerged as a key to Vatican II's understanding of the church. Communion ecclesiology was seen to be the underlying basis for episcopal collegiality, the relationship of the local to the universal church, the universal salvific will of God and the mystery of grace, and the relations among the various Christian churches and ecclesial communities. It was canonized by the Extraordinary Synod of Bishops of 1985 when the bishops taught, "The ecclesiology of communion is the central and fundamental idea of the council's documents."[7] The idea of communion, then, was espoused by the Anglican as well as the Roman Catholic members of ARCIC four years before the Extraordinary Synod of Bishops' statement. In the "Introduction" the members wrote: "Fundamental to all our Statements is the concept of *koinonia* (communion). In the early Christian tradition, reflection on the experience of *koinonia* opened the way to the understanding of the mystery of the Church. Although *'koinonia'* is never

---

6. "*The Church is apostolic* not only because its faith and life must reflect the witness to Jesus Christ given in the early church by the apostles, but because it is charged to continue the apostles' commission to communicate to the world what it has received." See "Ministry and Ordination," §4 (my italics). "Every individual act of ordination is therefore an expression of the continuing *apostolicity and catholicity of the whole Church.*" Ibid., §14 (my italics). "It is because the church is built up by the Spirit upon the foundation of the life, death and resurrection of Christ as these have been witnessed and transmitted by the apostles that the church is called *apostolic.*" "Church as Communion," §25 (italics in text). "Tradition expresses the *apostolicity of the church.* What the apostles received and proclaimed is now found in the Tradition of the church where the word of God is preached and the sacraments of Christ celebrated in the power of the Holy Spirit." "The Gift of Authority," §17 (my italics).

7. "The Final Report," C. 1. See *A Message to the People of God and The Final Report* (Washington, D.C.: National Conference of Catholic Bishops, 1986) 17.

equated with 'Church' in the New Testament, it is the term that most aptly expresses the mystery underlying the various New Testament images of the Church" (4). It then proceeds to apply the notion of communion to the issues discussed, namely, eucharistic *koinonia,* the ministry of leadership *(episkopē)* as service to the *koinonia,* and primacy as a focus within the *koinonia* (6). The "Introduction" concludes with the following summary statement: "Full visible communion between our two Churches [sic] cannot be achieved without mutual recognition of sacraments and ministry, together with the common acceptance of a universal primacy, at one with the episcopal college in the service of the *koinonia*" (9). We need to take cognizance of the fact that ARCIC-I sees "primacy" fundamentally in terms of communion and only secondarily in terms of the more juridical notion of "jurisdiction."

"Church as Communion"

The insight into the centrality of communion that dawned upon the participants of ARCIC-I in the course of their years of dialogue achieved prominence in ARCIC-II's "Church as Communion."[8] It begins with an affirmation of the communion that truly exists between both parties. Though it is imperfect, it is nonetheless very real (2).[9] What is this communion that the document speaks of? First of all, "Church as Communion" presents the biblical teaching about communion (6–15), giving special

8. Quite simply, it is one of the most theologically impressive documents produced in the postconciliar period. The Statement can be found in *Growth in Agreement II: Reports and Agreed Statements of Ecumenical Conversations on a World Level, 1982–1998,* eds. Jeffrey Gros, Harding Meyer, and William G. Rusch (Grand Rapids: Wm. B. Eerdmans Publishing Co., 2000) 328–43. See the "Agreed Report on the Local/Universal Church" of the Anglican-Roman Catholic Consultation in the U.S.A. (ARC-USA) dated November 15, 1999, in *Origins* 30/6 (June 22, 2000) 85–95.

9. In a footnote the document makes reference to the "Common Declaration" of Pope John Paul II and Archbishop Robert Runcie at their meeting in Rome in 1989: "We also urge our clergy and faithful not to neglect or undervalue that certain, yet imperfect, communion we already share. This communion already shared is grounded in faith in God our Father, in our Lord Jesus Christ and in the Holy Spirit; our common baptism into Christ; our sharing of the Holy Scriptures, of the Apostles' and Nicene creeds; the Chalcedonian definition and the teaching of the Fathers; our common Christian inheritance for many centuries. This communion should be cherished and guarded as we seek to grow into the fuller communion Christ wills. Even in the years of our separation we have been able to recognize gifts of the Spirit in each other. The ecumenical journey is not only about the removal of obstacles, but also about the sharing of gifts." See *Origins* 19/19 (October 12, 1989) 316–17, at 317.

attention to the Christian Scriptures. In the second section (16–24), the document develops the theme of communion more systematically. Communion represents our human vocation to be in communion with God and through us God's will to be in communion with all creation. Jesus Christ, "the eternal Word made incarnate," has reestablished and fulfilled this communion. The Holy Spirit, too, is intimately involved in the process of establishing divine communion with humankind. The Spirit unites us in the communion of the body of Christ, the church, so that the church shares in the mission of the Son and the Spirit, which is no less than creating humankind anew (see 18 and 22). "Church as Communion" sees no incompatibility between describing the church as a "sacrament" *(sacramentum)* and as "communion" *(communio* or *koinonia)*. In fact, the divine gift of communion comes to expression in the church as sacrament. This means that the church acts both as a sign and an instrument of human salvation, but always in dependence on the Lord and on the Holy Spirit: "The church is both the sign of salvation in Christ, for to be saved is to be brought into communion with God through him, and at the same time the instrument of salvation, as the community through which this salvation is offered and received" (19). The church then is an "effective sign" of God's will to save humankind, "given by God in the face of human sinfulness, division and alienation" (ibid.).

The sacramentality of the church is also a call to mission: "In the power of Christ's presence through the Spirit [the church] is caught up in the saving mission of Christ" (22). Yet, in the light of Christ's universal significance, the document cautions Christians against a narrow interpretation of salvation that refuses to accept salvation beyond the confines of the church: "To speak of the church as sacrament is to affirm that in and through the communion of all those who confess Jesus Christ and who live according to their confession, God realizes his plan of salvation for all the world. This is not to say that God's saving work is limited to those who confess Christ explicitly. By God's gift of the same Spirit who was at work in the earthly ministry of Christ Jesus, the church plays its part in bringing his work to its fulfilment" (ibid.). And finally, "Church as Communion" points to the eucharistic nature of communion. The celebration of the Eucharist profoundly expresses the Lord's communion with the Father, our communion with the Lord and each other in the fellowship of faith. It also celebrates in an anticipatory way the fullness of communion in God's kingdom when God will be "all in all" (24). This section succeeds admirably in unfolding some of the profound meaning of the mystery of divine-human communion.

The third section (25–41) is concerned with the interrelationships among apostolicity, catholicity, and holiness. To the authors of "Church as Communion," apostolicity rests on christological and pneumatological bases: "It is because the church is built up by the Spirit upon the foundation of the life, death and resurrection of Christ as these have been witnessed and transmitted by the apostles that the church is called *apostolic*. It is also called apostolic because it is equipped for its mission by sharing in the apostolic mandate" (25). This notion of apostolic mandate is developed from the point of view of the apostles' "memory of Jesus," which is more than mere accuracy of recall or the repeating of Jesus' words and deeds. It is a memory made alive by the Spirit of Jesus. The original apostolic community played an essential role by remaining faithful to the memory of Christ and open to the Holy Spirit. The document makes the important statement that "the living memory of the mystery of Christ is present and active within the church as a whole" (28). The section then stresses the importance of the diversity of cultures and experiences for a better understanding of the church's memory of Christ. Though every believer has responsibility for preserving the memory of Christ expressed in the church's living tradition, those who have the "ministry of oversight," the bishops, have a special duty of "preaching, explaining and applying its truth" (32) to the church's life. Episcopal succession is not some mechanical process of automatically handing on a fixed and static deposit of truths, but a true ministry of the whole church to the apostolic faith "received and transmitted from apostolic times." Moreover, the bishops assist in maintaining the local churches in the communion of all the churches (see 33).

Paragraphs 34–37 take up the church's catholicity and relate it to apostolicity. The church is catholic "because its mission is to teach universally and without omission all that has been revealed by God for the salvation and fulfilment of humankind" (34). Thus, catholicity is both quantitative and qualitative. The community's celebration of the Eucharist is the privileged expression of the church's catholicity: "At every eucharistic celebration of Christian communities dispersed throughout the world, in their variety of cultures, languages, social and political contexts, it is the same one and indivisible body of Christ reconciling divided humanity that is offered to believers. In this way this eucharist is the sacrament of the Church's catholicity in which God is glorified" (36). Finally, after dealing with holiness (38–40), the third section concludes with a treatment of how all three notions are interrelated:

> When the creed speaks of the church as holy, catholic and apostolic, it does not mean that these attributes are distinct and unrelated. On the contrary, they are so interwoven that there cannot be one without the others. The holiness of the church reflects the mission of the Spirit of God in Christ, the holy One of God, made known to all the world through the apostolic teaching. Catholicity is the realization of the church's proclamation of the fullness of the gospel to every nation throughout the ages. Apostolicity unites the church of all generations and in every place with the once-for-all sacrifice and resurrection of Christ, where God's holy love was supremely demonstrated (41).

Ecclesial communion needs to be fostered and safeguarded. All in the church have their role to play in maintaining the unity of the apostolic proclamation, but important, too, is the ministry of oversight, *episkope,* "the fullness of which is entrusted to the episcopate, which has the responsibility of maintaining and expressing the unity of the churches" (45b), a ministry which has various dimensions, including the collegial and primatial.[10] The forms of collegiality and primacy are reviewed in paragraph 45c, and the document is honest in not trying to dissimulate the degree of misunderstanding that still exists between Anglicans and Roman Catholics at the day-to-day, de facto, existential levels, even though there is general agreement on the de jure principles of unity. Any attempt to mislead Anglicans or Roman Catholics on this point is avoided: "If some element or important fact of visible communion is judged to be lacking, the communion between them, though it may be real, is incomplete" (47).

A final section deals with various practical issues of closer collaboration between the parties, as well as honesty about still divisive matters that will require further reflection, for example, questions coalescing around authority, and concludes with the following positive analysis:

---

10. The document is not thinking exclusively about the papal form of primacy but about the whole range of ecclesiastical authority, including that of the pope. The issue of primacy had been investigated earlier by ARCIC-I in its two statements on authority (Venice, 1976 and Windsor, 1981), and would become a major topic of consideration in ARCIC-II's "The Gift of Authority."

Grave obstacles from the past and of recent origin must not lead us into thinking that there is no further room for growth towards fuller communion. It is
clear to the commission, as we conclude this document, that, despite continuing obstacles, our two communions agree in their understanding of the church
as communion. Despite our distinct historical experiences, this firm basis
should encourage us to proceed to examine our continuing differences (56).

"The Gift of Authority"

The final document to be examined with relevance for the apostolicity of the church is ARCIC-II's "The Gift of Authority."[11] The document is the third to be issued by ARCIC on this topic and this fact points
to the difficulty of the issues. Already "Authority in the Church I" evoked
an "Elucidation" in 1981 in which a number of criticisms of "Authority
I" were addressed. The complexity and sensitivity surrounding collegiality,
the various forms of primacy in both communions, and papal jurisdiction in particular, precluded making much progress. A second statement,
"Authority in the Church II," also dating from 1981, which was longer
and attempted to clarify the issues of the biblical exegesis of certain passages concerning the figure of Peter, jurisdiction, what is of "divine law"
[*ius divinum*] in the church and not of merely human invention, and the
exercise of infallibility, though courageous on the part of both parties,
failed to garner much support or enthusiasm among Anglicans and Roman
Catholics. "The Gift of Authority" returned to these seemingly intractable
issues in 1999. Like its predecessors, "Authority III" is proving a hard
sell. Longer and more detailed, once again it seems to please neither Anglicans nor Catholics. What does it say about apostolicity, and is the
issue of authority a dead end?

"Authority III" goes into greater depth in pursuit of an understanding of tradition (14–18), in recommending the process of reception and
re-reception to the churches (24–25), and in addressing the nature of the
conciliar or synodal exercise of authority in the church. I think one must
also speak of a positive advance on the understanding of infallibility in
different terms, not the absence of error so much as the church's perse-
vering in the truth. The development of a new conceptual framework to
encompass the many issues of authority, namely, faith as our human

11. See *Origins* 29/2 (May 27, 1999) 17, 19–29. For commentaries on the statement,
see William Henn, "A Roman Catholic Commentary on ARCIC-II's *The Gift of Authority*,"
One in Christ 35 (1999) 267–91, and Adelbert Denaux, "Authority in the Church, A Challenge for Both Anglicans and Roman Catholics," *Ecumenical Trends* 30/4 (April 2001) 1–10.

"amen" to God's "yes" to us in Jesus Christ (7–13), has helped ARCIC-II make progress. The new conceptuality repositions issues of authority from the realm of obedience to God's representatives to the realm of obedience to God. There is much to recommend the new approach for its christological focus, but the text could do better by more thoroughly integrating it into its avowed ecclesiology of communion.[12] The role of the Spirit is unfortunately diminished in the more pronounced christological formulation that is preferred in paragraphs 7–13. I think this is unfortunate because the statement reverts to earlier, less clearly trinitarian perspectives.

Apostolicity is discussed in paragraphs 14–18, where we encounter the programmatic statement that "Tradition expresses the apostolicity of the church" (17). It is the entire church that is apostolic. The whole of this section continues to breathe from the communion theology of Vatican II and the postconciliar period, and the role of the Spirit remains central. The section offers a rich theology of tradition that is said to be

> a dynamic process, communicating to each generation what was delivered once for all to the apostolic community. Tradition is far more than the transmission of true propositions concerning salvation. . . . The church receives and must hand on all those elements that are constitutive of ecclesial communion. . . . Through it, from one generation to another and from one place to another, humanity shares communion in the Holy Trinity. By the process of tradition, the church ministers the grace of the Lord Jesus Christ and the *koinonia* of the Holy Spirit (14–15).

Indeed, the Spirit appears in this section to be the very force of tradition, while the "memory of Jesus" constitutes tradition's content. The bishops have a special role to play in fostering the tradition. What is interesting in "Authority III" is that the bishops are spoken of as belonging to a college—they are not isolated leaders or members of just any group—but of a college of bishops.[13] And secondly, their ministry is now described as a "ministry of memory"—not of leadership primarily. Or perhaps it is better

---

12. ARC-USA has captured the centrality of communion ecclesiology for both churches in its statement "Agreed Report on the Local/Universal Church." See *Origins* 30/6 (June 22, 2000) 85–95.

13. Later we read: "The ministry of bishop is crucial, for this ministry serves communion within and among local churches. Their communion with each other is expressed through the incorporation of each bishop into a college of bishops. Bishops are, both personally and collegially, at the service of communion and are concerned for synodality in all its expressions" (37).

to say that the college of bishops leads by guarding the "memory of Jesus," which "Church as Communion" had spoken about earlier. At any rate, it is evident how preeminent apostolic tradition is in "The Gift of Authority" and how the episcopal ministry is being repositioned in light of this shift. All in the church are called to faithfulness and service to apostolic tradition. It is remarkable that "The Gift of Authority," like its predecessors from ARCIC-I, has avoided concentrating on episcopal succession as the exclusive sign of apostolicity and pointed instead to the apostolicity of the whole church, without denying the very real authority and ministry of the bishops in preaching, defining, and guarding the truth of the apostolic tradition.

It is apparent that much still needs to be done before we can speak of any breakthrough on the issues surrounding ecclesiastical authority. To many readers, the observations of "The Gift of Authority" are too idealistic and too removed from current practices in the churches to convince the members of both communions that agreement has been reached on these tough issues.[14] Some practical suggestions in section four (especially 56–62) offer real possibilities for addressing the neuralgic issues by both communions. Continued patience, dialogue, and diligent study will be imperative in the future, and the issue of authority will certainly need to be revisited. However, apostolicity does not emerge as a church-dividing issue for ARCIC. Both communions accept the apostolic tradition, the apostolic faith, apostolic mission, and apostolic ministry. Both dialogue partners seem to assign priority to the apostolicity of the whole church, without rejecting the indispensable role of *episkopē* and episcopal succession.[15] Both Anglicans and Roman Catholics have endeavored to

14. See the comments of the Anglican-Roman Catholic Dialogue in the U.S.A. on "The Gift of Authority" in *Origins* 30/6 (June 22, 2000) 85–95. Jon Nilson says that "the text sometimes views the two Churches through rose-tinted glasses," and cites §§40, 48, 54, and 55. See "*The Gift of Authority:* An American, Roman Catholic Appreciation," *One in Christ* 36 (2000) 133–44, at 136. However, Nilson reserves his most pointed criticism for the document's claim regarding the issue of papal primacy; the document states: "The commission's work has resulted in sufficient agreement on universal primacy as a gift to be shared for us to propose that such a primacy could be offered and received even before our churches are in full communion" (§60). Nilson acknowledges the challenge in the statement but wonders how acceptable it is to the full Anglican Communion. See ibid., 137.

15. ARC-USA has maintained that "for both churches, not the bishops alone but the entire church hands on the apostolic tradition. However, each church gives different weight to the role of the episcopate in the transmission of the apostolic heritage. . . . The Roman Catholic church holds that there is an essential role for bishops: Episcopacy is not

rethink the historic episcopate[16] in terms broader than the validity of ordinations by repositioning episcopal ordination in reference to what I have called "substantive apostolicity," that is, the apostolicity of the whole life of a church.

The Roman Catholic-Lutheran Dialogue

One of the most fruitful and prolific of the bilateral dialogues has been between Roman Catholics and Lutherans. The dialogue has taken place at the national and international levels.[17] I intend to limit myself to an examination of apostolicity in the Roman Catholic/Lutheran Joint

---

the sole carrier of apostolicity, but it is the primary carrier. . . . Anglicans hold that episcopacy is one element among many that together ensure the church's fidelity to the apostolic inheritance. . . . For Anglicans, the episcopate is not necessarily the primary carrier of apostolicity. The Episcopal Church holds that apostolic ministry resides with all Christians by virtue of their baptism. Ordained ministries exist 'to serve, lead and enable this ministry.'" See "Agreed Report on the Local/Universal Church," *Origins* 30/6 (June 22, 2000) 85–95, here at 92. In my reading of the Statement, "Agreed Report on the Local/Universal Church" does not envision apostolicity and apostolic succession as church dividing. I share this view and would state the harmony between our two communions in stronger terms than the Statement does. I am not convinced that the Roman Catholic position is well served by simply saying that "Episcopacy . . . is the primary carrier" of apostolicity. I find the statement too bald, and hence in need of further nuance. My hesitation is not so much with the word "primary" but with "carrier." In my opinion, the primary carrier always remains the local church as a whole which necessarily includes the bishop's ministry of oversight. In the oft-cited case of Arianism, when many of the bishops seemed confused and careless in defence of Nicaea's teaching, Cardinal Newman maintained that it was largely the faithful who remained true to apostolic doctrine. Even if Newman has exaggerated the orthodoxy of the faithful, his intuition was correct in sensing the indispensable function of the *sensus fidelium* in this case. Not everyone agrees with Newman's claim, however. See Michael Slusser, "Does Newman's 'On Consulting the Faithful in Matters of Doctrine' Rest upon a Mistake?" *Horizons* 20 (1993) 234–40.

16. Robert W. Jenson has pointed to the problem of interpreting the exact meaning of the phrase "the historic(al) episcopate." According to Jenson, it can refer to the emergence of a separate figure holding a leadership position of a local community and thus a distinct office vis-à-vis the body of presbyters and the deacons. The *episkopos* is one member of the threefold ministry. Another meaning of *episkopos* can be discerned with the emergence of an *episkopos* who exercises responsibility over a larger region where many other local bishops reside. See "Episcopacy," in *Unbaptized God: The Basic Flaw in Ecumenical Theology* (Minneapolis: Fortress Press, 1992) 61–75, especially at 62, 69–71.

17. On the Roman Catholic-Lutheran dialogues, see Harding Meyer, "Roman Catholic/Lutheran Dialogue," *One in Christ* 22 (1986) 146–68, and George H. Tavard and John Reumann, "The Lutheran-Roman Catholic Dialogue in North America," *One in Christ* 34 (1998) 268–89.

[International] Commission's statements. These national and international dialogues have addressed the widespread misunderstanding by Catholics and Lutherans of each other's history and beliefs and have been highly successful in correcting errors of fact and interpretation of each other's belief.[18] The most recent statement, the "Joint Declaration on the Doctrine of Justification," issued in 1998[19] and officially signed by representatives of the World Lutheran Federation and the Pontifical Council for Promoting Christian Unity on October 31, 1999, in Augsburg, Germany,[20] is the culmination of years of patient discussion and the careful stating of each church's theological position. The document caps the efforts of the last thirty-five years of Roman Catholic-Lutheran ecumenical discussions, and represents the closing of a painful chapter of repeated misunderstandings between the two churches. It also represents the opening of a new chapter with momentous ramifications. The salvation of the person by the Lord's redemptive act of justification was the very heart of the magisterial Reformation.[21] Nothing else came close to expressing the radical character of this doctrine to Martin Luther (1483–1546) and the other Reformers.[22] The fact that Roman Catholics and Lutherans can

18. For general information on Lutheran ecclesiology, ministry, episcopacy, and ecumenical activities, see Michael Root, "The Lutheran Churches," in *The Christian Church: An Introduction to the Major Traditions,* ed. Paul Avis (London: SPCK, 2002) 186–213.

19. See *Origins* 28/8 (July 16, 1998) 120–27. The text is also available as the *Joint Declaration on the Doctrine of Justification* (Grand Rapids: Wm. B. Eerdmans Publishing Co., 2000).

20. Statements made on the occasion of the signing by Cardinal Edward Cassidy, President of the Pontifical Council for Promoting Christian Unity, Bishop Christian Krause, President of the Lutheran World Federation, Bishop Walter Kasper, Secretary of the Pontifical Council for Promoting Christian Unity, and the Rev. Ishmael Noko, General Secretary of the Lutheran World Federation, can be found in *Origins* 29/22 (November 11, 1999) 343–48. The event was preceded by the issuance of an "Official Common Statement with Appendix" and by remarks from Cardinal Cassidy and the Rev. Ishmael Noko earlier in June. See *Origins* 29/6 (June 24, 1999) 85, 87–92. The "Official Common Statement with Appendix" was approved by the Lutheran World Federation and by the Pontifical Council for Promoting Christian Unity and the Congregation for the Doctrine of the Faith, with the explicit approval of Pope John Paul II.

21. Cardinal Edward Cassidy has put it succinctly: "The consensus reached with the Lutheran World Federation on basic truths of the doctrine of justification is of great significance not only for the two parties directly involved, but also for the whole ecumenical movement since the doctrine of justification is at the very heart of the Christian faith. It was the different understanding of this fundamental Christian teaching, particularly, that resulted in the disputes that led to the Reformation." *Origins* 29/22 (November 11, 1999) 347.

22. See David C. Steinmetz, "The Intellectual Appeal of the Reformation," *Theology Today* 57 (2000–01) 459–72. See the collection of essays in Carl E. Braaten and Robert W.

now confess their "consensus [on] the basic truths of the doctrine of justification" means that when we re-read the earlier documents of the international dialogue, they take on added meaning. Let us examine some of the principal statements of the Roman Catholic-Lutheran dialogue.[23]

"The Gospel and the Church"

The issue of apostolicity has emerged repeatedly in the documents. Very early on, "The Gospel and the Church" (1972) remarked: "The church is apostolic insofar as it stands on this foundation [the apostles] and abides in the apostolic faith. The church's ministry, doctrine and order are apostolic insofar as they pass on and actualize the apostolic witness" (52).[24] The teaching of the apostles is rooted in the singularity of their being "witnesses of [the Lord's] resurrection." The document then goes on to speak of the "substance of apostolicity": "In the New Testament and the early fathers, the emphasis was obviously placed more on the substance of apostolicity, i.e., on succession in apostolic teaching. In this sense the entire church as the *ecclesia apostolica* stands in the apostolic succession" (57). Right from the start of the conversations, then, Catholics and Lutherans focused on the apostolicity of the whole church. The question of the historical forms of *episkopē* and the emergence of the historical episcopate was not neglected, but was considered only after the primary assertion of the whole church's apostolic character. Thus, the citation from paragraph 57 continues as follows:

> Within this general sense of succession, there is a more specific meaning: the succession of the uninterrupted line of the transmission of office. In the early church, primarily in connection with defence against heresies, it was a sign of the unimpaired transmission of the gospel and a sign of unity in the faith. It is in these terms that Catholics today are trying once again to develop a deeper understanding of apostolic succession in the ministerial office. Lutherans on their side can grant the importance of a special succession if the preeminence of succession in teaching is recognized and if the

---

Jenson, ed., *The Catholicity of the Reformation* (Grand Rapids: Wm B. Eerdmans Publishing Co., 1996).

23. For a well-informed presentation of the various statements issued by Lutherans and Roman Catholics, see Margaret O'Gara, "Apostolicity in Ecumenical Dialogue," *MidStream* 37 (1998) 175–212, at 177–93 ["Part One: Lutheran-Roman Catholic Agreed Statements"].

24. See *Growth in Agreement*, 180.

uninterrupted line of transmission of office is not viewed as an *ipso facto* certain guarantee of the continuity of the right proclamation of the gospel.[25]

The statement reveals both agreement and disagreement. The points of agreement are that substantive apostolicity is fundamental and grounds the apostolicity of the whole church and that the historical episcopate is not a foreign element introduced later into the church's structure. Somewhat problematic for Catholics was the statement about episcopacy as not being "an *ipso facto* certain guarantee" of the correct proclamation of the gospel. Today, in the light of the "Joint Declaration of the Doctrine of Justification," the remark need not be viewed as compromising the Catholic position regarding the authoritative preaching and the teaching office of the bishops, but that the episcopal office also must be understood in terms of the priority of what God always does to save us. Ecclesiastical authority is not excluded, but it is definitely not self-generating or self-referential. As a stable office, it is always God's gift and a sign of God's authority when it is exercised. A subsequent section, entitled "The Possibility of a Mutual Recognition of the Ministerial Office," seems to ignore the importance of the insight that more specific aspects of apostolicity, for example, ministerial office, must be viewed in the light of the apostolicity of the whole church. Unfortunately, it takes up the issue in isolation and evokes a "special statement" by four of the Catholic participants.[26] None of them, however, objects to the basic insight of the document that it is the church as a whole that is apostolic and that this must be our first statement regarding apostolicity. Though "The Gospel and the Church" addressed fundamental issues and oft-repeated misunderstandings of each other's positions theologically, it did not come to terms with the underlying ecclesiologies of each participant church.

"The Ministry in the Church"

A brief statement on the 450th anniversary of the Augsburg Confession, entitled "All Under One Christ" (1980), contained for the first time an important reference to the ecclesiology of communion. It stated: "By church we mean the communion of those whom God gathers together through Christ in the Holy Spirit, by the proclamation of the gospel

25. Ibid., 181–82.
26. Some of them also mention the following statement in §73: "Unclarity concerning a common doctrine of the ministerial office still makes for difficulties in reciprocal intercommunion agreements."

and the administration of the sacraments, and the ministry instituted by him for this purpose" (16).[27] The following year, in "The Ministry in the Church," the first detailed presentation on church ministry by Lutherans and Roman Catholics, was published. The document builds its theology of ministry on a doctrine dear to Lutherans and only recently retrieved by Catholics at Vatican II, namely, the priesthood of all the faithful.

> *Martyria, leiturgia* and *diakonia* (witness, worship and service to the neighbour) are tasks entrusted to the whole people of God. All Christians have their own charismata for service to God and to the world as well as for building up of the one body of Christ. . . . The doctrine of the common priesthood of all the baptized is amply attested in the church fathers and the theologians of the High Middle Ages. . . . In contemporary Protestant teaching regarding the church, the universal priesthood of all the baptized is once again stressed. The Second Vatican Council expressly emphasized the common priesthood of the faithful (13).[28]

The remainder of the document deals with issues of ecclesial ministry.[29] In the course of examining these issues, and the apostolicity of the ministry in particular, "The Ministry in the Church" does not hesitate to refer to the apostolicity of the entire church.

> The most important question regarding the theology of the episcopal office and regarding the mutual recognition of ministries is the problem of apostolic succession. This is normally taken to mean the unbroken ministerial succession of bishops in a church. But apostolic succession is also often understood to refer in the substantive sense to the apostolicity of the church in faith (59).
>
> The starting point must be the apostolicity of the church in the substantive sense. . . . The Lutheran tradition speaks in this connection of a *successio verbi*. In present-day Catholic theology, more and more often the view is adopted that the substantive understanding of apostolicity is primary. Far-reaching agreement on this understanding of apostolic succession is therefore developing (60).
>
> . . . The witness to the gospel has been entrusted to the church as a whole. Therefore, the whole church as the *ecclesia apostolica* stands in the apostolic

27. See *Growth in Agreement,* 244.
28. Ibid., 252–3.
29. "The Ordained Ministry in the Church" (16–39), "The Various Forms of Ministry" (40–73), and "Mutual Recognition of Ministries" (74–86).

succession. Succession in the sense of the succession of ministers must be seen within the succession of the whole church in the apostolic faith (61). . . . Catholic tradition holds that the episcopate as a whole is nevertheless kept firm in the truth of the gospel. In this sense, Catholic doctrine regards the apostolic succession in the episcopal office as a sign and ministry of the apostolicity of the church (62).[30]

Even though the bulk of the text is concerned with questions of the sacramental character of episcopal ordination, the emergence of episcopacy in the early church, the fact that episcopacy is constitutive of the church's organizational structure even though its concrete form is historically variable, the role of the bishop of Rome in the body of bishops, and sensitive matters relating to the mutual recognition of each other's ministers, "The Ministry in the Church" never ignores the fundamental insight of the Lutheran and Catholic participants that in the first instance it is the church as a whole that is apostolic. All other issues of apostolicity must be considered in the light of this basic datum. What "The Ministry in the Church" failed to do, however, was to develop adequately the underlying ecclesiology of the claim. The next two documents of the Joint Commission would go a long way in addressing the neglect of fundamental ecclesiological issues.

"Facing Unity"

"Facing Unity" (1984) consistently adopts an ecclesiology of communion: "The church is therefore a communion *(communio)* subsisting in a network of local churches. . . . This view of church unity as communion *(communio)* goes back to the early days of Christianity. It is determinative for the early church as well as for the life and ecclesiology of the Orthodox Churches. In recent times it has been particularly stressed in Catholic ecclesiology. . . . This view of the church and of ecclesial unity is also in accord with Lutheran ecclesiology" (5–7).[31] Basic consensus on communion ecclesiology allowed the authors to proceed to consider "models of comprehensive union" (13–30) and to conclude for "unity in reconciled diversity" (31–34 and 47–48). The community shared by Lutherans and Catholics includes community of faith (55–69), community in sacraments (70–85), and community of service (86–148). All three

30. See *Growth in Agreement*, 266–67.
31. See *Growth in Agreement II*, 445.

parts deal with the apostolicity of the church: community of faith with
the apostolic faith of the church, community in sacraments with the sacramental life bequeathed by the apostles, and community of service with
apostolic ministry. It is primarily in the third part that apostolic succession and the episcopal office is treated at length. But even in this section
that concentrates on the office of bishop in the church, the apostolicity of
the whole church is not forgotten.

> All this shows that the apostolic succession is not really to be understood
> as a succession of one individual to another, but rather as a succession in
> the church, to an episcopal see and to membership of the episcopal college,
> as shown by the lists of bishops.
>
> The responsibility of the congregation is not limited to the moment of
> ordination. Its full scope is illustrated by the exception "that one must
> deny one's consent even to bishops when it happens that they err and
> speak in a manner that contradicts the canonical texts." This means that
> the *episcope* is not exercised in isolation but normally in concert with the
> community of believers, i.e., within a diversity of ministries and services
> and in the synodal life of the local church.
>
> . . . Bishops thus both represent the universal church in their own church
> and represent their own church among all other churches (110–111).[32]

The remainder of "Facing Unity" deals with the joint exercise of
the bishop's ministry and makes a daring and detailed proposal for how
that ministry might be exercised by bishops of both churches (120–145).
And yet, in spite of all the attention paid to questions of episcopacy and
apostolic succession of the bishops, it is the apostolicity of the entire
church that remains the fundamental assertion.

"Church and Justification"

The Joint Commission directly engaged the theme of the church in
1993. Not unlike the Dogmatic Constitution on the Church of Vatican
II, "Church and Justification"[33] relies heavily on the biblical images of
the people of God, the body of Christ, and the temple of the Holy Spirit
(51–62). Reflecting on these images, the document sees the church as the

32. Ibid., 468. A footnote appended to the quotation refers to writings of Augustine
and Thomas Aquinas.

33. For a helpful overview and commentary, see Patrick Granfield, "Comments on
'Church and Justification,'" *One in Christ* 33 (1997) 35–46.

creation of the Trinity, with each image highlighting the role of the trinitarian persons (32–50). Here, too, it shows profound affinity of thought with Vatican II's Decree on the Missionary Activity of the Church, both in terms of its emphasis on the church and the Trinity, as well as the role of mission in defining the church (244–89). As its title indicates, it considers the church as an expression of salvation in Christ by justification of the sinner (4–31). The sensitive theme of the church as sacrament is honestly faced (107–34). How is the church a sacrament? How is it related to Christ as sacrament? How is the church a sign and an instrument of salvation, and does this detract from the centrality of Christ as savior (166–242)? "Church and Justification" manages to avoid being trapped by questions of ecclesiality and sacramentality by once again building on the ecclesial theme of "communion" (63–106). These paragraphs are of direct interest to our theme of apostolicity.

"Church and Justification" is the clearest of all the documents of the Roman Catholic/Lutheran Joint Commission in explaining the nature of *communio*.

> However one looks at the church, whether as "people of God" or "body of Christ" or "temple of the Holy Spirit", it is rooted in the inseparable communion or koinonia of the three divine persons and is thereby itself constituted as koinonia. It is not primarily the communion of believers with each other which makes the church koinonia; it is primarily and fundamentally the communion of believers with God, the triune God whose innermost being is koinonia. And yet the communion of believers with the triune God is inseparable from their communion with each other (65).[34]
>
> On both the Catholic and the Lutheran side, the concept of koinonia/communio has once more become important ecclesiologically; indeed it has become central (74).[35]

The primacy of communion ecclesiology is revealed in the acceptance by both parties of the fundamental importance of the local church, without detriment to the universal aspects of the church as a community of all the saved. The retrieval of the importance of the local church has helped Catholics better understand the dignity of local congregations and of their leaders, the bishops (91–104), while it has helped Lutherans better understand the unity of the church as founded in the *communio* of the Trinity

34. See *Growth in Agreement II*, 503.
35. Ibid., 505.

(84–90). Both parties have benefited enormously from communion ecclesiology, and new bonds of faith have been forged between the churches. How, then, does "Church and Justification" envision apostolicity?

The document treats apostolicity explicitly in two sections. Early on, "Church and Justification" grounds apostolicity on the role of the originary apostles (44–47). Though Jesus Christ is the church's true foundation (1 Cor 3:11), the apostles, too, have their role to play in laying the foundation of the church (Eph 2:20) by their proclamation of the gospel. What is interesting from the perspective of the ecumenical dialogue is that the preaching and teaching of the apostles is broadened to include apostolicity in a more all-inclusive sense: "Though Lutherans and Catholics think differently in many respects about the way in which the apostolic norm is safeguarded, the shared conviction nevertheless is that 'apostolicity' is an essential attribute of the church and the criterion par excellence of its faith, its proclamation, its teaching and *its life*" (46).[36] The implications are spelled out later when the document takes up the topic of episcopacy, the sacramental nature of ordination for both churches, and the historicity of ecclesial structures and the continuity of the church when it remains faithful to the gospel. Thus, the document finds no contradiction between the office of bishop and the norm of justification: "There is no contradiction between the doctrine of justification and the idea of an ordained ministry instituted by God and necessary for the church" (185).[37] Episcopacy even functions as a ministry to safeguard the purity of the gospel:

> . . . The episcopate and apostolic succession stand in service as ministry to what is necessary for salvation, so that the word will be authentically preached and the sacraments rightly celebrated. The episcopate and apostolic succession serve to safeguard the apostolic tradition, the content of which is expressed in the rule of faith. The Spirit of God uses the episcopate in order to identify the church in every historical situation with its apostolic origin, to integrate the faithful in the one universal faith of the church, and just so through the episcopate to make its liberating force effective (196).[38]

36. Ibid., 498 (my italics).

37. Ibid., 529. Furthermore, §183 remarks: "The critical assertion that the ordained ministry as an institution of continuity by its very existence runs counter to the doctrine of justification is thus repudiated fundamentally."

38. Ibid., 532.

On the ecumenically sensitive issue of the phrase of Vatican II that spoke of the ministry of the communities separated from Rome as suffering from *sacramenti ordinis defectum*,[39] "Church and Justification" challenges the Catholic Church to offer a better explanation of the statement in the light of its other claim that "the Lutheran churches are church."[40] Is the *defectus* to be understood as a "complete lack of the sacrament of orders" or as "a lack of completeness of the sacrament of orders"? The Council never defined the term exactly, leaving it up to further discussion between the separated churches.[41] In the light of the ecclesiology that has emerged from the Lutheran-Roman Catholic dialogue since "The Gospel and the Church" (1972) with its ever-increasing agreement on the priesthood of all the faithful, the ecclesiology of communion, and the apostolicity of the whole church, it is hard to believe that the dialogue partners see Protestant ministry as "lacking entirely the very reality of the apostolic ministry."

Finally, the document examines various aspects of the episcopal ministry: bishops as preachers and authoritative teachers of the faith (205–222) and as those who exercise a ministry of jurisdiction (223–242). In each instance, the document shows how Lutherans and Catholics understand the roles examined in different, but by no means in antithetically opposed, ways. Thus, Lutherans strive to understand episcopal juris-

39. See the Decree on Ecumenism, 22.

40. See the Decree on Ecumenism, 19–23. In 1981, the Lutheran-Roman Catholic Joint International Commission's "The Ministry in the Church" had already addressed this sensitive issue in §§ 75–80.

41. Walter Kasper has discussed this issue in his essay "The Apostolic Succession: An Ecumenical Problem," in *Leadership in the Church: How Traditional Roles Can Serve the Christian Community Today,* tr. Brian McNeil (New York: The Crossroad Publishing Company, 2003) 114–43. He writes: "What does this passage mean? It was observed soon after the council that *defectus* need not mean a total lack but can also mean a simple defect. . . . Hence both the vocabulary of the council and the logic of the matter show that *defectus ordinis* does not mean a total lack, but a defect in the full form of the ministry. The council does not define this defect; but in the light of what has been said above, it is surely not only the interruption of the apostolic succession in the episcopal office, since this may not be seen in isolation; ultimately, this break in continuity was the fruit of a different understanding of the church and of the connection between Gospel and church. . . . When we consider all those points where agreement exists or may soon be achieved, it becomes clear that the core of the remaining divergence between the separated churches remains the question of the relationship between the Gospel and the church—not the question of the validity of ordinations by non-episcopal ministers. The question is whether and to what extent the concrete church is the location, sign, and instrument of the Gospel of Jesus Christ." Ibid., at 135–38.

diction in a sense that respects the "freedom of the gospel," while Catholics stress the right of the bishop to legally order the communal life of the local church and to require obedience. The two interpretations should be viewed as offering complementary gospel perspectives. Each sees the bishop's ministry as a pastoral office, an expression of Christ who continues to shepherd his church.

BEM *Faith and Order of the World Council of Churches*

Undoubtedly, the single most important document to emerge from the ecumenical movement in the years following Vatican II is *Baptism, Eucharist and Ministry* [henceforth *BEM*].[42] It was the result of decades-long multilateral consultations enriched and broadened by the many churches that constituted the World Council of Churches[43] after its founding in 1948 and by the participation of the Roman Catholic Church in the Commission on Faith and Order[44] after Vatican II. *BEM* often goes by the title "The Lima Text," since it was approved by Faith and Order at its meeting in Lima, Peru, in 1982. *BEM* is really three studies linked by a common methodology and a formal process of reception of the document by the churches as explained in the "Preface" to *BEM*.[45] The process of reception extended from 1982 to 1989, and the responses were published in six volumes by the WCC between 1986 and 1988.[46] Two other documents, *The Church: Local and Universal* and *The Nature and Purpose of the Church: A Stage on the Way to a Common Statement,* seek to continue

42. Faith and Order Paper 111 (Geneva: WCC Publications, 1982), reprinted in *Growth in Agreement,* 466–503.

43. See Thomas Stransky, "World Council of Churches," in *Dictionary of the Ecumenical Movement,* ed. Nicholas Lossky and others (Grand Rapids: Wm. B. Eerdmans Publishing Co., 1991) 1083–90.

44. See Günther Gassmann, "Faith and Order," in ibid., 411–13.

45. On the preparatory history, nature of the process, and the responses to *BEM,* see Max Thurian, "Baptism, Eucharist and Ministry (the 'Lima text')," in ibid., 80–83. See also Michael Kinnamon, ed., *Towards Visible Unity: Commission on Faith and Order, Lima 1982,* vol. II: *Study Papers and Reports,* Faith and Order Paper 113 (Geneva: WCC Publications, 1982); Max Thurian, ed., *Ecumenical Perspectives on Baptism, Eucharist and Ministry,* Faith and Order Paper 116 (Geneva: WCC Publications, 1983); and Michael A. Fahey, ed., *Catholic Perspectives on 'Baptism, Eucharist and Ministry': A Study Commissioned by the Catholic Theological Society of America* (Lanham, Md.: University Press of America, 1986).

46. For a helpful summary of the voluminous responses and further proposals for clarification of issues, see *Baptism, Eucharist and Ministry 1982–1990: Report on the Process and Responses* (Geneva: WCC Publications, 1990).

the process inaugurated by *BEM*.[47] What do these documents state with regard to apostolicity?

BEM marks a clear advance over the ordinary presentation of who the apostles were. One of the peculiarities of *BEM* is the division of the text into a main text and a second series of "Commentaries" on the main text. The "commentaries" deal with historical matters and issues that do not rise to the level of convergence that *BEM* tries to express. As the "Preface" remarks:

> The agreed text purposely concentrates on those aspects of the theme that have been directly or indirectly related to the problems of mutual recognition leading to unity. The main text demonstrates the major areas of theological convergence; the added commentaries either indicate historical differences that have been overcome or identify disputed issues still in need of further research and reconciliation.[48]

In "Ministry," regarding the apostles we read:

> In the New Testament the term "apostle" is variously employed. It is used for the Twelve but also for a wider circle of disciples. It is applied to Paul and to others as they are sent out by the risen Christ to proclaim the Gospel. The roles of the apostles cover both foundation and mission.[49]

The distinction between the twelve apostles and "apostles" in a wider sense in the early church is helpful for purposes of elaborating a theology of ecclesiastical office. However, when "Ministry" speaks of apostolicity, it prefers to do so in terms of "apostolic tradition." *BEM* generally avoids a direct or explicit association of apostolicity with the whole church and gives the impression that the church of subsequent generations is apostolic because it remains in continuity with the faith proclaimed by the apostles. Nevertheless, in paragraph 34, in explaining what it means by apostolic tradition, "Ministry" opens the door to a wider interpretation:

> . . . Apostolic tradition in the Church means continuity in the permanent characteristics of the Church of the apostles: witness to the apostolic faith, proclamation and fresh interpretation of the Gospel, celebration of baptism

47. Faith and Order Paper 150 (Geneva: WCC Publications, 1990) [reprinted in *Growth in Agreement II*, 862–75] and Faith and Order Paper 181 (Geneva: WCC Publications, 1998).

48. See *Growth in Agreement*, 468–69.

49. Commentary on §9. See ibid., 499.

and the eucharist, the transmission of ministerial responsibilities, communion in prayer, love, joy and suffering, service to the sick and the needy, unity among the local churches and sharing the gifts which the Lord has given to each.

This description of apostolic tradition comes much closer to my understanding of "substantive apostolicity" as including the whole life of a community. Of course apostolicity refers to apostolic faith, but that faith is not disembodied. It assumes concrete form in sacramental life, liturgical actions, normative writings, acts of love, service, and promoting justice, suffering persecution for the faith, official and unofficial ministries in a community, and so forth.

BEM also grounds ministry in the common dignity of all who belong to the people of God, in the Holy Spirit's abundant sharing of charisms with all the faithful, and in a universal call to ministry. This last point does not exclude a special ministry of the ordained that shares in the power of Jesus Christ and that is more than a sign of the general ministry of the whole community. In the words of BEM:

> The Church has never been without persons holding specific authority and responsibility. . . . The very existence of the Twelve and other apostles shows that, from the beginning, there were differentiated roles in the community (M 9).
>
> Jesus called the Twelve to be representatives of the renewed Israel. At that moment they represent the whole people of God and at the same time exercise a special role in the midst of that community (M 10).
>
> All members of the believing community, ordained and lay, are interrelated. On the one hand, the community needs ordained ministers. Their presence reminds the community of the divine initiative, and of the dependence of the Church on Jesus Christ, who is the source of its mission and the foundation of its unity. They serve to build up the community in Christ and to strengthen its witness (M 12).[50]

BEM proceeds to show how the bishops, presbyters, and deacons of the second century continued the ministry of the apostles by remaining faithful to the gospel they proclaimed and by exercising *episkopē* (pastoral oversight or supervision) in the communities. The text concentrates on the issue of apostolic succession by the ordained ministers in the church, and

50. Ibid., 484–85.

preeminently by bishops in the early church, but not at the expense of seeing apostolic succession as something which the whole church participates in.

> The primary manifestation of apostolic succession is to be found in the apostolic tradition of the Church as a whole. The succession is an expression of the permanence and, therefore, of the continuity of Christ's own mission in which the Church participates. Within the Church the ordained ministry has a particular task of preserving and actualizing the apostolic faith. The orderly transmission of the ordained ministry is therefore a powerful expression of the continuity of the Church throughout history; it also underlines the calling of the ordained minister as guardian of the faith (M35).
>
> . . . Today churches, including those engaged in union negotiations, are expressing willingness to accept episcopal succession as a sign of the *apostolicity of the life of the whole Church* (M 38).[51]

Even though "Ministry" concentrates on episcopacy and on the thorny issue of the apostolic succession of the bishops, it does not entirely ignore the more basic truth of the succession of the whole church to the apostolic tradition of truth, life, and ecclesial ministry. On this point, *The Nature and Purpose of the Church* is perhaps even more explicit. There, we read:

> . . . [The Church] is apostolic because the Word of God that creates and sustains the Church is the Gospel primarily and normatively borne witness to by the apostles, making the communion of the faithful a community that lives in, and is responsible for, the succession of the apostolic truth throughout the ages (12).
>
> The primary manifestation of apostolic succession is to be found in the apostolic tradition of the Church as a whole. . . . The ministry of the ordained is to serve in a specific way the apostolic continuity of the Church as a whole. In this context, succession in ministry is a means of serving the apostolic continuity of the Church (88).
>
> . . . All the baptized share a responsibility for the apostolic faith and witness of the whole Church (98).[52]

The criticism frequently voiced concerning *BEM* is that the document lacks a clear and developed ecclesiology. As a result, the clarifications added to *BEM* called for Faith and Order to address this lack in future

---

51. Ibid., 491–92 (my italics).

52. *The Nature and Purpose of the Church: A Stage on the Way to a Common Statement* (Geneva: WCC Publications, 1998) 10, 42–42, and 49.

consultations. That explains why Faith and Order issued two further studies, *The Church: Local and Universal* and *The Nature and Purpose of the Church*. The first of these studies, *The Church: Local and Universal*, addressed an issue that had been given a prominent place in the Roman Catholic ecclesiology of Vatican II's Dogmatic Constitution on the Church (LG 23 and 26) and the Decree of the Pastoral Office of the Bishops in the Church (CD 11),[53] and which had always been a key ecclesiological doctrine of the churches of the East. In the wake of the magisterial Reform, the non-Catholic churches of the West also had stressed the local church. One can speak of a certain convergence of Roman Catholics, Orthodox Christians, and Christians of the Reform on the issue of the local church. *The Nature and Purpose of the Church* has attempted to address ecclesiological issues in a more comprehensive way than *BEM* and *The Church: Local and Universal* were able to do.

Nevertheless, in reading all three documents, I feel the criticism that *BEM* lacks a coherent ecclesiology is unfair.[54] The three statements of *BEM* are inextricably interconnected. To consider "Ministry" in isolation from "Baptism" and "Eucharist" is to do violence to the text's inner logic. This is especially true of what is said about the Eucharist.[55] To accept the basic convictions of "Eucharist" on sacrifice (E 4), anamnesis or "dynamic memory" (E 5–13), its statement about *communio* (E 19–21), the role of the Holy Spirit and the epiclesis or "invocation of the Spirit" (E 14–18), the eschatological and missionary dimensions of the Eucharist (E 22–26), and the question of the frequency of celebrating the Eucharist with its challenge to some churches to consider more frequent

53. On the recent discussions in the Catholic Church of the relationship of the local and universal church, see Kilian McDonnell, "The Ratzinger/Kasper Debate: The Universal Church and Local Churches," *Theological Studies* 63 (2002) 227–50.

54. The Vatican response to *BEM* often refers to the inadequacy of *BEM*'s ecclesiology. The following remark is typical: "For the Catholic Church, the truths of faith are not divided from one another. They constitute a unique organic whole. Therefore full agreement on the sacraments is related to agreement on the nature of the church. The sacraments, including baptism, receive their full significance and efficacy from the comprehensive ecclesial reality on which they depend and which they manifest. Nor can the goal of the unity of divided Christians be reached without agreement on the nature of the church" ("Conclusion"). See *Origins* 17/23 (November 19, 1987) 416. See the judgment of many churches on *BEM*'s ecclesiology summarized in *Baptism, Eucharist and Ministry 1982–1990: Report on the Process and Responses*, 87 [33 (a)].

55. See David N. Power, "Eucharistic Sacrifice in Ecumenical Dialogue," in *The Sacrifice We Offer: The Tridentine Dogma and Its Reinterpretation* (New York: The Crossroad Publishing Company, 1987) 1–26.

Sunday Eucharists (E 29–31) are already powerful ecclesiological statements. Can more be done with these elements of an ecclesiology? Certainly. This is true of the notion of "sacrament" and the sacramentality of the church in particular. Can it be said that *BEM* lacks a convincing ecclesiology? I think not. Considerations of apostolic succession in "Ministry" need to be based on this sound understanding of the church in *BEM*. The ecclesiology of *BEM* is clearly a eucharistic ecclesiology that has been nourished by the eucharistic ecclesiology of the churches of the East and that is intimately related to the eucharistic ecclesiology that comes to expression in Vatican II's Dogmatic Constitution on the Church (LG 3 and 11).[56] The ecclesiology of *BEM* is often implicit, and it is to be keenly desired that the discussions on the church will continue, but *BEM* truly represents a moment in which all the participating churches of Faith and Order can rejoice on the extent of convergence that has been reached.

56. In his commentary on LG 11, Aloys Grillmeier developed this eucharistic ecclesiology: "The Eucharist is the sacrament of the sacrifice of the Cross, that is, the sacramental insertion of Christ's death on the Cross, of his whole life and of his resurrection, into the total sacrament of the Church. By instituting the Eucharist Christ made the supreme act of his unique self-dedication an act of the Church, under the guise of symbolic action. As it performs this act, the Church offers to God the Father the Lord who is present there, and with this gift, the Church offers itself. . . . For in the Eucharist Christ gives himself to the 'Church' and thus constitutes from within, through the reality of the body and blood which is given to all, the unity of the people of God. The eucharistic body of Christ is thus the integrating and constructive principle of the mystical body of the Lord, the Church. But the eucharistic body is only the principle which unites and builds up because it works through the Church and its sacramental action. . . . We may no doubt deduce from this that incorporation into the unity of the mystical body is the primary effect of the Eucharist and the instrumental cause of all other effects." *Commentary on the Documents of Vatican II,* 5 vols., ed. Herbert Vorgrimler (New York: Herder and Herder, 1967) 1:160–61. Grillmeier refers to St. Augustine, William of St. Thierry, and Karl Rahner as advocates of eucharistic ecclesiology. For Karl Rahner, see *The Church and the Sacraments,* Quaestiones Disputatae 9, tr. W. J. O'Hara (New York: Herder and Herder, 1963) 82–87. There Rahner wrote: "Because he really gives himself in ever new sacramental manifestation as sacrifice for the Church (Eph. 5:25f.) and as sacrifice of the Church, because he exists in the Church in visible and tangible form, there *is* the Church. She is most manifest and in the most intensive form, she attains the highest actuality of her own nature, when she celebrates the eucharist. For here everything that goes to form the Church is found fully and manifestly present." Ibid., 84–85 (italics in text). See Robert W. Jenson, *God Baptized: The Basic Flaw in Ecumenical Theology,* 95–96. Finally, see the recent encyclical of John Paul II, *Ecclesia de Eucharistia* ("Church of the Eucharist), *Origins* 32/46 (May 1, 2003) 753, 755–68.

British and Irish Anglican Churches
and Nordic and Baltic Lutheran Churches

A regional bilateral dialogue between Anglicans and Lutherans published in 1993 has exerted an influence in ecumenical discussions well beyond its intended addressees. I am referring to "The Porvoo Common Statement" from conversations between the British and Irish Anglican Churches and the Nordic and Baltic Lutheran Churches.[57] Porvoo represents a culmination to date of recent discussions regarding apostolicity inasmuch as it draws widely from earlier bilateral and multilateral statements, especially from *BEM,* the Roman Catholic-Lutheran Joint Commission ("Facing Unity," 1985), Anglicans and the Evangelical Church in Germany ("The Meissen Common Statement," 1988), ARCIC- I ("The Final Report," 1982) and ARCIC-II "Salvation and the Church," 1987), Anglicans and Lutherans ("The Pullach Report," 1972, "The Helsinki Report," 1982, and "The Niagara Report," 1987), and the Anglican-Reformed International Commission ("God's Reign and Our Unity," 1984). It has offered the most concentrated theological focus on apostolicity and apostolic succession, and for this reason deserves careful study. What, then, does Porvoo say about apostolicity?

As we have seen, the various discussions of apostolicity since Vatican II have focused on the apostolicity of the whole church as the primary expression of apostolicity and apostolic succession. In fact, apostolic succession is often understood in this more fundamental sense and only then, in a second reflection on it, is it extended to the role of the historical episcopate as the most appropriate expression of the fundamental apostolicity of the whole church. Porvoo is crystal clear on the matter of the church's apostolicity:

---

57. *Together in Mission and Ministry: The Porvoo Common Statement with Essays on Church and Ministry in Northern Europe* (London: Church House Publishing, 1993). The Common Statement can be found on pages 6–29; the Porvoo Declaration itself follows on pages 30–33. In this section, I am concerned with the Common Statement only. On Porvoo, see Ola Tjørhom, "The Porvoo Statement–A Possible Ecumenical Breakthrough?" *One in Christ* 29 (1993) 302–9, and idem, "Apostolic Continuity and Apostolic Succession in the Porvoo Common Statement: A Challenge to the Nordic Lutheran Churches," *Louvain Studies* 21 (1996) 126–37; Henrik Roelvink, "The Apostolic Succession in the Porvoo Statement," *One in Christ* 30 (1994) 344–54; and Mary Tanner, "The Anglican Position on Apostolic Continuity and Apostolic Succession in the Porvoo Statement," *Louvain Studies* 21 (1996) 114–25.

Thus the whole Church, and every member, participates in and contributes to the communication of the gospel, by their faithful expression and embodiment of the permanent characteristics of the Church of the apostles in a given time and place (38).

Thus the primary manifestation of apostolic succession is to be found in the apostolic tradition of the Church as a whole. The succession is an expression of the permanence and, therefore, of the continuity of Christ's own mission in which the Church participates (39).

But Porvoo then proceeds to add a rather detailed reflection on the role of apostolic succession of the bishops (41–54).

The diversity of God's gifts requires their coordination so that they enrich the whole Church and its unity. This diversity and the multiplicity of tasks involved in serving it calls for a ministry of co-ordination. This is the ministry of oversight, *episcope,* a caring for the life of a whole community, a pasturing of the pastors and a true feeding of Christ's flock, in accordance with Christ's command across the ages and in unity with Christians in other places (42).

The ultimate ground of the fidelity of the Church, in continuity with the apostles, is the promise of the Lord and the presence of the Holy Spirit at work in the whole Church. The continuity of the ministry of oversight is to be understood within the continuity of the apostolic life and mission of the whole Church. Apostolic succession in the episcopal office is a visible and personal way of focusing the apostolicity of the whole Church (46).

Porvoo tries to keep both expressions of apostolicity in proper balance. Thus, though the apostolicity of the whole church is primary, the succession of the bishops is seen as necessary for expressing and preserving that very apostolicity. Both forms of apostolicity are related to each other and are held in a tensive relationship. The apostolic succession of the bishops makes sense only in terms of the apostolic life of the churches. Porvoo discerns the weakness of the presentation of apostolic succession in terms of an unbroken chain of episcopal ordinations in the course of history. The succession of bishops expresses the historicity of the church and its ministry but without isolating it from the total life of communities of Christians and thereby absolutizing it. On the other hand, the church's very apostolicity is incomplete in history where the office of episcopacy, willed by Christ and called forth anew by the Holy Spirit, is lacking. Apostolicity and apostolic succession are understood by Porvoo in relational terms. The priority is still with the apostolicity of the whole church, but that priority is embodied in a variety of historical expressions, including episcopacy, that relationally codetermine apostolicity.

Drawing on the insight of the priority of the whole church's apostolicity without sacrificing episcopal succession, Porvoo has also attempted to address the delicate issue of how episcopal churches can regard churches that in some sense accept a genuine form of *episcopē* but that have not preserved the historical episcopate and how these divergent positions can be reconciled in their shared life and common ministry. Doesn't the one alternative exclude the other? Porvoo judges not, and says:

> Faithfulness to the apostolic calling of the whole Church is carried by more than one means of continuity. Therefore a church which has preserved the sign of historical episcopal succession is free to acknowledge an authentic episcopal ministry in a church which has preserved continuity in the episcopal office by an occasional priestly/ presbyteral ordination at the time of the Reformation. Similarly, a church which has preserved continuity through such a succession is free to enter a relationship of mutual participation in episcopal ordinations with a church which has retained the historical episcopal succession, and to embrace this sign, without denying its past apostolic continuity (52).

Once again, the distinction of apostolicity into the notion of the apostolicity of the whole church and the apostolicity of episcopal ministry proves to be fruitful in overcoming a dichotomy by building on a prior intrinsic relationship. Each church truly "lacks" something that the other can give it because they both lack "visible ecclesial unity" and not because one lacks an essential element of being church that the other possesses.

The Catholic author Hendrik Roelvink has discerned the novelty of Porvoo's contribution to the vexing question of apostolic succession and its possible contribution to Roman Catholic discussions with other Christians regarding the apostolic ministry. He writes perceptively:

> . . . [I]f defects have arisen in elements of apostolic continuity, these defects can be "complemented" within the wholeness of the Church without especially dramatic measures. Formal unity can then be restored primarily by the enrichment of one Church with the goods that others have, followed by the recognition of each other as sister Churches, rather than by accepting the validity of each individual consecration from the past.

Since Vatican II the Catholic theology of ministry has clearly started from the thought that ministry is a ministry in the Church and thus in its essence depends on what the Church is. Also, Catholic theology sees apostolic succession in a strict sense as one of the many signs of the apostolicity of the Church. Nowadays it can—as the Tübingen school and Cardinal Newman did in the nineteenth century—look on this apostolicity as an organic and dynamic reality. Even within the Catholic Church the signs of apostolic ministry can change, and have done so in history, since there was already "absolute security in matters of sacraments" through the apostolicity of the whole Church.

. . . Our security does not lie in the apostolic succession of bishops as such, but in the life of the whole Church.[58]

The Orthodox-Roman Catholic Dialogue

Apostolicity and apostolic succession have also been discussed by Orthodox Christians and Roman Catholics both at the international and the regional levels.[59] In 1986 the Orthodox-Roman Catholic Consultation in the U.S.A. published a document entitled "Apostolicity as God's Gift in the Life of the Church."[60] Like so many of the statements we have examined above, the document emphasizes the apostolicity of the whole church without sacrificing the notion of the apostolic succession of bishops or by reducing it to a merely external representation of the Church's apostolicity. It succeeds by maintaining the balance between both expressions of apostolicity. After pointing to the two fundamental dimensions of apostolicity as grounded in the apostles' teaching and discipline in the past and in God's eschatological future as mysteriously present in the Eucharist in particular (7), "Apostolicity as God's Gift in the Life of the Church" goes on to say:

It is primordially within the mystery of Christian initiation that apostolicity is continually experienced in the life of the Church and in the life of

58. Roelvink, "The Apostolic Succession in the Porvoo Statement," 349.

59. For a comprehenhsive presentation, see Johannes Oeldemann, *Die Apostolizität der Kirche im ökumenischen Dialog mit der Orthodoxie. Der Beitrag russischer orthodoxer Theologen zum ökumenischen Gespräch über die apostolische Tradition und die Sukzession in der Kirche* (Paderborn: Bonifatius Verlag, 2000).

60. Orthodox-Roman Catholic Consultation in the U.S.A., "Apostolicity as God's Gift in the Life of the Church," in *The Quest for Unity: Orthodox and Catholics in Dialogue: Documents of the Joint International Commission and Official Dialogues in the United States 1965–1995,* eds. John Borelli and John H. Erickson (Crestwood, N.Y.: St. Vladimir's Seminary Press, 1996) 125–30.

each Christian. The baptismal act of receiving and giving back the Church's confession of faith *(traditio/redditio)* marks each Christian's entry into and appropriation of the apostolic life and faith of the Church. As an essential element in the life of the whole Church and of every Christian, apostolicity therefore is by no means unique or limited to the realm of hierarchical ministry. For just as we share by baptism in the royal and prophetic priesthood, so also by this baptismal confession we too become bearers of the Church's apostolicity (9).

In our consultation attention was drawn to at least two corollaries which may follow from this understanding of apostolic faith: (a) The apostolicity of ministry is generally seen as derived from the continuity of the community as a whole in apostolic life and faith; the succession of ministers in office is normally agreed to be subordinate to that ecclesial apostolicity. (b) Apostolicity seems to consist more in fidelity to the apostles' proclamation and mission than in any one form of handing on community office. These observations alert us once again to the danger of reducing apostolicity simply to forms and institutional structures (10).[61]

The document explains the importance of the succession of the bishops in relational terms by pointing to the incarnational order of salvation effected by Christ and thus its social character.[62] The church may not be reduced to purely individual relationships between Christ and the believer since it comes to expression as a social reality with a definite structure that includes leadership. Episcopal succession is not a pure accessory of the church, since it roots the church's apostolicity in historical continuity and permanence.

Surprisingly, these rich insights did not find any echo in the International Orthodox-Roman Catholic Commission's statement "The Sacrament of Order in the Sacramental Structure of the Church with Particular Reference to the Importance of Apostolic Succession for the Sanctification and Unity of the People of God" published in 1988.[63] The document preferred to remain within the standard terms of expression and considered the apostolic succession of the bishops as an isolated issue. After two rich sections that develop the relationship between Christ and

---

61. Ibid., 127–28.

62. I mean to point to the importance that emerges out of an "order of relationality" or of being in relationship to others. We considered this concept and its importance in postmodern thought above in Chapters Four [under John Zizioulas] and Six [under the "Other"].

63. See John Borelli and John H. Erickson, eds., *The Quest for Unity,* 131–42.

the Spirit in the order of salvation (6–14) and the ordained priesthood in the context of the scriptural and conciliar teaching that all believers participate in Christ's unique priesthood (15–23), the document proceeds to concentrate on the ministry of the bishop and his role in maintaining apostolic succession. To its credit the document approaches the office of bishop in terms of the college of bishops rather than by isolating the bishops as so many individuals who succeed to the apostles. Succession is by way of the episcopal college as an expression of the communion of the churches.

> This unity of the local church is inseparable from the universal communion of the churches. It is essential for a church to be in communion with the others. This communion is expressed and realized in and through the episcopal college. By his ordination, the bishop is made minister of a church which he represents in the universal communion (26).[64]

Then follows a passage that relates the bishop's office to the local church over which he presides and its antecedent apostolicity: "In ordination the bishops exercise their function as witnesses to the communion in the apostolic faith and sacramental life not only with respect to him whom they ordain, but also with respect to the church of which he will be bishop" (27).[65] Though the statement is cautious compared to those of the Orthodox-Roman Catholic Consultation in the U.S.A., it can be interpreted as making the same point by implication rather than by direct assertion. The concluding section on apostolic succession (44–55) also makes the point of the intrinsic relation between a bishop, his community, and the communion of churches. In paragraph 45 we read:

> The importance of this succession comes also from the fact that the apostolic tradition concerns the community and not only an isolated individual, ordained bishop. Apostolic succession is transmitted through local churches. . . .It is a matter of succession of persons in the community, because the *Una Sancta* is a communion of local churches and not of isolated individuals. It is within this mystery of *koinonia* that the episcopate appears as the central point of the apostolic succession (45).[66]

64. Ibid., 135–36.
65. Ibid., 136.
66. Ibid., 139. The Latin phrase *Una Sancta* refers to the universal church as "one" and "holy." See "Una Sancta," in *The Oxford Dictionary of the Christian Church*, eds. F. L. Cross and E. A. Livingstone (2nd ed.; New York: Oxford University Press, 1974) 1405.

The statements of the Orthodox-Roman Catholic dialogue are also in line with the general thrust of ideas developed in many of the other ecumenical dialogues we have examined. By contrast with these, however, its manner of expression is more cautious. But this impression would belie the context of the dialogue between two churches that see themselves as espousing an ecclesiology that is thoroughly sacramental, episcopal, and eucharistic. Against this background of a fundamentally shared understanding of the church, the Orthodox-Roman Catholic dialogue, too, breaks new ground. The former stereotype of apostolic succession as an unbroken chain of individual bishops ordained in time to succeed the apostles, who were also envisioned individualistically, has been transcended by the perceptions of episcopacy as inherently collegial and of the churches as constituting in the Spirit a communion of churches.

CHAPTER EIGHT

Apostolicity in an Ecumenical Church

By now, the thesis I have presented in this book should be evident to the reader: the apostolicity of the church that the Nicene-Constantinopolitan Creed expresses pertains to the church as a whole. The teaching is clear in the writings of the early church, in the statements of ecumenical conversations over the last forty years, and in recent Catholic, Orthodox, and Protestant theology. Apostolic succession in the classical sense of the succession of bishops in the course of the church's history as the primary expression of the church's apostolicity has been repositioned. In recent thought, apostolic succession of the bishops occupies a position after that of the apostolicity of the entire church. Still, the issue of apostolic episcopal succession is an unavoidable one, not because it is accessory to the question of the church's apostolicity, but precisely because it is included in it. To many Christians, apostolic episcopal succession is an intrinsic dimension of the church's own apostolicity. It is time that we now squarely address the issue of the apostolic succession of the bishops.

Apostolic Succession in Lutheranism

Before the magisterial Reformation, the succession of the bishops seemed to be in the secure possession of the church in the East and West. Martin Luther himself did not wish to depart from the church order that he had known to be a part of the church's life. Luther hoped that the bishops would participate in the reform and ordain presbyters who clearly espoused his reform proposals. When that course of action did not prove possible, Luther did not reject the episcopal structure of the church but had recourse to an equally early form of succession in office, the presbyteral one. In Luther's eyes this solution was an emergency one. But why were Luther and other Reformers convinced of the validity of recourse to the presbyteral form of succession in office? In order to answer this question, we must step back for a few moments and examine the theology of episcopacy and of the sacraments in late medieval Western theology.[1]

Prior to Vatican II, the teaching of the Council of Trent (1545–63) represented the culmination of efforts in the West to arrive at clear thinking about sacramental actions in the church initiated by Augustine in the fifth century. There was no unified vocabulary about the sacraments and no general theological tract dealing with "the sacraments in general." Answers to such issues as the definition of a sacrament, its matter, who the minister of a sacrament was and the minister's intentions, possible limitations of jurisdiction in administering a sacrament, the recipient of a sacrament and his/her dispositions toward the sacrament, the causality of the sacraments, the number of the sacraments, and so forth, were all largely elaborated in the course of the years stretching from the eleventh to the fifteenth centuries. It was really only with Trent that the Catholic Church came into the clear possession of a more or less full exposition of the sacraments.[2] The Reformers were not reacting to a well-reasoned,

1. The issue of episcopacy in the West suffered greatly from the West's isolation from the Eastern church after the break of 1054. The possibility of exercising a certain theological counterweight on the West by the Eastern churches was lost in practice. As East and West went their separate ways, the growing influence of juridical categories in the West in general tended to increase and confuse certain issues.

2. Trent drew on the teaching of the Council of Florence (1439–45). In its "Decree for the Armenians," Florence in turn drew heavily on Thomas Aquinas' *De articulis fidei et ecclesiae sacramentis*. Especially noteworthy are the teachings concerning the number of the sacraments; that the sacraments contain and confer grace; that a sacrament is characterized by its matter, form, and the minister's intention to do what the Church itself intends in administering the sacrament; and finally, that baptism, confirmation, and holy orders confer a "spiritual sign" *(spirituale quoddam signum)* or *character indelebile,* without its being further defined. See Herbert Vorgrimler, *Sacramental Theology,* tr. Linda M. Maloney (Collegeville, Minn.: The Liturgical Press, 1992) 57–58. For its part, Trent further summarized the medieval synthesis, addressed certain sacramental issues posed by the Reformers, but hardly provided a full systematization of sacramental doctrine. It was never Trent's intention to offer a complete and balanced sacramental theology, but only to address matters denied by the Reformers while providing certain minimal directions for a full and satisfactory sacramental theology. As Frans Jozef van Beeck has expressed the matter: "Individual doctrinal pronouncements are often antithetical, polemical, apologetical, which amounts to saying that they are often incomplete. This is particularly true in the case of the pronouncements made by the Council of Trent dealing with the sacraments. If one compares the sacramental

complete, and balanced theology of the sacraments, but to a series of minimal theological claims and a system of sacramental practices.[3] The question must be asked, then, whether Catholics have been entirely fair in treating the ambiguity of some of the Reformers on certain sacraments, for example, orders, matrimony, and the anointing of the sick. Luther himself was clear in identifying baptism, the Eucharist, and penance or absolution as sacraments, but then no one in the church at the time doubted their sacramental character.

The same was definitely not true of orders or ordination to the ministries of bishop and presbyter. As we saw earlier, the New Testament and the post-apostolic church evidence a variety of ministries in the church. Consistency of episcopal polity was not reached in general until late in the second century. The Reformers were not ignorant of emerging facts that paid greater attention to history and the texts of the Fathers and the early councils. The new theology represented at the University of Wittenberg, for instance, stressed the Scriptures and historical texts over the speculation of a late and often decadent Scholasticism. New sources were needed if university theology was to be enlisted in service of the church's faith. These "new sources" were none other than the Scriptures, the early church councils, and critical editions of the texts of the writings of the Fathers and other theologians of the early church. In these sources, however, they found a pluralism of opinions about the ministry. Thus, one of the giants of the early church, St. Jerome (348–420), had defended the position that originally there was no difference between presbyters and bishops.[4]

---

doctrine of Trent with, say, the very all-round and even ecumenical decree on justification, one cannot but be struck by its polemical tendency, especially in the *canones*." "Towards an Ecumenical Understanding of the Sacraments," *Journal of Ecumenical Studies* 3 (1966) 57–112, at 75. Similar reservations on the inadequacy of Trent's teaching on the sacraments are expressed by H. Vorgrimler, *Sacramental Theology,* 58–61. On sacraments in general, see Kevin W. Irwin, "Sacrament," in *The New Theological Dictionary,* eds. Joseph A. Komonchak, Mary Collins, and Dermot A. Lane (Wilmington, Del.: Michael Glazier, Inc., 1987) 910–22; Peter E. Fink, "Sacramental Theology after Vatican II," in *The New Dictionary of Sacramental Worship,* ed. Peter E. Fink (Collegeville, Minn.: The Liturgical Press, 1990) 1107–14; and idem, "Sacraments: Contemporary Issues," in *Handbook of Catholic Theology,* eds. Wolfgang Beinert and Francis Schüssler Fiorenza (New York: The Crossroad Publishing Co., 1995) 625–33.

3. See Susan J. White, "Sacraments in the Reformation Churches," in *The New Dictionary of Sacramental Worship,* 1130–35.

4. In his letter 146, "To Evangelus," Jerome wrote: ". . . the apostle clearly teaches that presbyters are the same as bishops. . . . When subsequently one presbyter was chosen

In itself, this opinion might have seemed merely an idiosyncratic one, but with the passing of the years the changes in the concrete order of church life from the late fifth to the twelfth centuries, meant that even an eminent theologian like Thomas Aquinas was not convinced of the sacramentality of the episcopal order.[5] With the introduction of the distinction between two separate "powers," that of order and of jurisdiction, the difference between bishop and presbyter seemed to belong to the realm of

---

to preside over the rest, this was done to remedy schism and to prevent each individual from rending the church of Christ by drawing it to himself. For even at Alexandria from the time of Mark the Evangelist until the episcopates of Heraclas and Dionysius the presbyters always named as bishop one of their own number chosen by themselves and set in a more exalted position. . . . For what function, excepting ordination, belongs to a bishop that does not belong to a presbyter?" *A Select Library of the Christian Church: Nicene and Post-Nicene Fathers,* 2nd Series, vol. 6: *Jerome: Letters and Select Works,* eds. Philip Schaff and Henry Wace (Peabody, Mass.: Hendrickson Publishers, Inc., 1994) 288–89. Apropos, Joseph Lécuyer has written: "St. Jerome and the anon[ymous] author known as Ambrosiaster, almost in the same terms, refuse to see the episcopate as a higher order than the presbyterate, save for the powers reserved to it: its ordination is merely a ceremony, without sacramental value." See "Ministries, Ordained Ministers," in *Encyclopedia of the Early Church,* 2 vols., ed. Angelo Di Berardino, tr. Adrian Walford (New York: Oxford University Press, 1992) 1:560–62, at 562.

5. See the *Summa theologiae* Supplementum, quaestio 40, ad 4. Later, the Council of Florence does not even list episcopacy among holy orders. It merely mentions that a bishop is the ordinary minister of orders, purportedly because he is a priest: "The sixth is the sacrament of orders. Its matter is the object by whose handing over the order is conferred. So the priesthood [*presbyteratus*] is bestowed by the handing over of a chalice with wine and a paten with bread; the diaconate by the giving of the book of the gospels; the subdiaconate by the handing over of an empty chalice with an empty paten on it; and similarly for the other orders by allotting things connected with their ministry. The form for a priest is: Receive the power of offering sacrifice in the church for the living and the dead, in the name of the Father and of the Son and of the holy Spirit. The forms for the other orders are contained in full in the Roman pontifical. The ordinary minister of this sacrament is a bishop. The effect is an increase of grace to make the person a suitable minister of Christ." Norman P. Tanner, ed., *Decrees of the Ecumenical Councils,* 2 vols. (Washington, D.C.: Georgetown University Press, 1990) 1:549–50. The strangeness of the teaching of Florence in its silence regarding episcopacy and its relationship to the presbyterate is striking to us, accustomed as we are to understanding the sacramentality of episcopacy. Still, we have to remember that it was only with Vatican II that the official church clearly taught the sacramentality of the office of bishop in the church. See the Dogmatic Constitution on the Church, arts. 21 and 26 (LG), and the Decree on the Pastoral Office of the Bishops in the Church, arts. 3 and 4 (CD). See Seamus Ryan, "Episcopal Consecration: The Fullness of the Sacrament of Order," *Irish Theological Quarterly* 32 (1965) 295–324; idem, "Vatican II: The Rediscovery of the Episcopate," *Irish Theological Quarterly* 33 (1966) 208–41; and Susan K. Wood, "The Sacramentality of Episcopal Consecration," *Theological Studies* 51 (1990) 479–96.

the power of jurisdiction, and not to holy order or sacramental power in which both shared.[6] In fact, a theology of ordained ministry based on the distinction of orders and jurisdiction was able to make sense also of the practice evidenced in the fifteenth century of abbots ordaining deacons and priests with appropriate papal permission. The abbots in question, who had been ordained priests but never bishops, had received permission from several popes to ordain members of their monasteries to the presbyterate.[7] This evidence came to light in the twentieth century and appeared in several scholarly theological works.[8] In the light of these facts, we have to realize that the theology of orders at the time of the outbreak of the magisterial Reformation was anything but fixed. There were many important questions still unanswered: Was episcopacy a sacrament? Can priests ordain? What is the essential nature of the priesthood?

It is clear that Luther wanted to have his pastors ordained by the German Catholic bishops, but they refused to do so. As an emergency measure, Luther turned to the not-unheard-of practice of presbyteral ordination of his pastors.[9] Luther and Philip Melanchthon (1497–1560) knew of Jerome's opinion regarding the equality of presbyters and bishops.

6. See the treatment of the history of episcopacy in medieval theology by Seamus Ryan, "Episcopal Consecration: The Legacy of the Schoolmen," *Irish Theological Quarterly* 33 (1966) 3–38, and idem; "Episcopal Consecration: Trent to Vatican II," ibid., 133–50. On the distinction between orders and jurisdiction, see Klaus Mörsdorf, "Ecclesiastical Authority," in *Sacramentum Mundi: An Encyclopedia of Theology,* ed. Karl Rahner, 6 vols. (New York: Herder and Herder, 1968–70) 2:133–39.

7. The monasteries were the Augustinians of St. Osyth, Essex, England (1400); the Cistercians of Altezelle, Meissen, Germany (1427); and Cîteaux (for the whole Cistercian Order!) and the abbeys of La Ferté, Pontingy, Clairvaux, and Mérimont, all in France (1489). The popes were Boniface IX, Martin V, and Innocent VIII. One can hardly say that the practice was widespread, but it continued sporadically for the greater part of a century, and was even widened toward the end of the century. The last papal permission was granted just seven years after the birth of Martin Luther in 1483.

8. The dossiers can be consulted in Heinrich Lennerz, *De sacramento ordinis* (2nd ed.; Rome: Apud aedem Universitatis Gregorianae, 1953) 142–44; and Charles Journet, *The Church of the Word Incarnate: An Essay in Speculative Theology,* vol. 1: *The Apostolic Hierarchy,* tr. A.H.C. Downes (New York: Sheed and Ward, 1955) 113–15 ["Two Bulls Authorizing Simple Priests to Confer the Priesthood"].

9. For the relevant historical facts, see Bernhard Lohse, "The Development of the Offices of Leadership in the German Lutheran Churches: 1517–1918," in *Episcopacy in the Lutheran Church? Studies in the Development and Definition of the Office of Church Leadership,* eds. Ivar Asheim and Victor R. Gold (Philadelphia: Fortress Press, 1970) 51–71. Robert J. Goeser presents a different explanation in "Augustana 28 and Lambeth 4: Episcopacy as Adiaphoron or Necessity," in *Concordat of Agreement: Supporting Essays,* ed. Daniel F. Martensen (Minneapolis: Augsburg Fortress, 1995) 31–54.

It is quite possible, then, to defend the ordination of priests by priests as an expression of apostolic succession in ministry. If Irenaeus could speak of succession by reason of the bishops and by reason of the presbyters,[10] it was not so far-fetched for Luther to defend the practice of presbyterial ordination—as an emergency measure. Holding on to the hope for intra-ecclesial reform, it appears that Luther did not envision the practice of presbyters ordaining presbyters as a permanent arrangement.[11] But what was Luther's position on office in the church and on the office of bishop in particular? The question is hotly disputed by scholars of Luther and the magisterial Reformation, and there are two schools of thought on the matter.

Some scholars point to Luther's insistence on the priesthood of all the faithful and maintain that the universal priesthood elicits the practical necessity of an ordained ministry. The ministry is understood in terms of a theory of delegation or transference by the community.[12] According to this interpretation, Lutheran ecclesiology is more congregational in nature. Others point to Luther's desire to remain within the Catholic ministerial structure while reforming it, so that it both served the gospel and broke down any class distinctions in the church between the ordained and the non-ordained faithful. At the time, the faithful experienced themselves as second-class citizens and as passive recipients of the ministerial actions of the ordained. The laity were not direct participants in spreading the gospel. Luther's intentions were not to pit the priesthood of the faithful against a divinely instituted special ministry in the church but to call believers to an awareness of their dignity as baptized Christians. For its part, the ministry of word and sacrament in the church also owes its existence to divine institution.[13] It serves the word of God and represents Christ to the congregation.

10. For the references to both forms of succession—episcopal and presbyteral—see the discussion of Irenaeus in chapter 3, p. 56.

11. For a while it looked as if the pope was going to call a general council to address issues of reform in the church.

12. The so-called "transference theory" was dominant in the nineteenth and early twentieth centuries. According to Brian A. Gerrish, "Those who derive the ministry from the common priesthood assign the ministerial functions to the whole congregation of believers. The necessity for the special office is then based mainly on the need for 'order,' treated by some as little more than a matter of expediency, as in the political theory of the social contract. The congregation has priority over the ministry both in time and rank." See his "Priesthood and Ministry in the Theology of Luther," *Church History* 34 (1965) 404–22, at 408.

13. This interpretation is called the "institution theory" of ministry and was championed by Wilhelm Brunotte in *Das geistliche Amt bei Luther* (Berlin: Lutherisches Verlagshaus,

Matters are also complicated regarding the office of bishop. Avery Dulles and George A. Lindbeck, in a jointly authored article, wrote the following:

> Luther in particular was notoriously varied in his utterances on this as on other topics. He did not, perhaps, contradict himself, but he said different things in different contexts that it is often difficult to discern the inner consistencies. Depending on which statements and which periods in his life one emphasizes, one can develop either protestantizing or catholicizing interpretations of his view of the ministry and of church order. It is doubtful that a consensus can be achieved on what the "real Luther" thought on these matters by a historical study of his writings.[14]

Their solution is to give priority to the text, in this case the *Augsburg Confession*, art. 28. What does the text itself maintain? Again, Dulles and Lindbeck write:

> The major claim of the CA [*Confessio Augustana*], as we have been repeatedly reminded in recent times, is to catholicity: "there is nothing here that departs from the Scriptures or the catholic church or the church of Rome." If one takes the stated purpose of the text seriously, this claim should be the controlling norm for interpreting every article, and for filling every gap. The interpreter is not at the mercy of competing historical and systematic opinions, but rather possesses a principle of selection in this hermeneutically normative claim to catholicity. The Reformation as represented at Augsburg wanted to retain the catholic substance of the ministry, and this intention is fundamental in determining what the CA would have said on those aspects of the ministry on which it is silent. It would have been, to put it simply, as catholic as possible.[15]

1959). Hellmut Lieberg, on the other hand, defended the interpretation that in Luther one finds both the "institution theory" and the superiority of the universal priesthood, but that this second position is subordinate to the first. See his *Amt und Ordination bei Luther und Melanchthon* (Göttingen: Vandenhoeck & Ruprecht, 1962). Brian Gerrish gives an explanation of the theses of both books in "Priesthood and Ministry in the Theology of Luther," at 408–409. See also John H. P. Reumann, "The Ministries of the Ordained and of the Laity in Lutheranism," in *Ministries Examined: Laity, Clergy, Women, and Bishops in a Time of Change* (Minneapolis: Augsburg Publishing House, 1987) 25–77, especially 35–50 ["Historical Development in Lutheranism"].

14. See "Bishops and the Ministry of the Gospel," in *Confessing One Faith: A Joint Commentary on the Augsburg Confession by Lutheran and Catholic Theologians,* eds. George Wolfgang Forell and James F. McCue (Minneapolis: Augsburg Publishing House, 1982) 147–72, at 158.

15. Ibid., 159. The authoritative commentary on the Augsburg Confession is Wilhelm Maurer, *Historical Commentary on the Augsburg Confession,* tr. H. George Anderson (Philadelphia:

After examining various issues related to episcopacy—the necessity of ordination, its relationship to the priesthood of the faithful, the sacramentality of office, and why the *Augsburg Confession* is silent about it—the authors conclude that in 1530 Luther and Melanchthon supported episcopacy and apostolic succession out of the conviction that it was God's will for the church, that it assured unity and peace in the church, and that it was always to be exercised in service to the gospel and never as lording it over God's word. They simply wanted to retain the episcopal office.[16] Their silence on the sacramentality of ordination, reflected in the silence of the *Augsburg Confession*, elicited the response of many Lutherans over the years that episcopacy was a theologically indifferent matter. Different Lutheran churches in different countries were free to adopt it or to discontinue it.[17] The episcopacy was a matter of theological indifference. This is certainly not the opinion of Dulles and Lindbeck, who write:

> . . . [The] failure to exclude a purely adiaphoristic [i.e., theologically indifferent] view of episcopal polity is probably the point at which the CA is . . . most obviously insufficient from the point of view of traditions which stress the historic succession.
>
> The CA, however, does not affirm an adiaphoristic view. It is also open to the contrary position that the apostolic succession in office is in principle

---

Fortress Press, 1986). See 59–64 ["Development of the Text of CA 28"] and 174–236 ["Ecclesiastical Order: Texts," "The Call to the Office of Preaching and Public Proclamation," "Ecclesiastical Order and Church Law," "The Theological Basis for New Church Orders," "Problems of Evangelical Church Law," and "Church Order and the Doctrine of Justification"]. Also, idem, "Die Entstehung und erste Auswirkung von Artikel 28 der Confessio Augustana," in *Volk Gottes. Zum Kirchenverständnis der katholischen, evangelischen und anglikanischen Theologie,* Festschrift Josef Höfer, eds. Remigius Bäumer and Heimo Dolch (Freiburg: Verlag Herder, 1967) 361–94.

16. Apropos, Bernhard Lohse has written: "In view of the Catholic bishops' resistance to reform, the evangelical prince in large measure took over the vacant episcopal see, and in the church tailored to the Reformation functioned as *summus episcopus.* Luther regarded this as a makeshift, for which he coined the term 'emergency bishop' *(Notbischof).* . . . Attempts to install an evangelical theologian as bishop in a vacated see, such as Luther undertook in Naumburg and Merseburg, indicate that he was struggling to arrive at his own structuring of the episcopal office, and to prevent the temporary assistance of princes from becoming a permanent arrangement." *Martin Luther's Theology: Its Historical and Systematic Development,* ed. and tr. by Roy A. Harrisville (Minneapolis: Fortress Press, 1999) 296–97.

17. In fact, in Sweden and Finland, the bishops did come over to the reform movement and ordained presbyters and bishops in proper historic succession. In Denmark, all the Catholic bishops were deposed and replaced by bishops of the Reform. See Martii Parvio, "The Post-Reformation Developments of the Episcopacy in Sweden, Finland, and the Baltic States," in *Episcopacy in the Lutheran Church?* 125–37.

positively desirable and, other things being equal, is preferable to alternatives. Episcopacy is a powerful symbol, an efficacious sign, of the unity of the church in space and time, and thereby strengthens the witness to the universality of the redemption in Christ. Such considerations, although formulated in contemporary rather than 16th-century terms, are in full harmony with the functional emphasis of the CA and the Lutheran Reformation. They do not grant any inalienable or divinely guaranteed indefectibility to the historic episcopacy, such as the Reformers deny, but they do recognize that it has a special potential for becoming a sign of great evangelical importance when it acts in obedience to the Word.

. . . It is no longer necessary, despite what many Lutherans have thought, to suppose that the resistance to bishops authorized by the CA implies that the historic episcopal structure of the church is of purely human origin. It may have developed under providential guidance and may, in its normal and proper functioning, be a God-willed means for helping to preserve the church in the apostolic faith. Such a view, although developed subsequently to the CA, does provide a basis for the positive attitude the latter adopts toward the restoration of episcopal jurisdiction once abuses are removed, and it is therefore more consistent with its fundamental tenor than is the adiaphoristic alternative.[18]

The Dulles-Lindbeck interpretation is not the only possible one, and many Luther scholars will be inclined to see their interpretation as too rosy. Still, the "catholicizing" interpretation that Dulles and Lindbeck represent is not without its supporters[19] and even has support in recent ecumenical dialogues, bilateral and international. For example, in the Joint Roman Catholic-Lutheran Commission's "The Ministry in the Church" (1981), we read:

> The *Lutheran Confessions* wanted to retain the episcopal polity of the church and with it the differentiation of the ministerial office on the condition that

18. Ibid., 165–66.

19. See Bernhard Lohse's comment: "Luther's view of the office of bishop can be tersely evaluated, since he believed it merely represented a particular instance of the ministerial office. It is significant that despite his attack on the papacy based on New Testament teaching as well as on development throughout church history, he never challenged the office of bishop." *Martin Luther's Theology,* 296. The Joint Roman Catholic-Lutheran Conversation, "The Ministry in the Church," says: "[The Lutheran tradition's] confessional writings claim to stand in the authentic Catholic tradition and emphasize the historical continuity of the church which has never ceased to exist" (art. 63). See Harding Meyer and Lukas Vischer, eds. *Growth in Agreement: Reports and Agreed Statements of Ecumenical Conversations on a World Level* (New York: Paulist Press, 1984) 268.

the bishops grant freedom and opportunity for the right proclamation of the gospel and the right administration of the sacraments and not prevent these by the formal requirement of obedience. The fact that it was impossible at this time to arrive at an agreement in doctrine and to persuade the bishops to ordain Reformation ministers led perforce to forsaking continuity with previous order (42).

. . .The Lutheran office of pastor, comparable to that of presbyter, has really taken over the spiritual functions of the bishop's office and was even at times theologically interpreted as identical with it. This was seen as a return to an earlier ministerial structure in church history in which the bishop's office was a local one. Within this context the function of *episcopé* was retained as necessary for the church; but its concrete ordering was taken to be a human and historical matter. . . (43).

We are, therefore, confronted with the empirical fact that in both churches there are local congregational ministers (priest, pastor) as well as also superordinated regional ministries [bishop, church president, superintendent]. These regional ministries have the function of pastoral supervision and of service of unity within a larger area. . . . . These tasks are entrusted to local ministries only in exceptional circumstances. In the two churches there thus exists a significant convergence as regards the actual character of ecclesical *[sic]* practice (44).[20]

Twelve years later, in their "Church and Justification," the Joint Commission wrote:

The difference between the Catholic and Lutheran views on the theological and ecclesiological evaluation of the episcopate is thus not so radical that a Lutheran rejection or even indifference towards this ministry [in as much as it pertains to the adiaphora] stands in opposition to the Catholic assertion of its ecclesial indispensability. The question is rather one of a clear gradation in the evaluation of this ministry, which can be and has been described on the Catholic side by predicates such as "necessary" or "indispensable", and on the Lutheran side as "important", "meaningful" and thus "desirable"(197).

This differentiation is also expressed regarding the ecclesial necessity of the episcopal office in apostolic succession, something which is not necessary for the salvation of individual persons. Because of a differentiation it is possible for Catholics to assert the necessity of this office without thereby contradicting the doctrine of justification. Thus the episcopal office is understood in the church as a necessary ministry of the gospel, which itself is necessary for salvation (202).

20. *Growth in Agreement,* 262–63.

The difference in the theological and ecclesiological evaluation of the episcopal office in historic succession loses its sharpness when Lutherans attribute
such a value to the episcopate that regaining full communion in this office
seems important and desirable, and when Catholics recognize that "the ministry in the Lutheran churches exercises essential functions of the ministry
that Jesus Christ instituted in his church" and does not contest the point that
the Lutheran churches are church. The difference in evaluating the historic
episcopate is thereby interpreted in such a way that the doctrine of justification is no longer at stake and consequently it is also possible to advocate
theologically the regaining of full communion in the episcopate (204).[21]

From what I have reported on the history of sacramental theology,
from the writings of Luther and the Lutheran confessional statements,
and from recent Roman Catholic-Lutheran ecumenical dialogues, it seems
reasonable to assert that there is widespread agreement among Lutherans and Catholics on the importance of the office of bishop and on the
pastoral and ecumenical appropriateness of its reinstatement as an expression of the apostolic succession of ministry in the Church.[22] I submit
that such a claim represents an important moment—a *kairos* in the true
theological sense of the word—for both communities to come to final
agreement on apostolic succession, a moment that should not be deferred
unnecessarily. Lutherans and Roman Catholics both have much to gain
from each other's experience and will be mutually enriched by agreement on episcopal apostolic succession—in service of the fundamental
apostolicity of the whole Church. But what do we mean when we speak
of "episcopacy"? Is episcopacy to be restricted to a single form or can it
be interpreted more broadly?

Episkopē *and Episcopacy*

One of the results of the historical-critical method of interpreting
the New Testament has been the recovery of the notion of pastoral oversight or *episkopē*. Before this retrieval, historians and theologians tended
to identify the Greek term e*piskopē* with the Latin *episcopatus* or episcopacy.

21. Jeffrey Gros, Harding Meyer and Wm. G. Rusch, eds., *Growth in Agreement II: Reports and Agreed Statements of Ecumenical Conversations on a World Level, 1982–1998* (Grand Rpids: Wm. B. Eerdmans Publishing Company, 2000) 532–33.
22. See Gunther Wenz, "Das kirchliche Amt in evangelischer Perspektive," *Stimmen der Zeit* 221 (2003) 376–85, for a clear and basic presentation of the Lutheran understanding of ministry that attempts to dispel common misunderstandings of the Lutheran position.

The recovery of the term *episkopē,* however, has meant that the English word "episcopacy" is not available as a translation. As a result, scholars prefer to simply use the Greek term untranslated. Our understanding of episcopacy has been influenced by the development of a specific form of the ministry of bishop generally called the "monarchical bishop." *Episkopē* does not necessarily include the monarchical aspect of the office of bishop.[23] What, then, does *episkopē* mean?

The nominal form *episkopē* appears in the New Testament four times with three different senses.[24] The most frequent meaning is a "visitation" or the "day of visitation" (Luke 19:44 and 1 Pet 2:12). My interest in *episkopē* is not related to this meaning. Acts 1:20 uses the term in a special sense to mean the office of apostle lost by Judas Iscariot but now meant to be assumed by Matthias. My interest does not include this restricted meaning either. However, in 1 Timothy 3:1 *episkopē* does have a special-ized meaning. According to Joachim Rohde:

> [*Episkopē*] has the meaning *office of overseer* or of *supervisor.* The word stands in the introductory verse of the list of qualifications for the Christian con-gregational overseer. It is improbable that the Pastorals, with this use of the term, already presuppose the existence of the monarchical episcopate. The impression is given that one does not, so to speak, automatically grow into this office through longer affiliation and testing, but rather that one can consciously strive for it.[25]

23. Apropos of the distinction, Jean M. R. Tillard has written: "It may happen that we shall discover how, under different forms and ideas, at least the main ideas of apostolic *episkopē* have reappeared in such communities [i.e., those deriving from the magisterial Reformation]. For it is not necessary for the threefold ministry—deacon , presbyter, bishop—to be attested in the classical form for apostolic *episkopē* to exist. The *id quod requiritur et sufficit* [i.e., the core con-tent necessary for being faithful to the apostolic tradition] would consist in such cases in the fact that all the functions and services essentially required by the life of the Church in confor-mity with the apostolic institution are present. The classical triad makes them actual in a form which has the burnish of the centuries upon it and quite certainly represents them in what we might call the full form. But it must be asked whether the essentially apostolic functions and services may not re-emerge in other forms." "Recognition of Ministries: What Is the Real Question?" *One in Christ* 21 (1985) 31–39, at 38–39. The distinction *episkopē* vis-à-vis episco-pacy is a common theological opinion among ecclesiologists and ecumenists.

24. See Joachim Rohde, "*episkopē* visitation; office; office of overseer," in *Exegetical Dictionary of the New Testament,* 3 vols., eds. Horst Balz and Gerhard Schneider, tr. James W. Thompson (Grand Rapids: Wm. B. Eerdmans Publishing Co., 1991) 2:35. In addition, see Rohde's articles "*episkopeō* look at; visit" and "*episkopos* bishop (overseer)," in ibid., 33–34 and 35–36.

25. Ibid., 35.

We arrive at the rather surprising result that a term so important to the later church—episcopacy—appears only once in the whole of the New Testament. Moreover, it isn't even certain that the office is clearly distinguished from that of the group of presbyters found in many local churches. The individual who enjoys *episkopē* is one among many and his *episkopē* is shared with others.[26] The situation soon changes in the second century, and our principal witness to the change is Ignatius of Antioch.

In the seven letters of Ignatius of Antioch,[27] we come across for the first time in post-apostolic literature the triad of a single *episkopos,* a group

26. The exegete and biblical theologian Frances Young says the following apropos of the word group *episkopē* and *episkopos/oi:* "The word *episkopos* itself simply meant someone who keeps an eye on things—it could even be used of God as the one who 'over-sees' the good and the bad; normally it referred to an 'overseer' or 'superintendent'. In putting the terminology together, it seems plausible to suggest that the household metaphor is of fundamental importance for understanding the duties of the *episkopos.* He is the one who is vested with God's authority to administer the church as God's household, to oversee the behaviour of the members of the household, to see that 'sound teaching' is promulgated, that proper order is maintained in gatherings for worship and in respectful, orderly interaction between members of the household community with different status and roles to perform. . . . So we learn little about the actual duties placed upon this metaphorical head-steward, or the functions he is expected to fulfil. But we do discover that he needs the qualities elsewhere required for a good general. That very metaphor is found in 2 Tim. 2.3–4, and developed in I Clement in direct application to the issue of authority in the church. . . . It is not yet clear that the *episkopos* has the kind of authority acquired later, but given the structures and assumptions of a hierarchically ordered society, the implication is that he is 'the chief cook and bottle-washer', under the authority of God. He is God's household manager, and the reputation of the household [church] depends upon his proper leadership and example." *The Theology of the Pastoral Letters,* New Testament Theology Series (New York: Cambridge University Press, 1994) 103–4. This picture is a far cry from the monarchical bishop of the third century and later. Are we even talking about a "bishop" in any technical sense?

27. Many questions still surround the figure of Ignatius of Antioch. The letters he wrote are undated, like so much of early Christian literature, and we have no information regarding his identity. Much of what we possess is surmise. Yet, the majority of scholars have not hesitated to locate his writings early in the second century, with the years 107 up to about 117 as the target dates. It is assumed that he was martyred during the reign of Trajan, who ruled from 98 to 117 C.E. Ignatius, however, never identifies the emperor or the exact circumstances of the persecution. Some scholars—invariably the minority—have departed from the consensus view and have located Ignatius closer to the middle of the second century. The *terminus ad quem* we have to work with is provided by Polycarp of Smyrna whose letter "To the Philippians" §9 refers to Ignatius. Polycarp's letter has been hypothetically dated around 140, but it could be much later, since we cannot be certain of Polycarp's dates either. Sometimes the date of his martyrdom is given as 156 C.E. (Robert M. Grant, *Augustus to Constantine* [New York: Harper & Row, 1970] 86–87) or 167 C.E. (Eusebius of Caesarea in his *Ecclesiastical History* Bk. 4, chap. 15 [324]). Thus, Charles Munier

of presbyters, and deacons. This threefold division of ministry eventually became standard in the early church and continued as the normative form of ministry for centuries. In some churches, such as Roman Catholicism, the Eastern Orthodox and Oriental churches, and Anglicanism, it has continued to our own day. *BEM* 25 advocates its restoration in churches that for one reason or another have departed from it,[28] and several churches have taken steps to implement it again. But recently, scholars have begun to examine the Ignatian form of the threefold ministry only to discover that the *episkopos* mentioned does not resemble the later monarchical *episkopos*.[29] Ignatius' bishop is a figure who exercises his

---

has argued that we are free to argue for a later date of Ignatius's letters and martyrdom. Working from the list of bishops from the church of Antioch and offering the second Jewish revolt (132–135 C.E.) as the possible context of the persecution Ignatius refers to, Munier argues for a date closer to 140. I accept this later dating of the Ignatian corpus as more reasonable. See Munier, "Où en est la question d'Ignace d'Antioch? Bilan d'un siècle de recherches: 1870–1988," in *Aufstieg und Niedergang der römischen Welt: Geschichte und Kultur Roms im Spiegel der neueren Forschung.* Teil II: *Principat,* vol. 27/1: *Vorkonstantinisches Christentum: Apostolische Väter und Apologeten,* ed. Wolfgang Haase (New York: Walter de Gruyter, 1993) 359–484. On Ignatius' letters, see the excellent summary in Régis Burnet, "Ignace d'Antioche dans la lignée de Paul," in *Épîtres et lettres Ier-IIe siècle. De Paul de Tarse à Polycarpe de Smyrne,* Lectio Divina 192 (Paris: Les Éditions du Cerf, 2003) 339–68. On Polycarp of Smyrna, see ibid., 370–75 ["La lettre de Polycarpe, achèvement de la pratique épistolaire du premier christianisme"]. The question is of more than mere academic interest because the early dating of Ignatius' letters has been used to establish as early a date as possible for the emergence of the regime of the single bishop (technically referred to as "monoepiscopacy") and thus to bring it as close as possible to the last living apostle, often thought to be the apostle John, or at the very least to the *viri probati* ["approved men," with the implication that they were "approved by the apostles"] *1 Clement* refers to. This would impart undoubted apostolic authority to the institution of episcopacy. The drawback of this procedure is that it obscures the real process of how episcopacy emerged, viz., the Lord's providential guiding of the church of the second century in the Spirit to the threefold ministry of bishop, presbyters, and deacons. Accustomed as we are today to think in historical terms, i.e., in terms of modern historical consciousness, retrieving an historical perspective on the church is not a loss but a clear gain. Historicity marks our human condition, whether personal, social, or institutional, as we saw above in chapter 6, pp. 145–50.

28. "The traditional threefold pattern thus raises questions for all the churches. Churches maintaining the threefold pattern will need to ask how its potential can be fully developed for the most effective witness of the church in this world. In this task churches not having the threefold pattern should also participate. They will further need to ask themselves whether the threefold pattern as developed does not have a powerful claim to be accepted by them." *Growth in Agreement,* 488–89.

29. On the emergence of monoepiscopacy in the early church, see Ernst Dassmann, "Zur Entstehung des Monepiskopats" and "Bischofsbestellung in der frühen Kirche," in *Ämter und Dienste in den frühchristlichen Gemeinden,* Hereditas. Studien zur alten Kirchengeschichte 8 (Bonn: Verlag Norbert M. Borengässer, 1994) 49–73 and 190–211 respectively.

episcopal ministry in close interrelationship with his presbyters and deacons. He is not above them, and there is no sense that the latter derive
their ministry from him. All three exercise the ministry in concert with
one another and so each is indispensable for the others.[30] The following
phrases are typical of Ignatius' view:

> Thus it is proper for you to act together in harmony with the mind of the
> bishop, as you are in fact doing. For your presbytery, which is worthy of its
> name and worthy of God, is attuned to the bishop as strings to a lyre. There-
> fore in your unanimity and harmonious love Jesus Christ is sung. You must
> join this chorus, every one of you, so that by being harmonious in unan-
> imity and taking your pitch from God you may sing in unison with one
> voice through Jesus Christ to the Father, in order that he may both hear
> you and, on the basis of what you do well, acknowledge that you are mem-
> bers of his Son. It is, therefore, advantageous for you to be in perfect unity,
> in order that you may always have a share in God.[31]
>
> Take care, therefore, to participate in one Eucharist (for there is one
> flesh of our Lord Jesus Christ, and one cup which leads to unity through
> his blood; there is one altar, just as there is one bishop, together with the
> presbytery and the deacons, my fellow servants), in order that whatever
> you do, you do in accordance with God.[32]

The ministerial functions of the Ignatian bishop, too, are simpler than
the third-century bishop's. He is clearly a liturgical figure, with responsibility principally for presiding at the community Eucharist and baptisms.
The teaching and governing functions, however, are still exercised by the
presbyters, and the deacons are clearly important assistants. The bishop's
eucharistic or liturgical activity is central to the life of the community,
and only in a situation of need is it delegated by him to another.[33] In a
word, the image of apostolic ministry we detect in Ignatius is one that is
shared by several different persons who act in clear concert with one another for the sake of the unity of the whole community. By the time we

30. See the discussion of the individual texts in Ignatius by Francis A. Sullivan,
"Ignatius of Antioch," in *From Apostles to Bishops: The Development of the Episcopacy in the Early
Church* (New York: Paulist Press, 2001) 103–25.

31. "To the Ephesians," §4. *The Apostolic Fathers,* tr. J. B. Lightfoot and J. R. Harmer,
ed. and rev. by Michael W. Holmes (2nd ed.; Grand Rapids: Baker Book House, 1989) 87.

32. "To the Philadelphians," §4. Ibid., 107.

33. See Ignatius' "To the Smyrneans" §8. James F. McCue discusses who these delegates might be in "Bishops, Presbyters, and Priests in Ignatius of Antioch," *Theological
Studies* 28 (1967) 828–34.

meet the "monarchical bishop" in the fourth century, we discern a clear division of responsibility and the dependence of the presbyters and the deacons on the *episkopos*.[34] The sense of mutual communion in the ministry has been lost. The hierarchical model in the strict sense is well on the way to being realized—the authority of the presbyters and the deacons depends on and flows from the fullness of the bishop's authority.[35] How did this come about and what did it mean in the early church?

John Zizioulas has made a proposal that is reasonable and makes sense out of the disparate information coming to us from the first three centuries of the church and the following centuries.[36] Zizioulas distinguishes between the Ignatian model of a bishop and the model of Cyprian of Carthage (c. 200–258). Ignatius' bishop is the single bishop (mono-episkopos) of a local church that is still small and whose members know each other rather intimately. The bishop is understood in a radically christological way, that is, he is the living symbol of Christ to the community, the Christ who reigns with the Father and whose kingdom is sacramentally present as an eschatological reality in the celebration of the Eucharist. The bishop mystically symbolizes the power and lure of Christ's eschatological future in the present life of his church. Present and future encounter each other in the Eucharist, the principal act of the community and the bishop who presides at it. Zizioulas contends that this Ignatian understanding has been maintained in its essentials by the Eastern churches. After Cyprian, and especially after the conversion of Constantine, another model of episcopacy emerged. With the spectacu-

34. For a brief but clear presentation of the barest historical data, see Charles Munier, "Authority in the Church," in *Encyclopedia of the Early Church*, 1:104–5; and Joseph Lécuyer, "Ministries, Ordained Ministers," in ibid., 560–62. For the emergence of the office of bishop and a concise history of episcopacy as it relates to the development of papal primacy, see William Henn, *The Honor of My Brothers: A Short History of the Relation between the Pope and the Bishops,* Ut Unum Sint: Studies on Papal Primacy (New York: The Crossroad Publishing Company, 2000).

35. See Hans Jorissen, "Reflections on the Structure of the Ordained Ministry and the Apostolic Succession from an Ecumenical Perspective," in *From Life to Law,* Concilium 1996/5, eds. James Provost and Knut Walf (Maryknoll, N.Y.: Orbis Books, 1996) 88–97, for a helpful discussion of the relationship between episcopacy and the presbyterate.

36. See John D. Zizioulas, "*Episkopē* and *Episkopos* in the Early Church: A Brief Survey of the Evidence," in *Episkopē and Episcopate in Ecumenical Perspective,* Faith and Order Paper 102 (Geneva: WCC, 1980) 30–42. See also Alvin F. Kimel, "Who Are the Bishops? Episkopé and the Church," *Anglican Theological Review* 77 (1995) 58–75, for a treatment of episcopacy that draws on Zizioulas's ideas and that poses some interesting questions on episcopacy in today's context.

lar growth of the church in terms of numbers, the presbyters began to assume the central role of the bishop as presider at the Eucharist. In turn, the bishop assumed the teaching (magisterium) and governing (jurisdiction) roles up to then largely exercised by the presbyters together with the bishop.

The late third and the fourth and fifth centuries were characterized by intense theological debates aimed at defining the primitive "rule of faith" in greater detail. The Trinitarian and christological controversies resulted in the emergence of an orthodox system of Christian beliefs. The up-to-then largely catechetical and kerygmatic activity of the presbyters was no longer adequate to the task of defining the faith, and so the bishops, who often came from the educated class, assumed this important and indispensable function. However, the role as the one who presided at the Eucharist became confused, and the intrinsic unity of ministry between the bishop and his presbyters, according to the Ignatian model, was broken in favor of pastoral expediency and effectiveness. This explains why Jerome saw no essential difference between a presbyter and a bishop. The model of episcopacy influenced by Cyprian came to be associated with the Western church and has dominated the theology of episcopacy ever since.

According to Zizioulas, even though the Western model influenced the understanding of Eastern Christianity, the liturgy of the East has always maintained the bishop as symbol of Christ's eschatological presence to his community. The consequence of Zizioulas' argument is that for centuries now there have been two understandings of a bishop—the Eastern (christological-eschatological) and the Western (monarchical-hierarchical). The former model is more symbolic in nature and in its exercise, the latter is more literal and comes to expression in juridical terms.[37] What is important for us to understand in the context of the thesis of this book is that de facto there is more than just one orthodox understanding of episcopacy in the church and therefore of apostolic succession in the ministry. This fact is almost uniformly ignored. Its consequences, however, are enormous. There are at least two ways of realizing *episkopē* in the church. The Ignatian way is more unified, since it stresses the oneness of ministry in the church, a ministry shared by a bishop who

37. This fact helps to explain why there was such heated debate at Vatican II on the notion of episcopal collegiality and why there has been little progress made in the postconciliar period on its nature, extent, limits, and interaction with the Petrine ministry of primacy.

is really a local pastor, his elders/presbyters or co-workers, and other helpers known as deacons. The Cyprianic way is of a ministry that is ultimately divisible and whose unity is assured by hierarchical ordering.

Zizioulas' theory is elegant in as much as it explains the historical emergence of the single bishop, the underlying unity of ecclesial ministry, the valid influence of differing historical experiences on different churches,[38] and a possible way of resolving our seemingly irreconcilable ways of understanding official ministry in our churches. I will turn to how the theory of John Zizioulas can help us resolve the ministerial issues that still divide us in the fourth section of this chapter. First, however, we need to examine certain terms associated with the sacraments, terms which often cause further misunderstanding, division, and hurt.

Meaning of the Term "Validity"

To many observers, the notion of validity affects the very existence of something: what is valid exists, what is invalid does not. According to this way of thinking, invalidity denotes non-existence—what is assumed to be simply does not exist. It is a sham. To others, validity has a more social function: personal or interpersonal actions can in fact lay claim to existence, but they are largely ineffectual or inauthentic. An invalid act is a mistake. The category of validity is generally applied to the sacramental actions of the church. These actions either take effect or not. What kind of claim are we making when we speak of the validity of the sacraments? Of the validity of holy orders? Of the validity of ministry outside the historical succession of the bishops? These questions cannot be answered unless we first note the emergence of the terms "valid" and "invalid," and unless we understand the notion of validity in terms of how we understand a "sacrament." First, then, to the history of the term.

John A. Gurrieri has shown the late appearance of the word group *validus* (adj.), *valide* (adv.), and *validitas* (noun) as applied to the sacraments.[39] Before Pope Benedict XIV (1740–58) one finds only passing ref-

---

38. E.g., the change from a bishop as a congregational leader to a regional leader of a larger entity or diocese, the emergence of the monarchical bishop in the fourth century, and the wrestling of the sixteenth-century Reformers with their experience that the bishops seemed to be impeding the proclamation of God's word in power and their refusal to ordain new pastors for the reform movement (which at the time was still a reform within the church).

39. John A. Gurrieri writes: "Up to the end of the thirteenth century *validus/invalidus* are not employed in a juridical sense, nor in a theological context either. . . . There was,

erences to it, but because the pope favored it, the term *validitas* soon became the favored expression for referring to the effects of the sacraments. Earlier terms used included such words as the Greek *akuros* (adj.)
used at the Council of Chalcedon (451) in its famous canon 6 and translated into Latin as *irritum* (adj.), or in English as "powerless" or "without
force"[40] and "useless" or "without effect"[41] respectively. For the most
part, in the history of the theology of the sacraments, the notion of validity was not intended to directly touch the very core or "substance of
the sacrament"–the *substantia sacramenti*–but was meant to address other
aspects of a sacrament, for example, the liturgical actions of its celebration, including the proper rubrics, and the applicability of jurisdiction to
its administration. Thus, "validity" emerged in the area of the sacrament

---

then, no discussion of the 'validity' of a sacrament in the Middle Ages, in the sense we
understand the term. A *sacramentum* was *verum* or *falsum*; a sacrament could be rendered *irritum*, if it was accomplished/celebrated contrary to its authentic meaning or contrary to
leges irritantes. This is not to say, on the other hand, that the principle of validity was never
employed in the medieval period, but only that its use did not extend to the sacraments *in
genere* or to the substance of the sacraments. . . . It is not until early in the fourteenth century that valid/invalid appear in connection with any of the sacraments, and then only in
connection with the sacrament of marriage." See "Sacramental Validity: The Origins and
Use of a Vocabulary," *The Jurist* 41 (1981) 21–58, at 30, 32 and 36. See also Pierre-Marie
Gy, "La notion de validité sacramentelle avant le Concile de Trente," *Revue de droit canonique* 28 (1978) 193–202. On the meaning of *lex irritans*, see Friedrich Merzbacher, "Zur
Rechtsgeschichte der lex irritans," in *Ius sacrum. Klaus Mörsdorf zum 60. Geburtstag*, eds. Au-
domar Scheuermann and Georg May (Munich: Verlag Ferdinand Schöningh, 1969) 101–10.
Catholics of a certain age will remember one of the examples of *leges irritantes* in the former
practice of announcing the "banns of marriage" from the pulpit on three successive Sun-
days in order to meet one of the requirements for the celebration of the sacrament. Another is the perfunctory call at a marriage or an ordination ceremony for anyone who has
knowledge of why the marriage or ordination should not take place to bring this information to the immediate attention of the presiding priest or bishop.
    40. See *"akuros,"* in *A Patristic Greek Lexikon*, ed. G. W. H. Lampe (Oxford: At the
Clarendon Press, 1978 [1961]) 68.
    41. See *"irritus,"* in *A Latin Dictionary*, eds. Charlton T. Lewis and Charles Short (Ox-
ford: At the Clarendon Press, 1962 [1879]) 1002–3. It should be remarked at this point
that *validitas/validum* comes from a different semantic background, viz., "that which is
healthy or sound." The Latin salutation *"Vale!"* means "Hail!" or "Be well!" More philo-
logical information can be found in P. G. W. Glare, ed., *Oxford Latin Dictionary* (Oxford: At
the Clarendon Press, 1982 [reprint 1994]) 968 ["*irritus*"] and 2008 ["*validus*"]. By the way,
in the accepted vocabulary the Latin *ratum* (adj.) was the contrary of *irritum*, and meant
"firm," "sure," or "certain." See *"reor, ratus,"* in *A Latin Dictionary*, 1566. A sacramental marriage was referred to as *"sacramentum ratum."*

of marriage and it referred originally to the marriage contract, that is, to that dimension of marriage that could be spelled out in legal terms.[42]

The Council of Trent marked an important point of departure for the church's teaching on the sacraments. The discussion shifted from marriage and its relation to the matrimonial contract to the issue of intention—the recipient's and the minister's. Such questions as the baptism of a non-believer by a Catholic and the absolution of a penitent by a priest who does not have a serious intention to absolve the sinner were typical examples regarding the sacraments after Trent. The issue was no longer that of the "substance of the sacrament," as in earlier times, but the matter of proper intention that governed the emergence of the new vocabulary of validity/invalidity. There is a shift from the institution of the sacrament by Christ to the conditions of receiving and administering the sacrament. The theological questions of the "substance of the sacrament" as willed by Christ and the validity of the sacrament as manifested in the "intention" of the recipient and the minister are not interchangeable. Luther and Calvin, for example, seem to have been more concerned with the sacraments as instituted by Christ, and thus with the "old problematic," while the bishops at Trent had moved into a "new problematic," that of intentionality. Eventually, the new problematic elicited a new vocabulary of "valid/invalid."[43] In the changed context of post-Tridentine sacramental theology, the distinction between the "validity" and the "liceity" of the sacraments becomes more pronounced as well. Gurrieri summarizes his discussion up to and including Benedict XIV in the following words:

> Benedict . . . established the classic distinction of validity/liceity in sacramental theology. Both validity and liceity are necessary for an authentic sacrament, a "sacramentum verum," a sacrament which is truly ecclesial.

42. Gurrieri writes: "It seems to be rather clear therefore that the origin and primitive use of *validus* and *invalidus* in canon law and later in theology comes from its usage with regard to contracts, especially the marriage contract. . . . On the eve of the Council of Trent theologians such as Cajetan and Domingo Soto have accepted into theology a terminology which was technical to canon law, more specifically to the marriage contract. And by the second third of the sixteenth century the vocabulary of validity is firmly in place among the theologians, although it is not yet the language of the papal magisterium." "Sacramental Validity: The Origins and Use of a Vocabulary," 39–40.

43. See Gurrieri's discussion on Benedict XIV's writings before he was elected pope and after his election. "Sacramental Validity: The Origins and Use of a Vocabulary," 51–56 ["The Sacramental Theology of Pope Benedict XIV"].

Yet a "valid sacrament" may be "confected" illicitly, that is, without the approbation of the "Ecclesia," and therefore "unecclesial." Sacramental validity is no longer another way of expressing a sacrament's authentic ecclesiality, as Schillebeeckx maintains, but rather "validitas sacramenti" has become mere objectivity—the divorce of the sacramental act from ecclesial sacramentality. Thus the vocabulary of validity, now fully accepted in the papal magisterium, deepens the trench between ecclesiology and sacramentology, a pit that began to open after Thomas Aquinas.[44]

It seems legitimate to distinguish a later ("modern") sacramental theology founded on validity from an earlier ("pre-modern") sacramentology founded on the *veritas* or "truth" of the sacrament. The latter points in the direction of the sacrament's connection with the mystery of the church, that is, its ecclesial nature. Thus, we need to address three distinct issues regarding the sacraments: validity (canonical/legal issues), liceity (the personal/existential dimensions), and what I will call "verity" (ecclesial dimensions). I propose to consider this third dimension in greater depth.

Finally, Gurrieri concludes his important study with several reflections on the applicability of his historical survey to the situation of the church after the Council. He writes:

> Perhaps what is needed today is a distinction proffered by B. J. Kidd in 1937: "validitas sacramentalis" and "validitas canonica." A concept of canonical validity based on the principle of "leges irritantes" might better explain the exact nature of the Church's authority over the "validitas sacramentalis," the "substance of the sacraments," their authentic ecclesiality. Moreover, in the light of ecumenism more needs to be said about the relationship between the principle of economy and the nature of the sacraments.[45]

I certainly support Gurrieri's call for such reconsideration and I propose in the next section to pursue the point of the connection between the church as sacrament and the church's sacraments in greater detail. Before proceeding to this larger topic, I wish to ask whether the invalidity of a sacrament might be better understood by us not in terms of existence/non-existence, and not in terms of what is licit/illicit, but in terms of what conforms to the church's understanding of a sacrament and consequently the regulations for properly celebrating a sacrament. To call a

44. Ibid., 55.
45. Ibid., 57–58.

sacrament "invalid" does not mean that nothing has occurred sacramentally, but that the celebration and administration of the sacrament has
not fully conformed to the church's understanding of the sacrament and
has not fulfilled all the conditions governing its celebration and administration. It suffers an "ecclesial lack" or *defectus* and not simply a canonical
irregularity. More precisely, what might such a *defectus* be? I propose that
it can be understood only in terms of the whole reality of what the
church is and not in terms of the sacraments as isolated acts.

In a study dedicated to the significance of validity, the Catholic theologian Charles Wackenheim distinguished three levels of meaning: the
canonical, the ecclesial, and the "theological."[46] He showed how there is
a clear hierarchy or ordering among the three levels. In the ordinary
Catholic understanding, however, priority is given the canonical, with
little or no regard to the other two issues of the relationship of an act to
the church (the christological/sacramental dimension) and also to the all-
embracing mystery of God's salvific will and presence, even beyond the
church (the pneumatological dimension). In fact, the canonical needs to
be understood against the backdrop of the larger reality of the church,
while the latter demands an opening or expansion of the notion of the
church to the greater mystery of salvation. Wackenheim further distinguishes the dimension of the role played by a person's decision of conscience within the "theological." His point is well made, but I think it
would be better to speak of two distinct meanings of validity with respect to the "theological": the personal (the dimension of conscience)
and the strictly "theological" (the mystery of God's saving humankind).
Thus, we can distinguish four levels of meaning, and each must be thought
through in relation to the others: the canonical, the ecclesial, the personal, and the "theological." Let us examine more closely the second
level of meaning, the ecclesial.

Wackenheim writes:

> What is characteristic of the ecclesial level is not the simple conformity to
> a law, but an organic reference of the believing community to Jesus Christ,
> the revealer of the indefectible love of God for the world. We can also call
> this reference the faith of the church. Sacraments are celebrated by a people
> who have been formed by the living word of the Gospel. Rather than speak
> of validity and nullity [in this sphere], we should speak of belonging (or of

46. "Validité et nullité des sacrements: le problème théologique," *Revue de droit canonique* 26 (1976) 15–22.

communion) and of refusal (or a certain rupture), always aware of the fact that such attitudes are never open to juridical verification.[47]

Though Wackenheim is primarily concerned with the sacrament of marriage in his article, at this point he turns to the vexing question of orders or ordination. Employing his distinction, he writes:

> It is said, for example, that a ministerial ordination is valid ecclesiologically if the ritual act and the pastoral commission conferred on someone enjoy an uncontested recognition by the church. Of course, the ecclesial dimension belongs integrally to canonical validity. But the theologian must also take into consideration situations where a certain disorder has resulted. This is the area where the question is posed regarding the ordinations conferred in other Christian churches and which oblige us at the very least to distinguish the canonical and the ecclesial. It would appear difficult today to declare without any reservations that ordinations celebrated in a church canonically separated [from Rome] are "null" because they depart from the normative rite. In this case, one must begin by examining the faith of the churches under consideration. Then, one must make the effort of evaluating the degree of consensus affecting this or that type of ordination and ministry. . . . I would simply like to point out that the reality of the church introduces an original dimension into the believer's existence, a dimension that cannot be reduced to the level of a canonical criterion.[48]

I consider Wackenheim's observations very important and relevant to the question of apostolic succession in ministry. In the following section, I propose to build on them and to examine the question in greater detail.

The Question of the Recognition of Ministry

In the last forty years, theologians, ecumenists, and historians have produced a series of excellent articles treating the issue of each church

47. Ibid., 16–17.

48. Ibid., 18. Hans Jorissen, too, renders a positive judgment on the validity of Lutheran orders when he writes: "Thus without conflicting with dogma, and with the support of statements by the Second Vatican Council, Catholic theology can respond that the essence of the apostolic ministry and the apostolic succession has been preserved in the churches of the Reformation, in the form of apostolic succession in the presbyterate, or, better, in the one ministry which by its sacramental nature is completely 'episcopal'. This raises the dogmatic possibility of the recognition of ministries. . . . Thus the Catholic church with its episcopal constitution can recognize a church with a 'presbyteral' constitution as a sister church and recognize its ministries as fully valid." "Reflections on the Structure of the Ordained Ministry and the Apostolic Succession from an Ecumenical Perspective," 94.

recognizing the ministry of the other churches.⁴⁹ And yet, little consensus has resulted from these studies. Why is it the case? Is it simply that each community wants to jealously guard its understanding of ministry

49. See Frans Jozef van Beeck, "Towards an Ecumenical Understanding of the Sacraments," *Journal of Ecumenical Studies* 3 (1966) 57–112; Harry J. McSorley, "Protestant Eucharistic Reality and Lack of Orders," *The Ecumenist* 5 (1966–67) 68–71 and 74–75; George H. Tavard, "Does the Protestant Ministry Have Sacramental Significance?" *Continuum* 6 (1968–69) 260–68; Harry J. McSorley, "The Roman Catholic Doctrine of the Competent Minister of the Eucharist in Ecumenical Perspective," in *Eucharist and Ministry,* Lutherans and Catholics in Dialogue 4, eds. Paul Empie and T. Austin Murphy (Washington, D.C.: USCC Publications, 1970) 120–37; idem, "Trent and the Question: Can Protestant Ministers Consecrate the Eucharist?" in ibid., 283–99; Arthur Carl Piepkorn, "A Lutheran View of the Validity of Lutheran Orders," in ibid., 209–26; George H. Tavard, "Roman Catholic Theology and 'Recognition of Ministry,'" in ibid., 301–5; Kilian McDonnell, "Ways of Validating Ministry," *Journal of Ecumenical Studies* 7 (1970) 209–65; Harry J. McSorley, "Recognition of a Presbyteral Succession?" in *The Plurality of Ministries,* Concilium 74, eds. Hans Küng and Walter Kasper (New York: Herder and Herder, 1972) 23–32, together with replies from the Orthodox, Lutheran, Methodist, Anglican, Free Church, and Catholic traditions to the question "How Can We Arrive at a Theological and Practical, Mutual Recognition of Ministries?" in the same issue, 63–114; Wilhelm Averbeck, "Gegenseitige Anerkennung des Amtes? Bemerkungen zu einem lutherisch-katholischen Dokument aus Amerika," *Catholica* 26 (1973) 172–91; Heribert Mühlen, "Wohin würde eine gegenseitige Anerkennung führen?" in *Amt im Widerstreit,* ed. Karlheinz Schuh (Berlin: Morus-Verlag, 1973) 91–102; Aloys Klein, "Von der Krise zur Anerkennung des kirchlichen Amtes," in ibid., 103–9; Heinrich Fries, "Was heißt Anerkennung?" in ibid., 110–21; George A. Maloney, "Validation of Catholic and Orthodox Ministry," *Diakonia* 8 (1973) 155–63; George H. Tavard, "The Recognition of Ministry," *Journal of Ecumenical Studies* 11 (1974) 65–83; Walter, Kasper, "Zur Frage der Anerkennung der Ämter in den lutherischen Kirchen," in *Evangelium–Welt–Kirche: Schlussbericht und Referate der römisch-katholisch/evangelisch-lutherischen Studienkommission "Das Evangelium und die Kirche", 1967–1971,* ed. Harding Meyer (Frankfurt am Main: Verlag Otto Lembeck; Frankfurt am Main: Verlag Josef Knecht, 1975) 401–14; George H. Tavard, "The Reconciliation of Ministries," *Journal of Ecumenical Studies* 18 (1981) 267–80; J.M.R. Tillard, "Recognition of Ministries: What Is the Real Question?" 31–39; Heinrich Fries and Karl Rahner, "Thesis VII (Recognition of Offices)," in *Unity of the Churches: An Actual Possibility,* trs. Ruth C. L. Gritsch and Eric W. Gritsch (Philadelphia: Fortress Press and New York: Paulist Press, 1985) 115–21; John D. Zizioulas, *Being as Communion: Studies in Personhood and the Church* (Crestwood, N.Y.: St. Vladimir's Semianry Press, 1985) 243–46 ["The 'Validity' of the Ministry"]; William J. Martyn, "Mutual Recognition of Ministry: Creating Another Rip Van Winkle?" *Journal of Ecumenical Studies* 23 (1986) 492–503; George H. Tavard, "The Recognition of Ministry: What Is the Priority?" *One in Christ* 23 (1987) 21–35; Gerard Kelly, "The Recognition of Ministries: A Shift in Ecumenical Thinking," *One in Christ* 30 (1994) 10–21; Heinrich Fries, *Fundamental Theology,* tr. Robert J. Daly (Washington, D.C.: The Catholic University of America Press, 1996) 556–59 ["The Meaning of 'Recognition'"]; and Thomas M. Kocik, *Apostolic Succession in an Ecumenical Context* (Staten Island, N.Y.: Alba House, 1996) 110–25 ["Proposals for Restoring Full Communion Following Doctrinal Consensus"].

because it is worried about maintaining its own ecclesial identity? Would changes in ministry result in the loss of ecclesial identity? Would acknowledging the mere possibility that one's ministry was in need of recognition by another church result in a sense that somehow or other this ministry is inferior or deficient? In the spectrum of ecumenical dialogues, each church believes that its ministry is genuine and conforms to Christ's will for the church. But how is it possible to acknowledge the authenticity of each church's ministry and still speak meaningfully of "ecclesial ministry" as something normative for the church, or at least as something that contributes to the church's claim that it is in continuity with the church of the Apostles? The churches seem to have arrived at an impasse on this difficult matter, and it is often called the "obstacle that defies resolution." It might seem foolhardy for me to try to address this ecumenical Gordian knot, but ignoring it is really not an option. I do not propose a complete solution to the problem but rather some reflections that I offer as elements toward a solution. I hope they will lead to further movement in addressing this urgent issue.

The language used in speaking about the underlying issue of different readings in the churches regarding official ministry is suggestive. At first, the vocabulary employed spoke about acknowledging the validity of each other's ministry or, where there were serious doubts regarding validity, about reestablishing validity through some act of rectification, either on the part of both churches or on the part of one church offering some element of "complementarity" or "validation." In some instances, the element was more of the historical order, that is, full reestablishment of the historic succession in ministry in terms of the succession of the bishops or the threefold ministry of bishop, presbyters, and deacons. At other times, it was seen as more sacramental in intent, that is, a necessary element for the fullness of the ministry was lacking, even though that did not necessarily mean that the ministry as a whole was contrary to Christ's founding will or that the fruitfulness of the ministry was to be denied. This approach proved to be a delicate path to walk since it was practically impossible to avoid the impression that one of the churches was deficient vis-à-vis the other(s). Official protestations to the contrary did not ring true—certainly not to the ordinary member of a church. Subsequent efforts moved away from considerations of a need to "validate" ministry toward examining the presuppositions of the ministry and the implied or stated ecclesiology within which the ministry was exercised. In this second move toward understanding, greater attention was paid to the apostolicity of the whole church and to the specialized ministry as an element of this greater sense of apostolicity—what I have called "substantive apostolicity" or "apostolicity of life." This second way has proven easier to pursue because it avoids invidious comparisons. However, it also has demonstrated shortcomings. For example, Roman Catholic authorities ask if apostolic succession of the bishops is still integral to ministry or a guarantee of the church's apostolicity of doctrine, or if it has become a mere "sign" of the church's own apostolicity in the sense that the "sign" is ultimately dispensable even though useful. How are we to understand these differing approaches?

We saw above the ambiguity surrounding the concept of validity, and yet somehow or other we seem bound to it, or to something like it, in trying to resolve the mutuality of ministry in the churches. Though the concept of validity is itself of late appearance, the concerns for discerning issues of authenticity of ministry, fruitfulness or effectiveness of ministry, reasons for dismissing a person from the ministry, and Christ as truly present and active in all forms of ministry—the word, the sacraments, acts of justice, charity, and so forth—can be found at almost any time in the church's history. In what follows, I will continue to speak of "validity," but I will be employing it in the broader senses developed by Charles Wackenheim.

In a pioneering article, Kilian McDonnell outlined three "ways of validating ministry": ritual, charismatic, and ecclesiological.[50] I find McDonnell's distinctions very helpful, but I suggest that they might better be thought of as three "models for validating ministry." The advantage of a models approach is that none is excluded, since each one emphasizes a dimension that the others find hard to express, yet the specificity of each model really adds something to our understanding of the richness of ministry.[51] A models approach does not mean that one must choose only one alternative from the many offered, but that they are to be understood "relationally."

Early on in the discussion regarding the mutual recognition of ministry, ritual validation played a major role. Much was learned by the serious studies of alternative ways of understanding how ministry was

50. Kilian McDonnell, "Ways of Validating Ministry," 209–65.
51. I discussed the notion of a "model" earlier in chapter 5, pp. 95–101.

transmitted in the early church, what was and was not officially taught by the Council of Trent regarding ministry and its *ius divinum,* that is, the explicit, divine ordering of the church either by Christ or by decisions rendered by the apostles as empowered by the Spirit. Moreover, by employing a process of a historical, doctrinal, and theological study of the sources of the Reformation, that is, what is commonly referred to as the *ressourcement* or "the return to the sources" method of study, Reformation scholars were better able to retrieve what Luther, the other leaders of the magisterial Reformation, and the confessional statements issuing from the Reformation really taught regarding ministry. In this way, misconceptions were discarded and oversimplifications were brought to the light of day. Most of this effort, however, concentrated on "ritual validation." It no longer seemed to be entirely correct to maintain that Luther's recourse to a presbyteral form of ordination was entirely out of the question or a heretical departure from the ordination practices of his time, especially if this was seen to be an "emergency solution." As hard as it might be to understand how an emergency situation could last for close to five hundred years, it was not entirely out of the question as an explanation.

Moreover, the rediscovery by Lutheran scholars of the importance of regarding installation in ministry as a form of ordination did not occur in an ecclesiological vacuum. The Second Vatican Council unleashed a flurry of interest and activity in renewing the liturgical life of the churches beyond the liturgical reforms of the Roman Catholic Church. Luther's own hesitant language about ministry now seemed less like a rejection of the medieval understanding and more an expression of the unresolved issues regarding ministry at the time, as well as an attempt to address the evident abuses in the church's offices—from top to bottom. In the light of these studies, Catholic authorities were challenged to stretch their understanding of entrance into ministry to include other forms of ordination as apostolic, even though they might be characterized as "archaic" and now demanded regularization after an intemperately long period of functioning as an "emergency solution." Is it really beyond the pale of Catholic principles of the ritual validity of ordination to see Lutheran forms—both presbyteral and episcopal—as also enjoying apostolicity? According to the generally accepted principles of a doubtful celebration of a sacrament, Catholic authorities need to seriously ask themselves if there really are sufficient reasons to entertain a doubt about the validity of Lutheran presbyteral and episcopal ordinations in a ritual sense. If there are reasons, then the doubt must still be addressed and the presumption that Lutheran ordinations are invalid must not be answered too hastily in terms of dogmatic assumptions that might need to be reexamined and possibly broadened. To restate it in positive terms, Catholic authorities need to keep an open stance on the validity of what they as Catholics would refer to as Lutheran ordinations. But that still leaves two other models to be considered in conjunction with my observations on ritual validity.

What can be said about McDonnell's second way of validating ministry, "charismatic validation"? Here, too, but seen as a model, charismatic forms of transmitting ministry have an important role to play. In terms of their histories of theology, Roman Catholicism, Lutheranism, and Anglicanism are all highly "christological" in orientation. The emergence of the charismatic movement in the 1960s was a source of genuine confusion to these churches. However, seeing the Second Vatican Council itself as an expression of the Spirit moving the churches, the teaching of the same council regarding the importance of charisms, as well as the vitality of charismatic groups, the churches eventually became reconciled to elements of the unpredictability of the Spirit in the life of the church. These influences opened the churches up to a reexamination of the pneumatological character of the church. Not everything about the church can be reduced to christological statements. Christ is not less Lord of the church and Head of the body because the Spirit breathes freely in the church as well. Little by little, the old antinomy between office and charism came to be seen as yet another polemical sharpening of the differences between two mutually coordinated movements—one of Christ, the other of the Spirit. Furthermore, the recovery of the richness of patristic trinitarian theology—largely mediated to us from the Eastern churches—led to the peaceful acceptance of the mutual roles of Christ and the Spirit in the return of humankind to the Father. In this light, office came to be understood as a stable charism, but still a charism. Office is always open to new forms and new responses. But little thought has as yet been given to the other possible direction of thought—from charism to office. Among Roman Catholics, Lutherans, and Anglicans, the area has been little explored. Is it also possible to see formally charismatic forms of entrance into ministry as expressions of the apostolic character of ministry?

I cannot pursue this question in depth, but I do need to dwell on the import of the question insofar as it highlights the significance of the charismatic model. Thus, for example, in the Roman Catholic Church, a

broad discussion has emerged on the relationship of the ordained ministry of a member of the diocesan presbyterate and the ministry of an ordained member of a religious institute or order. Are the priesthoods simply
mirror images of each other, where the religious profession of the religious clergy and the bonds of belonging to a local presbyterium on the
part of the diocesan presbyter function only as insignificant accessories
of their being priests? Among the ordained members of religious orders,
the differences are seen increasingly as fundamental, and not accidental.
There is not one generic sense of being a priest that is given definite direction by choosing to be a member of the diocesan clergy or by choosing to live out and exercise one's priesthood in the context of one's
religious community and its specific charism. Maybe there are two different, though mutually related, forms of being a priest. Thus, many religious priests understand their priesthood more under the sign of the
Spirit's freedom, creativity, the call to justice and the defense of the environment as God's good creation, the creating of a specific form of spirituality, and so forth. The call of the diocesan presbyter emerges more
clearly in terms of his permanent commitment to a local church, to collaboration with the bishop, to leading a community of the faithful, and to
the building up of the local church in a definite place.[52] These differences
are not negligible, but they are also not divisive. Each form of the ordained priesthood points to the importance of the local and the universal
church in complementary, but sometimes, too, in overlapping, ways. On
the basis of such experiences, can Roman Catholics open themselves to

52. The literature on this issue has grown considerably in the past twenty years. See
Ivan Havener, "Monastic Priesthood: Some Thoughts on Its Future in America," *Worship*
56 (1982) 431–41; John W. O'Malley, "Priesthood, Ministry, and Religious Life: Some
Historical and Historiographical Considerations," *Theological Studies* 49 (1988) 223–57;
idem, "Diocesan and Religious Models of Priestly Formation," in *Priests: Identity and Ministry,*
ed. Robert J. Wister (Wilmington, Del.: Michael Glazier, Inc., 1990) 54–70; Paul J. Philib-
ert, "Priesthood Within the Context of Religious Life," in *Being a Priest Today,* ed. Donald J.
Goergen (Collegeville, Minn.: The Liturgical Press, 1992) 73–96; Thomas P. Rausch,
"Priesthood in Apostolic Religious Communities," in *Priesthood Today: An Appraisal* (New
York: Paulist Press, 1992) 82–104; John W. O'Malley, "One Priesthood: Two Traditions,"
in *A Concert of Charisms: Ordained Ministry in Religious Life,* ed. Paul K. Hennessy (New York:
Paulist Press, 1997) 9–24; David N. Power, "Theologies of Religious Life and Priesthood,"
in ibid., 61–103; Kevin R. Seasoltz, "A Western Monastic Perspective on Ordained Ministry" and "Institutes of Consecrated Life and Ordained Ministry: Some Canonical Issues,"
in ibid., 25–60 and 139–68 respectively; and Thomas P. Rausch, "Priesthood in the Context of Apostolic Religious Life," in *The Theology of the Priesthood,* eds. Donald J. Goergen and
Ann Garrido (Collegeville, Minn.: The Liturgical Press, 2000) 105–11.

the possibility that in the ecumenical church of Christ there just might be something analogous in the churches that understand their ministry in terms of charismatic validation, for example, the Free churches? Are there different ways of being church that do not contradict but express the richness of the mystery of the church? I can only pose the question in a heuristic way, since the limitations of space and the focus of my work prevent me from entering into it at greater length.

In the third place, McDonnell speaks of "ecclesiological validation." At the same time that ritual validity was being studied, some early essays probed this dimension of apostolic ministry. However, the approach fully emerged only later, particularly as the various ecumenical statements concentrated on the apostolicity of the whole church—a question we have considered at length above. What might this form of "ecclesiological validation" mean in terms of my transposition of a "way" of validating ministry into a "model" of ecclesiological validation? Again, I do not need to dwell at length on the issue, but I do want to point to several applications of the model and then draw a general conclusion.

The model itself is based on the assumption that where ecclesiality—or "churchliness" as George H. Tavard has put it—is acknowledged, then official ministry must also be present in some meaningful sense. Theologians who support ecclesiological validation of ministry point to the teaching of Vatican II that real elements of ecclesiality are found in "churches or ecclesial communities" outside the Roman Catholic Church. They argue that these elements conduce to salvation precisely because they are expressions of the corporate character of salvation: a person is saved together with other persons, not in isolation. But to maintain that non-Catholic churches are means to salvation despite their ministries really involves a form of circular reasoning that leads nowhere. However difficult it is for theologians to resolve the question of "true" or "valid" ministry in conjunction with the question of installation or ordination to ministry, the challenge must be taken up.

The Council provides a clue for us in the distinction it makes between a person (1) being "incorporated" into the church, where the biblical image of church as "body of Christ" prevails, and (2) being "connected to" (or perhaps better translated as "affiliated to") the church, where the biblical image of church as "people of God" is predominant. The distinction intends to point out degrees of "really" or "truly" belonging to the church of Christ. There is a real difference between being "incorporated" into and being "affiliated" to Christ, but the difference is ecclesiological, not soteriological. We cannot judge God's actions to save, but salvation history reveals that God saves a person in a social and corporate way. In some way or other, then, we concede the fact that divine salvation is worked "also" in ecclesiological terms. Though these elements are not the same, they cannot be completely separated. They express different, though not radically opposed, ways of salvation being effected by God in and through the church. Here, I think, the reflections of Johannes Willebrands on "types" of churches are helpful. In a lecture universally judged to have been a seminal ecumenical talk, Willebrands spoke of a church "type" in the following words: "Where there is a long coherent tradition, commanding men's love and loyalty, creating and sustaining a harmonious and organic whole of complementary elements, each of which supports and strengths the other, you have the reality of a *typos*."[53] After almost five hundred years of existence, and in the face of clear evidence of vitality of faith, life, and faithful witness to Christ, the major churches that have issued from the Reformation must be acknowledged as "ecclesial types." To do so is not to maintain that *all* non-Catholic churches reveal the characteristics of an "ecclesial type." Only careful study among churches and sustained relations, not the least of which must include the element of mutual prayer, can hope to reveal this truth.

Eventually, Roman Catholics have to come to terms with whether or not these "ecclesial types" can rightly be called "churches." The knotty question of what the bishops at Vatican II intended by the phrase "churches and ecclesial communities" cannot be circumvented. The interpretations vary, but if one examines the early commentaries on the text, it appears that the bishops did not intend to draw a hard-and-fast line between a "church," understood rather narrowly in eucharistic terms and therefore necessarily including the validity of sacramental ordination, and an "ecclesial community," understood as a Christian community having genuine ecclesial elements but not including the Eucharist and the ordained sacramental ministry among them. Instead, the bishops appear only to have wanted to refer to the wide spectrum of "Christian

53. See "Cardinal Willebrand's Address in Cambridge, England, January 18, 1970," in *Called to Full Unity: Documents on Anglican-Roman Catholic Relations 1966–1983*, eds. Joseph W. Witmer and J. Robert Wright (Washington, D.C.: USCC Office of the Publishing and Promotion Services, 1986) 45–53, at 51. I will return to this issue of an ecclesial type below.

communities" as respectfully and comprehensively as possible. For their own reasons, some communities that issued from the Reformation preferred not to refer to themselves as "churches" but as "ecclesial communities." The bishops simply intended to show respect for the language used by other Christian communities and had no overarching fundamental distinction in mind.

In 1971 Jerome Hamer wrote an influential note on the meaning of the distinction between "church" and "ecclesial community" in the documents of Vatican II.[54] In this article Hamer examined the various places in the texts of Vatican II where the distinction was especially employed in the Decree on Ecumenism *(Unitatis redintegratio),* arts. 3, 19, and 22. In each case he cites the text in both Latin and in French translation, followed by his commentary. Hamer has been understood by some theologians to support a rigid separation between the two terms. A distinction, yes, but not a separation. I simply cannot find this interpretation in his note. Allow me to quote Hamer's article at several points. He writes apropos of UR 19:

> From the comparison [of official texts submitted to the bishops and their suggestions for emendations of the text], one can conclude that the authors of *Unitatis redintegratio* did not intend to introduce any innovation in regard to the terminology used in *Lumen gentium* but merely wanted to underscore the fact that the usual vocabulary used in referring to Oriental Christianity should also be extended to references made to Old Catholics as well. Moreover, and this is the important element, they wanted to cite a theological reason for this usage: the existence of a valid priesthood and eucharist.[55]

Hamer then quotes the remarks to the Council made by Archbishop J. C. Heenan, who was the official presenter or *relator* of the text on behalf of the Executive Committee, namely: "In speaking of churches and ecclesial communities in the title [to chapter 3, §2] we mean to include all who bear the name of Christian. It is not our intention in any way to enter into the disputed question of what elements are required for a Christian community to be theologically deserving to be called church." Hamer then continues his commentary:

> What is Archbishop Heenan trying to say here? Complete liberty is to be given theologians in their proper spheres. It is their responsibility to deter-

---

54. See "La terminologie ecclésiologique de Vatican II et les ministères protestants," *La Documentation Catholique* 68/13 No. 1589 (July 4, 1971) 625–28.
55. Ibid., 627.

mine which criteria are applicable when referring to a Christian community as "church" in the theological meaning of the term. The Council itself desires to employ terms it considers legitimate and already in common possession. For what remains, it is content that it not close any doors. If, beyond the Oriental and Old Catholic churches, theologians judge that other communities should bear the title of church in the formal and technical sense of the word, they are free to adduce whatever valid arguments they can. In any case, they cannot rely on the authority of *Unitatis redintegratio* in making their arguments.[56]

It seems evident to me that the Council is not imposing a single interpretation as the sole valid meaning of the distinction. Later on in his note, Hamer also explains why UR 22 only uses the expression "ecclesial communities" in a section that refers to the churches that issued from the Reformation. Again, for Hamer, this fact is no proof that they are not churches, but an indication that the bishops refused to enter into a disputed theological point by supplying grounds for some theologians to justify their own theological insights in maintaining that their views were identical with the teaching of the Council. He writes:

> If instead of speaking only of 'ecclesial communities' the Council here had employed the [ususal] formula 'churches and ecclesial communities,' it would have given serious support to one thesis that it did not want to pronounce on, viz., Are there churches in the theological sense of the word where the sacrament of order is lacking ["fait défaut" in the French text]?[57]

In other words, we need to beware of reading too much into the bishops' formulation at this point. In Hamer's words I read an openness of the Council to further theological discussion of the distinction by theologians. The bishops at Vatican II refused to settle the matter as a theological *quaestio disputata*, but warned theologians against relying on their statement of a distinction between church and ecclesial community as itself justifying the theologians' own opinions as to what constitutes the distinction, the limitations of the distinction, the possibility of better theological concepts or categories for discussing the relationships between communities of Christians, and so forth.

It appears that the bishops at Vatican II simply wanted to point out the evident fact that the church of Christ could not be limited to the Roman

56. Ibid.
57. Ibid., 628.

Catholic Church, even if they saw a certain meaning in also speaking of the church of Christ as coming to unique expression in the Roman Catholic Church—the famous statement of Vatican II that the church of Christ "subsists in" the Roman Catholic Church.[58] The Vatican II doctrine of "ecclesial subsistence" does not appear to exclude meaningful subsistence in other non-Catholic churches, but merely intends to express the bishops' faith conviction that the Roman Catholic Church enjoys certain God-given advantages, for example, in having maintained the Petrine ministry, but without wanting to claim that it alone deserves the name "church." A more restrictive theological distinction begins to emerge in the postconciliar period, especially in the late 1960s and the 1970s, as the Roman Catholic Church became a full and active participant in multiple ecumenical dialogues. To some extent, too, insistence on the distinction between a "church" and an "ecclesial community" was an official reaction to signs of exaggerated zeal in addressing certain issues of faith and practice. It lent itself to slowing down a train that sometimes seemed to be racing out of control. However defensible the intentions, they still do not justify a hard-and-fast separation of "church" and "ecclesial community."[59] To put it in the most direct way, "church" and "ecclesial commu-

58. See the Dogmatic Constitution on the Church, art. 8. The phrase is repeated in the Decree on Ecumenism, art. 4, with respect to the church's unity, which is said to "subsist in the Catholic Church as something she can never lose." Much has been written on the meaning of the Council's use of *"subsistit in."* See the studies by Francis A. Sullivan, "'Subsistit in': The Significance of Vatican II's Decision to Say of the Church of Christ Not that It 'Is' But that It 'Subsists in' the Roman Catholic Church," *One in Christ* 22 (1986) 115–23; idem, "The One Church of Christ 'Subsists' in the Catholic Church," in *The Church We Believe In: One, Holy, Catholic and Apostolic* (New York: Paulist Press, 1988) 23–33; and idem, "The Significance of the Vatican II Declaration that the Church of Christ 'Subsists in' the Roman Catholic Church," in *Vatican II: Assessment and Perspectives Twenty-Five Years After (1962–1987)*, 3 vols., ed. René Latourelle (New York: Paulist Press, 1989) 2:272–87. The pertinent literature can be found in Sullivan's studies of the question.

59. The letter *Dominus Iesus* of the Congregation for the Doctrine of the Faith (CDF) clearly goes in another direction from my understanding of the teaching of Vatican II. I want to make it clear that I do not reject outright the teaching of *Dominus Iesus* on the meaning of the same passages in the Dogmatic Constitution on the Church and the Decree on Ecumenism that I am examining. The letter of the CDF has clearly introduced a sharpening of the teaching regarding the difference between a "church" and an "ecclesial community" that emerged in the postconciliar church and has been interpreted as the official theology of the Vatican. Clearly, in the mind of the CDF the difference between church and ecclesial community is the *opinio communis* [the understanding common to many theologians]. No serious and responsible theological treatment can reject out of hand this *opinio communis,* but must strive to come to terms with it. However, there is a second opinion

nity" might be synonyms, and sometimes in fact are synonymous. That assertion still does not prove that non-Catholic churches possess the fullness of ministry willed by Christ, but it does mean that the distinction cannot be used to prove a priori this "lack" or "imperfection" (*defectus ordinis*) either.

Another teaching of Vatican II can help us better understand the issue of recognizing the ministry in other churches. In the Decree on Ecumenism, the Council refers us to a "hierarchy of truths" in the faith (UR 11).[60] In general, two images have been offered as a way of approaching the conciliar teaching of a certain "ordering" of the truths of faith: that of a foundation and a center. Certain truths of our faith are more "central" and more "fundamental" than others. All are true, and all are to be believed, but some truths are more important for understanding other truths because of where they are located in the ensemble of truths. Are we also at liberty to maintain an ordering of the truths that constitute a certain area or "common space" in our system of beliefs, for

that is also widely accepted which says that the difference enunciated by Vatican II has been changed from a distinction into a separation. In fact, in the intra-Catholic discussion at this moment we have a serious theological dialogue between two *opiniones theologicae,* one of which bears a certain weight that must be admitted because it emerges from a high Vatican Congregation. Which opinion is closer to the intentions of Vatican II will only emerge from the discussion within the church and how this discussion is refined by the day-to-day realities of continuing inter-ecclesial ecumenical discussions. I do not think that the process of theological sifting can take place while abstracting from these broader realities. The intra-Catholic debate cannot take place in isolation from broader needs and issues. The "ecumenical charge" of the Second Vatican Council to practice theology in a pastoral and an ecumenical spirit remains firmly in place and cannot seriously be contested. See the fine commentary on *Dominus Iesus* by the Lutheran-Catholic Covenant Commission of the Archdiocese of Saint Paul and Minneapolis and the Minneapolis Area Synod and Saint Paul Area Synod, Evangelical Lutheran Church of America in *Ecumenical Trends* 32/2 (February 2003) 1–7.

60. See George H. Tavard, "'Hierarchia veritatum': A Preliminary Investigation," *Theological Studies* 32 (1971) 278–89; Yves Congar, "The 'Hierarchy of Truths,'" in *Diversity and Communion,* tr. John Bowden (Mystic, Conn.: Twenty-Third Publications, 1985) 126–33; William Henn, "Hierarchy of Truths," in *Dictionary of Theology,* eds. Joseph A. Komonchak, Mary Collins, and Dermot A. Lane (Wilmington, Del.: Michael Glazier, Inc., 1986) 464–66; idem, "The Hierarchy of Truths Twenty Years Later," *Theological Studies* 48 (1987) 439–71; Karl Rahner, "A Hierarchy of Truths," in *Theological Investigations,* 23 vols., tr. Hugh T. Riley (New York: The Crossroad Publishing Company, 1988) 21:162–67; and the Joint Working Group between the Roman Catholic Church and the World Council of Churches, *The Notion of 'Hierarchy of Truths': An Ecumenical Interpretation, and The Church: Local and Universal: Two Studies,* Faith and Order Paper 150 (Geneva: WCC Publications, 1990) at 16–23.

example, sacraments?[61] In the area of ecclesiology, how might the doctrine of the "hierarchy of truths" help us to better discern the relationship between the apostolicity of the whole church and the apostolicity of office in the church?

The ecumenical statements of the last forty years make it abundantly clear that on the question of apostolicity, primacy is to be given to the apostolicity of the whole church. The claim seems to be well supported by what we observed in the church of the early centuries. Only later was apostolic office separated out from the encompassing apostolicity of the community and understood as fundamental. To return to the church's early self-understanding does not mean that the importance of apostolic succession in the narrower sense of the succession of the bishops to the ministry of the apostles is negligible or irrelevant, or that it can be denied. It does mean that its importance is always to be seen in relation to the more fundamental apostolicity of the whole believing community. The bishops retain leadership of the apostolic community, and this leadership is endowed with a sacramental quality and a uniqueness of function that the church needs, but they are still fellow believers who lead their fellow Christians. The temptation to dominance, to clericalism, and to triumphalism so characteristic of ordained office in the church is thereby greatly reduced. More importantly, the sense of passivity on the part of the community of believers is challenged by a view of apostolicity that sees that the roles of believers and bishops are mutually related and enriching, as well as complementary.

Finally, I said I would draw a general conclusion from my discussion. In dealing with the question of the validity of one another's ministry, all three models must be maintained. Though they cannot be reduced to a single "super-model," all three bring out different insights of a fuller and more complex reality. In comparing the models, however, I suggest that Roman Catholics would do better not to begin with ritual validation of ministry. They should consider ecclesial validation first, then charismatic validation, and finally ritual validation. What is primary does not come to expression in juridical terms, however necessary they are for a complete and balanced consideration of ecclesial office, but by looking at the underlying mystery of the church itself. I further suggest that churches

61. See Yves Congar, "The Idea of 'Major' or 'Principal' Sacraments," in *The Sacraments in General: A New Perspective,* Concilium 31, eds. Edward Schillebeeckx and Boniface Willems (New York: Paulist Press, 1968) 21–32.

issuing from the Reformation might also do better justice to ecclesial ministry by addressing some of the ambiguities found in their discussions of ritual validation.

The churches are called to acknowledge the reality of each other's ministry even while admitting a plurality of forms of the ministry. Practically speaking, this means that we refrain from caricaturing and condemning each other's understanding of ministry. This does not mean that we cannot challenge each other to deepen our understandings of ministry, but it does mean that we do so without implying that the other lacks something essential.

Apostolic Ministry and the Church as Fundamental Sacrament

One of the most far-reaching ecclesiological teachings of the Second Vatican Council was its statement that "the Church is in Christ as a sacrament or instrumental sign of intimate union with God and of the unity of all humanity."[62] The key term "sacrament" alludes to the fact that the church is a mystery, since the Latin *sacramentum* was a translation of the Greek term for "mystery"—*mysterion*. In the first chapter of *Lumen gentium*, the Council wanted to stress the fact that the church is best approached as a mystery. The church is a creation of the triune God, who associates the community of the faithful with the history of salvation. As such, the church points beyond itself, like a sign, to the divine reality—a mystery of communion of divine persons who draw all men and women into the divine communion of life. Because the church is ultimately a mystery, it is best approached by way of the images and metaphors we encounter in the Bible. But there is also a second reason why the Council employs the word "sacrament," and that is because the church helps us to understand the special actions that we call "sacraments." There is an intrinsic relationship between these privileged acts and the church itself as sacrament of faith and salvation. The sacraments are not so much free-floating divine actions on our behalf, not so much disparate gifts of God's grace drawing us to our individual salvation, but, to a person of faith, expressions of what God is ceaselessly doing in behalf of the human race.[63]

62. The Dogmatic Constitution on the Church, 1. Cf. LG 9 and 48; the Decree on the Missionary Activity of the Church *(Ad gentes),* 1 and 5; and the Pastoral Constitution on the Church in the World of Today *(Gaudium et spes),* 42 and 45.

63. Karl Rahner addresses the issue of God's will to redeem all men and women in terms of the essential unity of humankind. He writes: "What is meant by the people of

The uniqueness of these sacramental acts is real and Christians need to be grateful for the sacramental grace. But Christians must also remain aware that God's grace is not restricted to the sacraments, nor is it limited to the Christian economy of salvation and its sacraments.[64] Sacramental grace bursts the boundaries of its own self-expression.

In the post-World War II years, several theologians began to develop ideas about the church as a sacrament.[65] To an extent, it was an effort to retrieve some of the ecclesiological depth of meaning these theologians had rediscovered in the patristic and medieval sources. But it was also an attempt to break out of the restrictive juridical and narrow socio-political categories that were characteristic of explanations of the church at the time.[66] Karl Rahner was one of these pioneering theolo-

---

God? The eternal Word of the Father, born of the virgin Mary, one of the daughters of Eve, has become of one race and family with us (Heb. 2:11), not merely of the same nature in the abstract as it were. He belongs to the one human race which is not merely the logical sum of the multitude of individual human beings, but an actually real unity by the will of God. . . . That unity is confirmed, increased and made definitive by the incarnation of the Logos. . . . But because this man Jesus is a member of the one human race, this itself is called to a supernatural destiny in and through him, even if it were not so called in Adam, or not called in Adam because called in Christ as first willed by God. God maintains this vocation of all humanity, despite sin, on account of Christ, who by what he is and what he does, the sacrificial death on the cross, is a member of this single human race." See Karl Rahner, *The Church and the Sacraments,* Quaestiones Disputatae 9, tr. W. J. O'Hara (New York: Herder and Herder, 1963) 11–19 ["The Church as the Fundamental Sacrament"], at 12–13.

64. As Rahner writes: "Supernatural activity where grace is conferred and promised to us by God, infallibly on his part, and sacramental activity, are not identical. The second is only one of the possible kinds of the first." See *The Church and the Sacraments,* 28.

65. See Otto Semmelroth, *Die Kirche als Ursakrament* (Frankfurt: Verlag Josef Knecht, 1953); Piet Smulders, "Sakramenten en Kerk: kerkelijk recht, kultus, pneuma." *Bijdragen* 17 (1956) 391–418; idem, "Die sakramental-kirchliche Struktur der christlichen Gnade," *Bijdragen* 18 (1957) 333–41; Boniface Willems, "Der sakramentale Kirchenbegriff," *Freiburger Zeitschrift für Philosophie und Theologie* 5 (1958) 274–96; Otto Semmelroth, *Church and Sacrament,* tr. Emily Schossberger (Notre Dame, Ind.: Fides Publishers, Inc., 1965); Piet Smulders, "Die Kirche as Sakrament des Heils," in *De Ecclesia. Beiträge zur Konstitution 'Über die Kirche' des Zweiten Vatikanischen Konzils,* 2 vols., ed. G. Baraúna (Freiburg: Verlag Herder and Frankfurt: Verlag Josef Knecht, 1966) 1:289–312; and Avery Dulles, "The Church as Sacrament," in *Models of the Church* (Garden City, N.Y.: Doubleday & Company, Inc., 1974) 58–70.

66. This was true particularly of the approach to the church as a "perfect society"–the *societas perfecta inequalium.* See Knut Walf, "Die katholische Kirche–eine 'societas perfecta'?" *Theologische Quartalschrift* 157 (1977) 107–18; Patrick Granfield, "The Church as *Societas Perfecta* in the Schemata of Vatican I," *Church History* 48 (1979) 431–46; and Jean Rigal, *L'ecclésiologie de communion. Son évolution historique et ses fondements,* Cogitatio fidei 202 (Paris: Les Éditions du Cerf, 1997) 33–37 ["La 'societas perfecta'"]. But it was also true of a narrowly

gians who discerned the underlying unity of the church's sacramental life.[67] But he also saw how the church itself came to life and was actualized in the celebration of the sacraments.[68] Each sacramental act is eo ipso an ecclesial act as well, or in Rahner's terms, a "Grundvollzug der Kirche"—an action in which the church is realized or actualized. In the celebration of the sacraments, believers encounter the church *in actu*—as active here and now. The church is experienced not so much in its creeds and doctrines—though they are of course important from another perspective—as in the church's rich sacramental and liturgical life. Rahner also rethought the mystery of grace at several levels,[69] and since the sacraments are also means of grace, his theology of grace necessarily affected his sacramentology. How?

To Rahner, grace is primarily God's gift to us of God's own infinite life. Grace is "uncreated grace," that is, *gratia increata*—the triune life of the communion of the divine persons and the ever-present invitation to humans to share in that life. Grace, then, is best understood in personal terms as an encounter between ourselves and God and the relationship that is established by that encounter. Quantitative terms, or terms referring to grace in a material sense as "some*thing*," are inappropriate for grasping the mystery of grace. Personal, interpersonal, and relational terms are more helpful in expressing what grace is. The church's sacraments are not just so many acts of administering the sacraments to individual recipients. Rather, they are symbols of the human encounter with

---

hierarchical way of viewing the church, according to which the phrase "the Church" came to be synonymous with "the hierarchy" or the official church.

67. See Karl Rahner, *The Church and the Sacraments,* and idem, "What Is a Sacrament?" in *Theological Investigations,* tr. David Bourke (New York: The Seabury Press, 1976) 14:135–48. An excellent introduction to Rahner's sacramental theology can be found in Michael Skelley, *The Liturgy of the World: Karl Rahner's Theology of Worship* (Collegeville, Minn.: The Liturgical Press, 1991).

68. See Karl Rahner, "The Word and the Eucharist," in *Theological Investigations,* tr. Kevin Smyth (reprint, New York: The Crossroad Publishing Company, 1982) 4:253–86.

69. See Karl Rahner, "Concerning the Relationship between Nature and Grace," in *Theological Investigations,* tr. Cornelius Ernst (reprint, New York: The Seabury Press, 1974) 1:297–317; idem, "Some Implications of the Scholastic Concept of Grace," in ibid., 319–46; and idem, "Nature and Grace," in *Theological Investigations,* tr. Kevin Smyth, 4:165–88. For a good introduction to Rahner's theology of grace, see John P. Galvin, "The Invitation of Grace," in *A World of Grace: An Introduction to the Themes and Foundations of Karl Rahner's Theology,* ed. Leo J. O'Donovan (New York: The Crossroad Publishing Company, 1981) 64–75.

the divine—an encounter that is always very concrete for men and women. Each celebration or ministration of a sacrament is a simultaneous celebration of church. Therefore, it is not incorrect to speak about the church as the "fundamental sacrament"—"Grundsakrament" in German—in which all celebrations and ministrations of the sacraments find their unity, ultimate meaning, and foundational reference to grace. The church is not another sacrament—a kind of "super-sacrament" in addition to the seven sacraments Catholics traditionally enumerate—but the graced reality that embraces all of them and fashions God's eschatologically triumphant and unsurpassable community of grace and salvation. Moreover, the church is "only" the fundamental sacrament, it is not itself the "primordial sacrament"—"Ursakrament" in German.[70] Jesus the Lord is himself the primordial sacrament, in whom the church and the individual sacraments are rooted.[71] The mystery of Christ's being, or what in the

70. See the discussion of this important distinction by Walter Kasper, "The Church as a Universal Sacrament of Salvation," in *Theology and Church,* tr. Margaret Kohl (New York: The Crossroad Publishing Company, 1989) 111–28. In his earlier writings, Karl Rahner referred to the church as the "Ursakrament," but later changed this to the church as the "Grundsakrament." For the latter usage, see Rahner's *Foundations of Christian Faith: An Introduction to the Idea of Christianity,* tr. William V. Dych (New York: The Seabury Press, 1976), at 411, where Dych translates Rahner's section heading "Die Kirche als Grundsakrament und die sieben Sakramente" as "The Church as Basic Sacrament and the Seven Sacraments." I have preferred the translation "fundamental sacrament" to Dych's "basic sacrament." It needs to be noted, however, that Rahner was always careful in his writings prior to his *Foundations of Christian Faith* to relate the church to Christ as primary. See his contribution to *Handbuch der Pastoraltheologie. Praktische Theologie der Kirche in ihrer Gegenwart,* 4 vols., ed. Franz Xaver Arnold and others (Freiburg: Verlag Herder, 1964) 1:117–48 ["Ekklesiologische Grundlegung"], at 133.

71. Some, though by no means all, Lutheran and Reformed theologians have difficulties with the designation of the church as a sacrament, since many are highly sensitive to the idea that the church always runs the risk of interposing itself in God's own act of salvation. There is an excellent discussion of the issue by André Birmelé, in *Le salut en Jésus Christ dans les dialogues oecuméniques,* Cogitatio fidei 141 (Paris: Les Éditions du Cerf, 1986) 203–53 ["La sacramentalité de l'Église"]. For both sides of the Lutheran understanding, see Günther Gassmann, "The Church as Sacrament, Sign and Instrument: The Reception of This Ecclesiological Understanding in Ecumenical Debate," in *Church, Kingdom, World: The Church as Mystery and Prophetic Sign,* Faith and Order Paper 130, ed. Gennadios Limouris (Geneva: WCC Publications, 1986) 1–17, for a more positive assessment; and Eberhard Jüngel, "The Church as Sacrament?" *Theological Essays,* ed. and tr. J. B. Webster (Edinburgh: T&T Clark Ltd., 1989) 189–213, who is highly critical of sacramental vocabulary being applied to the church. Geoffrey Wainwright pointedly takes exception to Jüngel's criticism of the concept of sacrament being applied to the church in "Church and Sacrament(s)," in *The Possibilities of Theology: Studies in the Theology of Eberhard Jüngel in his*

christological tradition is called the "Hypostatic Union," alone is ultimate and underived. The church makes no sense apart from the mystery of the unity of human and divine, of historicity and absolute freedom, of sacrificial obedience and absolute love encountered in Jesus Christ. For that reason, Christ is the personal sacrament that precedes and grounds the church itself as sacrament of (graced) persons. This is why the Council can move spontaneously from sacramental language to the language of *communio*. Each says something different about the church, but that difference helps to realize the other dimension it is incapable of expressing by itself. Church as sacrament needs the dialectically "other" of church as communion, and vice versa. Are there any implications of Vatican II's teaching on the church as sacrament for apostolic succession in official ministry? I believe the implications are profound.[72]

Sixtieth Year, ed. John Webster (Edinburgh: T&T Clark Ltd., 1994) 90–105. In his most recent contribution on sacramental theology, written after Wainwright's contribution to his English *Festschrift*, Jüngel appears more open to the sacraments as "events" of God's gracing human beings. Still, Jüngel urges caution in understanding sacramental activity as always God's saving activity. The church's representative activity must be totally open to God as the principal agent, so that the church does not understand its activity as perfecting or completing God's action. See "Sakrament und Repräsentation. Wesen und Funktion der sakramentalen Handlung," in *Ganz werden. Theologische Erörterungen*, vol. 5 (Tübingen: J. C. B. Mohr [Paul Siebeck], 2003) 274–87. Very helpful, too, is Otto Hermann Pesch, "Das katholische Sakramentsverständnis im Urteil gegenwärtiger evangelischer Theologie," in *Verifikationen. Festschrift für Gerhard Ebeling zum 70. Geburtstag*, eds. E. Jüngel, J. Wallmann, and W. Werbeck (Tübingen: J. C. B. Mohr [Paul Siebeck], 1982) 317–40. Kasper's insistence on the difference between the church as "Grundsakrament" and Christ as the "Ursakrament" can help allay this anxiety. In another article, Kasper also writes of the openness of some Protestant theologians to understanding the character of the church as sacrament. He writes: "Protestant theology too has reflected on the sacramental structure of the church." See Walter Kasper, "The Apostolic Succession: An Ecumenical Problem," *Leadership in the Church: How Traditional Roles Can Serve the Christian Community Today*, tr. Brian McNeil (New York: The Crossroad Publishing Company, 2003) 114–43, at 133. Jean Rigal also has discussed this ecumenically neuralgic issue with caution and sensitivity in *L'ecclésiologie de communion*, 318–29 ["La communion sous le signe de la sacramentalité"], as has Bernard Sesboüé, "Les sacrements de la foi. L'économie sacramentelle, célébration ecclésiale de la justification par la foi," in *Pour une théologie oecuménique. Église et sacrements, Eucharistie et ministères, La Vierge Marie*, Cogitatio fidei 160 (Paris: Les Éditions du Cerf, 1990) 91–125.

72. Avery Dulles has written: "I have here contended that Scripture alone, read without prior commitment to a particular denominational position, presents the Church as the Body and Spouse of Christ, animated by his Spirit, who dwells in individual members and in the Church as a whole, making it into a mysterious communion of grace and love. As a kind of corporate sacrament, the Church is a sign and instrument of Christ's abiding presence with the community and its leaders. The sacramentality of the Church

I have argued that sacramental actions are eo ipso acts of the church. I would also like to argue in the other direction, that where one finds the reality of church, those acts that, in an especially concentrated way, most directly engage it are eo ipso sacraments. It does not matter that some non-Catholic churches find it hard to identify them as sacraments, for example, marriage, penance, ordination, or the anointing of the sick; these actions so engage the person that necessarily more than that individual's salvific situation comes into play. The point of naming the sacraments is not to be able to say that here and here alone God's grace is to be found, but to be able to move towards the conviction that these sacramental works in us help us acknowledge that we live in a "sacramental world." Both the church as fundamental sacrament and the various individual sacraments we celebrate evoke in us a "sacramental sensibility," that is, awareness of the mystery of grace all around us and openness to the transcendent. This graced "sacramental sensibility" comes to a certain clarity or density of expression in the specific situations we call "the sacraments." We can detect the contours of "the sacraments" but not the limits of God's graced actions, and therefore we can speak of sacraments in a wider or more open-ended sense.

Even when we think that we have really identified "the sacraments," we run the risk of misunderstanding them if we place them outside of all God's other salvific actions. Thus, there is no competition here between proclaiming God's word and receiving the sacraments. I think it is misleading to accept a dichotomy that understands the Catholic Church as church of the sacraments, and Protestant churches as churches of the word of God. Such a formulation shortchanges the churches of the Reform in terms of their real sacramental life, and shortchanges the Catholic Church in as much as it lives from the word of God and constantly meditates on it. It would be helpful here to return to an understanding of

pervades all dimensions of its life, but is especially manifest in baptism, whereby its members are consecrated to the Lord, and in the Eucharist, whereby they enter into the heart of the Paschal mystery. If Evangelical Christians could accept the measure of sacramentality that is attested by Scripture itself, the present dialogue would be rich in promise. The way would be clear for a discussion whether the post-biblical developments in Catholic faith and order are consonant with the biblical foundations or at odds with them." "Church, Ministry, and Sacraments in Catholic-Evangelical Dialogue," in *Catholics and Evangelicals: Do They Share a Common Future?* ed. Thomas P. Rausch (Downers Grove, Ill.: InterVarsity Press, 2000) 101–21, at 118–19.

the sacraments as acts of faith, in which God's word plays an indispensable role.[73]

The sacraments are always acts of faith, that is, acts inspired by God in us *and* human actions that are expressed through our mind, will, imagination, memory, emotions, and our dependence on sense realities. Sometimes the word of God acts to save apart from the sacraments, while at other times it acts in such a way as to come to term in a sacramental act—speaking both narrowly and more globally.[74] Thus, the Catholic penchant for "sacramentals," for example, medals, statues, novenas, blessed

73. The Catholic theologian Edward J. Kilmartin in particular has emphasized this aspect of sacramental theology in order to offset an approach to the sacraments that in the pre-conciliar church tended to stress the *opus operatum* dimension of the sacraments in a one-sided way. See his "Sacraments as Liturgy of the Church," *Theological Studies* 50 (1989) 527–47. In Catholic sacramental theology, the sacrament as *opus operatum* is intended to stress the sovereignty of God in the sacrament and the fact that the recipient has solid grounds to rely on God's promise of grace in the sacrament. Unfortunately, over time it came to signify in the minds of many a theology of the sacraments that paid little or no attention to the actions of the recipient, especially the faith of the recipient and the faith of the church. This aspect is often called the *opus operantis* dimension of the sacrament. Again, one must note Karl Rahner's contribution to the deepening of this controversial aspect of sacramental theology. He writes: "Consequently *opus operatum* means the unambiguous, abiding promise irrevocably made by God, and as such recognizable and historically manifest, of grace for the individual human being, a promise made by the God of the new and eternal covenant. The statement that it is a conferring of God's grace without the subjective merit of the minister or the recipient of the sign, is only the negative and therefore secondary formulation of this positive content of the concept." See *The Church and the Sacraments,* 24–33 [*"Opus operatum"*], at 32–33. On the theology of the *opus operatum* as a subject of controversy between Catholic and Protestant theologians, Rahner further remarks: *"Opus operatum* is only the plainest expression in Catholic dogmatic theology to affirm that God gives his grace of himself, on his own initiative; man's answer is truly only an answer, deriving its whole meaning and existence from God's word to man. It is quite surprising that this expression has provoked such contradiction in Protestant theology. *Opus operatum* is not a concept in opposition to faith. It states that God *sola gratia,* out of pure grace, gives this faith and utters this gracious summons to man plainly and simply in this historically visible form of the sacraments." Ibid., 33–34.

74. Karl Rahner's approach to the sacraments in particular has emphasized the dimension of the word in confecting a sacrament. According to Rahner, it is impossible to completely separate word from sacramental action or the matter of a sacrament, e.g., water, bread, and oil, and in fact only the word can indicate unambiguously what is happening in the sacramental moment. He writes: "A theology of the word in this sense could perfectly well become the basis for a theology of the sacraments in which the sacrament figures as the supreme human and ecclesiastical stage of the word in all its dimensions which has been uttered in the Church as such. . . . According to Catholic teaching there are sacraments which are enacted in words alone, and it follows that the true nature of sacraments as such must consist in the word." See Karl Rahner, "What Is a Sacrament?" 137–38.

water, strives to express the connection between "the sacraments" and the wider "sacramental world" perceived by faith's sacramental sensibility. To the extent that "sacramentals" do this, they are healthy expressions of faith. In fact, Catholics are called to understand them in such a way that they see the world itself as an expression of God dealing with us sacramentally.

After Vatican II, theologians began to consider how the ministries in our various churches could be reconciled with each other. Once agreement had been reached on the role, importance, and official transmission of ecclesial ministry, particularly the ministry of directing a local community, what form of reconciling our ministries would be followed: conditional reordination, a public act of reconciliation, a statement from the leaders at the highest levels of mutual acceptance of each other's ministries? None of the suggestions met with general acceptance. Each harbored difficulties for the other churches. For example, reordination, even conditionally, seemed to imply that the ministry practiced in another church up to that point had not measured up to the office as willed by Christ. This was an ecumenical dead end. But if one paid attention to one's ecclesiology first of all, official ministry in the churches would emerge in a new light.

Ordained ministry is rooted in the character of the believing community as church. The church itself is primary, and ministry serves the church and does not found it first of all. True, there would be no church today without the "founding ministry" of the originary apostles, but all post-apostolic ministry differs from that of the apostles in that it is bound forever to their witness—a witness itself engendered by God's word that they proclaimed and the continuing presence and action of the Spirit. Further communities of Christians were founded, but only in terms of their being in communion with the churches the apostles themselves had founded and endowed with the apostolic tradition. Pursuing the logic of such ideas, theologians began to concentrate on the ecclesiality of the churches themselves. Did one truly encounter an expression of the church of Christ in a particular church or ecclesial community? Could one say that here one really encountered the body of Christ in a more-than-purely-individual way, in a genuinely corporate and communal form? Could one say that here, in this instance, are found the essentials of what the church is, even if their ideal expression is less than perfect? If one can answer yes to these questions, then the way seems open to recognizing the different forms of ministry in these churches and its transmission.[75] From ancient times the church has known various forms of organized ministry and forms of transmitting that ministry.[76] If true ecclesiality is found in a church, is it possible to accept a variety of ministries as not incompatible with that fundamental ecclesiality? In this way, an irenic, yet serious, way is opened for recognizing each other's ministerial structures.

75. Some might ask whether the criterion of ecclesiality is specific enough. Is any church that claims to be "church" to be simply acknowledged as such by the other churches, or must so-called "churches" meet certain definite criteria? The issue is a delicate one and deserves a more in-depth analysis than I can give here. However, two things need to be said on the matter. First of all, I would apply the criterion of an ecclesial *typos* as developed by Johannes Willebrands. Apropos an ecclesial *typos*, let us recall what Willebrands wrote: "Where there is a long coherent tradition, commanding men's love and loyalty, creating and sustaining a harmonious and organic whole of complementary elements, each of which supports and strengthens the other, you have the reality of a *typos*." Each word in this definition is carefully weighed and related to the others. The definition is admirable for its balance, conciseness, comprehensiveness, and for its lack of polemic, and I submit that it might function as a criterion in helping our communities decide on the presence of true ecclesial qualities in the other(s). See "Cardinal Willebrand's Address in Cambridge, England, January 18, 1970," in *Called to Full Unity*, 45–53, at 51. And second, I would not be too hasty in denying genuine ecclesiality to a community of Christians but would accord the presumption of belonging to the church of Christ unless problems, grave misunderstandings, a persistent lack of openness and failures at communicating with other ecclesial communities, hostile rejection of the beliefs and practices of the other churches, or an evident contradiction of something the other churches regard as an essential feature of the church of Christ, would argue for a negative judgment. Moreover, the element of time is important in this regard. In some cases, a positive judgment can be rendered in a relatively short period of time, especially where bilateral dialogues have been pursued over a number of years. In other cases, however, a positive judgment might demand a rather prolonged period of reflection, prayer, and dialogue. What I am proposing in terms of a criterion of ecclesiality, then, is not something automatic or something that lacks real seriousness in being applied. It is evident that much more needs to be said about defining ecclesiality and recognizing it. Thus, applying both these norms to the issue of apostolic succession in ministry, it is not inconceivable that an ecclesial community that has preserved official ministry by way of a long-standing form of ordination to office as part of its ecclesial *typos* and that does not reject the possibility of other, let us say complementary, forms of ministry of the other churches, e.g., episcopacy or the Petrine ministry, would be a logical candidate for recognition of its ministry by the other churches because of its inherent ecclesiality and thus of its ministry as well.

76. See Hans Conzelmann, "Die Vielfalt der neutestamentlichen Kirchenstrukturen und die Frage ihrer Einheit: eine Problemskizze," in *Evangelium–Welt–Kirche*, 205–11; and Heinrich Fries, "Structures of the Church at the Beginning of the Church" and "The Pluriform Development of Christian Origins," in *Fundamental Theology*, 510–20 and 521–31 respectively.

246 APOSTOLICITY THEN AND NOW

Apostolic Succession in Postconciliar Roman Catholicism

Numerous studies by Roman Catholic theologians in the postconciliar period point in the direction of a new synthesis of apostolic succession in the sense of the succession of the bishops of the local churches. Gone is the insistence on the idea of a strict historical chain of ordinations reaching from the present all the way back to the originary apostles. Joseph Ratzinger can serve here as an example of the desire to take leave of ideas of a "chain of succession of bishops" or a "pipeline of episcopal ordinations." Reflecting on the laudable intentions of some non-Catholic hierarchs already in the nineteenth century to assure the historic episcopate by including at least one bishop of unimpeachable episcopal pedigree among the ordaining bishops during their ceremonies, Ratzinger speaks of such ordinations rather caustically as "apocryphal ordinations" and as "liturgical Romanticism" by reason of the ritual and doctrinal formalism of their expression.[77] Such ideas tend to inculcate an unhealthy or mechanical sense of the causality of the sacraments and end up expressing a profound theological insight in an abject form of historical reductionism. In this section, I propose to summarize the ideas of Walter Kasper, who will serve as a representative example of a renewed Roman Catholic theology of apostolic succession. In a number of articles over the years, Kasper has continued to deepen his theology of the episcopacy.[78] In articles written in the 1990s, he has offered us a balanced and updated exposition of apostolic succession, yet one that is theologically fully in line with the apostolic tradition.[79] Kasper's theology represents

77. See Joseph Ratzinger, "Bemerkungen zur Frage der apostolischen Sukzession," in *Amt im Widerstreit,* ed. Karlheinz Schuh, 42. In popular presentations of episcopacy and apostolic succession, these theologically outmoded ideas continue to be repeated.

78. See "Ökumenischer Fortschritt im Amstversändnis?" in *Amt im Widerstreit,* 52–58; and "Episcopal Office, in *Leadership in the Church,* 76–113. In 1989 Walter Kasper, then Professor of Dogmatic Theology at the University of Tübingen, was ordained bishop of the diocese of Rottenburg-Stuttgart. Kasper functioned as the ordinary of the diocese until his recent appointments to Vatican Curial positions, most recently as Prefect of the Pontifical Council for Church Unity. It is probable that Kasper's experience as a local bishop helped in deepening his ideas on episcopacy and on the theological value of the local church.

79. See Walter Kasper, "The Apostolic Succession: An Ecumenical Problem," *Leadership in the Church,* 114–43 [=an English translation of an article that appeared in *Lehrverurteilungen kirchentrennend?* vol. 3, ed. Wolfhart Pannenberg (Freiburg: Verlag Herder, 1990) 329–49]; idem, "Apostolic Succession in Episcopacy in an Ecumenical Context," the Bicentennial Lecture delivered on the occasion of the bicentenary of St. Mary's Seminary & University, 1791–1991, 16 pages (available from St. Mary's Seminary & University,

the best of Roman Catholic ideas about the development of dogma.[80] What, then, does he say about apostolic succession?

Kasper recasts episcopal succession in terms of the succession of the college of bishops. Gone is the insistence on the bishop as a successor to an apostle or to the apostles in some generic sense. The bishop today "succeeds to" the apostles by being incorporated, through the sacrament of episcopal ordination, into the college of bishops. For him, episcopal collegiality plays one of the dominant roles in his rethinking episcopacy. It is the universal college of bishops that genuinely succeeds to the apostles of the early church, who are now themselves seen to have constituted a college.[81] The bishops, past and present, know themselves to be bound to the *traditio apostolica* deriving from the apostles, and their apostolic succession is really in service of the *traditio*. Here is how Kasper expresses it:

> [Apostolic succession] is not a succession in the linear sense, where one office-bearer follows another; rather, new members are coopted and integrated into the apostolic college with its mission that is carried on from age to age.[82]
>
> When a bishop enters the apostolic succession, he does not receive some private channel (or "pipeline") connecting him to the apostles. Rather, he enters the fellowship of bishops. The individual bishop is a successor of the apostles, not thanks to an unbroken chain going back from his predecessors to one of the apostles, but because he is in communion [*communio*] with the entire *ordo episcoporum* [body of bishops], which as a whole is the successor of the apostolic college and of the apostles' mission. This is why the mutual agreement of the bishops is a decisive sign of the apostolicity of their teaching. Catholicity is an instrument and expression of apostolicity.[83]

Baltimore, Md.); and idem, "Das Zweite Vatikanum weiterkenken. Die apostolische Sukzession im Bischofsamt als ökumenisches Problem," *Kerygma und Dogma* 44 (1998) 207–18.

80. See also Heinrich Fries, "The Question of Office in Contemporary Ecumenical Discussion," in *Fundamental Theology*, 544–59; and Francis A. Sullivan, "Apostolic Succession in the Episcopate: A Church-Dividing Issue," in *From Apostles to Bishops*, 1–16.

81. One should not press the point of a "college" unduly. I do not intend it in any juridical sense, but merely to point out that the originary apostles, far from being so many isolated plenipotentiary individuals, were "one body of ministers" in their proclamation of the word and in their founding of churches. All the apostles from the earliest years of the church of the first century did not have to meet in a council, as it were, to really be a body of ministers sent by Christ and empowered by the Spirit for this crucial founding period without which we could not speak meaningfully of the church.

82. "The Apostolic Succession: An Ecumenical Problem," 121.

83. Ibid., 125.

The second conciliar teaching that has enriched Kasper's theology of apostolic succession is, as we just read, the idea of *communio*. The college is an expression of the ecclesial "communion" that is the church. Kasper emphasizes how episcopal ordinations in the patristic church were always performed by several bishops of a given region whose joint action pointed to their will to be in communion with the new bishop, and to welcome him into their communion and the communion among their churches. Other bishops of the region participated in the process of extending communion by themselves sending "letters of communion" to the new bishop, thereby indicating their welcoming him into the body of bishops and into ecclesial communion. Kasper envisions apostolic succession of the bishops in the interchange of ideas that are expressed in the Latin triad *successio–traditio–communio*. Any complete meaning of apostolicity of office includes all three notions in their rich interplay among themselves. Again, here is how he puts the matter: "We need to begin with the fundamental insight that *successio, traditio,* and *communio* constitute an interconnected construct and form a whole. This interconnectedness is based on the biblically attested interconnection among Christology, pneumatology, and ecclesiology."[84]

Kasper's theology offers a better starting point for further ecumenical reflections on apostolic succession. At the very heart of the collegiality and the sense of communion of the bishops is the notion of relationality. No bishop, not even the pope as Bishop of Rome, stands entirely outside the circle of the college. In participatory and communication-oriented cultures, these ideas regarding collegiality take on new meaning and importance. The alone-at-the-top, omni-competent, unchallenged Church Manager (CEO) is no longer an ideal leader in today's church. Episcopal collegiality creates space for a new image of the bishop to emerge that can also incorporate the idea of synodality or conciliarity, so dear to the churches of the East and increasingly, too, expressly desired by the churches that have issued from the Reformation.

Kasper's ideas can help us better understand the papacy also. In the light of episcopal collegiality, the pope, as successor to the one who was understood to have "recapitulated" the founding college of apostles, continues this role as head of the college of bishops. His office makes little sense apart from this role, and the role of uniting as head the vast body

84. "Das Zweite Vatikanum weiterdenken," 212.

of bishops—themselves indicating the catholicity of the church—is the foundation of all the other papal responsibilities. By their intrinsic relationships the bishops together constitute the body, while the pope has a relation on all the bishops while he himself is acted upon reciprocally by reason of his relations with the body of bishops. No office in the church exists in isolation from the others.

Again, Postmodernism

In conclusion, I want to return to the topic of postmodernity and its pertinence to apostolic succession. I am convinced that contemporary Western society—and probably beyond Western society also—has turned the corner from modernity to postmodernity. As we saw in chapter 6 (pp. 127–45), this change is accompanied by dangers, threats, and possible disasters. But these negative effects are not the whole picture, since postmodernity also holds promise and creates new possibilities. The Christian faith, so long unsure of itself and held in check by the spell of modernity, is now free to pursue new paths of evangelization and theological vitality. Ours is the task of discerning and preserving the genuine contributions of the classical worldview in its rich variety of forms and of modernity's contributions to humankind and to the well-being of the cosmos. Of equal importance is our task of summoning up the courage to apply our mental acumen to the problems and possibilities that postmodernity presents to us. Perhaps today's postmodernisms will free us to embrace the possibilities of pluralism, of radical historicity rooted in our human freedom, and of relationality as the fundamental condition of human self-realization.

Each of these ideas can also be applied to this book's topic of the apostolicity of the church and help to move it in new directions. Postmodern pluralism challenges us to openness in the face of there being more than one insight or solution to the complexity of reality. Maybe a pluralism of views does better justice to reality than a rigid systematization that must necessarily leave many perspectives out of consideration. In the case of apostolicity, our churches need to be more genuinely open to the insights of the other churches. There is something we can really learn from each other. Perhaps our acceptance of historicity will connect us more deeply and more meaningfully with the vast flow of God's evolving creation. In the case of apostolicity, we can come to the insight that historical development is not always organic and predictable. It often obeys different laws. Can we be open to the ambiguity and complexities of historical development that also reveal God to us? And finally, relationality can help us to see how the humanly other, the socially other, the religiously other, the ecclesially other—not to speak of the divine Other—will help us to discover the mystery of human being-with-others (co-being) and emancipate us from the tyranny of self-destructive individualism. We can learn anew what it is to be a person in a deep and satisfying way, and so come to see how our personhood is a reflection of the communion of personal relations that is the Trinity—Father, Son, and Spirit. In the case of apostolicity, we can come to accept the other churches for the reality of their otherness, an otherness that helps to create our ecclesial identities in genuine relationship with each other. We can begin to loosen our tight grasp on our "churchliness" and accept the other Christian communities as truly "church" as well.